Struggling Adolescent Readers

A Collection of Teaching Strategies

David W. Moore
Arizona State University West
Phoenix, Arizona, USA

Donna E. Alvermann
University of Georgia
Athens, Georgia, USA

Kathleen A. Hinchman
Syracuse University
Syracuse, New York, USA

INTERNATIONAL
Reading
Association

800 Barksdale Road, PO Box 8139
Newark, Delaware 19714-8139, USA
www.reading.org

The International Reading Association attempts, through its publications, to provide a forum for a wide spectrum of opinions on reading. This policy permits divergent viewpoints without implying the endorsement of the Association.

Director of Publications   Joan M. Irwin
Editor in Chief, Books   Matthew W. Baker
Permissions Editor   Janet S. Parrack
Associate Editor   Tori Mello
Publications Coordinator   Beth Doughty
Association Editor   David K. Roberts
Production Department Manager   Iona Sauscermen
Art Director   Boni Nash
Senior Electronic Publishing Specialist   Anette Schütz-Ruff
Electronic Publishing Specialist   Cheryl J. Strum
Electronic Publishing Assistant   Jeanine K. McGann

Project Editor   Matthew W. Baker

Cover   JAM Photography–Jonathan A. Meyers

Library of Congress Cataloging in Publication Data
Struggling adolescent readers: a collection of teaching strategies/David W. Moore, Donna E. Alvermann, Kathleen A. Hinchman, editors.
    p.   cm.
   Includes bibliographical references and index.
    1. Reading (Middle school)—United States.   2. Reading (Secondary)—United States.   3. Teacher effectiveness—United States.   I. Moore, David W.   II. Alvermann, Donna E.   III. Hinchman, Kathleen A.
LB1632.39.S87   2000   00-028138
428.4'071'2—dc21
ISBN 0-87207-272-X
Fifth Printing, May 2003

CONTENTS

iii

SECTION 4
Supporting Classroom Writing and Inquiry / 197

David W. Moore, Donna E. Alvermann, and Kathleen A. Hinchman

Introduction

Quotations can express ideas compellingly. The following quotations we use as headings are from adolescents speaking about real-life dimensions of reading and schooling. We offer these comments and our reactions to them to crystallize issues that are addressed in this compilation.

"I just didn't understand it!"

After one of us, David Moore, earned his initial teaching certificate in the early 1970s, he landed his first job teaching social studies at a rural Arizona high school. As with many beginning teachers, classroom life got off to a good start the first few days, but then troubles began. Class discussions began sputtering after only a few minutes, writing was meager, and students were getting restless. By the time evolution came up as one of the topics to cover, David decided that he needed to energize things. He stayed up late one night reproducing the beginning pages of Arthur C. Clarke's science fiction novel, *2001: A Space Odyssey*, because it lyrically portrayed an ape discovering tools and beginning the evolutionary changes that tools enhanced. "This is sure to work!" he thought.

The next day David presented the passage for students to read in class, played the soundtrack from the *2001* movie, and eagerly awaited what was expected to be a lively discussion of the passage. However, the discussion fizzled; few students expressed thoughts about the passage or about one another's comments. As the class members left this especially disappointing lesson, David pressed Eleanor, an approachable and serious student, about why she had not reacted to the passage.

When Eleanor eventually–and tearfully–exclaimed that she just did not understand it, David had an epiphany, a change in his understanding of secondary school teaching. Until that moment he never suspected that well-intentioned, hard-working adolescents actually might struggle with reading. He eventually returned to the university for a master's degree in reading education and has been involved in this area ever since.

The main point of this account is that some adolescents perennially struggle with reading in middle school and high school, so educators and the public should address this issue directly and compassionately. U.S. standardized tests of the early 1900s revealed large numbers of adolescents reading well below expectations (Kibby, 1995). More recently, the 1998 Reading Report Card produced by the National Assessment of Educational Progress (NAEP) (1999) showed that approximately 40% of U.S. adolescents have difficulty comprehending specific factual information. And few teenagers have gone beyond the basics to advanced reading and writing. Fewer than 5% of the adolescents NAEP assessed could appropriately extend or elaborate the meanings of the materials they read.

Many students continue to struggle with basic reading processes beyond third grade, and those who have mastered basic processes by the time they reach secondary school still have much to learn about the different reading practices associated with subject matter disciplines, texts, and life situations. To illustrate, Kathy Hinchman remembers observing a group of students in a high school biology classroom. These adolescents, many of whom struggled with reading, were doggedly completing a set of written directions for completing a laboratory experiment. They looked through their textbook and then through their microscope, confused. Eventually, they plaintively asked Kathy, "Do we write what they want us to write, or do we write what we see?" Kathy took this question to mean that the students had turned over all authority for interpretation to the textbook authors, unwilling or unable to realize that the point of the experiment was to see for themselves and critique the textbook accordingly.

Even with the best instruction early in a child's schooling, differences in reading ability increase as students develop from year to year. Additionally, adolescents enter school speaking many different languages and coming from many different backgrounds and experiences, so their academic progress differs substantially. This situation is especially pressing as more and more states enact or consider enacting reading requirements for promotion and graduation.

The articles in this collection directly address the teaching and learning of adoles-

cents who struggle with reading. An important feature of these articles is their focus on adolescents. All but one article comes from past issues of the *Journal of Adolescent & Adult Literacy* (*JAAL*) (formerly *Journal of Reading*) whose masthead states, "*JAAL* serves those interested in the teaching of reading to adolescents and adults." The one article in this collection that comes from *The Reading Teacher*, a journal that predominantly addresses the literacy learning of elementary-age children, is about a middle school student with a reading disability.

Staying focused on the teaching and learning of adolescents is especially appropriate because a teaching practice that seems effective for all ages might not be so. The teaching and learning of adolescents differs in subtle ways from other age groups. For instance, a noteworthy 1998 NAEP Reading Report Card finding is that fourth-grade students who read self-selected books in school on a daily basis average higher reading scores than those who do not do such reading (National Assessment of Educational Progress, 1999). However, students in grades 8 and 12 did not demonstrate similar benefits from daily self-selected reading in school. Providing access to materials adolescents can and will read is a well-established principle of instruction (Moore, Bean, Birdyshaw, & Rycik, 1999), but the everyday practice of daily self-selected reading in middle schools and high schools—along with many other practices—deserves scrutiny.

Most educators would agree that productively engaging low-achieving adolescents in lively print-rich classrooms is complicated (O'Brien, 1998; Rossi & Pace, 1998). Although the articles in this compilation go far in describing teaching-learning environments that engage middle school and high school students who struggle with reading, we believe they represent only the tip of the iceberg in terms of what is needed. We are acutely aware of a paradigm shift in reading education from an emphasis on the psychology of reading to the social world, with labels changing from *remediation* to *intervention* and from *disabled* to *struggling* reader. Much more needs to be researched, written, and published with regard to struggling adolescent readers. The piece *Adolescent Literacy: A Position Statement*, developed by IRA's Commission on Adolescent Literacy, explicitly calls for increased support and funding in research, staff development, and program leadership (Moore, Bean, Birdyshaw, & Rycik, 1999).

"Hey, I'm not as dumb as I thought!"

When teaching reading at a Tucson, Arizona, high school, David regularly explained standardized test scores so students knew where they stood according to these assessments. After one such session, a student who scored above the 50th percentile was so ecstatic that he called out to the class the quotation presented above. David took to heart this person's statement as an indication of years of seeing himself not measuring up to expectations. It opened David's eyes to the intensely personal dimensions of reading difficulties.

Similarly, Kathy recalls a student she met at an awards ceremony for adult students at a local Literacy Volunteers of America affiliate. The student, speaking as an award-winning Student of the Year with this group, noted that the *only* success he remembered from his public school education was serving as a sixth-grade dismissal helper for a kindergarten classroom, helping children get coats and boots on in time to catch the bus. And Richard Vacca, past-president of the International Reading Association, tells of meeting

a young man who had been in his high school English class but who dropped out of school. When Vacca mentioned reading, the teen remarked "somewhat wistfully, somewhat defiantly, 'F_____ reading. Reading robbed me of my manhood'" (Vacca, 1998, p. 608).

Specifics about all the personal events and feelings underlying these comments and memories are left unsaid, but scenes come to mind where classmates might have ridiculed the individuals' reading and where low track placements might have embarrassed them. Like other adolescents who have struggled with reading (Kos, 1991; Rose, 1989), these individuals probably experienced stress and anxiety and doubted their potential effectiveness in the world. Literacy failures can hurt adolescents deeply.

Reading development does not occur in a vacuum. It mixes with the ways adolescents identify their roles as learners, friends, employees, and citizens (Alvermann, Hinchman, Moore, Phelps, & Waff, 1998). Adolescents with a history of literacy difficulties often generate identities that interfere with future literacy learning. Students who see themselves as academic failures and nonreaders require special conditions to shape new productive identities. When reporting on longitudinal studies of adolescents learning to read, Meek (1983) put it this way:

> Readers in secondary school who want to learn to read have to subject themselves to a particular kind of metaphysical distress. Nothing written about it can fully convey the strain of what, hitherto, has been superficially described as "reluctance," "failure," "poor motivation." The real condition of these pupils was not lack of desire to learn, or poor basic skills, but absolute conviction that they could not be successful no matter what they did. (p. 214)

Many of the articles in this collection focus on this condition. They suggest ways to generate academic engagement and success, ways to break cycles of failure. They acknowledge students' beliefs and situations that interfere with learning while presenting ways to inspire teens to be resilient and take charge of their learning.

"That's just the way it is"

One way of breaking cycles of failure and low self-esteem is to create spaces in which students can express themselves and their reactions to assigned class readings. For example, Donna Alvermann vividly recalls the following incident in which a group of eighth graders were asked to respond to John Steinbeck's *The Pearl* (Alvermann, Commeyras, Hinson, & Randall, 1996). Students were to consider who was the more dominant character–Kino or Juana, Kino's wife. Most students concluded that it had to be Kino because he was the man, and he made all the decisions for his family. When asked, "Do you think this is pretty common in literature for the man to be the dominant one?" the students nodded their heads in agreement, with a student named Paula explaining the phenomenon this way: "Well, it kind of just started in the beginning. Adam was made first, and that was kind of like the man was the head of the family. And so it was just kind of in all the stories. That's just likely to be applied to real life. That's just the way it is."

This example shows how the language of the classroom and the language of the text conspire to socially construct what it means to be male, and, by implication, what it means to be female. Here, the weight of religion, literary history, and culture combine to leave little doubt in Paula's mind that this is just the way life is, always has been, and always will be.

With regard to classroom life, a group of high school students reported to Kathy how easy it was to read their teachers' expectations and biases and how doing well in some classes only meant playing to those readings in uncritical subservient ways. Certain girls were treated disparagingly in some classes, male "jocks" were treated so in others. White students seemed to receive preferential treatment in some classes, while students of color seemed to do so in others. Students could see the way stereotypes played out in classrooms to the benefit or detriment of certain groups.

But need this be the case? We do not think so. Creating spaces for students to explore multiple perspectives and interpretations of their texts and their classrooms is a starting point. This compilation of articles presents numerous examples of strategies for building an awareness among adolescents of the need to explore differences and to honor diversity as these students work toward interpreting texts and achieving a sense of community in classrooms.

"I am getting so-o-o tired of answering your cardboard questions!"

When David began as a high school Title I reading teacher, he inherited a classroom full of commercial skill-building kits and a few paperbacks. He dutifully directed each student through individualized programs of reading passages, answering questions, checking answers for accuracy, then moving up or down in the kits to new sets of passages and questions.

One day, one of the more unconventional students with whom David shared good rapport trudged from her desk to the reading kit. She looked him directly in the eye and expressed her disdain for the cardboard questions, as quoted above. David was beginning to realize that this program was unproductive, and this student's comment inspired him to take action. With the help of some like-minded teachers, he began moving to a curriculum of inquiry, response, and group interaction.

Adolescents with and without reading difficulties often comment on being bored with schoolwork (Farrell, Peguero, Lindsey, & White, 1988). Boredom seems at least partly implicated with assignments that make little sense, materials that barely connect with students' worlds, and limited opportunities for self expression. For instance, Kathy observed students in a high school social studies class who did not feel the study guide questions they were completing were helpful. Instead, they indicated that the questions were like work in a factory that demanded only partial consciousness. As one student acknowledged, "When you have other subjects, it's hard (to get all the required work done). I like it when I understand."

Concluding Thoughts

The articles included here present ways to foster a spirit of inquiry and to provide needed support as students use print for exploring the world as well as their lives. They present multiple strategies for enhancing reading. Many articles describe networks that connect adolescents with teachers and peers, younger and older acquaintances, and family and community members. The works are practical. Acknowledging the complexity of teaching adolescents who struggle with reading, the articles are grounded in classroom applications.

REFERENCES

Alvermann, D., Commeyras, M., Hinson, D., & Randall, S. (1996). *The gendered language of texts and classrooms: Teachers and students exploring multiple perspectives and interpretations* (Instructional Resource No. 23). Athens, GA: National Reading Research Center.

Alvermann, D.E., Hinchman, K.A., Moore, D.W., Phelps, S.F., & Waff, D.R. (Eds.). (1998). *Reconceptualizing the literacies in adolescents' lives*. Mahwah, NJ: Erlbaum.

Farrell, E., Peguero, G., Lindsey, R., & White, R. (1988). Giving voice to high school students: Pressure and boredom, ya know what I'm sayin'? *American Educational Research Journal*, *25*, 489–502.

Kibby, M.W. (1995). *Student literacy: Myths and realities*. Bloomington, IN: Phi Delta Kappa Educational Foundation.

Kos, R. (1991). Persistence of reading difficulties: The voices of four middle school students. *American Educational Research Journal*, *28*, 875–895.

Meek, M. (1983). *Achieving literacy: Longitudinal studies of adolescents learning to read*. London: Routledge & Kegan Paul.

Moore, D.W., Bean, T.W., Birdyshaw, D., & Rycik, J.A. (1999). *Adolescent literacy: A position statement*. Newark, DE: International Reading Association.

National Assessment of Educational Progress. (1999). *NAEP 1998 reading report card for the nation and the states* [Online]. Available Internet: http://www.ed.gov/NCES/NAEP

O'Brien, D. (1998). Multiple literacies in a high-school program for "at-risk" adolescents. In D.E. Alvermann, K.A. Hinchman, D.W. Moore, S.F. Phelps, & D.R. Waff (Eds.), *Reconceptualizing the literacies in adolescents' lives* (pp. 27–49). Mahwah, NJ: Erlbaum.

Rose, M. (1989). *Lives on the boundary: The struggles and achievements of America's underprepared*. New York: Free Press

Rossi, J.A., & Pace, C.M. (1998). Issues-centered instruction with low achieving high school students: The dilemmas of two teachers. *Theory and Research in Social Education*, *26*, 380–409.

Vacca, R. (1998). Let's not marginalize adolescent literacy. *Journal of Adolescent & Adult Literacy*, *41*, 604–609.

SECTION 1

Working With Struggling Adolescent Readers

At teachers' conferences and among prospective teachers in undergraduate classes, one can regularly hear comments such as, "I LOVE working with high school students!" or "I could NEVER work with middle school students!" Students who are establishing personal identities in a complex and often dangerous world readily elicit emotionally charged responses. To be sure, adolescents can be complicated and provocative. Moreover, teenagers who struggle with reading often are developing multilayered identities and perspectives that differ considerably from more academically successful peers—even as they differ from one another. Yet the varied nature of their identities and perspectives is easily overlooked in the academically driven world of secondary schooling.

The authors of the five articles in this section share the insight that understanding individual perspectives is critical if we are to help adolescents who struggle with reading. These articles address connections between adolescents' burgeoning identities and their classroom literacy behaviors. The authors share students' views of their literacy-related actions. Most importantly, these authors introduce us to instructional responses that are constructed with respect for adolescents' particular viewpoints.

We encourage you to consider the themes of this section as you review instructional ideas in the rest of this book and elsewhere. As complicated and provocative as adolescents might seem, respect for who they are and what they understand is an important starting point for any pedagogy meant to help them be more successful readers.

Darrell Morris, Criss Ervin, and Kim Conrad

A Case Study of Middle School Reading Disability

As director of a university reading clinic, each year I (Morris) see scores of children who experience difficulty with reading. Our clinical program is straightforward and short on frills; it consists of a parent interview (1 hour), informal testing to determine each student's reading level (1 hour), and intensive one-to-one tutoring (two times per week during the school year) to help the student improve his/her reading ability. Some of the students we tutor improve rapidly in reading, others make slow but steady progress, and a few show little gain despite our best efforts.

Sometimes a specific clinic case captures my attention. Usually it is a child who is having an undue amount of difficulty processing written language. But on occasion, a case stands out not so much for its exceptionality as for its seeming generality. That is, in getting to know a particular disabled reader and his or her family, and reflecting on the educational havoc caused by the reading problem, I recognize that this one student is representative of many others in the public schools.

This article describes such a case. Brett (not his true name), a sixth-grade boy of average intelligence, came to us reading at the second-grade level. His school diagnosis was learning disabled; his chances for becoming fully literate appeared slim. This case study report includes (a) a summary of the initial parent interview, (b) a detailed description of the student's tutoring program (including assessment), and (c) commentary on the public school's responsibility to provide effective remedial reading instruction.

Parent Interview

Mrs. Stacey (also a pseudonym) took off from work early on a Friday afternoon and drove 60 miles to have her sixth-grade son, Brett, evaluated at our reading clinic. As Brett was being tested, I interviewed her. Mrs. Stacey lived with her husband and three children in a small town in western North Carolina. She informed me that though neither she nor her husband had attended college, her oldest daughter was now a freshman at a state university and her other daughter was doing well academically in junior high school. It was Brett, her youngest, that she was concerned about. A rising seventh grader, he had scored at the second-grade level (2.8) on a recent, school-administered standardized reading test.

According to Mrs. Stacey, Brett had repeated kindergarten and experienced difficulty learning to read in first grade. ("He would memorize the basal stories but he couldn't read them.") In December of second grade,

Reprinted From *The Reading Teacher*, *49*(5), 368–377, February 1996.

Brett was tested for a possible learning disability and diagnosed as dyslexic. He spent his third- and fourth-grade years in a self-contained special education class but advanced little in reading despite the help of an after-school tutor. In the fifth and sixth grades Brett was mainstreamed into the regular classroom, receiving resource help 90 minutes per day. Mrs. Stacey approved of her son's placement in the regular academic classes; however, the special education assistance program in Brett's middle school was changing, and Mrs. Stacey did not like the changes.

In the sixth grade, Mrs. Stacey explained, the special education resource teacher no longer provided Brett with direct instruction in reading but instead concentrated on helping him understand and complete assignments in his academic subjects. Mrs. Stacey recognized the need for such academic assistance, but she stated adamantly:

> Brett is finishing the sixth grade and he can't read his textbooks. If the resource teacher isn't helping him improve his reading skills, then who is going to do it? I think the school is giving up on reading, and I'm not going to have it. I've come up here [to the university] to get some help.

I must admit that I, the interviewer, had nothing but admiration for this forceful, straight-talking mother. Not only had Mrs. Stacey diligently supported her child through 6 trying years in school, but now she was interpreting and rightly confronting a change in school policy that could adversely affect her son's chances of achieving literacy. If the learning disabilities resource teacher was no longer going to provide direct reading instruction to Brett (a rising seventh grader reading on a second-grade level), then who was going to teach him to read–his middle-school English teacher, science teacher, math teacher? This seemed highly unlikely.

At this point in my interview with Mrs. Stacey, I was handed some early and tentative results from Brett's reading evaluation. His word recognition, passage reading, and spelling scores all pointed to a second-grade instructional level. I explained to Mrs. Stacey that Brett was 5 years below grade level in reading; however, I also told her that I could not be sure about the severity or intractability of his reading problem without working with him over a few weeks in a clinical teaching situation. I mentioned that we ran a 4-week reading clinic each summer and was about to say that the distance might be prohibitive. Mrs. Stacey interrupted me in mid-sentence: "Brett will be here this summer."

Reading Instruction

Summer 1992. I assigned Mrs. Ervin, an experienced first-grade teacher taking a reading practicum course, to work with Brett during the summer. We began by looking back at Brett's performance on the spring reading evaluation (see Table 1).

On the initial informal reading inventory (IRI), Brett's oral reading was slow, labored, and barely audible. He consistently waited for examiner help on difficult words, not wanting to risk a mistake. Brett's silent reading was little better. His silent comprehension of the second- and third-grade passages was poor, and his silent reading rates approximated those of a first grader. Notice in Table 1 that Brett's oral reading accuracy and oral reading rate dropped significantly at second grade. However, he did show some strength in word recognition at the second grade level (flash 70%; untimed 85%).

Mrs. Ervin tutored Brett 1 hour per day, Monday through Thursday, during the 14-day summer practicum (2 days, week 1; 4 days per week, weeks 2-4). The principles that guid-

Table 1
Brett's initial test results in word recognition, passage reading, and spelling (May 1992)

| Grade level | Word recognition | | Passage reading | | | | | Spelling |
| | | | Oral | | | Silent | | |
	Flash (%)	Untimed (%)	Accuracy (%)	Comp. (%)	Rate (wpm)	Comp. (%)	Rate (wpm)	(%)
First	70	90	94	80	69	80	72	65
Second	70	85	90	80	55	60	63	44
Third	30	60	84	60	51	50	65	20

Note: Instructional level criteria (%) varied by assessment task: word recognition (flash) 70%, oral reading accuracy 92%, oral and silent reading comprehension 75%, and spelling 40%.

ed her instruction were traditional but time-less in their importance:

- Determine the student's reading instructional level–the level where he is challenged but not frustrated–and present instruction accordingly.

- Use reading material that is of personal interest and significance to the student.

- Build comprehension through informal discussions of stories or articles as they are being read.

- Assess the student's word recognition along a continuum of written word knowledge (e.g., beginning consonants, word families, vowel patterns, multisyllable words) and then, over time, provide systematic, developmentally appropriate word study.

- Explore ways of getting the student to practice reading when he is away from the tutorial setting.

Mrs. Ervin's lesson plans, which did not vary across the 14-day summer session, reflected these principles (see Figure 1).

1. *Guided reading.* After previewing a second-grade story (or book chapter), Brett and his tutor would alternate reading pages orally, stopping now and then to check comprehension. After four or five pages of this partner reading, Mrs. Ervin would elicit a plot prediction from Brett and then have him read silently the remaining three or four pages of the story. He was encouraged to ask for help on difficult words. Again, comprehension was checked.

Brett began the summer by reading four stories in an old second-grade basal reader (*Tricky Troll*, Eller & Hester, 1976). He then read two chapter books, *The Stories Julian Tells* (Cameron, 1981) and *Shoeshine Girl* (Bulla, 1975), both written at a second-grade reading level. Mrs. Ervin developed an interesting and effective plan for supporting Brett's reading in the chapter books:

- Brett read a chapter with Mrs. Ervin in the tutoring session.

- Brett then took the next chapter home on cassette audiotape. His task was not just to listen to the taped chapter (six to eight pages), but to practice reading it in preparation for an oral reading check the next day.

- Brett began the next tutoring session by reading a 200-word sample from the practiced chapter. Mrs. Ervin recorded his oral reading accuracy and rate, and shared this information with Brett.

- The content of the practiced chapter was then discussed. A third chapter was partner read in the tutoring session, and a tape of the fourth chapter sent home.

By reading the same book in the tutoring sessions and at home (with the taped support), Brett was able to finish both chapter books in the short 4-week session. Not only did his reading ability improve, but his self-concept as a reader changed. He was completing, possibly for the first time in his life, meaningful reading assignments.

2. *Word study*. At each tutoring session Brett spent a few minutes sorting one-syllable words into vowel patterns (see Figure 2).

Brett enjoyed these brief lessons where he and his tutor categorized words by pattern. He also benefited from the short spelling checks (five or six words) that followed each sort. Over 3 weeks, he worked across the common *a*, *e*, and *i* vowel patterns (see Invernizzi, Abouzeid, & Gill, 1994; Morris, 1982; or Schlagal & Schlagal, 1992, for more information on word sorting).

3. *Writing*. At first Brett was reluctant to write, and writing did prove to be a slow, arduous process for him. Mrs. Ervin was firm but encouraging. She allowed Brett to select his own writing topics and emphasized the expression of ideas, not mechanical correctness, on first drafts. Choosing to write about sports and later a family trip to Atlanta, Brett progressed from short three-sentence accounts at the beginning of the summer to two-paragraph stories several weeks later. Mrs. Ervin helped him revise and edit two of his favorite pieces, which were then typed and illustrated.

4. *Easy reading*. Brett quickly became hooked on the Starpol books (Tully, 1987), a series of space adventures written at a late-first- to late-second-grade difficulty level. (Each Starpol book is 24 pages with engaging, colorful illustrations on each page.) Brett and his tutor would begin a Starpol story in the tutoring

Figure 1
Sample lesson plan

1. *Guided reading*

   Begin by having Brett orally read a 200-word sample from Chapter 2 of *Shoeshine Girl* (graph accuracy and rate).

   Review content of Chapter 2, and then begin Chapter 3 (partner read first three pages; Brett reads last three pages silently).

   Send Chapter 4 home on tape.

2. *Word sort*

   Sort *a* patterns (*a*, *a-e*, *ar*, *all*).

   Play Concentration game with 12 of the words.

   Do spelling check on 6 words.

3. *Writing*

   Have Brett add to, and possibly finish, his story on Atlanta trip.

4. *Easy reading*

   Introduce new Starpol book *Testing Hunter 4* (partner read first four pages, then let Brett proceed independently).

session and on most days he would finish the story at home. This easy but meaningful reading in a single series served to improve Brett's word recognition, fluency, and confidence.

At the end of the summer session it was apparent to everyone involved that Brett had made gains in reading and self-confidence. Mrs. Stacey was very pleased, but at the same time concerned about the summer clinic coming to an end. I suggested that she ask Mrs. Ervin to continue tutoring Brett during the upcoming school year (the Staceys lived approxi-

Figure 2
Word sort example

mat	rake	card	(?)
fan	made	park	fall
bag	face	far	ball
flat		dart	

name

Figure 3
Number of words read across repeated readings

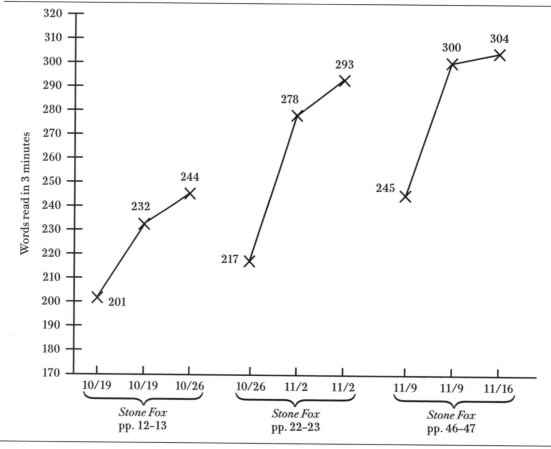

mately 45 minutes from Mrs. Ervin's school). To my delight, Mrs. Ervin agreed to tutor Brett after school if I would provide professional assistance now and then. I readily agreed.

School year 1992–1993. Brett was tutored once per week during the school year; the busy work schedules of his mother and tutor precluded more frequent sessions. Mrs. Ervin, for the most part, followed the tutoring plan that she had developed for the summer reading clinic. This included guided reading of chapter books, word study, repeated readings of familiar passages, writing, and taped readings for homework.

Brett read third- and fourth-grade chapter books during the year. In order, these were *Mustard* (Graeber, 1983), *Stone Fox* (Gardiner, 1983), *How to Eat Fried Worms* (Rockwell, 1973), *Owls in the Family* (Mowat, 1981), and *Skinnybones* (Park, 1982). He again alternated reading a chapter in the tutoring session and the following chapter at home (with the support of an audiotape). Brett's comprehension of these books was excellent, his oral reading accuracy and rate adequate, and his interest high.

To improve Brett's reading fluency (or rate), Mrs. Ervin employed the method of repeated readings (Samuels, 1979). In this activity Brett read a familiar passage for 3 minutes. The number of words read was graphed. He then read the same passage again, and then a third time in the following tutoring session. Each time the number of words read in 3 minutes was graphed (see Figure 3).

Brett benefited from the repeated readings in several ways: (a) the timed trials heightened his concentration, (b) rereadings of the same passage consistently increased his fluency or rate, and (c) the immediate graphing of results provided Brett with much-needed performance feedback.

After a few weeks of tutoring, Mrs. Ervin shared with me the difficulty Brett was having with spelling instruction in school. He was being asked to learn 10 seventh-grade words per week (e.g., *horrible*, *elegant*, *brilliant*, *companion*, *doubtful*); however, Brett was unsure of even third-grade spellings (i.e., whether *boil* was spelled "boil," "bole," or "boyl"). Frustration over weekly spelling assignments was building rapidly.

At this point Mrs. Ervin and I devised a plan for helping Brett with spelling. First, we assessed his spelling ability by administering the first three levels of a diagnostic spelling inventory (Schlagal, 1989). Results showed that Brett was functioning at a second-grade level in spelling. With these results in hand, Mrs. Ervin approached the school about having Brett's spelling instruction provided during his tutoring sessions. The classroom teacher and learning disabilities resource teacher readily consented, with the stipulation that some type of weekly assessment be turned in to the school.

In late October, Mrs. Ervin located a third-grade spelling book and used this as a resource to provide Brett with both spelling and word study instruction for the remainder of the school year. Each Monday, in the tutoring session, Brett took a pretest on a unit of 15 words from the spelling book. (Note: The first six units in the book reviewed second-grade spelling patterns.) Brett, on average, misspelled 4 to 6 words on the weekly pretest. He immediately self-corrected the pretest, writing each misspelled word correctly three times, and then sorted the 15 spelling words into patterns (see Figure 4).

Figure 4
Example of third-grade spelling unit and accompanying word sort activity

Spelling pretest		Word sort activity			
1. tray	+				
2. feel	+				
3. paint	PANT				
4. sneak	SNEK				
5. seem	+	*fail*	*lay*	*sweet*	*real*
6. real	+				
7. hay	+	paint	hay	seem	treat
8. chain	CHANE	chain	tray	feel	wheat
9. free	+				
10. lay	+		train		
11. fail	+				
12. treat	TREET				
13. train	TRANE				
14. sweet	+				
15. wheat	WHET				

Brett's homework assignment was to use each misspelled pretest word in a meaningful sentence and to review the entire spelling unit for a Friday posttest to be administered at school by his resource teacher. The following Monday, a new spelling unit was introduced in the tutoring lesson. From November through May, Brett worked through 20 of the 36 units in the third-grade book. He consistently scored 93% or better on the Friday posttests.

School year 1993–1994. Mrs. Ervin and a colleague, Mrs. Conrad, continued to tutor Brett once per week during the following school year. Brett was now a stronger reader and, consequently, his tutors increased the challenge level of his assignments. In Year 2, Brett read narrative and content material written at a fourth- or fifth-grade level; he studied spelling patterns selected from a fourth-grade spelling book. Basic tutoring procedures did not change significantly from Year 1 to Year 2.

Posttesting. Mrs. Ervin evaluated Brett's reading progress once per year. Each time, she administered the same word recognition and spelling lists, along with different but equivalent sets of reading passages.

Table 2 summarizes Brett's posttutoring (May 1994) performance. Comparing this performance against his initial assessment (Table 1) shows that Brett made considerable improvement in all areas of contextual reading: word reading accuracy, rate, and comprehension. A plodding second-grade-level reader in 1992, 2 years later he was reading fluently at the fourth-grade level. Brett also improved in spelling. Using 40% accuracy as an instructional level criterion (Morris, Blanton, Blanton, & Perney, 1995), Table 2 shows that Brett progressed 2 years in spelling, from a second-grade to a fourth-grade level. Interestingly, Brett's smallest gain was in decontextualized word recognition (flashed and untimed). Here, he ad-

vanced from a second- to a third-grade level, with most of this gain coming in the first year of tutoring.

Summary of reading instruction and test results. Brett received 78 hours of tutorial instruction over the 2-year period. His reading lessons were characterized by balance, support, and adherence to instructional level. Balance was reflected in the consistent lesson routine of (a) reading for meaning, (b) word study, (c) fluency drill, and (d) writing. Although reading for meaning in narrative and content materials dominated, the systematic study of word patterns was not neglected. In fact, a unique feature of the after-school lessons was the tutor's skillful integration of spelling and word study instruction.

When tutoring began in the summer of 1992, Brett was a struggling reader, severely lacking in confidence. He required tutorial support to read in context, and this support was provided in several ways: *partner reading* in which tutor and child alternated reading aloud pages at the beginning of a story; *taped reading* in which Brett, at home, read along with a tape-recorded version of a story or chapter; *repeated readings* in which he read aloud one short passage three successive times, working on fluency; and finally *guided reading* in which the tutor's questions and probes facilitated Brett's silent reading of a story. It is significant that much of this contextual reading support was phased out as Brett became a stronger reader over the 2-year period. For example, in Year 1 Brett often read an assigned chapter at home with the assistance of a tape recorder; in Year 2 he was able to read a chapter at home without the tape recorder.

Balanced instruction and appropriate tutor support were important, but the essential element in Brett's successful reading program was the tutor's diligent, unrelenting attention to instructional level. Initial testing

Table 2
Test results after 2 years of tutoring (May 1994)

| Grade level | Word recognition | | Passage reading | | | | | Spelling |
| | Flash (%) | Untimed (%) | Oral | | | Silent | | (%) |
			Accuracy (%)	Comp. (%)	Rate (wpm)	Comp. (%)	Rate (wpm)	
First								95
Second								76
Third	55	100	98	100	110	93	116	70
Fourth	30	70	99	93	104	100	112	48
Fifth	–	–	94	100	55	100	89	–

Note: Instructional level criteria (%) varied by assessment task: word recognition (flash) 70%, oral reading accuracy 92%, oral and silent reading comprehension 75%, and spelling 40%.

showed Brett to have, at best, a second-grade reading level. Mrs. Ervin, putting aside age and grade expectations, began working with Brett at the second-grade level. In effect, she dropped back (five levels below Brett's grade placement) to enable him to move forward. Over a 2-year period, Brett progressed steadily–from a second- to a fourth-grade instructional level in both reading and spelling. Progress was slow but foundational, and, importantly, it was sensed and appreciated by the tutor and student alike.

Brett's 2-year gain in reading and spelling was encouraging, particularly in light of the minimal reading/spelling progress he had made during his first 6 years in school. One not-so-positive test finding, however, warrants mention. It was noted earlier that Brett's ability to recognize isolated words lagged behind his contextual word recognition ability, particularly in the second year of tutoring. It can be argued that the second-year gain in reading skill was contextual in nature and that the underlying word recognition competence stalled (Chall, Jacobs, & Baldwin, 1990). Such an interpretation is certainly consistent with Brett's longstanding problem with word recognition. It also highlights the necessity of a continuing word study program–systematic study of developmentally appropriate word patterns–if Brett is to make further advances in reading and spelling.

Commentary

If this case study is representative of only a minute population of students, then its value is limited. However, I believe the opposite to be true. I believe that there are many thousands of Bretts sitting in middle school classrooms. These students struggle mightily with grade-level reading assignments and, because they are forced to read at frustration level most of the school day, their reading skill may improve little from year to year; in effect, they fall further behind their peers. Some of these students are labeled learning disabled and some slow learners, but the inescapable fact remains that *they have the potential to learn if they receive appropriate instruction.*

Appropriate instruction in Brett's case rested, in large part, on his tutor's knowledge of how to teach reading. Mrs. Ervin understood the fundamental importance of reading instructional level, she exercised good judgment in selecting interesting reading material, she was skillful in getting Brett to search for meaning in text, and she possessed knowledge of the English orthographic system and of appropriate strategies for teaching that system. Moreover, Mrs. Ervin's summer practicum experience, although short in duration, allowed her to practice her teaching—to refine her understanding of the process—in a one-to-one context under the watchful eye of an experienced clinician.

Obviously we need more Mrs. Ervins in our schools if the needs of students like Brett are to be met. I have no formula for producing such teachers, but I do think it must be done at the graduate level and at least two conditions must be satisfied. First, graduate methods courses in reading instruction must be rigorous and provide teachers with a balanced, comprehensive view of the reading process. Reading teachers must understand both word recognition and comprehension development and be able to facilitate growth in both areas through thoughtful, carefully planned instruction. Second, reading teachers-in-training must be provided with carefully supervised clinical teaching experiences. Henderson (1981) addressed this issue eloquently:

> I am convinced that a year-long practicum should be required for all reading specialists. The work should be carried on under the direct supervision of an experienced clinician who can show by example both the techniques and the exercise of judgment that are needed. No formula will suffice nor will practice by a teacher alone convey what must be mastered.... It is only by experiencing the effects of refined teaching that students learning to be teachers are gradually able to free themselves from the false belief that it is the method rather than they themselves that must control the set for learning.... Such teaching skill is learned only gradually, by example and practice. (pp. 129-130)

There are no shortcuts. One learns to teach reading by teaching—and reflecting on the teaching act—under the supervision of an experienced guide. For those who believe that clinical training is an unneeded relic from reading education's past, keep in mind that today such training receives impressive theoretical support from the "reflective practitioner" work of Schon (1987) and the "assisted learning" work of Tharp and Gallimore (1988). Also note that Reading Recovery (Clay, 1985), the most successful early reading intervention program to come along in years, is a pure example of clinical teacher training.

Are we then providing prospective reading and learning disabilities teachers with rigorous, balanced reading methods courses and carefully supervised clinical teaching experiences? This question must be answered by individual graduate programs. In U.S. reading education, I do know that there has been a general lessening of interest and vitality in clinical training over the last 2 decades. I also know that in the three states in which I have worked (Virginia, Illinois, and North Carolina), only *one* graduate course in reading has been required for a master's degree in learning disabilities (and that one course was not a teaching practicum). This is an unfortunate situation. Expertise is needed to help disabled readers. Until reading and special education faculty members in colleges of education commit themselves to developing teaching expertise in their graduate students, I do not foresee significant improvements in the quality of school-based remedial reading instruction (see Kauffman, 1994).

Given adequate training in teaching reading (a crucial assumption), a Title I or learning disabilities teacher can make a positive difference with students like Brett. The same general principles apply to tutoring and to small-group instruction; that is, identify students' instructional levels, put them in interesting books that they can read, and pace them efficiently in accordance with their advancing reading skill. Moreover, several of the specific tutoring activities mentioned in this case study can be easily adapted to small-group contexts (e.g., guided reading, taped reading, writing, word study).

Unfortunately, many Title I and most learning disabilities teachers have difficulty assembling workable instructional groups during the day (i.e., a small group of students working at a similar reading level). Disabled readers come to the resource room when their academic schedule allows, not necessarily when there is an optimal time (or context) for teaching them to read. Yet, it is next to impossible to conduct an effective 40-minute reading lesson with four students from two different grades who read at three different reading levels. And a year's worth of ineffective lessons adds up to minimal reading growth. Note, however, that this is a school scheduling problem (how to prioritize instructional time for students), not a student learning problem. If reading improvement were *the* priority for students like Brett, then scheduling conflicts could be resolved at the beginning of the year through discussion among teachers and principal.

A current trend in special education (inclusion) is to deemphasize "pull-out" programs, where direct reading instruction has traditionally been provided, and instead to have the resource teacher assist the student with academic assignments in the regular classroom. But, as Brett's mother observed in the parent interview, "That's fine, but who is going to teach Brett how to read?" It may be possible to provide appropriate instruction to remedial readers within the inclusion model, but it will be difficult. At a minimum, there will need to be coordinated planning of lessons by the classroom and resource teachers, textbook materials written at several difficulty levels, and opportunities for small-group teaching within the regular classroom (Walsmley & Walp, 1990). Anyone who has been around schools recognizes that this is a tall order. If the inclusion model leads to resource teachers abandoning direct instruction in reading to become teacher consultants or academic subject facilitators, then students like Brett will pay a huge price in terms of their reading development.

An alternative to total inclusion models, and one that I favor, is a specialist position that combines small-group pull-out teaching with some classroom consultation. If we can assume expertise on the part of the specialist, there are several advantages to this role. By continuing to provide direct reading instruction to small groups on a daily basis, the specialist teacher continually refines her/his teaching skills. By sharing expertise with classroom teachers (through conferences and model teaching), the specialist can influence a larger number of students in the school. My own experience points to a third advantage to this reading teacher/consultant role. Regular classroom teachers listen most attentively to those consultants who work directly with at-risk students on a regular basis and make a difference in their learning.

Allington (1994) points out that, historically, U.S. public schools have not been successful in meeting the needs of students like Brett. He suggests that we disband the current remediation system (Title I and learning disabilities) and start over. My concern with this radical analysis is that I am not sure we have given the current system a fair chance. There is plenty of blame to go around and, to my mind, much of it should be assigned to graduate teacher-training programs. If *all* Title I and learning disabilities teachers were well trained in teaching reading (and not all are), and if these teachers had adequate freedom in scheduling workable instructional groups during the school day (and they do not), then I see no reason why they could not make a significant difference in their students' learning.

One thing is clear from the present case study: Even a child who has fallen 4 years behind in reading can make substantial progress if s/he receives good instruction. As Mrs. Ervin stated:

> In many ways I have changed after working with Brett.... Certainly I have learned things from the tutoring experience, but more important I have come to believe even more strongly that it is never too late to help a child learn to read.

REFERENCES

Allington, R. (1994). Critical issues: What's special about special programs for children who find learning to read difficult? *Journal of Reading Behavior, 26*, 95-115.

Chall, J., Jacobs, V., & Baldwin, L. (1990). *Reading crisis: Why poor children fall behind.* Cambridge, MA: Harvard University Press.

Clay, M. (1985). *The early detection of reading difficulties* (3rd ed.). Auckland, NZ: Heinemann.

Henderson, E.H. (1981). *Learning to read and spell: The child's knowledge of words.* DeKalb, IL: Northern Illinois University Press.

Invernizzi, M., Abouzeid, M., & Gill, J.T. (1994). Using students' invented spellings as a guide for spelling instruction that emphasizes word study. *The Elementary School Journal, 95*, 155-167.

Kauffman, J.M. (1994). Places of change: Special education's power and identity in an era of educational reform. *Journal of Learning Disabilities, 27*, 610-618.

Morris, D. (1982). Word sort: A categorization strategy for improving word recognition ability. *Reading Psychology, 3*, 247-259.

Morris, D., Blanton, L., Blanton, W., & Perney, J. (1995). Spelling instruction and achievement in six elementary classrooms. *The Elementary School Journal, 96*, 145-162.

Samuels, S.J. (1979). The method of repeated readings. *The Reading Teacher, 32*, 403-408.

Schlagal, R. (1989). Constancy and change in spelling development. *Reading Psychology, 10*, 207-232.

Schlagal, R., & Schlagal, J. (1992). The integrated character of spelling: Teaching strategies for multiple purposes. *Language Arts, 69*, 418-424.

Schon, D. (1987). *Educating the reflective practitioner.* San Francisco: Jossey-Bass.

Tharp, R., & Gallimore, R. (1988). *Rousing minds to life: Teaching, learning, and schooling in social context.* New York: Cambridge University Press.

Walmsley, S., & Walp, T. (1990). Integrating literature and composing into the language arts curriculum: Philosophy and practice. *The Elementary School Journal, 90*, 251-274.

READING MATERIALS USED WITH BRETT

Bulla, C.R. (1975). *Shoeshine girl.* New York: Harper Trophy.

Cameron, A. (1981). *The stories Julian tells.* New York: Knopf.

Eller, W., & Hester, K. (1976). *Tricky troll.* River Forest, IL: Laidlaw.

Gardiner, J.R. (1983). *Stone fox.* New York: Harper Trophy.

Graeber, C. (1983). *Mustard.* New York: Bantam Skylark.

Mowat, F. (1981). *Owls in the family.* New York: Bantam Skylark.

Park, B. (1982). *Skinnybones.* New York: Knopf.

Rockwell, T. (1973). *How to eat fried worms.* New York: Dell Yearling.

Tully, J. (1987). *The Starpol series.* San Diego, CA: Wright Group.

Nancy G. Lee and Judith C. Neal

Case Study
Reading Rescue: Intervention for a Student "At Promise"

David spoke with animation and his face lit up. "I really like reading. It doesn't stress me out any more. And I really like authors! Right now, I'm reading *It* by Stephen King. It's so *exciting*!"

This remarkable conversation took place a year after we worked with David in a university clinic setting. We met with him to determine how he was faring as a freshman in high school after receiving intensive intervention for literacy improvement in our clinic. Although not unusual, perhaps, for accomplished readers, these comments were gratifying because of the nature of David's reading difficulties when we first met him.

We were contacted initially by David's middle school resource teacher who indicated that David had received special help in reading since third grade. As his eighth-grade resource teacher, she claimed that she had never worked with a student so lacking in reading skills or devoid of comprehension strategies. She stated that she was at a loss to help this student with his reading: and, although she was doubtful that a plan of intensive intervention would make a difference in his proficiency, she wholeheartedly appreciated our interest in his specific needs.

Early in our relationship with David, we discovered that he regularly attends school, has no health problems or a history of them, does not wear or need glasses, is not a behavior problem at school or at home, enjoys a stable home life, and is well liked by his peers. Thus we were able to eliminate physical or emotional factors which could be influencing his poor reading achievement (Wilson & Cleland, 1989). David demonstrated an active curiosity, self-confident social skills, and avid interest in participating in tutorial sessions. (He was thrilled to be able to brag to his friends that he was going to class at the university!)

We decided that David was "at promise" even though a single measure of his reading achievement would have labeled him "at risk." With the perspective that he had strong interpersonal skills, excellent home and school support, and a willingness to focus on what was admittedly an area of frustration to him, we believed all the ingredients were in place to allow a breakthrough in his reading performance.

Preliminary Literacy Assessment

Assessment of David's specific reading capabilities was multifaceted. We administered an informal reading inventory (IRI) for a miscue analysis and to determine his independent and instructional levels. However, when he experienced frustration on the Level I pas-

Reprinted From the *Journal of Reading*, *36*(4), 276–282, December 1992/January 1993.

sage of the IRI, we chose additional basic literacy assessments including a letter identification task and a teacher-constructed dictation task. On these two tasks, David accurately identified the sounds of the letters of the alphabet and was able to write two thirds of the words in dictated sentences. A phonics survey had to be discontinued when he was unable to blend three-letter words in a preliminary check of his phonic knowledge.

To assess comprehension strategies, we selected two relatively new procedures, the "think aloud" and the Metacomprehension Strategy Index (MSI) (Schmitt, 1990). A think aloud consists of asking students to read a short passage and then describe what they were thinking about as they read. Typically, students read a sentence at a time, and then report what was going on in their minds as they read. Students' responses can be analyzed to determine the kinds of strategies they are using to obtain meaning (see Wade, 1990). The MSI measures metacognitive behavior by assessing the types of activities in which students engage before, during, and after reading.

Results from both the think aloud activity and the MSI indicated that David was functioning almost entirely at the letter and word analysis level of reading. He exhibited no awareness of other strategies for getting meaning from print and very little knowledge of what to do to promote his understanding of print.

We returned to the IRI for listening comprehension to determine David's potential reading achievement. Although only able to read at a primer level on his own, he was able to comprehend passages up to Level 9 when they were read to him. This confirmed our belief that David was at promise in terms of his overall literacy development, exclusive of reading performance.

We also used teacher observation to note that, although interested in improving his reading, he found even attempting to read stressful. He tapped his fingers, jiggled his knees, and sat hunched over the desk with crossed arms and legs during most of the early sessions. In addition, we observed an unusual coping strategy when he read aloud. He held his breath to the point where, after several words, he was gasping for air. These behaviors led us to hypothesize that the very act of reading created a level of stress that was debilitating (Gentile & McMillan, 1987). When discussing the stress that reading represented for him, David acknowledged that he was aware of his actions and how they were affecting his ability to improve.

These assessments revealed an extremely stressed reader who had a basic knowledge of the alphabet, limited sight vocabulary, virtually no word analysis skills, and limited strategies for coping with print, yet who could comprehend eight levels beyond the ability to read on his own. We viewed our task with him as one of empowerment, enabling him to gain a sense of control over print after many years of being overwhelmed.

Instructional Model: One-on-One

We selected Clay's (1985) model of one-on-one intervention for adapting to the learning needs of a middle grade student. Clay's instructional model is intended for first graders; in a 12- to 16-week program, children receive intensive intervention, after which time they demonstrate proficiency equal to their peers. Longitudinal research data indicate that most children retain the positive effects of the intervention over time (Clay, 1985). The long-term benefits achieved by a relatively short-term form of intervention made Clay's model

Two models of reading intervention

Marie Clay's model	Reading Rescue model
Intended grade level: 1	Intended grade levels: 6-8
Instructional components:	Instructional components:
1. Reading familiar material. (Pupil selects from previously mastered books.)	1. Reading familiar material. (Pupil selects from chapter book excerpts and LEA stories.)
2. Taking a running record on a book introduced in the previous session.	2. Reading aloud to the student. (Teacher continues reading from chapter book.)
3. Developing letter identification knowledge. (Use of magnetic board, plastic letters.)	3. Taking a running record on a portion of new material introduced in the previous session.
4. Writing a story. (Composing 1-2 sentences: then cutting up the sentence(s) and rearranging words in correct order.)	4. Working with words and letters. (Use of magnetic board, plastic letters.)
5. Reading new material.	5. Writing through language experience. (Use of computer and word processing software.)
	6. Reading new material.
Materials:	Materials:
Primary level books	Chapter books in Scholastic Action Series.

appear particularly promising for adapting to the learning needs of an older student.

In Clay's model, the following components are combined within a daily 30-minute session: reading familiar material, taking a running record, developing letter identification knowledge, writing a brief story and cutting it apart to rearrange, and reading new material. Each of the components is structured or based on materials for first-grade children. In adapting the model, we determined each component's relevance for an older student and the specific materials we would use.

In the following paragraphs, we describe the unique tutoring approach, Reading Rescue, that we derived from Clay's instructional components and additional ones that we added as the need for them emerged from interacting with David. We named our model Reading Rescue because of the intensive nature of intervention required for middle school students who will soon confront the rigors of the high school curriculum. For many reading disabled students in Grades 6-8, the middle grades represent their last chance to catch up in their literacy development.

The components described below are those that compose the final instructional model developed from our experience with David. (See Figure for a comparison of Clay's model and the model we developed for older students.)

Reading familiar material. We began each session with the initial instructional component of Clay's model, rereading material already introduced to the student. Rereading familiar material is intended to build confidence and fluency, two important aspects of reading that troubled readers may rarely have experienced.

Early on, we realized that a key element for rereading material would be determining materials that would interest a middle grade student. We selected stories from the Scholastic Action Library series; these stories are written at low readability levels, yet the storylines are contemporary and reflect common concerns of preteens and teenagers. Each story is illustrated with photographs and divided into short chapters.

David began each session with rereading portions of the book that had been read as new material at the end of the previous session (see

Figure). Typically, he reread a portion of a chapter that was a favorite episode. To provide a choice of materials for this beginning activity, we also encouraged David to reread stories that he had written as part of the language experience portion of each lesson.

Reading aloud to the student. Because David was using a chapter book with a motivating storyline, we added this component to the original instructional model. His own reading of new material in the book was so labored that we spent the second part of each session reading aloud to him, picking up where we had stopped reading new material from the book the day before. (Reading new material is the final component of each session.) We wanted to maintain David's interest in the story and considered developing his appreciation of reading as a pleasurable activity to be a priority. Also, we wanted to model regular breathing during reading and appropriate expression to match the meaning.

This lesson element proved to be a favorite of David's. We observed his rapt attention as he listened and responded by laughing or asking questions about story events.

Taking a running record. This feature of Clay's instructional model was retained. In this procedure, the pupil reads aloud a selected portion of material while the teacher notes any discrepancies between print and pronunciation. Each word pronounced accurately is marked with a check; any mispronunciation is indicated by writing the word that is given above the printed word. Successful self-corrections are also indicated.

The running record provided a window on David's reading. By performing a running record during each session, a focus was established for the next part of the lesson, working with words and letters, and changes in David's strategies over the period of intervention were closely monitored.

Working with words and letters. This lesson component was not planned, just as Clay advocates. Rather, the specific focus emerged from the running record. Typical activities included identifying word parts, developing awareness of sounds in words, examining similarly spelled words, and developing various strategies for pronouncing unfamiliar words. Instruction was provided using plastic letters that David could manipulate for spelling words and constructing short sentences on a magnetic board.

After assisting him to develop specific understanding of letters and words, we encouraged the immediate contextualization of the skills work in the next instructional segment, writing through language experience.

Writing through language experience. This component is analogous to the activity of Clay's model in which students write a brief story, usually a single sentence, which is cut up and rearranged in correct order. We expanded the idea of composing a single sentence, appropriate for younger students, to writing a full story, an age-appropriate task for older students. (Because of story length, we did not cut up the stories David wrote.)

Because we wanted to take advantage of David's exceptional oral language development, we decided to have him dictate stories to us about events in his life in order to create reading materials he would be capable of reading. Hence, we referred to this as the language experience segment of the instructional model.

We combined the language experience approach (LEA) with the use of a computer and word processing software. The benefits of implementing LEA through word processing are many: Text editing can be done easily, thereby encouraging more risk taking; written text appears immediately on the screen to reinforce reading/writing connections; and immediate accessibility to what has been written promotes better story development and longer stories, prolonging the time spent in writing (Anderson-Inman, 1986; Grabe & Grabe, 1985; Smith, 1985).

For this part of each session, David dictated stories while the teacher typed what he said. During a single segment of LEA, he would start a story; the next session, he continued the story; during the third session, he would complete and edit the story. Each day, the story in progress was printed out so that he could read over it and decide what changes or additions he wanted to make in the next session. When the story was completed to his satisfaction, a final printout became part of his collection of stories that he could choose from for rereading at the beginning of each session.

The LEA activity culminated in a collection of stories, one of which was published in the format of a big book for sharing with ESL students in his school. David was proud of this book, and dedicated it to his resource teacher.

Reading new material. For this last component of each session, we returned to the low-readability, high-interest chapter book at the point where we had stopped reading aloud earlier in the session. As we introduced the new material, the story passage was overviewed for words and unfamiliar concepts.

Then, following Clay's recommended procedure, we first read a portion of the new material to David. Next, he was encouraged to read the same portion aloud as the tutor reread it. The paired unison reading was repeated as necessary to give David a sense of fluency and mastery. It was this "new" rehearsed material that we used for taking a running record in the next session.

We tutored David 2 hours a week, in two 1-hour sessions, for 15 weeks, using the Reading Rescue lesson sequence described above, for a total of 30 hours. (This matches the average length of instruction of young children in Clay's intervention program: 2.5 hours per week for 12 weeks.) To assure accuracy of the records made of each session, we also audio- and videotaped each session inconspicuously through a one way glass, as we did not want David to be distracted by taping equipment.

Progress and Results

One aspect of assessing David's progress consisted of reattempting the informal inventory. On it, David's postassessment instructional score was Level 3, a marked improvement from the frustration range on Level I for preassessment. After several years of near nonperformance in reading, this progress over 15 weeks was especially heartening. Although he continued to have many word recognition errors, he employed a range of strategies to cope with unfamiliar words and to get meaning from print.

David's new ability to use various strategies was observed also through reexamining the running records and reviewing the audio- and videotaped records taken during the final 2 weeks of instruction. His skills had improved to the point that he was willing to tackle any word, and he demonstrated the ability and willingness to solve most of his difficulties without prompting.

A postassessment of the Metacomprehension Strategy Index revealed that David had developed several new metacognitive behaviors. He acquired four effective strategies for before reading, five for during reading, and three effective strategies for after reading.

Perhaps the most significant change, however, was in the affective domain, that is, David's changed response and reaction to reading as a literacy activity. Because a major element in his inability to read was the level of stress he was experiencing, we maintained anecdotal records throughout the tutoring sessions to capture any changes in our initial observations of his behavior. By the end of the 15 weeks, David showed a relaxed posture during reading and breathed normally. He was eager to read aloud for the teacher and frequently expressed regret when the session ended. A real turning point appeared to be when one day, after 10 weeks, he took the book out of the teacher's hand in order to "read it faster" for himself.

Conversations with both his mother and resource teacher confirmed our conclusion that David had made a breakthrough regarding stress. David's mother exclaimed that he was reading at home on his own for the first time and was taking a book to bed with him! The resource teacher reported a dramatic change at school: He was willing to read aloud to others and offered to help other students. She asked to receive training in the procedures we had used with David.

To obtain final case study data, we met with David for a follow-up interview a year later. The nature of his comments and his attitude toward school and learning confirmed that the changes in his affective response to reading had been maintained over time.

Guidelines for Others

For clinical settings and reading resource classrooms, the Reading Rescue model represents a structured sequence of instructional intervention that can be implemented with middle school students. In clinical settings, the model as described appears powerful for tutorial assistance. In resource classrooms, we envision teachers working with one or two students at a time daily while other students do independent activities.

For regular classroom teachers, David's case suggests some important guidelines for providing literacy instruction.

1. *Emphasize the student's strengths.* Although teachers know to do this with regular classroom instruction, it is easy to become focused on what an older remedial student cannot do. Older students frequently exhibit idiosyncratic patterns of literacy achievement; each one is a separate case of unfulfilled potential. However, because they are older, they have more life experiences to draw upon which provide a greater store of background knowledge for applying to literacy activities.

In keeping with the idea of viewing students as "at promise," we constantly made David aware of what he could do and what he already knew about reading. This was done in the context of daily lessons by pointing out the strengths he was using: guessing at unknown words, building hypotheses related to meaning by using background knowledge, applying basic phonics knowledge, and persevering in attending to reading tasks. For David, understanding that there are different kinds of strategies was critical to his more relaxed response to reading.

2. *Use several indicators of literacy development to assess students' learning needs.* A single indicator of literacy, such as a standardized test score, provides a very narrow sample of a student's achievement, one that is obtained under the duress of formal testing. We view a standardized score as a beginning point to be considered along with other indicators.

Additional measures suitable for classroom use include an informal reading inventory, a dictation task, a writing sample, and a metacognitive survey such as the Metacomprehension Strategy Index. Except for the IRI, each of these can be group administered. Results of these varied assessments will provide insights into students' phonic awareness, ability to pronounce unfamiliar words, independent and instructional levels of reading, listening (potential) level of comprehension, writing performance, and awareness of strategic comprehension processes.

3. *Incorporate reading aloud as a regular feature of classroom instruction.* Reading aloud is a critical factor in children's early literacy development and contributes directly to achievement in reading (Anderson, Hiebert, Scott, & Wilkinson, 1985; Trelease, 1989). Although elementary teachers recognize the importance of reading aloud to younger children, many times teachers in the middle school overlook it as a vital literacy development activity. Listening to wonderful stories needs to continue throughout the grades in order to create interest in reading and to expose pupils to literature that is beyond their own level of reading.

From David's response to the reading aloud segment of each lesson, we can attest to its appeal for older students. Reading aloud also provides an opportunity for sharing ideas and discussion. As David became involved in the events of the story, we were able to explore ideas related to the main character's values and decisions.

4. *Plan opportunities for students to reread familiar favorite material.* Just as students do not outgrow having teachers read aloud to them daily, so they do not outgrow the need for reexperiencing familiar tasks. If the task was once difficult but the student has mastered it, each repetition is a reinforcement of the initial success. Also, if the story was exciting the first time, it will continue to be so. Teachers may worry too much about rereading being boring. Our experience has been that students more likely will claim ''This is boring'' when they cannot perform the planned task.

5. *Plan instruction that will reinforce the reading/writing connection.* Perhaps the most successful component of instruction for David was the opportunity to write and then read his own stories. As we worked with him

at the computer, he glowed with pleasure at choosing words and seeing them appear on the screen. At first his stories were short but he progressed rapidly to longer retellings of events at school or at home. Of course, this provided him with even more choices for reading familiar material at the beginning of each session.

In addition to creating material that he could read, the language experience component provided a way to build David's confidence and fluency, which in turn encouraged risk-taking behavior required for reading other stories. He quickly moved from reading his own stories to displaying a willingness to try harder reading. At the same time, his breathing became regular and gradually other indications of stress subsided as well. Our opinion, based on careful observation, is that the language experience component might have been the single greatest factor in David's improvement.

This case study was a preliminary investigation into the efficacy of intensive literacy intervention for a disabled reader at the middle school level. Until all children receive early intervention and disabled readers are anomalies rather than commonalities in the upper grades, the Reading Rescue model holds promise for settings in which one-on-one instruction is feasible. In addition, insights from this case study are applicable to language arts teachers who plan instruction for remedial readers.

Has David been rescued from a future of frustration with reading? Results of the intensive intervention he received and our follow-up interview with him a year later indicate that he has.

REFERENCES

Anderson, R.C., Hiebert, E.H., Scott, J., & Wilkinson, I.A.G. (1985). *Becoming a nation of readers*. Washington, DC: National Institute of Education, U.S. Department of Education.

Anderson-Inman, L. (1986). The reading-writing connection: Classroom applications for the computer. *Computing Teacher*, *14*(3), 23–26.

Clay, M.M. (1985). *The early detection of reading difficulties* (3rd ed.). Auckland, New Zealand: Heinemann.

Gentile, L.M., & McMillan, M.M. (1987). *Stress and reading difficulties*. Newark, DE: International Reading Association.

Grabe, M., & Grabe, C. (1985). The microcomputer and the language experience approach. *The Reading Teacher*, *38*, 508–511.

Schmitt, M.C. (1990). A questionnaire to measure children's awareness of strategic reading processes. *The Reading Teacher*, *43*, 454–461.

Smith, N.J. (1985). The word processing approach to language experience. *The Reading Teacher*, *38*, 556–559.

Trelease, J. (1989). Jim Trelease speaks on reading aloud to children. *The Reading Teacher*, *42*, 200–206.

Wade, S.E. (1990). Using think alouds to assess comprehension. *The Reading Teacher*, *43*, 442–451.

Wilson, R.M., & Cleland, C.J. (1989). *Diagnostic and remedial reading for classroom and clinic* (6th ed.). Columbus, OH: Merrill.

Gay Ivey

Reflections on Teaching Struggling Middle School Readers

Clark [all names are pseudonyms] told me he is interested in historical fiction. He said he guessed that *The Highwayman* (Noyes, 1981), which I read to the class today, was set during the American Revolution because Redcoats were mentioned. During free reading time we explored the classroom library for more historical fiction. I suggested that he take a look at *My Brother Sam Is Dead* (Collier & Collier, 1974).

This afternoon I read *The Little Match Girl* (Andersen, 1975) with Katie and Robin. There was a huge difference in the way these two girls read the story. Robin read very fluently, with no problems. Katie, on the other hand, stumbled through the story. Robin helped her out with every few words. I noticed that, in some instances, Katie was not using beginning consonant sounds to help her figure out words.

At the end of class today, Sarah Ann asked me if I planned to be in their classroom tomorrow. I assured her that I would. She said she likes it when I'm there because the students in the class get to do "fun things." Then she said she really doesn't like reading, though. But she pulled out a picture book, *The Wolf's Chicken Stew* (Kasza, 1987), and asked, "Do we get to read tomorrow? I want to read this book." I wonder how she really feels about reading.

These excerpts from my research journal were recorded during the first several weeks of a 5-month naturalistic investigation

on sixth-grade readers (Ivey, in press). These three separate incidents exemplify the interesting and complex nature of what I discovered about sixth-grade readers. Clark shows that middle school students can have specific reading preferences. Katie and Robin demonstrate the wide range of abilities among middle school readers. Sarah Ann reveals that some middle school students have mixed attitudes toward reading. As demonstrated by these children and their sixth-grade classmates, middle school students exhibit great range and diversity in their reading behaviors.

What my study revealed, that middle school students as readers are complex, was not surprising to me given my previous experiences with young adolescent readers and their teachers. During my training as a reading specialist, I had the opportunity to work with scores of elementary and middle school students in a university reading clinic. I learned some particularly important lessons about literacy development from tutoring for an entire academic year a fourth-grade student who enrolled in the clinic as an emergent reader. As a middle school Title I (then Chapter 1) reading/language arts teacher, I worked primarily with struggling readers, and I discovered some of the obstacles to learning for students who have not learned

Reprinted From the *Journal of Adolescent & Adult Literacy*, *42*(5), 372–381, February 1999.

27

to read strategically and purposefully by sixth grade. However, I also saw many students learn to love reading. Now, as a university instructor, I am developing a sense of what concerns preservice and inservice teachers about teaching reading to middle school students.

Through all these experiences, along with my recent research, I have reflected on what it takes for middle school students with persistent reading difficulties to become successful, engaged readers. Throughout these reflections are recurring themes that have led me to form some working generalizations about teaching struggling middle school readers.

My purpose here is to share these working generalizations. In the remainder of this article, I will elaborate on these themes, not because I think they are unique, but because I think they will be recognizable to other middle grades educators who have reflected on how to help young adolescents become readers. Although young adolescent readers do represent a wide range of abilities and habits, those of us who work closely with them are beginning to solve the puzzle of who they are as a group by identifying some important commonalties across students. The ones I mention in this article are from a variety of U.S. classrooms in three different states, and I have known them at different points in my 10 years as a reading educator, but their experiences and voices reveal what they have in common.

Recurring Themes

Struggling middle school readers like to read when they have access to materials that span the gamut of interests and difficulty levels. Numerous studies have reported that by the time students reach the middle grades, they have become uninterested in reading (Ley, Schaer, & Dismukes, 1994; McKenna, Kear, & Ellsworth, 1995). However, I agree with Bintz (1993), who suggested that many

secondary students "do not lose interest in reading per se" (p. 613), but instead they lose interest in the kinds of reading they are typically required to do in school, such as reading textbooks and certain teacher-selected texts. Worthy (1996) discussed the importance of making available interesting materials that "hook" reluctant readers, and in my experience, getting the right books into middle school students' hands has made a world of difference in their inclination to read.

One of the first books to convince me that interesting materials can inspire otherwise reluctant readers was Walter Dean Myers's *Scorpions* (1988). During my first year of teaching Title I classes I bought six copies of this book at a local bookstore. Several of the seventh-grade boys were drawn to it because of its interesting cover, which portrayed two African American teenagers at the front steps of an urban apartment building. My students were fascinated by the story, which is about a boy their own age who reluctantly joins a gang. However, they liked the book mostly because it struck a chord of familiarity with them. Students could relate, for example, to the following excerpt in which Jamal, the main character, is being harassed by Dwayne, his nemesis at school:

> "Yo, Jamal, what kind of sneakers you wearin'?" ...
> "Why don't you shut your mouth?" Jamal said. There were only fifteen minutes of school left, and he didn't want any garbage out of Dwayne.
> "All I did was ask a question," Dwayne said, looking in the direction of Billy Ware. "What kind of sneakers you wearing?"
> "None of your business," Jamal said.
> "They look like Brand X sneakers to me," Dwayne said.
> "I think you got a Brand X face," Jamal said.
> "Hey, Billy, I think he got them sneakers from the Salvation Army."
> Billy giggled and looked down at Jamal's sneakers. (Myers, 1988, p. 21)

The boys continue to taunt Jamal, and at the end of the scene, Myers writes that "Dwayne made Jamal feel small inside" (p. 22). This scenario was not new to my seventh-grade students who, like many other young adolescents, witnessed and experienced many similar real-life situations daily in school. Real-life language and incidents like these kept my students reading Scorpions, which was, for some, the first chapter book they had ever read from cover to cover. Humorous books, such as Roald Dahl's *The Twits* (1980) and Jon Scieszka's Time Warp Trio series (e.g., *Knights of the Kitchen Table*, 1991), have also been popular choices for students who have not previously read an entire chapter book.

Often picture books are the key to motivating middle school students to read. Charlie, a sixth-grade struggling reader, proclaimed *Willy the Wimp* (Browne, 1984) the "book of the year," and his sentiments were shared not only by the other students in Title I, but also by some of my homeroom students identified as gifted who chose to read the book during Sustained Silent Reading (SSR). While spending time in a sixth-grade classroom during a recent study (Ivey, in press), I read aloud to the class *Officer Buckle and Gloria* (Rathmann, 1995). After the reading many students elected to read that book during independent free reading time, and others subsequently checked it out from the school library. Other middle school favorites have been *Buz* (Egielski, 1995), *The Great White Man-Eating Shark* (Mahy, 1989), *The Stinky Cheese Man and Other Fairly Stupid Tales* (Scieszka, 1992), *Meanwhile Back at the Ranch* (Noble, 1987), and *Prince Cinders* (Cole, 1987), to name a few.

The matter of interest pertains not only to reluctant readers, but also to avid and successful middle school readers. Casey, a sixth-grade student who is a capable and highly motivated reader, wrote this note to her teacher:

I used to love to read. But this year it's not as enjoyable. I don't know why but I plainly don't like it anymore. I guess it is because I have better things to do. Another reason may be that I can't find a book in the library that interests me. I mean the school library would be the only place I could get books right now. I have already read my books at home.

I can relate to those people who say reading is boring now. I guess after you read so much you just get tired of it.

Reading is kind of like a boy. You like (him) or reading for a long while. Then after so long you just don't like (him) or reading any longer.

I thought you were suppose to enjoy reading as you got older. But it's just the opposite for me. As I get older reading is starting to interest me the least little bit.

A few weeks later, Casey found a new series of books to read, and she reported that she liked reading again. Thus, regardless of ability or general inclination to read, interesting materials are needed to develop and sustain engaged middle school readers.

Instructional-level materials have similar importance. In order for students to get better at reading, they need many opportunities to read materials they can read with 95% accuracy in word recognition (e.g., Betts, 1954). For middle school students who may be 3 to 4 or more years behind their peers in terms of reading ability, this may present a problem given the difficult materials typically found in their classrooms, but this need not be the case. Fielding and Roller's (1992) *making difficult books accessible and easy books acceptable* principle should apply beyond the early grades and into the upper elementary and middle grades in order to give all students what they need.

Lori Ann, a sixth-grade student who scored a first-grade instructional level on an informal reading inventory, had experienced only embarrassment, frustration, and failure with the grade-level texts she was asked to read year after year in school. When she discovered *The Magic Fish* (Littledale, 1986), an easy-to-read, predictable picture book in her sixth-grade classroom, she experienced fluent reading for the first time, and she asked if she could take the book home to read. Lawrence, a seventh grader whose instructional reading level was second grade, moved from frustration to success when he completed all the books in Marshall's easy-to-read Fox series (e.g., *Fox and His Friends*, 1982; *Fox on Wheels*, 1983).

Preservice teachers often ask, "Aren't middle school students embarrassed to read easy books in front of their peers?" My typical response is consistent with what Worthy, Patterson, Turner, Prater, and Salas (1997) reported about struggling readers in their after-school tutoring program. Like the middle school students I have known, these readers "approached the reading of easy texts with pleasure and a sense of relief," and they read easy books "with gusto and not a hint of embarrassment" (p. 5).

Still, some struggling middle school readers want to read texts that are difficult far beyond their comfort levels. Brock, for instance, my former sixth-grade student who read most comfortably in third-grade materials, wanted to read more challenging and sophisticated books such as Carolyn Reeder's (1989) *Shades of Gray*. Because high interest in a book's topic can often help students transcend their reading level (Hunt, 1971), students like Brock can access the things they want to read, especially with some support from a teacher or a peer.

Transitional chapter books are appropriate for middle students who are just slightly below their grade level in reading and for those who are quite capable of reading, but who are inexperienced or reluctant to read. Books such as Patricia Reilly Giff's The Kids of the Polk Street School series (e.g., *The*

Secret at the Polk Street School, 1987), Betsy Byars's *Beans on the Roof* (1988), and Clyde R. Bulla's *Shoeshine Girl* (1975) are particularly appealing because they are fairly short and easy to read so that they do not overwhelm inexperienced readers, and they also bridge the gap between picture books and chapter books. Elizabeth, a seventh-grade student in a learning disabilities resource class, read Roald Dahl's *The Magic Finger* (1993) within a 24-hour period, and when she returned the book to me, she reported proudly that it was the first book she had read.

Allington (1994) discussed how limited experience in reading is commonly misperceived as limited ability. It may seem shocking that students who have been in school for 6, 7, or 8 years could be inexperienced with print, but they cannot become experienced until they actually engage in sustained periods of reading. This can be facilitated only when students are provided time to read and access to books they really can read.

Struggling middle school readers want opportunities to share reading experiences with their teachers and their classmates. If you imagined a classroom scene in which the teacher is sitting on a stool or in a rocking chair reading aloud a story or picture book, with students sitting all around on a rug or on big, comfortable pillows or beanbag chairs, you might assume it must be an early elementary classroom. I have come to believe that this is a perfectly appropriate and desirable scene for middle school classrooms.

Successful environments for struggling middle school readers involve interaction among students and interaction between students and teachers during literacy activities. One of these activities, alluded to previously, is the teacher read-aloud. There is no doubt that reading aloud to students is a powerful practice for promoting literacy appreciation and development, but I have found that read-alouds have specific benefits for struggling middle school readers.

Introducing books and reading aloud to the class gives teachers a chance to show students that teachers themselves value the books they bring to the classroom, thus giving students the impression that reading is pleasurable and worthwhile. Far too often, teachers reveal a lack of enthusiasm for school reading materials, as Casey, a sixth-grade student, aptly observed: "I've had teachers before that just, like, hated to read. It's like 'Uhhh, here's the new book we're going to read today, class.' And that made it even boring-er because you can tell that they're not interested, so you're not going to be interested" (Ivey, in press).

When teachers read aloud interesting books and demonstrate their own enthusiasm for reading, however, their zeal may become contagious. The preservice teachers in my literacy development methods course are becoming convinced of this phenomenon, as one student, Jamie, wrote after reading a story aloud to a group of fourth-grade students for the first time: "I began telling the class that this book was one of my favorites, and as soon as I said that some of the girls were like, 'If it's your favorite, then it's my favorite, too.' It was really funny, but I told them to wait and discover if they like the book themselves." Later, she added, "It really made me smile inside when the story was over and students asked to borrow the book."

I have also observed that when middle school teachers share books regularly, students become inspired to do the same. Dora, a sixth-grade teacher, found that soon after she honored one or two students' requests to share books from home and the school library, she had to create a waiting list for students to read aloud to their classmates. The books they shared ranged from childhood favorites, such as *The Giving Tree* (Silverstein, 1994) and *The Jolly Postman* (Ahlberg & Ahlberg, 1986) to all-time middle school favorites, such as *Scary Stories to Tell in the Dark* (Schwartz, 1981). Still some students introduced their classmates to less familiar genres, such as collections of Greek mythology.

Sharing favorite books with peers is especially appealing to less successful and reluctant readers whose prior experiences with public reading consisted mainly of whole-class, round-robin readings of texts that were either too difficult, uninteresting, or both. When students have a chance to choose the books they will share and to rehearse before they read aloud, they can feel like competent, valued members of their classroom literacy communities. For instance, Joshua, a frustrated seventh-grade student in a learning disabilities resource class, had severely limited word knowledge and had never read a book on his own. Needless to say, his oral reading experiences in school had been torturous. What he desperately needed was plenty of supported reading in simple texts, since there was probably no book he could pick up and read on his own.

What worked for Joshua was echo and choral reading. For example, in an echo reading of the predictable pattern book *Hattie and the Fox* (Fox, 1986), the teacher started by reading a short section of the text, and then Joshua read the same lines, and they continued in this manner until the end of the book. After Joshua gained some confidence through echo reading the book in its entirety several times, they tried choral reading, in which Joshua and his teacher read in unison, with the teacher taking the lead until Joshua felt comfortable enough to do so. After a couple of choral readings, Joshua requested to read it aloud to his class, an incident that ignited a pattern book read-aloud frenzy among his classmates who were also extremely inexperienced as readers in the seventh grade.

A sixth-grade student, Ronnie, who I had assumed was uninterested in all the reading and writing activities in his class, asked me to listen to him read *Private I. Guana: The Case of the Missing Chameleon* (Laden, 1995) in the hallway before he read it to the class. I jumped to the conclusion that this often mischievous student was using this opportunity to get out of the classroom, but he proved me wrong when after practicing his reading on several pages he announced that he felt he was ready to share. He went back into the classroom, took a seat on the stool at the front of the class, and read the story to his classmates, cover to cover.

Shared reading times are also good opportunities for students to learn from their teachers and classmates about how to season their oral reading. I have often noticed students trying to mimic the way the teacher reads, using different voices for different characters. A sixth-grade boy once told me as I read aloud *Johnny Appleseed* (Kellogg, 1988), "When you read, it's like a story." After hearing her sixth-grade teacher read aloud *Elbert's Bad Word* (Wood, 1988), Allison decided to read the book on her own, and she announced, "I'm going to try to read this with expression." One of my preservice teachers reflected on how her reading style affected the fifth-grade students who listened to her: "As I read the book, I noticed that the kids really liked to hear different voices and characters throughout the story, which I thought was fun to do and also seemed to help link the characters with a persona."

Equally important to struggling middle school readers are opportunities to read one-on-one with a peer or a teacher. For many students who struggle with reading, individualization has meant going to a remedial reading class and working alone to complete skill sheets, with the teacher rarely intervening with explanations or instructional support (McGill-Franzen & Allington, 1990). There are obvious instructional benefits to one-on-one reading times, such as impromptu lessons on word identification and comprehension strategies, but perhaps their fundamental value is that they are shared literacy experiences that are both personalized and individualized. If students who struggle with reading are to become better and more enthusiastic, they need many opportunities just to enjoy the literate experience with peers and teachers when they are not also being monitored, corrected, or tested.

Struggling middle school readers need real purposes for reading. When surveyed about their most memorable school assignments, one group of middle school students rated hands-on science and independent research projects as their favorites (Wasserstein, 1995). Although reading and writing were scarcely mentioned as favorites, students did not complain about reading and writing when they were used to accomplish some meaningful task. It is not surprising that middle school readers need real purposes for reading, given that motivation is highest when students engage in tasks for their own intrinsic reasons (Deci & Ryan, 1985).

For middle school students who struggle with reading, having authentic purposes is especially crucial. Unfortunately, the remediation programs provided to struggling readers when they were in the elementary grades may have focused on specific skills and other nonacademic activities rather than on reading for meaning (Johnston & Allington, 1991), and students are likely to encounter a similar skill-and-drill approach in the middle grades (Becker, 1990).

Round-robin reading, a practice that persists in schools despite uncertainty about the origin of its popularity (Hoffman & Segel,

1982), is especially problematic for struggling middle school readers. Many students may share the sentiments of Allison, a sixth-grade student who avoids oral reading because of her limited word identification skills: "I think [other students] be staring at me and stuff" (Ivey, in press). Ryan, a fairly fluent sixth-grade reader, senses the frustration of less able readers in his class during round-robin reading, and he explained why he volunteers to read: "I raise my hand 'cause I want to read and get it done with 'cause the slow people read, and it takes them forever to get it done" (Ivey, in press). If struggling readers' agenda is to avoid being called on to read during round-robin readings, and fluent readers' agenda is to "get it done," the ultimate purpose for the reading, to actively construct meaning, must be lost to most of the class.

In my experience, struggling middle school readers enjoy oral reading activities that culminate with a performance. For instance, Allison, the sixth-grade student mentioned previously, vehemently disliked traditional oral reading activities such as round-robin reading. However, after collaborating with a classmate on an original poem patterned after selections from *Joyful Noise: Poems for Two Voices* (Fleischman, 1988), she voluntarily read it aloud to the class. What made the difference for Allison in this situation was the fact that she was able to rehearse the poem at least a dozen times before performing it, or, as she put it, "I got to practice" (Ivey, in press). Moreover, sharing something she had written gave her an authentic purpose for reading. Readers Theatre performances of a wide range of texts, including poetry (e.g., *Revolting Rhymes*, Dahl, 1983), excerpts from novels (e.g., *Goodbye Chicken Little*, Byars, 1979), and short stories (e.g., *Fables*, Lobel, 1980), provide opportunities for students to practice reading toward a goal. In this activity the text is read aloud as a script, with each student assuming the role of a character or some other part.

I have also come to believe that struggling middle school readers do find their own purposes for reading, but not necessarily for in-school, teacher-assigned reading. For example, Allison, who said she "hates to read," read *Jet* magazine regularly at home and often read aloud to her younger brother. Daisy, a sixth-grade struggling reader, checked out books on cooking from the school library and experimented with brownie baking at home. Joey, a sixth-grade sports fanatic, counted on me to bring the morning newspaper to school each day so that he could borrow the sports section during SSR. Ricky and Tim read books on how to draw and make paper airplanes. Given the importance of students' personal preferences, out-of-school reading interests ought to be welcomed into the classroom and integrated into the reading curriculum.

The strong influence of self-selection on motivation to read makes a good case for free-choice reading, especially for struggling middle school readers. Still, for ease of dealing with comprehension instruction, promoting literary discussions, and developing content knowledge, teacher-selected, whole-class, common texts are sometimes necessary in middle school classrooms, so a balance between teacher-selected and student-selected reading must be maintained. However, many struggling middle school readers may succeed at reading teacher-assigned texts only when teachers help them set purposes for reading and support their reading by showing them ways to become active, strategic readers. I have found that Directed Reading-Thinking Activities (Stauffer, 1969) help less successful readers become engaged in reading texts they would not necessarily choose for themselves because predicting, based on clues from the book and their prior knowledge, along with monitoring their hypotheses, gives them the purpose they need to keep reading. Still, though, materials for guided reading and discussion must be on students' instructional reading levels.

Struggling middle school readers want to be and can become good readers. In general, students' attitudes toward reading may decline during the middle school years, and they may choose to read less than in previous years (Ley, Schaer, & Dismukes, 1994). For struggling middle school readers, increasingly negative attitudes toward reading are even more pronounced than for average and above-average readers (McKenna, Kear, & Ellsworth, 1995). However, their pessimism toward reading may be caused by feelings of helplessness and hopelessness (e.g., Johnston & Winograd, 1985) rather than by a general dislike of reading (Kos, 1991).

Conversely, I have some lasting recollections of sixth-, seventh-, and eighth-grade students who, despite significant odds and low expectations, actually became willing, skilled readers during the middle grades. Antoine, a frustrated, reluctant seventh-grade reader, began the school year reading on the second-grade level, mainly due to his limited word knowledge. A spelling inventory revealed that Antoine was in the within-word-pattern stage of development (Bear, Invernizzi, Templeton, & Johnston, 1996). His instructional program was multifaceted, but it included two main foci: word study and independent reading.

I taught Antoine within a small pull-out group for just 40 minutes each day, so roughly 30 minutes of that time was devoted to a combination of those two activities. Antoine's word study group, which included three or four other students, began the school year by examining long vowel patterns, one vowel at a time (e.g., v*a*se, tr*ai*n, w*a*y), through conceptual word sorting activities and games (see Bear, Invernizzi, Templeton, & Johnston, 1996).

The books Antoine chose for independent reading were mainly easy-to-read picture books, such as *Henry and Mudge in the Green Time* (Rylant, 1987). As Antoine's word knowledge developed, he began to read more challenging titles, such as the short novel *Mystery in the Night Woods* (Peterson, 1991). The most convincing evidence of his growth, however, was his mother's happy and tearful report that she came home from work one day to find Antoine reading to his preschool-aged sister.

There were many students who blossomed as readers like Antoine did, but there were also those who did not. But even my failure to find what worked for these children did not destroy their desire to become more literate nor did it diminish the value they placed on what they could do as readers and writers. I remember vividly Darryl, who was in my Title I class for sixth and seventh grades, but who was placed in a special education program for his eighth-grade year and could not receive both services. Although, despite our efforts, he had not made tremendous progress in reading and writing by eighth grade, he still had the desire to improve and the desire to read and write, which he demonstrated often by skipping lunch to read picture books and to write poems on the computer in my classroom. I am convinced that helping Darryl with his persistent reading problem was my responsibility, and that he was fully capable of becoming a skilled reader if he had been provided with appropriate instruction. I can only hope that now, 7 years later and much more knowledgeable and experienced as a reading educator, I would know how to help Darryl match his motivation to read with good reading skills.

Perhaps the most compelling story I have read with respect to struggling middle school readers chronicled one sixth-grade boy's growth from a second-grade instructional level to a fourth-grade instructional level during 2 years of tutoring (Morris, Ervin, & Conrad, 1996). Instruction for this student included comprehension practice, word study, fluency practice, and writing, but all were balanced within the context of interesting literature he could read and wanted to read. Morris et al. (1996) attributed this success story, in large part, to the fact that the tutor was well trained and knowledgeable about teaching reading. If we placed struggling middle school readers in classrooms where they could experience good teaching, I believe their potential to improve and their motivation to be literate would become increasingly apparent.

In my experiences, struggling middle school students do want to become better at reading, but this happens only when they experience instructional environments that foster optimism for improvement. I believe the most beneficial learning contexts for struggling readers, whether they are regular classrooms, pull-out programs, or one-on-one tutoring sessions, are those that promote both skill and will (Paris, Lipson, & Wixson, 1983) and combine enablement and engagement (Roe, 1997) for reading and writing.

One barrier to providing struggling middle school readers with the instruction they need is the wide range of reading abilities in any one middle school classroom. In order for middle school teachers to see the potential of struggling readers to improve, they must reconceptualize how the reading/language arts class looks, both physically and instructionally. Roller (1996) described how a workshop concept can facilitate reading and writing growth for all students within the regular classroom. The organization of a workshop classroom is particularly appropriate for struggling readers because it is grounded in the notion that individual children within the same classroom can do a variety of literacy activities at once, thus accommodating vari-

Children's Books

Ahlberg, J., & Ahlberg, A. (1986). *The jolly postman*. Ill. A. Ahlberg. New York: Little, Brown.

Andersen, H.C. (1975). *The little match girl*. Ill. B. Lent. Boston: Houghton Mifflin.

Browne, A. (1984). *Willy the wimp*. New York: Knopf.

Bulla, R.C. (1975). *Shoeshine girl*. New York: HarperCollins.

Byars, B. (1979). *Goodbye, Chicken Little*. New York: Harper & Row.

Byars, B. (1988). *Beans on the roof*. New York: Dell.

Cole, B. (1987). *Prince Cinders*. New York: G.P. Putnam's Sons.

Collier, J.L., & Collier, C. (1974). *My brother Sam is dead*. New York: Macmillan.

Dahl, R. (1980). *The Twits*. Ill. Q. Blake. New York: Bantam-Skylark.

Dahl, R. (1983). *Revolting rhymes*. Ill. Q. Blake. New York: Bantam.

Dahl, R. (1993). *The magic finger*. Ill. T. Ross. New York: Puffin.

Egielski, R. (1995). *Buz*. New York: HarperCollins.

Fleischman, P. (1988). *Joyful noise: Poems for two voices*. New York: HarperCollins.

Fox, M. (1986). *Hattie and the fox*. Ill. P. Mullins. New York: Simon & Schuster.

Giff, P.R. (1987). *The secrets at the Polk Street School*. Ill. B. Sims. New York: Dell.

Kasza, K. (1987). *The wolf's chicken stew*. New York: G.P. Putnam's Sons.

Kellogg, S. (1988). *Johnny Appleseed*. New York: Morrow.

Laden, N. (1995). *Private I. Guana: The case of the missing chameleon*. San Francisco: Chronicle.

Littledale, F. (1986). *The magic fish*. Ill. W.P. Pels. New York: Scholastic.

Lobel, A. (1980). *Fables*. New York: Harper & Row.

Mahy, M. (1989). *The great white man-eating shark*. Ill. J. Allen. New York: Dial.

Marshall, E. (1982). *Fox and his friends*. Ill. J. Marshall. New York: Dial.

(continued)

Children's Books (continued)

Marshall, E. (1983). *Fox on wheels*. Ill. J. Marshall. New York: Dial.

Myers, W.D. (1988). *Scorpions*. New York: Harper & Row.

Noble, T.H. (1987). *Meanwhile back at the ranch*. Ill. T. Ross. New York: Dial.

Noyes, A. (1981). *The highwayman*. Ill. C. Keeping. Oxford, England: Oxford University Press.

Peterson, J. (1991). *Mystery in the night woods*. Ill. C. Szekeres. New York: Scholastic.

Rathmann, P. (1995). *Officer Buckle and Gloria*. New York: G.P. Putman's Sons.

Reeder, C. (1989). *Shades of gray*. New York: Avon.

Rylant, C. (1987). *Henry and Mudge in the green time*. Ill. S. Stevenson. New York: Macmillan.

Schwartz, A. (1981). *Scary stories to tell in the dark*. Ill. S. Gammell. New York: HarperCollins.

Scieszka, J. (1991). *Knights of the kitchen table*. Ill. L. Smith). New York: Puffin.

Scieszka, J., & Smith, L. (1992). *The stinky cheese man and other fairly stupid tales*. New York: Viking.

Silverstein, S. (1994). *The giving tree*. New York: HarperCollins.

Wood, A. (1988). *Elbert's bad word*. Ill. A. Wood & D. Wood. New York: Harcourt Brace.

ability between students. Reading and writing skills can be taught individually, in small groups, or in whole-class minilessons while students are reading and responding to self-selected, personally interesting children's literature on their independent or instructional reading levels. From a teaching perspective, I value the workshop design because it allows me to work in close proximity to small groups of students and, most importantly, to individual students.

A second organizational plan that allows for struggling readers' needs to be met in the regular classroom is the circle-seat-center format (Bear et al., 1996), with students placed in one of three rotating groups based on their instructional needs. During circle time, the teacher meets with a small group of students for instructional-level, guided reading and word study activities. At seat time, students practice what the teacher modeled or taught in a previous circle time. For instance, students might work independently on word study activities (e.g., word sorts, word hunts, writing sorts) dealing with whatever spelling pattern or concept they are studying, or they might read books on their independent reading level. Center time might consist of writing projects students can work on individually or with partners. Although developmental grouping should not be the only way of grouping students during the school day, struggling readers in particular benefit from developmentally appropriate instruction that is difficult to accomplish in a whole-class, heterogeneous format.

Final Thoughts

My working generalizations on teaching struggling middle school readers are not intended to oversimplify the very serious and complex problem of children reaching the middle grades lacking the basic skills, confidence, and motivation they need to learn from the increasingly difficult and diverse materials they are expected to read. Morris et al. (1996) called for improved and more intensive training for reading specialists and learning disabilities teachers who work with struggling readers. I would extend that recommendation to include regular classroom teachers in the middle school. I believe middle school language arts teachers ought to be knowledgeable about how literacy develops from the early years on, and only then will they understand struggling readers' histories and what they need to progress toward independence in reading.

Do current teacher education programs prepare new middle school teachers to be good teachers of struggling readers? Probably not. We still have a long way to go in offering adequate reading methods coursework in general for preservice middle school teachers (Romine, McKenna, & Robinson, 1996). What I hope my working generalizations offer to new and experienced middle school teachers is a place to start with students whose situations seem otherwise hopeless or, at best, extremely difficult. The more I learn about middle school readers the more I am convinced that all of them, even those who have struggled with reading since kindergarten, can become successful, engaged readers with the right kind of instruction and with teachers who are attuned to what they need.

REFERENCES

Allington, R.L. (1994). The schools we have. The schools we need. *The Reading Teacher, 48,* 14–29.

Bear, D.R., Invernizzi, M., Templeton, S., & Johnston, F. (1996). *Words their way: Word study for phonics, vocabulary, and spelling instruction.* Englewood Cliffs, NJ: Prentice-Hall.

Becker, H.J. (1990). Curriculum and instruction in middle-grades schools. *Phi Delta Kappan, 71,* 450–457.

Betts, E.A. (1954). *Foundations of reading instruction.* New York: American Books.

Bintz, W.P. (1993). Resistant readers in secondary education: Some insights and implications. *Journal of Reading, 36,* 604–615.

Deci, E.L., & Ryan, R.M. (1985). *Intrinsic motivation and self-determination in human behavior.* New York: Plenum Press.

Fielding, L., & Roller, C. (1992). Making difficult books accessible and easy books acceptable. *The Reading Teacher, 46,* 678–685.

Hoffman, J.V., & Segel, K.W. (1982). *Oral reading instruction: A century of controversy.* (ERIC Document Reproduction Service No. ED 239 277)

Hunt, L.C. (1971). The effect of self-selection, interest, and motivation upon independent, instructional, and frustration levels. *The Reading Teacher, 24,* 146–151.

Ivey, G. (in press). A multicase study of middle school readers. *Reading Research Quarterly.*

Johnston, P., & Allington, R. (1991). Remediation. In R. Barr, M.L. Kamil, P. Mosenthal, & P.D. Pearson (Eds.), *Handbook of reading research, Vol. 2* (pp. 984–1012). White Plains, NY: Longman.

Johnston, P.H., & Winograd, P.N. (1985). Passive failure in reading. *Journal of Reading Behavior, 17,* 279–299.

Kos, R. (1991). Persistence of reading disabilities: The voices of four middle school students. *American Educational Research Journal, 28,* 875–895.

Ley, T.C., Schaer, B.B., & Dismukes, B.W. (1994). Longitudinal study of the reading attitudes and behaviors of middle school students. *Reading Psychology, 15,* 11–38.

McGill-Franzen, A., & Allington, R.L. (1990). Comprehension and coherence: Neglected elements of literacy instruction in remedial and resource room services. *Journal of Reading, Writing, and Learning Disabilities, 6,* 149–180.

McKenna, M.C., Kear, D.J., & Ellsworth, R.A. (1995). Children's attitudes toward reading: A national survey. *Reading Research Quarterly, 30,* 934–955.

Morris, D., Ervin, C., & Conrad, K. (1996). A case study of middle school reading disability. *The Reading Teacher, 49,* 368–377.

Paris, S.G., Lipson, M.Y., & Wixson, K.K. (1983). Becoming a strategic reader. *Contemporary Educational Psychology, 8,* 296–316.

Roe, M.F. (1997). Combining enablement and engagement to assist students who do not read and write well. *Middle School Journal, 28*(3), 35–41.

Roller, C.M. (1996). *Variability not disability: Struggling readers in a workshop classroom.* Newark, DE: International Reading Association.

Romine, B.G.C., McKenna, M.C., & Robinson, R.D. (1996). Reading coursework requirements for middle and high school content area teachers: A U.S. survey. *Journal of Adolescent & Adult Literacy, 40,* 194–198.

Stauffer, R.G. (1969). *Directing the reading-thinking process*. New York: Harper & Row.

Wasserstein, P. (1995). What middle schoolers say about their schoolwork. *Educational Leadership*, *53*(1), 41–43.

Worthy, J. (1996). A matter of interest: Literature that hooks reluctant readers and keeps them reading. *The Reading Teacher*, *50*, 204–212.

Worthy, J., Patterson, E., Turner, M., Prater, S., & Salas, R. (1997, December). *Coming to love books: Reading preferences of struggling readers*. Paper presented at the annual meeting of the National Reading Conference, Scottsdale, AZ.

Carolyn Colvin and Linda Kramer Schlosser

Developing Academic Confidence to Build Literacy: What Teachers Can Do

The school day is about to begin at Southwestern Middle School (pseudonym), a neighborhood school in an older, low-income urban area in southern California, USA. The school's main office is a hub of activity in the minutes just before the bell rings to signal the start of the first class. As one enters this aging stucco structure, the scene might resemble that of many schools. What makes this one unique is the ethnic and linguistic mix of the local neighborhood as represented by the approximately 850 students in Grades 7–9. Many families are recent immigrants from camps in Laos and Vietnam. Almost half of the students are Asian or Asian American, with a substantial number who are of Mexican origin or Latino/a. The majority of neighborhood families speak English as their second language.

Approximately 45 minutes before the first bell, a phone call from a parent rings through the school switchboard, the first of many calls that continue well into the morning after classes begin. The parent calls are often to explain a child's absence, but the content of their queries also ranges across a wide variety of topics related to school. In order to negotiate the variety of languages spoken in the neighborhood, students have been recruited to help in communicating with parents whose English is limited. One such student is Maria Torres (pseudonym).

Maria is a ninth-grade student assistant who arrives well before the start of school to serve as a translator and who remains at the phone desk through the first hour talking with Spanish-speaking parents whose English is limited. Because Maria is very dependable and responsible in her skillful handling of the translation between English and Spanish, the office staff has come to rely on her expertise. Maria has acquired high status among the other student assistants because she is so effective and confident in her duties.

The bell rings to begin the second class period and marks the transition to Maria's other life at school, her life as a student. In the 5 minutes it takes for Maria to gather her books in the office and walk to the second floor of the school, her entire persona changes. In the office, Maria has been confident and assured, smiling and talking easily with parents and the school staff. She gives the appearance of being in complete control. By the time Maria arrives on the second floor, however, she has become somber and silent, not making eye contact with anyone as she enters the room. She silently chooses a seat at the back of the room and slumps in the desk. On the basis of her academic performance, Maria has been designated as a "student at risk," who may fail ninth grade. With the start of second period, Maria's academic day begins.

Reprinted From the *Journal of Adolescent & Adult Literacy*, *41*(4), 272–281, December 1997/January 1998.

In Maria's junior high school, those students who have received failing marks in three or more classes during the last grading period are identified by school administrators as at risk. Maria is one of 13 students who attend a specially designated second-period class to receive extra help with academic coursework. (During fifth period, another 18 students declared by the school to be at risk for similar reasons also gather for study skill assistance.)

In a matter of only minutes, Maria has been transformed into an uninterested student visible in the back or corner chairs of our classrooms, a student whose behaviors convey to teachers a lack of engagement in school. As the second period begins, Maria's school day essentially has come to an end. What lies ahead for her in the next 5 hours will be a series of academic disappointments and failures.

The school struggle of Maria and students like her is often enmeshed in a struggle with literacy, the ability to handle the academic demands of reading and writing tasks in school. Classroom observations of Maria reveal the extent and depth of her literacy struggles. Since the intermediate years in elementary school, Maria's literacy abilities have not kept pace with those of her peers or with what the academic tasks demand for her to be successful as a literacy learner. By her own report, Maria's link with literacy has been tenuous since second or third grade, and is further complicated by her ongoing efforts to become fluent in English.

One characteristic shared by most less proficient readers and writers is an eroding set of beliefs about their own abilities to achieve success in school (Shell, Colvin, & Bruning, 1995). Maria, like others in her second-period class, struggles with the reading and writing tasks that form the basis for succeeding in most content discipline areas, so she has come to believe that academic success is not within her reach. Bandura (1986), a social learning theorist, has said that the element of success is the greatest single predictor for engagement in school tasks. According to Bandura, success serves to further develop one's sense of competence. We believe that this element of success is pivotal in adolescents' development of their sense of self, particularly the academic self.

In this article, we will discuss how students' literacy behaviors in the classroom relate to their academic success or lack thereof, how these behaviors reinforce students' developing sense of self, and how teachers can support perceived and actual academic competence in their students. The theoretic grounding for our work and the ideas presented in this article are informed by Bandura's theory of self-efficacy as it relates to individual student performance in a given situation. The basic premise in self-efficacy theory is that one's confidence to perform a given task is likely to influence actual performance. Bandura would tell us that confidence is specific to the task, so that one's confidence in succeeding with mathematics may not be the same as for comprehending a novel. We will explore the relationship between beliefs about literacy tasks and performance and the degree of success that results.

We will begin by sharing information from yearlong classroom observations and interviews with students at Southwestern Middle School that illuminates how students' beliefs about literacy (literacy self-efficacy) and their performance (ability to actually perform the specific literacy task) are related. Observations were focused on understanding how adolescents' literacy beliefs affected their performance in school. We interviewed students in the at-risk classes, their more academically successful classmates, and teachers to gather impressions regarding students' academic performance. Finally, we will discuss the strategies teachers can use to create classroom settings that are more likely to assist students in strengthening their academic performance, particularly as it relates to successfully performing reading and writing tasks in school.

Theoretical Framework

Although beliefs concerning one's self-efficacy can affect performance throughout life, the particular impact of these beliefs during early adolescence is widely recognized (Eccles et al., 1993). Self-conscious and struggling with self-esteem, young adolescents are greatly concerned with gaining acceptance (Elkind, 1984; George & Alexander, 1993). In this developmental stage, competency beliefs can undergo dramatic changes (Kramer Schlosser, 1991; Shell et al., 1995). The changes in school structure they encounter in moving from the elementary to the middle school may exacerbate any negative competency beliefs. Upon entering the middle grades, students leave predominantly self-contained learning environments for multiple classrooms with different teachers, expectations, and rules; a wider, more diverse set of peers; and a greater sense of anonymity (Allington, 1990; Eccles & Midgley, 1989; Kramer Schlosser, 1992).

For many adolescents, social interactions serve as a gauge of their connection to school, one measure of their engagement in learning. Our own work demonstrates that in the course of the school day middle school students do attend to academics; however, their primary focus is on the social context of school. Thus, adolescents are developing critical beliefs about themselves as learners at the same time they are constructing multiple dimensions of self, including their self-worth and importance as viewed through the lenses of others. Perhaps it is an artifact of development, but the merging of the personal and

academic selves appears particularly critical for the middle school student and may portend a student's future academic success. In Maria's case, her sense of self as a confident and able student assistant in the school office stands in stark contrast to the invisible person Maria became once she assumed her role as a student.

Teachers' Influence on Efficacious Behavior

Middle-level students' interactions with teachers help to form the context within which their sense of self is fostered (Bandura, 1986; Brantlinger, 1993). Achieving success in school is related, in large part, to the extent and depth of interactions with teachers, because young adolescents' attitudes and beliefs about competence are strongly influenced by teachers' messages (Kramer Schlosser, 1992). Teachers are powerful individuals in the lives of adolescents; they critique academic work, clarify expectations, enforce rules, and provide support. Students are also recipients of teachers' nonverbal messages contained in written feedback on academic work; in strategies used in calling on, in praising, and in recognizing them publicly; and in the facial expressions and voice tones used in and outside the classroom. Students negotiate the institution of school and experience a sense of success or failure based on these interactions.

For students, teachers are the personification of the institution of school; messages from teachers may be interpreted as though they represent the entity of school itself (Brantlinger, 1993). Students are likely to cast past and present experiences with teachers and school in powerful ways, resulting in beliefs that may become permanent and unchangeable over time. From students' beliefs come the enacting of classroom behaviors, and it is these behaviors that clearly distinguish the more academically successful students from those who are less successful.

We believe that the ways in which students approach reading and writing tasks, in part, may be understood in terms of the level of self-efficacy or confidence they have acquired. According to Bandura (1986), self-efficacy beliefs are generative and draw on behavioral, cognitive, and social elements, all of which come together in a course of action–in our case, some dimension of literacy learning. As we have indicated, teachers play a pivotal role in the way these beliefs coalesce for students. In many respects, teachers orchestrate the social interactions in the classroom and beyond, exerting a strong influence on the academic or literate selves adolescents are constructing.

How Do Students and Teachers Work Together?

As university colleagues engaged in efforts to prepare effective teachers to teach at the middle grades, we devoted one school year to specifically observing the ways in which students and teachers worked together on literacy learning tasks. To gather data, we observed classes, interviewed both students and teachers, and documented the kinds of assignments involving literacy learning. We kept field notes to document classroom observations and interviews. In addition, we audiotaped student and teacher interviews and transcribed them for analysis. These data were collected in an attempt to better understand how adolescents' literacy beliefs affect their performance in school. Our analysis of the data was an ongoing process throughout the project. Individually, we searched for themes that evolved from the data, compared

these themes with one another and across data sets, and looked for counterexamples that would necessitate the revision of themes.

We closely observed the relationship between literacy performance and beliefs for academically successful and academically marginal students. As we analyzed the themes that began to emerge during the course of observing and interviewing, we created a working list of literacy behaviors that we had observed or that students had described using. Because Bandura's work was influential in our theoretical frame, we focused on instructional settings and student behaviors that would support the self-efficacy theory and for those examples that would run counter to Bandura's work.

With an array of literacy behaviors, we were able to display along a continuum those behaviors that appeared to result in success and those that gave students no direct or indirect *success* with literacy tasks. We defined success as a student action or a classroom event that reinforced or maintained the focal student's efforts with literacy. An example of such a response is a verbal comment or nonverbal response from a teacher or one's peers that provided assistance or clarity regarding a student's literacy attempt. Using self-efficacy theory as the frame for understanding how adolescents approach academic literacy tasks, we were able to explore how interactions with teachers are central to the formation of students' competency literacy beliefs.

Students' Beliefs About Themselves

Academically
successful
student: I just keep doing what I am supposed to do and I get good grades.

Researcher:	What are you supposed to do?
Student:	Basically all your work. Trying it, I mean. And asking questions when there's something you don't understand. Get help from your teachers. Pay attention in class. Those things. I pay attention a lot. And I study at night. I read over my notes or even my textbook sometimes.
Academically marginal student:	I have to develop good study habits. I know that and I want to do better to get my credits (for high school).
Researcher:	How can you do better?
Student:	Well...what I do is I always use the phone or go out or listen to the radio. What I have to do now is figure out how I'm going to do my homework first. And I need to study harder.
Researcher:	How do you do that?
Student:	I guess I just stop messing around with people. Don't do drugs. You know. Like that. Respect the teachers so they notice you and give you a good grade.

When students were interviewed regarding their sense of competency with regard to school literacy tasks, we found their self-reports to be revealing not only because of what their comments suggested about school literacy tasks but, importantly, because students were fairly good judges of when they were struggling with literacy tasks. Observations and interviews indicated that academically marginal students, despite their enrollment in special skills classes, lacked the repertoire of knowledge about learning strategies that was easily articulated by their more successful classmates. When academically marginal students did call on literacy strategies, these strategies were limited in scope and provided little assistance for a struggling literacy learner. Those more academically successful students, on the other hand, appeared to be well aware of behaviors that were likely to bring about success. These students described a series of routines that, when implemented, would likely result in a successful experience with literacy.

Academically successful student:	I will have to do good in school to go to collage [sic] and save time so I don't neglect my friends, and save money to out on my own and lurn [sic] to use it wisely. Preparing for this dose [sic] not only take education but it takes the will to want to do this. You have to put your mind to it and believe in yourself.
Academically marginal student:	Read? I never read a book in my life.
Researcher:	Do your mom and your uncles read?
Student:	Yeah. I guess so.
Researcher:	What about writing? Do you like it?
Student:	No, I hardly ever write. It's like reading. I just hate it and I'm no good at it.
Researcher:	You never do it outside school?
Student:	Maybe I read letters girls write to my friends, but that's it.

The Table on the following page summarizes the literacy behaviors/beliefs documented for efficacious (more likely to experience academic success) and less efficacious (academically marginal) students. To distinguish between the more academically successful students and those students like Maria, who

Characteristics of efficacious and less efficacious literacy learners

Students with greater literacy self-efficacy will...	Students with less literacy self-efficacy will...
• take greater risks in reading and writing because of the likelihood for success; • establish valuable social networks among peers and actively seek feedback, assistance, and support; • define reading and writing as acts of meaning-making; • persist in completing literacy tasks in spite of failure or task ambiguity; • anticipate success, attribute literacy success to their own hard work; • express value for literacy and demonstrate a sense that they are in control.	• avoid risks with reading and writing because they anticipate failure; • seek isolation in the classroom and opt for silence, avoid opportunities for feedback and talk; • define reading and writing as discrete performances, as a set of skills or discrete tasks not based on meaning-making efforts; • make attempts to initiate literacy tasks but rarely complete tasks; • be surprised by literacy success without understanding the means to replicate success; • express value for literacy but seem uncertain how to achieve it.

experienced little academic success, we selected characteristics that would represent the dramatic differences in student efficacy beliefs/behaviors. During our observations, we noted several students who would be positioned somewhere in the middle of our efficacy continuum and, depending on individual characteristics of literacy behaviors/beliefs and literacy tasks, might shift along the continuum from efficacious to less efficacious.

For example, it is likely that a particular student positioned somewhere in the middle of this continuum might accurately gauge the likelihood of his/her successful literacy performance (item 6) and anticipate a less-than-successful experience with literacy and thus take very few risks (item 1). In other words, it was not uncommon to observe students who demonstrated efficacious characteristics and yet, in a slightly different context, their literacy behavior might be interpreted as less efficacious. Literacy self-efficacy for such a student might be interpreted as evolving, as shifting or changeable. Upon reflection, it is the student with shifting, emerging efficacy for literacy that caught our attention. These students best exemplify the power of applying Bandura's theory for middle-grade students,

because teachers have opportunities to make an impact on these students' beliefs while their efficacy for literacy appears to be in flux.

An additional complication in our attempts to understand student beliefs and performance came with the realization that students might have a different self-efficacy profile in another content area. Therefore, the information contained in the Table should not necessarily be interpreted as revealing static, all-encompassing profiles of individual students (although it does for some students in our study). Our goal in this article is to explore the kinds of literacy behaviors likely to be observed in middle-level classrooms in order to promote greater understanding of the manner in which such behaviors may be interpreted and understood by teachers when applying Bandura's lens of self-efficacy.

As mentioned earlier, examining beliefs and behaviors of efficacious students in contrast with less efficacious students can also provide clear distinctions between those students who are academically successful versus those who regularly experience little academic success. We share first a typical profile of an efficacious student who regularly experiences academic success.

Profile of Efficacious Students

> Ten years from now, I will be working on my internship at Emory University in Atlanta, Georgia. I will be interning to be a child psychiatrist. I will have just completed college and am almost ready to start in the working world.
>
> In order to prepare for the future, I must first get a good education. I must try my best in school and then go to college. I need to have the self-confidence and desire to achieve my goals in life.

For those students who confirmed in interviews a strong or stable sense of self-efficacy for school literacy tasks, we were able to note classroom behaviors that seemed to reinforce these students' beliefs about themselves as literacy learners. From our observations, key characteristics that seemed to define efficacious students were (a) their sense of risk taking, (b) their flexibility in implementing a range of strategies to ensure academic success, and (c) their definitions of reading and writing as meaning-making activities.

Efficacious students were confident, strategic, and organized in the way they approached classroom literacy tasks. Strategies mentioned by these academically successful students often involved working with others, rereading text material (silently and aloud), posing questions of the text and themselves as readers, and requesting help (from peers and teachers). In large part, these students experienced academic success and were adept at establishing effective social networks that provided another avenue for constructing meaning as readers and writers. These students were also likely to attribute their successful performance to their willingness to persevere with an assignment or task and moving on to a new behavior or strategy if one they selected seemed to be ineffective. In a word, literacy seemed to be something they knew they could control and manipulate for their own purposes.

Profile of Less Efficacious Students

In contrast, those students who were less successful academically and less confident of their literacy abilities presented a much different classroom profile. While efficacious students were seen as flexible risk takers, these students were observed to be circumspect, hesitant, and rigid.

Researcher:	Can you make a prediction for me about how school is going for you this year?
Student:	No, not really. I never know.
Researcher:	There's no way to tell if you are doing OK? If you will pass?
Student:	Well, I guess it's if you get your homework done... Or if you can sit and listen to the teacher talking for a long time and expecting you to understand everything she said, just exactly like she said it. That's just all.
Researcher:	So do you take notes when they talk?
Student:	Sometimes, but no, not a lot. In some of our classes we're not supposed to take notes. They say it is impolite to write while they talk.
Researcher:	Oh. Do you think there should be someone who looks over your grades and pulls kids out to warn them and help them when they aren't doing well just so they know?
Student:	Yeah. That would help. That way you would know when to work.

Less efficacious students were more likely to be cautious in placing themselves in classroom arenas where their literacy proficiency would be revealed. Often, their tendency was to stay out of the literacy spotlight in order to avoid showing their peers and the teacher their struggles with literacy. For less efficacious students there was less pain involved in being removed from class because of incomplete assignments than to endure the public show often made of their literacy struggles. We speculated that less efficacious students avoided peer feedback because they seemed unable to negotiate the classroom context for knowing how to ask for help. To persevere with an academic literacy task, one must understand where and how to begin; lacking that knowledge, some students found it easier to never start.

The strategies used by less efficacious students provided critical information to us about their understanding of literacy. Because they usually avoided feedback from peers, they were left to their own devices when confronted with challenging literacy tasks. Their range of literacy strategies, as compared with efficacious students, was constrained and rigid. During our conversations, many less successful students could suggest only one reading strategy–rereading–when confronted with uncertainty. Often, even subsequent rereadings did not help students acquire the level of understanding necessary for school success.

Perhaps the most revealing aspects of our talks with these students were their definitions of good reading and writing. Less efficacious students defined successful reading and writing as something related to the performance of reading and writing; in other words, the ability to pronounce all the words when reading aloud and the use of appropriate and legible penmanship. Students guided by these definitions of reading and writing are less likely to experience the level of academic success necessary for doing well in school.

> I'm not good at reading out loud but to myself, I can read good. 'Cause when I read out loud, I skip sentences and stuff. Skip words, like put words into other words.

Clearly, all students approach literacy tasks with varying sets of beliefs regarding their competency and the likelihood for success. These beliefs stem from interactions with teachers and school experiences that have accumulated over time, and result in students' conscious and unconscious decisions concerning the way they manage school literacy tasks.

We believe middle-grade teachers are particularly well positioned to influence the self-efficacy beliefs students have acquired and continue to acquire through those developmentally crucial middle grades. Teachers have the power to address students' competency beliefs and to mitigate the negative changes that may occur as a result of the transition to middle school if they understand how confidence can be built.

Confident Classrooms: Suggestions for Teachers

The following is an academically marginal student's advice to teachers:

> Well, first of all I would tell them that they should at least give me some credit for making an effort to complete whatever I had to accomplish. No matter if it was a D– or F. All they would have to just show me how to do the work.

What can teachers do to create classrooms in which students behave with greater efficacy?

First, teachers must understand the relationship between student literacy beliefs and the behaviors that follow in order to develop new perspectives for interpreting student behavior. Learning how to interpret specific behaviors related to literacy learning is perhaps the first step in moving toward creating confident classrooms. Teachers who understand this critically important developmental relationship can provide opportunities to showcase students' strengths and, in turn, address students' weaknesses in ways that encourage risk taking and persistence.

Second, teachers *must believe* that students can be competent and capable literacy learners. Students will find it impossible to believe in themselves as literacy learners if they detect that teachers lack the belief that literacy success is within a student's reach. In our interviews, the students with less efficacy for literacy reported they *knew* when teachers assumed they would be unable to accomplish academic tasks. Breaking rather cleanly along lines of greater and less literacy efficacy, students would describe situations where they simply gave up on a task because they knew teachers did not feel they were capable. On the other hand, some students reported being inspired to higher levels of persistence if they perceived teacher support. Rather than assuming that a student's literacy performance reflects diminished ability, teachers should first assess the adequacy of a student's prior knowledge for a given task.

Third, conventional wisdom often encourages us to believe that tasks considered to be easy will motivate students. In fact, the opposite is often true. Students' perceptions of themselves as less able readers and writers are often reinforced when they are given literacy tasks that are less involved or less challenging than those assigned to their peers. Students will respond positively to material that challenges them and requires an investment of their efforts as learners. When defining what

texts might be challenging, we have found it particularly helpful to think in terms of Vygotsky's (1986) zone of proximal development. In other words, we recommend that students be given material that is slightly beyond their ability to complete when working alone but that they can successfully complete when they receive assistance from a teacher or a peer. Individually, students might become defeated by silently reading paragraphs in a general science textbook, but when they are asked to orally read the text with another student, the task may seem less daunting. Teachers who are equally invested in the process of creating academic success will reward student efforts with encouragement and attention.

Fourth, accomplishing a task may require that it be broken down into its component steps and addressed one step at a time. Less efficacious students in our study were unable to envision literacy tasks in parts that they could accomplish and thus became overwhelmed by the whole. The most effective teachers intercede by talking with students as they devise a plan that includes a step-by-step process for success. ("What have you decided you should do first? How long will that take? What will you do next?") These plans can be paired with appropriate problem-solving strategies ("If you find you are not understanding the reading, what will you do?") so that students persist, evaluating their performance as they go. Becoming a strategic reader/writer requires knowing when to stop the process and evaluate whether one's goals have been accomplished. It is critical that students have input in developing these learning plans, with options to indicate how to begin with monitoring points along the way.

Fifth, be honest and direct. Teachers who begin by discussing the difficulty of the task with students rather than avoiding such a discussion may find the honesty pays off. Implied throughout such discussions between teachers and students should be the belief that students are capable of success if they understand what to do when they encounter difficulties with reading and writing. Strategies such as reading to the end of the sentence to see if meaning is more apparent, reading with a peer, and generating questions are effective. Students need to be assured that they have support in literacy tasks and that teachers trust their ability to handle the task.

We believe some students have experienced less success with literacy tasks because they have incomplete information about how to be successful. Explicit instruction of any valued classroom literacy task is crucial if we are to expect less efficacious students to devise new literacy behaviors in response to their efficacy beliefs. (One student who spoke Spanish as his first language in our study was convinced he was a poor reader because he did not know phonics. In an effort to respect his request for more phonics information, we provided a few minilessons on phonics concepts that would support his reading efforts. Once he could demonstrate this knowledge of letter-sound relationships, he went on to develop other strategies that might be more effective. Central to this story is that his confidence for reading wavered less and his repertoire of strategies was increased.)

Students ought to be encouraged to evaluate their own work from plans they have had a role in developing prior to beginning a task. When students are encouraged to join in the evaluation process, they can become invested in designating where they would like to improve as readers and writers.

Our final point centers on applying Bandura's notion of self-efficacy for literacy tasks in order to better understand the performance of linguistically diverse students. We believe that self-efficacy is likely to be influenced by culture and language. For students like Maria, interpreting literacy behaviors requires that teachers consider the additional linguistic layers that students must negotiate in the process of learning the dominant language (English) while being asked to perform academically. Other research (Colvin, 1993) with middle-grade students using self-efficacy as the lens for understanding academic performance indicates that L2 students on first glance may appear to have diminished efficacy for literacy as they make the transition from expertise with their first language to fluency in two languages. In reality, notions of self-efficacy become complicated, as students negotiate between first and second language while they are also asked to successfully perform with academic discourse. Teachers who strive to better understand how self-efficacy for literacy learning for L2 students can be supported in classroom learning are likely to help students like Maria create new visions for how learning may happen.

What Maria's Portrait Tells Us

The authenticity of Maria's work outside the classroom is evident in the lives she affected in positive ways and in the immediate affirmation she received from her work in the school office. As a student assistant, Maria's efforts were constantly focused at the level of communicating in meaningful settings. However, her classroom literacy tasks rarely achieved the same level of consistent meaningful interactions. In the school office, Maria was challenged by her work and accorded respect by her associates as she moved between diverse language settings and groups. The majority of her teachers were unaware of her language abilities with Spanish and, instead, viewed her as an unskilled student who lacked the requisite ability with English.

Upon close examination, what was missing from Maria's classroom experiences was critical to her emerging beliefs about literacy and competence. She needed the means to connect the literacy efficacy and meaningful literacy understanding in her setting of success with the academic setting of school.

Possibility and Uncertainty

Because we began with Maria's story, it seems fitting that we return to the ways in which her teachers might help her write a new ending to the school journey she begins with every second-period class. If Maria were encouraged to think of herself as a reader and a writer in Spanish, she might then come to think of herself as having the ability–with assistance–to be a reader and writer in English. Maria informed us that she was already writing English and Spanish children's stories at home for her siblings. If, for example, her reading teacher could build on this literacy knowledge, connections could be made to school literacy tasks. Her language arts teacher might help her discover the similarity between the children's stories she is writing and the narrative texts she is asked to read in school. If Maria's teachers could find the means to bring her literacy outside of school into her classroom, Maria might be able to connect these multiple literacy performances and reconstruct her self-efficacy as a reader and a writer.

Maria and her peers in the classroom for at-risk students could benefit from having many forms of literacy made available to them, including the school and city newspapers, stories recounted by family members or peers that could be recorded on tape, and paired journal-writing activities. In this way, Maria and her peers might understand the many forms that school reading and writing might take. With access to the computer lab at their school, their concerns with poor penmanship might become secondary to expressing their own opinions and reading and responding to what their peers have written. Bandura reminds us that for students like Maria, opportunities for performance provide the most powerful arena for experiencing success, thereby creating opportunities to revise one's sense of competency. "Whether these opportunities are exploited depends, in large measure, on teachers' collective beliefs about how young adolescents learn and about their own ability to influence the student, particularly marginal students" (Kramer Schlosser, 1992, p. 129).

When one observes the many key tensions with which middle school students must contend, it becomes increasingly apparent how the middle grades are critical, filled both with possibility and great uncertainty. The likelihood for school success depends on what sense students make of the many competing demands–academic and social, personal and public. Finally, success may hinge on teachers who believe that the strength of their own instruction influences students' perceptions of themselves as competent and confident learners.

REFERENCES

Allington, R.L. (1990). What have we done in the middle? In G. Duffy (Ed.), *Reading in the middle school* (pp. 32-40). Newark, DE: International Reading Association.

Bandura, A. (1986). *Social foundations of thought and action: A social cognitive theory*. Englewood Cliffs, NJ: Prentice-Hall.

Brantlinger, E. (1993). *The politics of social class in secondary school: Views of affluent and impoverished youth*. New York: Teachers College Press.

Colvin, C. (1993). *Negotiating school in rural America: Issues of confidence and literacy for Mexican American adolescents*. Paper presented to the National Reading Conference, Charleston, SC.

Eccles, J.S., & Midgley, C. (1989). Stage-environment fit: Developmentally appropriate classrooms for young adolescents. In C. Ames & R.

Ames (Eds.), *Research on motivation in education: Vol. 3 Goals and cognitions* (pp. 139–185). San Diego, CA: Academic.

Eccles, J.S., Midgley, C., Wigfield, A., Buchman, C., Reuman, D., Flanagan, C., & MacIver, D. (1993). Development during adolescence: The impact of stage-environment fit on young adolescents' experiences in schools and in families. *American Psychologist, 48*(2), 90–101.

Elkind, D. (1984). *All grown up and no place to go: Teenagers in crisis*. Reading, MA: Addison Wesley.

George, P.S., & Alexander, W.M. (1993). *The exemplary middle school* (2nd ed.). New York: Harcourt Brace Jovanovich.

Kramer Schlosser, L. (1991). *Academic performance, ethnicity, and motivation for successful and marginal middle school students*. Paper presented at the American Educational Research Association Annual Conference, Chicago.

Kramer Schlosser, L. (1992). Teacher distance and student disengagement: School lives on the margin. *Journal of Teacher Education, 43*, 128–140.

Shell, D., Colvin, C., & Bruning, R. (1995). Self-efficacy, attribution, and outcome expectancy mechanisms in reading and writing achievement: Grade-level and achievement-level differences. *Journal of Educational Psychology, 87*, 386–398.

Vygotsky, L.S. (1986). *Thought and language* (Rev. ed.; A. Kozulin, Trans. & Ed.). Cambridge, MA: MIT Press.

William G. Brozo

Hiding Out in Secondary Content Classrooms: Coping Strategies of Unsuccessful Readers

These are the words of Scott, an unsuccessful 11th-grade reader: "Yeah, I'm always scared the teacher is going to call on me. I'll fool around...and she tells me to shut up...you can do that or act sick or something. Most of the time I just get the answer from Andrea."

Scott, like countless other poor readers, has developed a complex repertoire of coping strategies designed to avoid reading or being held accountable for reading. Young adults who lack literacy skills are often painfully aware of their own inadequacies (Johnston, 1985); to avoid ridicule by exposing their "stupidity" in the classroom, many resort to hiding out and bluffing behaviors. These behaviors fit into a cycle of failure that ensures the individual will have few if any opportunities to practice or expand upon the reading skills he/she does possess. With little practice, skills decline further, leading to more hiding out and more bluffing.

This article describes my observations of a high school classroom and subsequent interviews of the poor readers in the class in an attempt to uncover their coping strategies. First, I discuss conflicting evidence from classroom observational research, depending upon whether it's from the teacher's or the student's perspective. I argue that teachers who focus on effective instruction from only their perspectives fail to appreciate the needs of unsuccessful readers and may inadvertently reinforce students' reading failure. I conclude with recommendations for improving teacher interactions with poor readers.

Conflicting Evidence

Classroom observational research from the teacher's perspective (see the reviews of Brophy & Good, 1985, and Rosenshine & Stevens, 1984) has revealed a great deal about what is happening during instructional events. The focus has been on identifying teacher behaviors that correlate with student achievement, as well as on teachers' perceptions of and reactions to student behaviors.

A common outgrowth of this research has been the specification of characteristics of quality or effective instruction. Some typical examples of teaching effectiveness prescriptions that have derived from classroom observation studies are Brophy's (1981) 24 guidelines for effective praise, Good and Grouws's (1979) 14 guidelines for math instruction, and Anderson, Evertson, and Brophy's (1982) elaborate list of 26 specific principles for small group instruction in reading, including such behaviors as (a) praising in moderation, (b) requiring ordered-turn

Reprinted From the *Journal of Reading*,
33(5), 324–328, February 1990.

51

responding, and (c) brisk pacing of the instructional sequence.

A growing number of researchers (Bloome, 1984; Davidson, 1985; Green & Wallat, 1981; McCutcheon, 1981), however, have voiced criticisms of classroom observations from the teacher's perspective only and the teacher effectiveness prescriptions that are deprived from such research. These critics point out that the classroom dynamics of teacher-student verbal and nonverbal interaction must be viewed from both the teacher's and the students' perspectives if observations are to be "contextualized."

This is a vital point in light of findings from school ethnographies suggesting that what a teacher might think is going on with his/her students may not be going on at all (Davidson, 1985). For example, Bloome (1983) has identified the phenomenon of "mock participation"–behaviors exhibited by students that on the surface appear to be task oriented but may in fact be totally unrelated to the task. Rist (1980) has determined that because teachers base their inferences about students' attention on observable clues such as eye gaze, body movements (e.g., head nodding), and body orientation, students can easily deceive the teacher by creating the impression of academic engagement.

How do we know what a student is thinking when nodding his head while staring at the teacher with apparent undivided attention? How do we know the student is engrossed in seatwork simply because her eyes are fixed on the page and her pencil is busy? Observations of what the teacher is doing during classroom events cannot answer these questions. Furthermore, so-called effective teaching guidelines are useful only to the extent that students are actually engaged in teacher-directed tasks instead of creating the appearance of academic engagement.

Geertz (1973) has urged researchers to conduct "thick" description of observed behaviors. In other words, observational researchers should do more than simply describe head nodding, for instance, by attempting to determine what this nodding means. Nodding could mean (a) following the teacher's train of thought, (b) agreeing with the teacher's point of view, (c) projecting an interest that isn't there, or (d) falling asleep (McCutcheon, 1981).

One way to do thick description is through case studies and interviews. Interviews can corroborate, extend or correct misimpressions from gross behavior observations (Geertz, 1973). In subsequent sections of this article, I describe the results of classroom observations and interviews of three high school readers of low ability. The intent was to determine if they actively engaged in mock participation and other coping strategies in order to avoid reading.

Short Term Survival

Poor high school readers have two choices for dealing with their problem. They can try to improve, or they can continue to use and refine their coping strategies. Johnston (1985), having identified a group of adult disabled readers who were otherwise socially adept and intellectually able, gathered retrospectives from them of their own classroom coping strategies. Their behaviors included:

(1) Apple polishing–manipulating the teacher by creating positive perceptions outside the classroom, such as walking the teacher to her car.

(2) Sitting right up front in order to give the impression of attentiveness, because it is felt that the teacher picks on students who sit in the back of the room.

(3) Exploiting alternatives to reading: using nonprint sources, listening well, and talking with others.

As Johnston insightfully notes, listening for oral instructions and bluffing are effective only for attaining short term survival goals, but are self defeating in terms of the long term goal of learning to read. The danger is that the survival strategies poor high school readers employ will systematically exclude print from their lives. As adults they may lead lives of silent desperation in which the goal becomes avoiding situations where reading is required or expected.

Interviewing Poor Readers

Twice per week for one semester a research assistant and I observed an 11th-grade history classroom in a large U.S. suburban high school in the Midwest in an attempt to identify unsuccessful readers' classroom survival strategies. We split the room in two to limit our observations and traded sides of the room each session. Notes were taken on a seating chart grid so we could make brief coded inscriptions next to an individual student whose behavior was being observed. To avoid biasing our observations, we did not know in advance who were the low-level readers in the class.

At the conclusion of the semester, we identified the three poorest readers in the class using reading test scores and teacher information. We then went back through our field notes, listed all the behaviors we observed for these three students, and categorized them. When we interviewed the students, we asked them to respond to the behaviors we had observed and to provide additional information about their perceptions of their own classroom coping strategies. Each student was interviewed three times for approximately 30 minutes per session.

Coping Strategies

(1) The most common way these poor readers coped with their inability to read well was to *avoid eye contact with the teacher*, especially when the teacher asked questions about the class reading assignments. All three students we interviewed employed this strategy to varying degrees. One student, diffident by nature, suggested that by keeping his eyes focused on his textbook, desk, or notebook he had frequently avoided being called on to answer questions or read. He reported, in fact, that the teacher rarely initiated any contact with him in the classroom.

In his summary of related observational research, Brophy (1983) described many interesting inferences teachers drew from the presence or lack of eye contact. They regarded students who made eye contact as intelligent, social leaders, creative, and likely to come from good homes. On the other hand, students who avoided eye contact were described as active, inattentive, nonvolunteers, frequently absent, and untrustworthy, as well as failing to participate actively in academic activities and requiring prodding to continue to work. Teachers frequently criticized these students for poor answers and poor work.

There was little evidence of teachers reaching out to students who avoided eye contact. Apparently, these students conditioned teachers and the teachers preferred to keep their interactions impersonal. Brophy found that teachers were more likely to call on a high achiever volunteer than the poor achiever nonvolunteer, which implies that avoiding eye contact may be a strategy that often works.

(2) The next most frequent coping behavior was to *engage in disruptive behavior*. For two of the poor readers we observed, this took the form of frequently leaving their seats, snatching personal items from neighbors, throwing items across the room, and making inappropriate or defiant statements to the teacher.

Brophy's (1983) review of studies concerning teachers' perceptions of disruptive student behavior showed that teachers were less likely to seek academic contact with these students. When these students attempted to initiate academic interactions, they were often rebuffed. It is possible that a history of hostile interactions could condition teachers to avoid contact with these students.

Interestingly, even though disruptive behavior does elicit teacher attention, and places the low-level reader under scrutiny, the teacher-student interactions are generally irrelevant to the task. Thus, engaging in disruptive behavior seems to be a very effective strategy to avoid classroom reading.

Five other coping strategies we identified through our student interviews appear to be common:

(3) *Become a good listener*. The students indicated that they learned to pay attention to the teacher when necessary.

(4) *Rely on a "with it" classmate or a good reader*. Poor readers reported using these individuals when they needed to quickly tune in to classroom activities, get directions for completing assignments in class, and get help finding their place in the textbook. At times the poor readers would gather procedural information by asking questions of the teacher through other students.

(5) *Seek help from friends*. One student reported that his girlfriend did his homework for him.

(6) *Forget to bring to class books and other materials that may be needed for oral reading*. The students reported that more times than not the teacher will call on another student to read instead of asking them to read from their neighbor's book.

(7) *Use manipulative techniques in and out of class to gain teachers' positive perceptions*. One student described how talking with his teacher about current events, which he picked up from television news, seemed to leave the teacher with the impression that he was actually an avid reader of news magazines.

Reaching Poor Readers

Many poor secondary readers bring to the classroom a long history of failure and, likely, a repertoire of strategies designed to avoid reading, so solutions are not simple. Nevertheless, there are teacher-student interactions as well as classroom instructional strategies that can help promote greater feelings of trust between poor readers and teachers, lead to broader self awareness, and encourage these students to make genuine attempts to improve their reading and learning.

• *Develop a personal rapport with less able readers*. Teachers should try to get to know poor readers as individuals. Extended and frequent informal discussions before, after, and outside of class will help the teacher better understand the student's needs and could reduce the student's tendency to bluff. These frequent informal exchanges can also be used to monitor the student's progress. Often, informal, personal contact with a student can make the difference between giving up and trying. In a nonthreatening, informal atmosphere, teachers can offer and suggest alternative reading materials related to the class topics or to the student's outside interests.

• *Become more aware of behaviors and biases*. Teachers should do some soul searching in order to become more self aware of their biases toward certain students and unconscious behaviors that may be estranging poor readers from the main flow of instructional activities in the classroom. Research on self fulfilling prophecy and teacher expectations (Brophy, 1983) has revealed that when teachers are made aware of maladaptive behaviors they can and do change.

• *Teach poor, passive readers to monitor their own performance*. Poor readers are often passive, that is, they are unwilling to exert the effort to improve their reading because of a history of critical and abundant failure (Brozo & Curtis, 1987). Johnston and Winograd (1985) recommend that passive readers be encouraged to monitor their own reading performance so as to see the connection between effort and its consequences. Teaching students textbook study strategies that are metacognitive in nature may be very useful in helping to break cycles of passivity and failure.

• *Adapt instruction to low-ability students*. Teachers can ask questions of these students that they can answer successfully, such as opinion questions or questions that ask them to relate their own experience to the ideas being discussed in class. This strategy along with engaging poor readers in frequent cooperative learning activities will help them see that their input is valued. In turn, this will buoy confidence and may catalyze poor readers to keep trying.

• *Refer to and cooperate with the reading specialist*. Poor readers should be referred to a reading specialist for extra help. However, classroom teachers should not assume that special reading instruction alone will take care of the students' problems. Working together, the classroom teacher and the specialist can dovetail their efforts to more effectively meet the literacy needs of less able students. For example, the reading specialist can help the classroom teacher generate and plan individual assignments. In the specialist's classroom, poor readers can be shown how to use literacy tools to expand their understanding of subject area concepts.

Confronting the Problem

Classroom observational researchers have determined that teachers tend not to reach out to less able students, though there may be frequent nonacademic interactions, disciplinary in nature. In fact, teachers behave in a variety of ways that reinforce distance, such as paying less attention to them, calling on them less often, seating them further away, and demanding less from them (Johnston & Winograd, 1985).

It should not come as a surprise to anyone that teachers simply find it more stimulating to work with better students. An important philosophical question needs to be asked here, however: Should we allow less able students to avoid confronting their reading problems? Poor readers who are running scared in secondary classrooms will continue to run if they are ignored. And after high school they are likely to find themselves running as adults, avoiding situations in which they might be expected to read.

A teacher who follows effective instructional guidelines may be reaching most of his/her students, while inadvertently overlooking the serious needs of the poor readers in class who are trying to blend into the walls, precipitate task-irrelevant interchanges, employ apple polishing strategies to manipulate perceptions, or fake academic engagement.

Teachers need to demonstrate that they genuinely care about poor readers and are interested in more than forcing these students to expose their most vulnerable areas of weakness again and again in the classroom. Only then, I believe, will poor readers like Scott be inclined to come out from hiding and, with the help of teachers, take realistic and adaptive measures to deal with their literacy problems.

REFERENCES

Anderson, L., Evertson, C., & Brophy, J. (1982). *Principles of small group instruction in elementary reading* (Occasional Paper No. 58). East Lansing, MI: Michigan State University, Institute for Research on Teaching.

Bloome, D. (1983). Classroom reading instruction: A socio-communicative analysis of time on task. In J. Niles & L. Harris (Eds.), *Searches for meaning in reading/language processing and instruction*. Thirty-second Yearbook of the National Reading Conference. Rochester, NY: National Reading Conference.

Bloome, D. (1984). A socio-communicative perspective of formal and informal classroom reading events. In J. Niles & L. Harris (Eds.), *Changing perspectives on research in reading/ language processing and instruction*. Thirty-third Yearbook of the National Reading Conference. Rochester, NY: National Reading Conference.

Brophy, J. (1981). Teacher praise: A functional analysis. *Review of Educational Research*, *51*, 5–32.

Brophy, J. (1983). Research on the self-fulfilling prophecy and teacher expectations. *Journal of Educational Psychology*, *75*, 631–661.

Brophy, J., & Good, T. (1985). Teacher behavior and student achievement. In M. Wittrock (Ed.), *Handbook of research on teaching* (3rd ed.). New York: Macmillan.

Brozo, W.G., & Curtis, C.L. (1987). Coping strategies of four successful learning disabled college students: A case study approach. In J. Readence & R.S. Baldwin (Eds.), *Research in literacy: Merging perspectives*. Thirty-sixth Yearbook of the National Reading Conference. Rochester, NY: National Reading Conference.

Davidson, J.L. (1985). What you think is going on, isn't: Eighth grade students' introspections of discussion in science and social studies lessons. In J. Niles & R. Lalik (Eds.), *Issues in literacy: A research perspective*. Thirty-fourth Yearbook of the National Reading Conference. Rochester, NY: National Reading Conference.

Geertz, C. (1973). *The interpretation of cultures*. New York: Basic Books.

Good, T, & Grouws, D. (1979). The Missouri Mathematics Effectiveness Project: An experimental study in fourth grade classrooms. *Journal of Educational Psychology*, *71*, 355–362.

Green, J., & Wallat, C. (1981). Mapping instructional conversations-a sociolinguistic ethnography. In J. Green & C. Wallat (Eds.), *Ethnography and language in educational settings*, Vol. 5. Norwood, NJ: Ablex.

Johnston, P. (1985). Understanding reading disability: A case study approach. *Harvard Educational Review*, *55*, 153–177.

Johnston, P., & Winograd, P. (1985). Passive failure in reading. *Journal of Reading Behavior*, *17*, 279–301.

McCutcheon, G. (1981). On the interpretation of classroom observations. *Educational Researcher*, *10*, 5–10.

Rist, R. (1980). Blitzkrieg ethnography: On the transformation of a method into a movement. *Educational Researcher*, *9*, 8–10.

Rosenshine, B., & Stevens, R. (1984). Classroom instruction in reading. In P.D. Pearson (Ed.), *Handbook of reading research*. New York: Longman.

SECTION 2
Acknowledging Cultural Ties

Focusing on readers who struggle is bound to be tied to the cultural and linguistic milieu in which adolescents go about their lives. Living in an era known for its technological wizardry, consumer capitalism, and popular culture icons, adolescents who struggle to read and learn from their assigned texts at school are often considerably more literate in the everyday world outside of school. Yet, without schooled literacy as a base on which to build, these same adolescents are at risk of remaining marginalized in terms of their ability to communicate with their peers and teachers, especially if they carry markers of cultural and linguistic differences.

The articles in this section address such differences, first through their attention to culturally and linguistically sensitive instructional materials, and second through their insistence on embedding these materials in literacy activities that bring the outside world into the classroom. The authors of these nine articles are particularly adept at situating reading instruction within social contexts that matter greatly to adolescents. Although the authors do not deny the cognitive or behavioral aspects of reading, they portray them as attendant processes in a much larger scheme of things—that is, in the cultural environment in which adolescents find themselves.

Trevor H. Cairney

Developing Parent Partnerships in Secondary Literacy Learning

Parent involvement in children's education has long been accepted as an important element in effective schooling (Delgado-Gaitan, 1991; Schneider & Coleman, 1993). Many studies have shown that there is a high positive correlation between parent knowledge, beliefs, and interactive styles with children's school achievement (see Schaefer, 1991 for a detailed review). Although attempts to explain this relationship have varied, explanations that represent a deficit model are often emphasized. These explanations are based on the assumption that some children receive "good" or "appropriate" preparation for schooling, while others receive "poor" or "inappropriate" preparation. This view has been criticised because of its failure to recognise that schooling is a cultural practice (Auerbach, 1989; Taylor, 1993), and consequently, much of the variability of student achievement in school reflects differences and discrepancies in the cultures of home and school (Au & Kawakami, 1984; Cazden, 1988; Heath, 1983; Moll, 1988).

Bourdieu (1977), for example, argues that schools inconsistently tap the social and cultural resources of society, privileging specific groups by emphasising particular linguistic styles, curricula, and authority patterns. Similarly, Gee (1990) notes that to be a teacher in any school demands specific ways of using language, behaving, interacting, and adherence to sets of values and attitudes. There is obvious potential for mismatches between these discourses and those which have been characteristic of some children's homes and communities.

Scribner and Cole (1981) describe literacy as a social practice into which people are enculturated or apprenticed as members of specific groups. Since one gets better at specific social practices as one practices them, it would seem that those children who enter school already having been partially apprenticed into the social practices of schooling (of which literacy is a part) invariably perform better at the practices of schooling right from the start.

But how should one respond to the cultural mismatches of home and school? Should one focus on developing initiatives that provide parents with the cultural practices that enable them to cope with the limited practices of the school (Lareau, 1991), or find ways to help schools recognise the cultural practices of the home and community and build effective communication among these parties (Delgado-Gaitan, 1992)?

It is the combination of these strategies that this article addresses. Involving parents more closely in school education at both elementary and secondary levels has the poten-

58

Reprinted From the *Journal of Reading*, *38*(7), 520–526, April 1995.

tial to develop new understanding by each party of the other's specific cultural practices. This in turn may enable both teachers and parents to understand the ways each defines, values, and uses literacy as part of cultural practices. In this way schooling can be adjusted to meet the needs of families. Parents, in turn, can also be given the opportunity to observe and understand the definitions of literacy that schools support, and which ultimately empower individuals to take their places in society.

Developing Programs That Facilitate Partnership

The importance of mutually supportive relationships between schools and families has received increasing attention in the past 10 years. In summarising this work, Epstein and Dauber (1991) group parent initiatives into six specific typologies. They argue that whilst each type of home-school involvement is quite different, each can lead to genuine partnerships with parents and the wider community. Their typologies cover basic obligations of families (e.g., provision for health and safety), basic obligations of schools (e.g., provision of information about school programs), involvement at school (e.g, use of parents as volunteers within the classroom), involvement in learning activities at home (e.g., assistance with homework), involvement in decision making (e.g., through committees or groups), and collaboration and exchanges with community organisations (e.g., access to community and support services).

Although there may be a rich array of initiatives, some educators have begun to question the programs that have been implemented. Auerbach (1989) has argued that some programs are based on a model designed simply to transmit school practices to the home. Considerable criticism has been levelled at programs that are designed to exert a central influence on parents' caregiving roles. Many of these programs aim to improve the education of caregivers in order to bring about intergenerational changes in learning.

Whilst accepting the concern that such programs risk intruding on families' own cultural practices, many educators see that specific literacy practices do have the potential to empower individuals. Studies of low-income families have shown that parents who often have limited needs for print literacy may not encourage particular literacy practices of their children, thus setting up an intergenerational pattern of literacy difficulties (Goldenberg, 1987). Not surprisingly, some have therefore argued that the best way to empower students from minority groups is to change the nature of education to equip students with the knowledge and skills necessary to gain power over their own community (Briggs & Potter, 1990). This, they argue, requires the transformation of primary schools into focal points for their communities, thus bringing teachers and parents closer together, and leading subsequently to changed attitudes on the part of both parties.

Several educators, however, argue not for the transmission of knowledge from schools to parents and their children, but rather for a process of reaching mutual consensus between the partners. This process of reaching shared understanding is what Vygotsky (1978) called "intersubjectivity." It requires a shared focus of attention and mutual understanding of any joint activity. Fitzgerald and Goncu (in press) suggest that this requires reaching agreement on the selection of activities, their goals, and plans for reaching the goal. Programs that are imposed by teachers on communities "for their own good" obviously fail to meet the conditions necessary for intersubjectivity to occur. Such programs frequently end with no appreciable impact on teachers and the school and with little long-term benefit for parents and their children.

A recurring theme in the recent literature is that parents must be viewed as equal partners and that there must be a reciprocal relationship. It has been argued that we need to go beyond token involvement and recognise the vital role that parents play in education (Cairney & Munsie, in press). Harry (1992) argues that parent initiatives must forge collaborative relationships that create mutual understanding between parents and teachers, a "posture of reciprocity."

An Initiative for Parents of Secondary School Students

While research into home influences has addressed a comprehensive range of forms of involvement in children's learning and development, there has been a strong interest in parental participation in early language and literacy development. This has been influenced strongly by the well-documented influence of parents on the early language development of children (Cairney, 1989a, 1989b; Teale, 1986; Wells, 1986).

There has been considerably less attention to the involvement of secondary parents in their children's literacy development. A small number of programs have been developed for use in the middle school (e.g., Montgomery, 1992; Thomas, 1992) that have been of some relevance to adolescents, but these are not focussed specifically on literacy. Indeed, there is little evidence of concerted work concerning the development of family literacy programs at the secondary level.

The reasons for this lack of work at the secondary level are difficult to gauge, but it would seem that they include a belief that it is more difficult to involve parents of secondary-

aged students and that adolescents do not appreciate the active involvement of their parents in their schooling. My own research has provided little reason to support these assumptions. There is clear evidence that parents of secondary students have quite specific needs. Furthermore, there seems little justification to believe that there is any less reason to expect a solid partnership between parents and the school just because the students are older.

During 1992, this was demonstrated quite clearly to me when a parent from a local high school called to seek help on behalf of a small group of secondary school parents. This group of six people was made up largely of parents who had been involved in an elementary school parent literacy program called Talk To A Literacy Learner (TTALL) (see Cairney & Munsie, 1992a, 1992b). The small deputation noted: TTALL helped us so much, now we need some practical help with secondary school.

In response to the request, we planned a meeting of teachers, parents, and a community liaison officer who was based at the school. At this first meeting, the parents outlined their needs, and a decision was made to seek state government funding under the Disadvantaged Schools Program. Over a period of 6 weeks, a submission was prepared by the combined group of parents, teachers, my collaborator on the TTALL program, Lynne Munsie, and myself. The application was completed and ultimately proved successful.

The outcome was a program which was largely developed week by week and was then monitored and adapted by a small group of teachers, parents, and researchers. It is worth noting that in this group the parents were equal in number to the researchers and teachers and were involved in the setting of goals for the program and the activities to be undertaken.

The program that resulted was called Effective Partners in Secondary Literacy Learning (EPISLL). It was designed to support and raise parent participation in children's literacy learning and study skills in Grades 7 to 10. The participants were 17 adults (16 mothers and 1 father) and their 57 children, aged 12 to 17 years. The parents and their children volunteered to participate in the program following advertising in school newsletters and verbal presentations by the full-time coordinator of the program at an information day for parents and during visits to roll call classes.

The community from which the parents were drawn is in the western suburbs of Sydney and is seen as socioeconomically disadvantaged. It has a high proportion of welfare housing and higher than average community levels of crime, family crises, vandalism, and juvenile problems. The school academic attainments are well below state averages.

The parents who chose to participate in the EPISLL program were as diverse as the community itself. They had on average three children, were largely Australian-born, and all but one had left school before year 11 (the second-last year of high school).

The specific objectives identified by the planning group were to:

- increase community awareness of literacy learning and its importance for schooling and entry into society;

- develop more positive attitudes towards reading and writing in the school and within the community;

- encourage members of the school and local community to see reading and writing as relevant to themselves and society;

- develop and maintain an educational program which could have widespread use within the school community and other disadvantaged schools;

- encourage teachers, parents and students to work together to provide all with access to literacy practices used across the whole curriculum; and

- increase parent involvement in schooling leading to greater mutual understanding by parents and teachers of the reciprocal nature of their relationships.

The program was designed to be conducted by a part-time coordinator and selected school and community resource people. Based on an interactive learning model which was developed as part of the TTALL Program (Cairney & Munsie, 1995), the program contained a mixture of short lectures, workshop activities, and demonstrations. The final program consisted of eleven 2-hour sessions designed to be spread over a 6-week period. A critical part of the program was the practical demonstration of all strategies and involvement of parents with their children at home.

The content of the program covered the importance of positive relationships, setting realistic personal goals, learning, the nature of the reading and writing processes, strategies for assisting with their work (summarising, notetaking, understanding the textbook), organising time for study and strategies for researching information, locating and using community resources, and the use of computers for word processing.

In a typical session, parents would meet first for coffee in a designated community room within the school for approximately half an hour. The session would then begin with a discussion of the previous session's home task. Tasks typically required parents to talk with students about their work, sometimes to try out a specific strategy (e.g., notetaking), or perhaps just to chat about issues raised in sessions (e.g., What did their children see as the most important subjects, and why? What did they, as parents, see as most important?). Each session would then normally begin with some form of presentation. This could include a short talk by the coordinator, the use of a guest speaker (school or community), or a video. The rest of each session would then normally be made up of short segments of discussion, shared observation of classrooms or demonstrated literacy strategies, reflection on specific input or observations, and practice at literacy strategies (e.g., finding reference material or editing one's work). Each session contained a great deal of discussion and a format that was fastmoving and highly interactive.

While the impact of the program is still being evaluated at a number of sites (it is now being implemented in approximately 50 communities), early analysis of data for the first group of 17 parents and 57 children indicates that the program has achieved its objectives. Initially, the program's effectiveness was evaluated in writing by all parent participants at the end of each program and through interviews with various participants. The written evaluation required the completion of 35 multiple choice and open-ended questions, the provision of background information, and an opportunity to offer more extended comments. Assistance was provided for parents with literacy difficulties. The evaluation took approximately 30 minutes to complete.

A number of structured interviews were also conducted with a variety of staff and parents associated with the project. These people included the leading teacher, the head teacher of mathematics, the community liaison officer, the support teacher for learning difficulties, parent participants, and some of their children. The interviews were conducted by a part-time research assistant using a structured schedule of questions for each interview. Two slightly different schedules were used, one for parents and one for school staff. Interviews ranged from 15 to 30 minutes.

Our analysis of data showed that the program had influenced parents, students, and teachers alike (for a full description see Cairney & Munsie, 1993, 1994). Because the program was designed essentially to be conducted with parents, it was expected that the greatest impact would be upon this group. Six major influences were evident in relation to the impact of the EPISLL program on parents:

- The program was seen as well planned, structured, and suited to their needs.
- Parents gained new strategies to use to assist their children.
- Parents experienced improved communication with their children and better personal relationships with them.
- Parents gained new knowledge about literacy and learning.
- Parents grew personally as a consequence of the program.
- Parents gained confidence.

While it is difficult to quantify the effect that EPISLL has had on the school, staff are overwhelmingly supportive of the program. One of the most significant effects seems to be the development of a greater sense of partnership between the home and school. One teacher expressed this effect in the following way:

EPISLL has helped to develop that partnership with the community. It allowed better communication between community and the teaching staff and senior executive of the school. It allowed a focus in the school that has been schoolwide rather than just faculty based, which has truly meant more involvement of the community.

There is evidence that the increased partnership has led to:

- an increased understanding of parent perceptions and expectations of schooling;

- attitudes and expectations concerning the significant role that parents play in student learning;
- an increased understanding of student needs; and
- greater participation of parents in school activities (e.g., decision making, classroom support, fund-raising activities).

The following two comments provide insight into the nature of these changes:

> It's probably embellished our curriculum a little in that we are thinking more clearly and getting better feedback from the parents as to what they believe children should be learning. Pretty good evaluators are parents…. (leading teacher)

> I think there's been a big impact for the school in terms of community involvement. I think it's another avenue where parents can get involved in the school process instead of just covering textbooks and fete days. It gives them real empowerment, gives them skills really to run the school. (math teacher)

While one of the expected outcomes of the EPISLL program was an effect on student literacy and study skills, this part of the evaluation is still to be completed due to the need to conduct longitudinal observations and monitoring of student achievement. Nevertheless, data from teachers and parents indicate that they have observed a number of positive influences on students. The major effects observed at this stage are that:

- students have acquired new skills as result of their parents' involvement (e.g., study skills);
- students have shown evidence of raised expectations;
- parents and students have reported improved relationships; and
- students have grown in confidence and self-esteem.

Although these data are yet tentative, the apparent benefits that have accrued for parents, the school and the students would suggest that programs like EPISLL have the potential to make a significant difference in students' literacy and learning.

The success of EPISLL has probably been due as much to the development of community support networks as to the day-to-day quality of program activities. One of the positive outcomes is that EPISLL seems to have broken down the barriers that schools unknowingly erect around themselves. In the words of one parent:

> Because my eldest is nearly 25, there was none of this sort of thing when he went to school. The schools weren't open to parents except on Education Day, and maybe sports day. You weren't encouraged to interfere. You couldn't go up and ask the teacher what was wrong, or how could you help or something, you were virtually told–you know–more or less, that we're the teacher, you're only the mother.

Parent partnership programs like EPISLL appear to have the potential to act as vehicles for breaking down barriers between the school and home so that parents can take their place as partners in their children's learning.

Achieving Evolutionary Development

Parent and family literacy initiatives provide considerable promise and offer potential to achieve the "posture of reciprocity" which Harry (1992) argues parents and teachers must forge. Those interested in partnerships between parents and schools need to continue to ask themselves a number of basic questions about their literacy practices: Do the literacy practices of my classroom disempower some and empower others? If so, which students are disadvantaged most by the types of literacy practices I support and legitimise? How must I change my practices in order to ensure that literacy is empowering for all? How can I set up an environment that permits greater intersubjectivity to develop between myself and parents?

As teachers we need to come up with a response to the accusation that schools, and teachers as their chief agents, act as gate keepers, letting some children in and keeping others out. How do we respond to the claim that "short of radical social change," there is "no access to power in society without control of the social practices in thought, speech and writing essay-text literacy and its attendant world view" (Gee, 1990, p. 67)?

Such ideological concerns are anathema to some teachers, as they strive to get on with the everyday practices of teaching. But the challenge of these ideas cannot be denied. Schools are amongst the most stable institutions in society, and short of a total transformation in the society within which they are embedded, they will not move quickly. However, move they must.

I believe that the response to this dilemma is not to keep telling teachers that they need to change, but rather to engage in social evolutionary development by providing opportunities and alternative programs and curricula that challenge existing educational practices. The work in parent and family literacy in the past 2 decades has given me some hope that long-term reform of the practices of schooling is possible. I hope these practices will lead to a greater sense of partnership between schools and their communities.

REFERENCES

Au, K., & Kawakami, A. (1984). Vygotskian perspectives on discussion processes in small-group reading lessons. In P. Peterson & L.C. Wilkinson (Eds.), *The social context of instruction* (pp. 209–225). Portsmouth, NH: Heinemann.

Auerbach, E. (1989). Toward a social-contextual approach to family literacy. *Harvard Educational Review*, *59*, 165–181.

Bourdieu, P. (1977). Cultural reproduction and social reproduction. In J. Karabel & A.H. Halsey (Eds.), *Power and ideology in education* (pp. 487–511). New York: Oxford University Press.

Briggs, F., & Potter, G. (1990). *Teaching children in the first three years of school*. Melbourne: Longman Cheshire.

Cairney, T.H. (1989a). Building communities of readers and writers. *The Reading Teacher*, *42*, 560–567.

Cairney, T.H. (1989b). Text talk: Helping students to learn about language. *English in Australia*, *92*, 60–69.

Cairney, T.H., & Munsie, L. (1992a). *Talk to a literacy learner*. Sydney: UWS Press.

Cairney, T.H., & Munsie, L. (1992b). Talking to literacy learners: A parent education project. *Reading*, *26*, 34–47.

Cairney, T.H., & Munsie, L. (1993). *Effective partners in secondary literacy learning: Final report to the Disadvantaged Schools Program*. Sydney: UWS Press.

Cairney, T.H., & Munsie, L. (1994, April). *Parents as partners in secondary literacy learning*. Paper presented to the American Educational Research Association Conference, New Orleans, LA.

Cairney, T.H., & Munsie, L. (1995). Parent participation in literacy learning. *The Reading Teacher*, *48*, 392–403.

Cairney, T.H., & Munsie, L. (in press). *Beyond tokenism: Parents as partners in literacy*. Portsmouth, NH: Heinemann.

Cazden, C. (1988). *Classroom discourse*. Portsmouth, NH: Heinemann.

Delgado-Gaitan, C. (1991). Involving parents in schools: A process of empowerment. *American Journal of Education*, *100*, 20–45.

Delgado-Gaitan, C. (1992). School matters in the Mexican-American home: Socializing children to education. *American Educational Research Journal*, *29*, 495–516.

Epstein, J., & Dauber, S.L. (1991). School programs and teacher practices of parent involvement in inner-city elementary and middle schools. *The Elementary School Journal*, *91*, 289–305.

Fitzgerald, L.M., & Goncu, A. (in press). Parent involvement in urban early childhood education: A

Vygotskian approach. In S. Reifel (Ed.), *Advances in early childhood education and day care: A research annual*. Greenwich,CT: JAI Press.

Gee, J. (1990). *Social linguistics and literacies: Ideology in discourses*. London: The Falmer Press.

Goldenberg, C.N. (1987). Low-income Hispanic parents' contributions to their first-grade children's word-recognition skills. *Anthropology and Education Quarterly*, *18*, 149–179.

Harry, B. (1992). An ethnographic study of cross-cultural communication with Puerto Rican-American families in the special education system. *American Educational Research Journal*, *29*, 471–494.

Heath, S.B. (1983). *Ways with words: Language, life and work in community and classrooms*. Cambridge, UK: Cambridge University Press.

Lareau, A. (1991). *Home advantage*. New York: Falmer Press.

Moll, L. (1988). Some key issues in teaching Latino students. *Language Arts*, *65*, 465–472.

Montgomery, D. (1992). EPIC: Helping school life and family support each other. *Schools in the Middle*, *1*, 3-5.

Schaefer, E. (1991). Goals for parent and future parent education: Research on parental beliefs and behaviour. *The Elementary School Journal*, *91*, 239–247.

Schneider, B., & Coleman, J.S. (1993). *Parents, their children, and schools*. San Francisco, CA: Westview Press.

Scribner, S., & Cole, M. (1981). *The psychology of literacy*. Cambridge, MA: Harvard University Press.

Taylor, D. (1993). Family literacy: Resisting deficit models. *TESOL Quarterly*, *27*, 550–553.

Teale, W.H. (1986). Home background and young children's literacy development. In W. Teale & E. Sulzby (Eds.), *Emergent literacy* (pp. 173–206). Norwood, NJ: Ablex.

Thomas, K. (1992). The parents' institute: Helping parents understand their early adolescent. *Schools in the Middle*, *1*, 12-14.

Vygotsky, L.S. (1978). *Mind and society: The development of higher psychological processes*. Cambridge, MA: Harvard University Press.

Wells, G. (1986). *The meaning makers*. Portsmouth, NH: Heinemann.

William G. Brozo, Paul Cantú Valerio, and Minerva M. Salazar

A Walk Through Gracie's Garden: Literacy and Cultural Explorations in a Mexican American Junior High School

Two blocks from West Oso Junior High School, Gracie Mendoza, a Mexican American faith healer, stands under a Chinese plum tree, holding one of its tender light green leaves up to the sun. Smiling, she says, "Estas hojas tiernas se hierven para hacer un te. Este te es para los diabeticos. Ellos lo toman para su enfermedad." (These tender leaves are boiled to make a tea. This tea is for diabetics. They drink it for their illness.) Gracie's weathered dark brown skin attests to the many hours spent tending her garden under the hot and humid south Texas sun. Yet her eyes, behind her large plastic-framed glasses, are crystal clear and shine with an honest passion as she attempts to educate her audience.

In the early morning hours that make up second period, Gracie finds herself surrounded by a group of 22 eighth-grade students. Their attention drifts from Gracie's instruction to the enticing aroma of tortillas and chorizo in the air of the neighborhood they know so well. "Listen up," says Minerva, their teacher. "Mrs. Mendoza is talking about making a tea of herbs just like in the stories we've been reading with Mr. Valerio and Dr. Brazos." [sic]

"But, Miss, I don't understand Spanish, and that smell is making me hungry—Yes, Miss, me too!" most of the class chimes in.

"I speak English, pero no muy bien. Como se dice, en boca cerrada no entran moscas?" (...but not too well, how do you say, a closed mouth will not draw flies?) Gracie asks. Immediately 6 or 7 students who understand Spanish well start laughing along with Paul and Minerva, who steer the group towards the entrance of Gracie's garden. As they walk toward what appears from the street to be a yard overgrown with weeds and brush, Gracie continues to describe the benefits of the medicinal plants that lace many of the small trees in her garden, stopping now and again to pluck samples of mint, basil, and other herbs for our students to smell and taste.

A School on the Boundary

West Oso Junior High School is situated in the Molina area of Corpus Christi, Texas, USA. This community was made famous recently with the tragic death of the Tejano singer, Selena, who resided with her family a few blocks from the school. In spite of its ephemeral association with this glamorous music star, Molina is a community "on the boundary" (Rose, 1989). According to Rose, these are communities with isolated neighborhoods, economic and information poverty, and limited means of protecting children

Reprinted From the *Journal of Adolescent & Adult Literacy*, *40*(3), 164–170, November 1996.

from family disasters. Children and adults in these communities harbor strong feelings of scholastic inadequacy.

Out of some 45,000 Molina residents around West Oso Junior High School, nearly 90% are Latino/a, of which 70% speak English as a second language. Sixty percent of adults 18 and older have no high school diploma or General Equivalency Diploma. Unemployment is at 16.6%, more than double the state average, and 40% of the residents of Molina live below the poverty level with a per capita income of between US$5,000 and $11,000 annually.

The junior high school has been perpetually in danger of losing its accreditation due to low scores on state-mandated tests. Two years ago, however, with a strong commitment from the principal, the school managed to demonstrate substantial gains in math and writing and modest gains in reading. With the arrival of a new district superintendent has come another strong push to continue to elevate test scores in all areas.

Part of this push has been to elicit the assistance of the local university, which traditionally held a tacit "hands off" policy toward the West Oso school district. University education students were routinely discouraged from student teaching there and warned of the difficulties and dangers they would face working in Molina. This practice isolated schools like West Oso Junior High. Consequently, educational innovations—with which its staff might have been familiar had there been frequent exchanges and collaboration between university and school personnel such as those enjoyed by its much larger parent school district of Corpus Christi—were less evident.

It is within this community that Gracie Mendoza lives and our collaborative work took place.

Getting Started

In the early summer of 1994, Paul, one of the coauthors, introduced Bill to Minerva (the other coauthors). Paul was a graduate student specializing in reading and had taken a few classes with Bill, who is an associate professor at the local university. Paul, a Mexican American and native of Molina, had children who attended school in the West Oso district. He became an active community member of the Site Based Decision Management team for West Oso Junior High; that is where he met Minerva. Paul represents a Molina success story. By dint of remarkable effort on his part, he is now embarking on doctoral studies in literacy at a major university. He was well suited to offer the eighth graders the kind of literacy model needed to help stretch their vision of future educational and career possibilities.

Minerva, a Mexican American as well, expressed to Bill and Paul a strong desire to engage in a collaborative project to work with her eighth-grade reading classes. She was preparing for her second year of teaching at the junior high level after 3 years as a second-grade teacher. By her own admission, Minerva was not entirely pleased with the teaching approach she had used with the eighth graders the year before. Stressed by the abrupt change in her teaching assignment, she had spent her first year at the junior high in "survival" mode, relying principally on turn-taking oral reading, whole-class discussion questions, and worksheets for preparing for state reading tests. Minerva said she was open to any new strategies for reaching her students.

The three of us spent the balance of the summer planning our project. For the duration of the school year, Paul and Bill became participant-observers in one of Minerva's eighth-grade classrooms. The class was composed of 19 Mexican American students, 1

Filipino American, 1 African American, and 1 Anglo student. As participant-observers, Bill and Paul gathered information about the class, got to know the students, provided Minerva with feedback on classroom dynamics, offered recommendations for improving literacy instruction, and gave teaching demonstrations of literacy innovations. The idea was that by focusing intently on one class, Minerva would be able to draw on this experience for developing similar learning activities in her other reading classes.

Though Minerva was slowly incorporating new teaching strategies into her class activities, such as journal writing, she decided that our work should culminate in the integration of these new strategies within a learning unit on Hispanic American culture. The description of that unit, the quality of literacy behavior demonstrated by the eighth-grade students, the students' heightened awareness of positive cultural identities, and implications for teaching comprise the remainder of this article. (Note: Pseudonyms have been used for the names of students mentioned in the following sections.)

Becoming a Community of Learners

All of us, everyone here, need to think of ways like this of becoming partners in our children's education.

Ms. Garcia,
Principal of West Oso Junior High

With those words, Ms. Garcia inaugurated our Hispanic culture unit. It was early in April 1995, and we were hosting a party and information session in Minerva's classroom. Parents, school and university administrators, students, other teachers, and the three of us shared punch and pan dulce (sweet bread; pastries made in a Mexican American bakery) over friendly conversation.

By this time, Paul and Bill were accepted members of Minerva's eighth-grade classroom culture, and they spoke with a legitimate sense of propriety and enthusiasm about the upcoming unit. Each of us told the guests about our planned activities with the students during the unit and stressed to parents the need for their involvement in assuring the success of the learning experiences we had prepared for their sons and daughters.

Minerva had received a small grant through the Texas State Reading Association that she used to purchase a class set of Rudolfo Anaya's novel, *Bless Me, Ultima* (1972). Rife with *curanderismo* (traditional Mexican American faith healing) and the practice of folk medicines, this book became the core text of the unit around which reading, writing, and field activities were structured. In addition, students read and engaged in activities associated with several short stories and informational texts by Hispanic authors such as Sandra Cisneros and Gary Soto.

Because the unit was about Hispanic cultural identity, it was critical that the eighth graders had opportunities to explore their cultural roots within their families. Saravia-Shore and Arvizu's (1992) extensive investigation of cross-cultural literacy plans for Hispanic students led to their contention that instructional approaches are not adequate without parent participation. They argue further that it is only through home-school linkages that cultural resources from the surrounding community are utilized. They assert that in order for programs for Hispanic children to succeed "students and parents need to participate actively with school personnel in creating and testing innovative approaches" (p. 50).

We kept the focus of the unit on the cultural resources of the community as much as possible. The walk to Gracie Mendoza's home; a field trip to the university to celebrate Cinco do Mayo; and a talk by Dr. Carrillo, a local Mexican American scholar, on "green medicines" were all critical to the success of the unit.

Another way we were able to bring about a community-school dialogue and exchange of cultural resources was through the use of Integrated Parent Involvement Packets or IPIPs (Prouty & Irby, 1995). The IPIPs we used were housed in a three-ring binder with the following components. Introducing the IPIP was a letter to the parents thanking them for taking the time and energy to participate in this unit. On the flip side of the letter was a sign-out chart with a place for the parents' and students' signatures when they completed the IPIP. Next, there was an explanation of what was required to successfully complete the IPIP. This was followed by a story by a Hispanic author along with a short biography of the author. The stories reflected authentic Hispanic cultural experiences and were meant to be read aloud by the parents and the students to one another (Hayden, 1995).

The final component of the IPIP was a hands-on activity for student and parents to share. The activities were typically suggested by the IPIP readings. For example, in one of the stories we included in the IPIPs, Sandra Cisneros's (1990) "Three Wise Guys: Un Cuento de Navidad," a Mexican American family celebrates Christmas with the smell of cinnamon in the holiday air. We then asked parents and students to make cinnamon sticks from the ingredients we provided in a zippered plastic pouch in the IPIP binder. After reading Rudolfo Anaya's (1990) "Salomon's Story," which contains information about brewing traditional teas from local herbs, parents and students were given directions and ingredients for making their own native tea, manzanilla.

Noelia initially expressed skepticism about the value of the IPIP in making the unit more enjoyable and meaningful on a personal and family level. She lived with her mother, whom she doubted would be interested in reading with her and completing assignments together. However, after returning the IPIP binder with the Anaya short story and tea-brewing activity, she wrote in her journal:

> I wasn't too interested in the very beginning of this story, but my mom said she wanted to hear what happened in the end. When I finished we were really surprised and we felt what it was like if we were in Salomon's place. It was cool that afternoon so we made the tea together. While we drank it my mom told me about her parents from the valley and how they had to struggle to get by. She said she remembered drinking tea when she was sick that her mom, mi abuelita, made for her from herbs that grew wild around their house.

Noelia's response was typical of those we received from students who seemed to rediscover the pleasure of experiencing stories and family culture with their parents.

Cooperative Meaning Making With Literature

Bill and Paul's observations of Minerva and her class led them to recommend that students be given more opportunities to learn from one another. Early in the school year, the primary way stories and books were explored was through turn-taking oral reading and whole-class discussion questions. Minerva had already expressed dissatisfaction with this way of teaching reading but was unsure about her own knowledge of and skills in using alternatives. Nevertheless, we all came to recognize that this approach tended to disguise the real thinking abilities of the less effusive students in class.

With Paul and Bill's assistance, Minerva experimented with alternative ways of exploring literature with her students, including peer-led discussion (McMahon, 1992) and paired reading and responding (Marshall, Smagorinsky, & Smith, 1994). By the time the Hispanic culture unit began, she felt ready to use a cooperative learning approach (Eeds & Wells, 1991; Jules, 1990) for helping her students make meaning from the novel and other texts they were reading.

The cooperative learning approach she adopted was based on a method used successfully by a couple of teachers with whom Bill had worked extensively (Brozo, Brobst, & Moje, 1994/1995; Brozo & Simpson, 1995). For each chapter of *Bless Me, Ultima*, the eighth graders, in groups of four, fulfilled clearly defined roles that were independent of one another yet mutually supportive. The student assigned to be "literary luminary" identified passages in that day's assignment for discussion and oral reading. The "vocabulary enricher" prepared a list of unfamiliar words or word usages for sharing and teaching. The "discussion director" prepared questions about the assignments for stimulating group dialogue. The "checker" questioned group members about completion of their assignment, evaluated participation, and urged everyone to enter into the discussion. Students came to their groups having read the assignments and filled in a form that asked for information appropriate to their role. Group work preparation was usually completed the day before at home.

In the beginning, we modeled each cooperative group assignment extensively. Then, as students began learning their roles, we moved around frequently from group to group providing assistance and clarification.

It was particularly pleasing to watch students become more thoughtful and self-directed learners through cooperation.

Blanca taught her group such words as *ambushed*, *relished*, *impending*, *nebulous*, and *incessant* in Chapter 16 by directing students to the context, giving examples, and relating the word to a meaningful synonym. Gloria, typically diffident in social settings, was directing discussion about Chapter 3 when she recounted this tale to her group:

> I live with my grandfather and when I read this chapter to him he said it reminded him when he use to go to the river with his friends and his parents use to tell him not to go because he couldn't swim—one day he was down there and his friends would taunt and make fun of him and some of the older boys would tell him not to go but he went anyway and he fell down into a deep hole into the river, he almost drowned and one of the older boys grabbed him and pulled him out—then he remembered what his parents said, so he was scared to tell them but he did tell them eventually.

As literary luminary, Claudia organized an impromptu Readers Theatre on a critical section of Chapter 11 that related to an important recurring symbol in the story—a golden carp—and had her group members perform it for the rest of the class.

These demonstrations of literary engagement were at a level unseen among Minerva's eighth graders before the Hispanic culture unit and the reading of books and stories authored by Hispanic Americans. Strong support for the cooperative learning approach came from students like Andrea, a checker, who commented on her group's performance: "In groups I read more and we help each other understand better."

Everybody's a Winner

Another area of mutual discovery for the three of us early in the school year was that Minerva's students seemed to have limited opportunities for writing. This was a major concern for Minerva, who recognized the vital need to build a stronger writing component into her overall literacy curriculum. The only writing students did regularly was 5 minutes of journal writing at the beginning of each class. Gradually, she increased the amount of time students had to write in their journals, so that when the Hispanic culture unit began they were comfortable generating one to two pages of continuous text daily. This was important for the principal writing strategy we used in the unit.

The writing strategy evolved out of a concern Paul had about finding ways to raise the self-esteem of Minerva's students. Messages of scholastic inferiority invade settings like West Oso Junior High School as the local media reports frequently on the relative standing of area school districts' state test scores–West Oso is always near the bottom. To promote a positive sense of academic accomplishment, Paul devised a writing strategy expressly for the Hispanic culture unit called WINNER (Ways of Integrating the New to the kNown by Evoking Reflection). In completing WINNER log sheets, students made both text- and reader-based entries (Petrosky, 1982) about the culturally relevant literature they were reading.

We introduced students to WINNER through modeling and demonstrating possible responses using think-alouds, as well as with sample answers in handouts and on overheads. There are six prompts to the WINNER log that ask students to move from lower levels of thinking through increasingly sophisticated interpretations and ultimately to reader response.

1. Who are the main characters, and what are their roles in the chapter you've just read?

2. Briefly summarize the chapter you have just read.

3. What do you think is going to happen in the next chapter?

4. Compose three questions that you would like to have answered in the next chapter.

5. Did this reading remind you of something that has happened in your own life? Describe the incident.

6. Do the values, ideas, thoughts, or actions in this story confirm or conflict with your own personal values? How?

Students completed WINNER logs after each chapter of *Bless Me, Ultima* and kept their log sheets in a writing folder. To our delight, the eighth graders took full advantage of the WINNER prompts, generating thoughtful and heartfelt responses to each of the six questions. Consider how the following response from Gavino to question 5 brings out his own family connections to *curanderismo* and witchcraft described in the story.

> This part about Ultima curing the uncle reminds me when my mother and father got divorced someone payed a man to do bad things to my mother. She got ill and had a hard time for about a year, but I found out who it was and told my grandmother. She told about witches and stuff. She told a story about a lady she knew who did stuff like that and that she got what she had coming. One night an owl or something just like in the story was outside our house and my grandmother told it was the person who was doing that bad stuff to my mother.

Lettie's response to question 6 after reading Chapter 14 reflects a sophisticated understanding of the moral dilemma facing the characters in the story and deep personal connection with the events:

> If I were Tony's Uncle Pedro I would have defied my father's wishes and gone to warn Ultima of the trouble that was coming her way. I wouldn't have thought twice if I was indebted to Ultima for a loved one's life.

A Year and Unit Reconsidered

When the three of us met in early June (1995) to reflect on the year's events in Minerva's classroom, we began by reading aloud the final journal entries made by the eighth graders. Before long we were blending the students' impressions and feelings with our own thoughts about what made the Hispanic culture unit a success. We believe the following implications for teaching, which are supportable by the work we did at West Oso Junior High School, can be useful to anyone planning instruction for learners in similar settings.

Give students a greater range of options for responding to text. When Minerva began shifting the responsibility from herself as teacher to her students for asking questions and exploring meaning, we found a much greater level of involvement and motivation. Students like Jamie and Eliseo who held back during whole-class discussion became active meaning makers and involved partners when opportunities were created for student-student dialogue and group problem solving. We found that cooperative learning was especially useful in helping students become more enthusiastic discoverers of their own interpretive powers.

Use literature that is culturally relevant and appealing. It became immediately apparent to us that the heart of what made the Hispanic culture unit a success was the high-quality, culturally relevant literature the students read. Our adolescents from Molina found they could intimately identify with the characters and conflicts of *Bless Me, Ultima* and the other stories by Hispanic authors. Roel, a formerly uninvolved class member, summed up the students' reactions to Anaya's novel when he wrote in his journal: "*Ultima* is one of the coolest books I have ever read. I haven't even finished the whole book and I know it rules!"

Establish home-school connections. Teachers are well aware of the importance of parental support for achieving their instructional goals. And although we know this is especially true at the junior high and high school levels, we generally fail to be proactive about establishing or eliciting parental support for the academic growth of adolescents. Through the use of IPIPs we were able to bring our eighth graders' parents into the learning process. As a result, students were better able to connect the ideas from the novel and stories in our unit to their own families and heritage. In this way, learning became more personal and memorable. Claudia wrote in her WINNER log: "When my mother and I read this part about mal ojo, she reminded me of when my sister's baby was ill and my mother placed a raw egg under his crib to heal him."

Use the community as a cultural resource. Nearly all students noted in their final journal entries that the most memorable aspect of the Hispanic culture unit was the opportunity to experience the learning firsthand. The tour of Gracie Mendoza's garden and Dr. Carrillo's presentation of folk medicines stood out in the collective memories of the eighth graders. Members of the community became "touchable role models" (Hilliard, 1989) for our students, while they brought to life the words and ideas being explored in the classroom. The field trip to the university to celebrate Cinco de Mayo was also a favorite activity that helped reinforce the cultural linkages to the unit.

Provide regular and frequent opportunities for writing. We felt the unit was successful simply because of the variety of thoughtful and insightful written pieces generated by the eighth graders. By linking their reading and writing using cooperative learning forms, reflective journals, and WINNER logs, the students were able to explore story content as well as their own personal, familial, and cultural connections to that content.

Some Final Thoughts: A Return to Gracie

When we said our goodbyes to Gracie Mendoza and walked from her garden back to the junior high, the students immediately expressed a desire to write her a letter of appreciation. In their letters the eighth graders wrote about what they had learned from the wise woman and more significantly what they were learning about themselves as Hispanic youth and their rich cultural heritage. We felt it was fitting, then, to end this article with the words of Nelda:

> Dear Ms. Mendoza,
>
> I am one of the fortunate students from West Oso Junior High who had a chance to visit your house and learn about healing plants. Before I took this trip I didn't know how useful nature can be. I realize now why many Hispanics value nature's gifts so deeply. It's simply because nature's gifts are wonderful. Thank you for helping me better understand the depth of my Mexican culture. I enjoyed the tour of your garden very much. I hope I can do it again.

REFERENCES

Anaya, R. (1972). *Bless me, Ultima*. New York: Warner.

Anaya, R. (1990). "Salomon's story." In C. Tatum (Ed.), *Mexican-American literature* (pp. 179–185). Orlando, FL: Harcourt Brace Jovanovich.

Brozo, W.G., Brobst, A., & Moje, E. (1994/1995). A personal story of teacher change. *Childhood Education, 71*, 70–73.

Brozo, W.G., & Simpson, M.L. (1995). *Readers, teachers, learners: Expanding literacy in secondary schools*. Columbus, OH: Merrill.

Cisneros, S. (1990). Three wise guys: Un cuento de navidad. In C. Tatum (Ed.), *Mexican-American literature* (pp. 27–33). Orlando, FL: Harcourt Brace Jovanovich.

Eeds, M., & Wells, D. (1991). Talking, thinking and cooperative learning: Lessons learned from listening to children talk about books. *Social Education, 55*, 134–137.

Hayden, R. (1995). Training parents as reading facilitators. *The Reading Teacher, 49*, 334–336.

Hilliard, A.G. (1989). Teaching and cultural styles in a pluralistic society. *National Education Association, 7*, 65–69.

Jules, V. (1990). Cooperative learning and workmate preferences in classrooms in secondary schools. *Contemporary Education, 61*, 65–70.

Marshall, J.D., Smagorinsky, P., & Smith, M.W. (1994). *The language of interpretation: Patterns of discourse in discussions of literature*. Urbana, IL: National Council of Teachers of English.

McMahon, S.I. (1992, April). *Classroom discourse during social studies: Students' purposes and topics of interest in peer-led discussion groups*. Paper presented at the annual meeting of the American Educational Research Association, San Francisco, CA.

Petrosky, A.R. (1982). From story to essay: Reading and writing. College *Composition and Communication, 33*, 19–36.

Prouty, J.L., & Irby, B. (1995, February). *Parent involvement: Integrated packets*. Paper presented at the Student/Beginning Teacher Conference, Nacogdoches, TX.

Rose, M. (1989). *Lives on the boundary*. New York: Penguin.

Saravia-Shore, M., & Arvizu, S.F. (1992). *Cross-cultural literacy: Ethnographies of communication in multiethnic classrooms*. New York: Garland.

Robert T. Jiménez and Arturo Gámez

Literature-Based Cognitive Strategy Instruction for Middle School Latina/o Students

In a provocative statement, Donaldo Macedo (1994) challenges U.S. teachers and others involved in the education of students from culturally and linguistically diverse communities:

> I am increasingly convinced that the U.S. educational system is not a failure. The failure that it generates represents its ultimate victory to the extent that large groups of people, including the so-called minorities, were never intended to be educated. (p. 36)

Macedo's challenge is not easy to dismiss, especially when one examines the literacy learning and educational opportunities available to Latina/o students. The U.S. Census reports that during the last decade there has been a 30% increase in the number of persons who identify themselves as Latina/o, and the number of Latina/o teachers in the United States is less than 3% (de la Rosa, Maw, & Yzaguirre, 1990). Waggoner (1991) points out that approximately 35% of all Latina/o students discontinue their education before completing high school and that these dismal rates are much higher in urban areas. In spite of the tremendous need for high-quality instructional programs for students from culturally and linguistically diverse backgrounds, only about 15% of the close to 10 million such students in the U.S. actually have access to English as a Second Language classes or bilingual education (National Education Association, 1990; Waggoner, 1994).

Without a doubt, much more could be done to improve the literacy learning of Latina/o students. Yet, even if a national commitment to such an endeavor were to emerge right now, it is not clear that concrete, practical information is available to teachers and others who see these students daily (Goldenberg, 1996).

The problem is exacerbated for those who work with middle school students because of the assumption that students at this level have already received necessary literacy instruction (García et al., 1995). This article reports one effort to learn about and improve the literacy instruction provided to Latina/o students.

We visited a middle school for 1 school year during which time we observed students and teachers, interviewed them, and, finally, taught the students for approximately 2 school weeks. Information reported here is derived primarily from the 2-week period that we worked directly with the students. The instruction we designed and delivered was characterized by use of culturally relevant and familiar text, a focus on comprehension, and provision of opportunities to build reading fluency.

Reprinted From the *Journal of Adolescent & Adult Literacy*, 40(2), 84–91, October 1996.

The School and the Students

We asked the bilingual program director of a large midwestern U.S. urban school district if we could work collaboratively with one or two teachers of Latina/o students. We explained that we were most interested in students who were experiencing difficulties with literacy learning. The bilingual program director introduced us to the principal of Swanson Middle School. The principal invited us to observe Grade 7 students in Ms. Holden's self-contained special education classroom (all names used are pseudonyms). In the fall of 1994, the enrollment at Swanson Middle School consisted of 819 students, 407 of whom were Latina/o.

There were approximately 14 students in Ms. Holden's classroom, all of whom were Latina/o. The teacher's aide, Ms. Ramirez, who assisted Ms. Holden was bilingual and occasionally spoke to the students in Spanish. We asked Ms. Holden if she could identify between three and five of her students whom she believed were experiencing the most problems with reading and writing. She told us that all of her students performed at low levels in English language literacy, but she gave us the names of Victor, Sara, and Adán.

All three of these students had grown up in the United States. They had completed all of their schooling in the U.S. and spoke English fluently according to their teacher and her teaching assistant. Yet although these students were enrolled in Grade 7, they were reading at about a Grade 3 level in English, as determined by teacher judgment and standardized test scores. These students were not currently receiving any formal instruction in Spanish except for occasional comments made to them by the teacher's aide.

Our Approach

We visited Swanson Middle School on 9 different occasions for a total of 17 school days. During our last visit, we were at the school for 8 days (Tuesday through Friday of each week).

On four separate occasions, we observed the three students in their classroom, during which time we targeted language arts activities. We observed the students for at least 1 hour during each visit. Activities included reading, writing, and an English language grammar exercise. We took extensive field notes during these observations; during three of the four visits, we took notes jointly. These observations spanned 3 months.

We then met with the three students as a group. During that meeting we showed the students five or six trade books and asked them to choose one. We asked them to read a short portion of their book silently. Next, we demonstrated the think-aloud procedure for them and we asked them to try it as well. The think-aloud procedure is described in more depth later in this article.

During later meetings, we interviewed each of the three students individually. We asked students about their language learning histories, their language preferences, and their school experiences. Prior to the interview, we had also asked the students to select a text, either a book or a magazine from their classroom, that they felt comfortable reading. We asked them to read the text a line at a time and then to tell us what they thought about as they read (G.E. García, personal communication, January 10, 1995). We used this information, along with our observations, to begin to get a sense of the students as readers. We taped and later transcribed all of our interviews with the students. Our analysis of this information revealed that the students' word recognition and oral reading fluency were rudimentary (Grade 2–3 level), and their

Corn is found in a rancho. There are millions of them on the rancho. You have to help corn grow by giving it water. Once it grows you must clean it, wash it, cut it, and then take it to the store. Corn can be used to make masa. Masa is then used to make tortillas and tamales. Tamales are made on special days. Tamales are made during Christmas, birthdays and 5 de Mayo. Many family members help make tamales like moms, sisters, aunts, grandmothers, and cousins.

We did tamales de chile, dulce, carne de chivo, carne de marrano y a veces hacemos gorditas, tortillas, arroz y frijoles. Los elotes los siembran y les echan agua y despues los echaban a las tiendas para venderlos. El último día que mi familia hizo tamales fue el viernes que acaba de pasar. Mi prima le ayuda y también mi tía. Estas comidas se hacen cuando festejamos algún día especial como el día de las madres y los cumpleaños.

knowledge and implementation of strategic reading processes were very limited.

After we completed the observations, interviews, and initial think-alouds, we arranged to spend 8 school days at Swanson Middle School so that we could meet with the students for one full period a day during that time. This article focuses primarily on the instruction and interaction with the students that occurred during these 8 days. We taped and transcribed all of the instruction that we conducted with the students for later analysis.

Developing Rapport With Students

Because we purposely chose to work with three students who did not have a history of success with literacy, we knew we would have to devote attention to winning their confidence and gaining their trust. This task, it turned out, was more difficult than we originally thought (Bos & Vaughn, 1988). The students were not initially enthusiastic about the project. At our first group meeting, for example, I (Jiménez) informed the students that their involvement was voluntary and that it

was their choice whether to participate. All of the students immediately stood up and asked to return to their classroom. I told them that it was their decision but I asked them to first listen to what we had in mind. Fortunately for us, after hearing more about the project, they decided to continue.

We decided to begin by simply engaging the students in conversation. We asked about their families, their favorite foods, special holidays, and the menus for such events.

We then put four objects on the table. These were corn flour (masa harina), two ears of corn, and a package of tortillas. We purposely chose items that we were certain the students would recognize, that we knew were culturally familiar, and that were mentioned or discussed in the texts we planned to present to the students later. Because both of us were raised within close proximity to Swanson, we were familiar with the broader Latina/o community and its customs.

Our main concern during this phase of the work was to ensure that students would be able to engage in conversation. We wanted to be able to encourage, support, and gently push students to produce extended discourse. We were only moderately successful in eliciting quantities of student-produced language. The Figure displays the written text that was produced as a result of the students' conversation with us. In essence, we used the language experience approach (Allen, 1968; Tierney, Readence, & Dishner, 1990). We typed the students' language into a computer and provided each of them with a printed copy, which we then used as the basis for teaching the think-aloud procedure.

The Think-Aloud Procedure

We demonstrated the think-aloud procedure for the students and provided them with multiple opportunities to try the technique on their own (Ericsson & Simon, 1984; Wade, 1990). We spent 2 class periods working with students on this technique. The following is an example of how we modeled the procedure. (R1 = first author, R2 = second author, other letters represent names of students.)

Text: Estas comidas se hacen cuando festejamos algún día especial como el día de las madres y los cumpleaños. (These dishes are prepared when we celebrate some special day like Mother's Day or a birthday.)

R2: Esta frase me hace pensar en los días festivos como los cumpleaños y día de las madres. En estos días nuestra familia acostumbra reunirse y estar juntos. Especialmente en los cumpleaños; siempre celebramos los cumpleaños de mi mamá, mi papá y mis hermanos. Y hacemos comida. Casi siempre mi mamá y mis hermanas son las que cocinan, hacen comidas como tamales, pozole, menudo, comidas típicas. También el día de las madres le hacemos una comida a mi mamá o celebramos el día de las madres y nos reunimos. Toda la familia se reune. Es lo que me hace pensar esta frase. (This sentence makes me think about holidays like birthdays or Mother's Day. On those days it is our family custom to get together. This is especially true of birthdays; we always celebrate my mother's birthday and my father's and my brothers' and sisters'. And we make food. It is almost always my mother and my brothers who cook, who make food like tamales, pozole, menudo, typical foods. Also on Mother's Day we make a meal for my mother or we celebrate Mother's Day and we get together. All of the family gets together. That is what this sentence makes me think about.)

The students initially had problems implementing the procedure, as the following examples drawn from Sara's transcript testify.

These examples also illustrate that by creating a text that reflected recognizable and culturally familiar information, we could persist in asking that students participate in the dialogue. The transcripts also bear witness that this is not easy work; it definitely requires persistence and ample amounts of time. Although our early comments may appear somewhat harsh when read as transcript and separated from their total communicative context, we were determined to do everything possible to engage these students in literacy learning. As indicated in the final example, our efforts appeared to pay off.

R1: What does it make you think about, Sara?

Sara: Nothing.

R1: Well, think a little harder....

R1: Habla, habla, habla. Eres muy inteligente Sara, y lo puedes hacer. (Talk, talk, talk. You are very intelligent, Sara, and you can do it.)

S: I don't know about any....

R1: Te voy a seguir molestando hasta que me hables. (I'm going to keep bothering you until you talk to me.)

S: OK, I think of music and there are people sitting around and they are eating. And that's it.

R1: That's it. You did it, that's cool! You know how to do it! Thank you. Can you do that next time?

S: I'll try.

We found that use of both Spanish and English during this time was extremely helpful. We believed that by using both languages we could provide opportunities for students to make use of their full linguistic repertoire. Of special interest to us was that the students seemed to appreciate the opportunity to use Spanish and that its use may have improved rapport and student participation. In addition, we believed that by using both languages, we were able to encourage students to discuss their previous experiences. The following are some examples of how students used both languages:

R1: ¿Qué te pasó en Navidad? (What happened to you at Christmas?)

S: Comí tamales y different kinds of food. (I ate tamales and different kinds of food.)

Victor: Unos estan creciendo. Hay morados, allá where I live. Hay unos woods you go walking a lot y hay bien hartos elotes. You can grab thousands of them. (Some are growing. There are purple ones, over there where I live. There are some woods. You can go walking a lot and there are lots and lots of ears of corn.)

R1: What's leather?

S: It's like...

Adán: Como piel de animal. (Like animal skin.)

Culturally Relevant Text and Selected Reading Strategies

After we finished our initial efforts to demonstrate the think-aloud procedure, we introduced the students to trade books that contained what we considered culturally relevant text (Au, 1993; Harris, 1993). As much as possible, we tried to provide students with text that was also culturally recognizable, that is, mention was made of events or information that was within their experience. We put together a thematic strand of literature that we selected in order to build on and take advantage of the initial work we did in building students' prior knowledge and making connections with their community experience.

We used three books for this purpose: *A Quetzalcóatl Tale of Corn* (Parke & Panik, 1992), *The Day It Snowed Tortillas* (Hayes, 1985), and *Aztec, Inca and Maya* (Baquedano,

1993). All three of these books included stories that involved corn, corn flour, tortillas, and many other food items commonly used in Mexican cuisine, or they discussed these items in an expository text format.

We emphasized three cognitive and metacognitive strategies during the reading of all three texts. These were (a) approaching unknown vocabulary, which included using context, looking for cognate relationships, and making sure students could approximate pronunciations of words; (b) asking questions, which was often accompanied by overt comprehension monitoring; and (c) making inferences, which involved the integration of their prior knowledge with information found in print. These strategies have been identified and shown to be present in the think-aloud protocols of successful bilingual Latina/o readers of English (Jiménez, García, & Pearson, 1995, 1996). One example of our approach to present and teach each of these strategies follows.

Approaching unknown vocabulary

R1: You know that word in Spanish, so we can use a Spanish clue to help us figure out what it means. Victor, what does espectacular mean?

V: That it's useful?

R1: It's something very...

S: Special?

R1: Special, you got it! I like this. So [for] something very special, you can say wonderful, maravilloso. The Spanish clue helped us with spectacular because that is exactly the same in English and Spanish. Have you guys heard that word on the radio, spectacular? (The researcher writes this on the chalkboard.) That's English, and here's Spanish espectacular. The only difference between English and Spanish is that we put an e in the front in Spanish. That's exactly the same word. It almost sounds exactly the same, only a little bit different. But when you guys can do this you're taking advantage of your bilingualism and you're using what you already know to help you understand. OK? I think it's really cool when Latino kids do that. That makes a lot of sense to me.

Asking questions

S: Quetzalcóatl wanted very much to help the people that he loved.

R1: OK. What's your question now? What kind of question would you ask yourself? He wants very much to help the people that he loves so you wonder, well....

S: Is it gonna happen or not?

Making inferences

S: "The people of the Earth will starve unless they get food" said Quetzalcóatl.

R1: What does that mean, "the people of the Earth will starve"?

S: I don't know. Well, they don't have any food. They will starve.

R1: Starve means what?

S: They don't have food. They don't eat food.

R1: What happens if you don't eat?

S: You die.

R1: Exactly. So that's what it makes you think about. See, you're using what you know. You're integrating it with what you're reading here. You know that if people don't eat they're going to die. They will starve. That's making an inference, OK? Putting together what you know with what you read.

Building Reading Fluency

Our classroom observations and individual student interviews revealed that all three students were experiencing major difficulties with word recognition and reading fluency. As a result, we decided to work with

students on these abilities with the goal of helping them achieve what Samuels (1988) calls automaticity.

It was our belief that this work needed to be embedded within an overall context of meaningful, culturally relevant text, student-generated discourse, and instruction designed to promote comprehension. We always asked students to first read text silently. We then, on occasion, asked individual students to read orally. We viewed the building of reading fluency as one means toward helping students more carefully monitor their reading comprehension.

We did not continually interrupt students' oral reading every time they had difficulty pronouncing a word. Instead, we waited until they stopped because they were unable to pronounce a word or got to the end of a sentence. If students demonstrated difficulty with word recognition or overall fluency in reading (overly slow, choppy, meaning-altering miscues), then we asked them to orally reread specific phrases. At times, we asked them to do this two to three times. We took care not to embarrass students by also occasionally asking the other students present to read chorally with the group. The purpose of rereading was focused squarely on the larger goal of comprehension. Whenever students were asked to reread any portion of the text, we made sure that they then reread silently the problematic section within its larger context.

We explicitly emphasized that reading fluency was a means to comprehension, not an end in itself. We explained to the students that a consequence of poor reading fluency is an inability to understand. By the seventh and eighth day, we noticed that students appeared to be experiencing fewer problems with word recognition. The following is an example that was produced on the third day of working with the students:

V: The people began the children cried and Quetzalcóatl and those who had been.... (Text: *The people begged*, *the children cried*, *and Quetzalcóatl*, *the feathered serpent*, *heard their sadness.*)

R1: OK, read it again a little bit faster.

V: The people began, the children cried, and Quetzalcóatl, the feathered serpent, heard their sentence.

R1: OK, read it again.

V: The people began, the children... (student pauses)

R1: Does that make sense, "The people began"?

V: No.

R1: What's that word? The people what?

S: Begun.

R1: Look at it [carefully].

S: Began.

R1: Is that *began*?

S: No.

V: Begged.

R1: You got it; what is the meaning of *begged*?

V: They were begging for something. The people begged, the children cried, and Quetzalcóatl, the feathered serpent, heard their sadness.

Promising Results

By the end of our time working with the students, we began to notice some encouraging changes in their statements about reading. Sara's statement appeared to reflect added confidence in her ability to read and in her desire to read. Statements made by all three students also reflected increased metacognitive knowledge about themselves as readers and about useful strategies for increasing comprehension of text (Baker & Brown, 1984). These statements occurred during the last 2 days of our involvement with them.

R1: Yesterday, Sara was telling me what she used to think about reading.

S: I didn't like it.

R1: What was it that you didn't like?

S: [It was] hard.

R1: Hard. It was very hard for you to read, OK. How about now?

S: I kind of like it.

R1: How come?

S: Because it makes a little more sense, sort of. And I can read better.

We found that encouraging students to reflect on the activity of reading was also an excellent opportunity to review important information concerning cognitive and metacognitive reading strategies. The following two examples indicate that these three students began to discuss reading in ways similar to more experienced or successful readers (Jiménez, García, & Pearson, 1995, 1996). We found their statements very encouraging:

R1: What do you think you need to do to become a really good reader?

A: Read a lot.

R1: Yeah, read a lot. What else do you have to do when you're reading?

S: Picture things in your head.

R1: Yeah, you have to picture things in your head and what else?

S: Try and look for clues for words you don't know.

R1: Look for clues....

S: Try the words out in Spanish.

R1: Try it in Spanish, yeah. That's really smart. What else, Victor, what do you do to become a good reader? These are good answers because the first time I talked to you guys....

V: Imagine it and ask yourself questions....

R1: How about you, Victor? What's the difference between someone who is a good reader and someone who isn't? What do good readers do?

V: [They make] pictures in their head.

S: They ask questions.

R1: They ask questions, they make pictures in their head, and they do what....

V: Mix what we know....

R1: Mix what they know with what they're reading about. Mix it together and they understand.

Instruction Must Make Sense

Based on our experience, we believe that an emphasis on comprehension, use of culturally relevant texts, and instruction in and practice of reading fluency has strong potential for promoting and fostering the reading abilities of Latina/o students who are performing at low levels of literacy in the middle school grades.

Our earlier classroom observations and individual student interviews provided evidence that the students we worked with were reading and comprehending at quite rudimentary levels. Towards the end of this project, there were indications of changes in their motivation to read and their ability to verbalize important information about reading strategies. We believe that this preliminary work provides encouragement for those working with Latina/o students who are performing at low levels of literacy. These students are too often viewed simply as at risk for school failure, when, in fact, they may possess untapped potential for success in literacy.

We also strove to provide concrete examples of where to start and what to do with middle school students who are experiencing these kinds of problems. Instruction—defined broadly as interaction with and among students, information provided in the form of demonstrations, and focused attention and practice of specific strategies and other literate behaviors—still appears to be a crucial element necessary for the academic success of Latina/o students (Reyes, 1992).

For us, the most exciting aspect of this work was that these students were willing and eager to work hard and to participate in activities designed to improve their reading comprehension. Instruction, however, had to make sense to them. Macedo's (1994) challenge to provide Latina/o students with a worthwhile education may be met, at least in part, by literacy instruction that emphasizes culturally relevant quality literature and that focuses heavily on comprehension-enhancing strategies.

REFERENCES

Allen, R.V. (1968). How a language experience program works. In E.C. Vilscek (Ed.), *A decade of innovations: Approaches to beginning reading* (pp. 1-8). Newark, DE: International Reading Association.

Au, K.H. (1993). *Literacy instruction in multicultural settings*. Fort Worth, TX: Harcourt Brace Jovanovich.

Baker, L., & Brown, A.L. (1984). Metacognitive skills and reading. In P.D. Pearson (Ed.), *Handbook of reading research* (pp. 353-394). New York: Longman.

Bos, C.S., & Vaughn, S. (1988). *Strategies for teaching students with learning and behavioral problems*. Needham Heights, MA: Allyn & Bacon.

de la Rosa, D., Maw, C.E., & Yzaguirre, R. (1990). *Hispanic education: A statistical portrait 1990*. Washington, DC: Policy Analysis Center, Office of Research, Advocacy, and Legislation, National Council of La Raza.

Ericsson, K.A., & Simon, H.A. (1984). *Protocol analysis: Verbal reports as data*. Cambridge, MA: MIT Press.

García, G.E., Stephens, D.L., Koenke, K.R., Harris, V.J., Pearson, P.D., Jiménez, R.T., & Janisch, C. (1995). *Reading instruction and educational opportunity at the middle school level* (Tech. Rep. 622). Urbana-Champaign, IL: University of Illinois, Center for the Study of Reading.

Goldenberg, C. (1996). The education of language minority children: Where are we and where do we need to go? *Elementary School Journal, 96*, 353-361.

Harris, V.J. (1993). *Teaching multicultural literature*. Norwood, MA: Christopher-Gordon.

Jiménez, R.T., García, G.E., & Pearson, P.D. (1995). Three children, two languages, and strategic reading: Case studies in bilingual/monolingual reading. *American Educational Research Journal, 32*(1), 31-61.

Jiménez, R.T., García, G.E., & Pearson, P.D. (1996). The reading strategies of Latina/o students who are successful English readers: Opportunities and obstacles. *Reading Research Quarterly, 31*, 90-112.

Macedo, D. (1994). *Literacies of power*. Boulder, CO: Westview.

National Education Association. (1990). *Federal education funding: The cost of excellence*. Washington, DC: Author.

Reyes, M. de la Luz. (1992). Challenging venerable assumptions: Literacy instruction for linguistically different students. *Harvard Educational Review, 62*, 427-446.

Samuels, S.J. (1988). Decoding and automaticity: Helping poor readers become automatic at word recognition. *The Reading Teacher, 41*, 756-760.

Tierney, R.J., Readence, J.E., & Dishner, E.K. (1990). *Reading strategies and practices* (3rd ed.). Boston: Allyn & Bacon.

Wade, S.E. (1990). Using think alouds to assess comprehension. *The Reading Teacher, 43*, 442-453.

Waggoner, D. (1991). *Undereducation in America: The demography of high school dropouts*. New York: Auburn House.

Waggoner, D. (1994). Language-minority school-age population now totals 9.9 million. *NABE News, 18*(1), 1, 24-26.

CULTURALLY RELEVANT BOOKS USED FOR THINK-ALOUDS

Baquedano, E. (1993). *Aztec, Inca and Maya*. New York: Knopf.

Hayes, J. (1985). *The day it snowed tortillas: Tales from Spanish New Mexico*. Santa Fe, NM: Mariposa.

Parke, M., & Panik, S. (1992). *A Quetzalcóatl tale of corn*. Carthage, IL: Fearon Teacher Aids, Simon & Schuster Supplementary Education Group.

Nancy L. Hadaway and Jane Mundy

Children's Informational Picture Books Visit a Secondary ESL Classroom

The idea of literature-based instruction is not new to elementary classrooms. Numerous theoretical articles and teacher-researcher accounts chronicle the transition from textbook- and basal-driven instruction in the elementary grades to a literature-based emphasis (Cullinan, 1992; Freeman, 1991; Guzzetti, Kowalinski, & McGowan, 1992; McGee, 1992; Neal & Moore; 1991/1992; Scharer & Detwiler, 1992). Rather than reducing language to a series of isolated rules and skill sequences with texts that are simplified, literature-rich classrooms offer students a wealth of language and visual appeal along with current, relevant, and interesting information (Cullinan, 1992; Hedgecock & Pucci, 1993/1994; Rigg & Allen, 1989; Vardell & Copeland, 1992). Accompanying this move toward literature-based instruction is an explosion of outstanding children's books. "We have more good books on more diverse topics than we have ever had before; this makes it possible to develop programs that use literature across the curriculum" (Cullinan, 1993, p. 2).

While the literature-based approach has been focused primarily on the elementary schools, secondary teachers have also begun to dabble in this territory spurred by the recent emphasis on integrating the curriculum and in consideration of their students' diverse needs. Much effort at the secondary level centers around young adult literature; however, we are beginning to realize the many possibilities of children's literature as well. Picture books, especially, hold exceptional appeal for supporting students with diverse language proficiencies and reading levels and for assisting them to actively participate (Allen, 1989, 1994; Coonrod & Hughes, 1992, 1994; Maclean, 1990; Roser, 1990; Silverman, 1990).

English language learners (ELL), in particular, who might be intimidated by the amount of text in a novel with no subheadings or other visual cues for meaning require reading material that is comprehensible, material that is fine-tuned to approximate the learner's English language proficiency (Krashen, 1985; Rigg & Allen, 1989; Scarcella, 1990). Informational picture books provide that optimal input—chunks of text in a digestible format—through their solid information, short length, small amount of text, and use of illustrations as comprehension aids (Greenlaw, Shepperson, & Nistler, 1992; Neal & Moore, 1991/1992; Richard-Amato, 1996).

The focus of this article is to illustrate how research can inform and transform practice. Using the research base on literature-based instruction and effective instructional strategies for ELL, both authors, a university

Reprinted From the *Journal of Adolescent & Adult Literacy*, *42*(6), 464–475, March 1999.

teacher educator and a high school English as a Second Language (ESL) teacher, embark on a collaborative venture. The article chronicles our steps through the process as we plan and implement a unit using informational picture books in a high school ESL class.

Getting Started: A Rationale

Through reading professional journals and attending conferences, a public school colleague (Mundy) and I (Hadaway) became excited about applying the literature-based approach to secondary classrooms. I was seeking to encourage preservice teachers to try this method, and she was interested in testing the approach with her ESL students at the high school level. This was not our first collaboration or attempt at using literature with ELL. Our first unit on folklore centered on personal experience narratives of family and the journey to America with a limited use of literature. But, in viewing such positive student response to the literature and the type of models it provided for student writing (Allen, 1989), we wanted to extend our efforts, using more literature and moving to informational text with its strong link to the curriculum and potential benefit to ELL.

We knew that informational text provided an excellent literacy vehicle for English language learners, reinforcing language through content concepts that students encounter outside the sheltered environment of the ESL classroom. Indeed, Chamot and O'Malley (1994, p. 102) argue "that ESL instruction is moving in the direction of greater integration of language and content and that the development of academic-language proficiency will become the major objective of ESL instruction in schools." Clearly, continued progress in academic language proficiency is crucial to the success of ELL as they mainstream into regular classrooms and deal with the content curriculum and standardized tests.

Planning for Student Engagement

After discussing our idea at length, my colleague and I headed to the local public library, a valuable resource for secondary teachers because high school libraries house very little children's literature. We used the library shelves as a resource file of ideas and spent time talking and reflecting about possible topics as well as the students, their language backgrounds, and their potential interest in various fields of study. After brainstorming options, we looked at a long list of possibilities, everything from the environment to aging, and finally decided to focus on weather, integrating the related areas of seasons, weather phenomena, and weather disasters.

Although student choice certainly can drive unit selection, we based our decision on the link to the curriculum and the familiarity of concepts, knowing that the more background knowledge students bring to the page, the easier the process of comprehension (Allen, 1994). So, even if the English labels for weather concepts were not familiar, all English language learners would have experienced the concepts—some degree of seasonal change along with various weather phenomena and perhaps some weather disasters—wherever they had lived. The interplay of the culturally diverse students' geographic backgrounds would add another element of interest. Finally, linking informational picture books with environmental print resources, current magazine and newspaper accounts of local weather-related happenings, could pique student interest even further.

Our planning process was straightforward. After the initial expedition to the library, I visited the high school on a regular basis because preservice teachers from the university were assigned to that campus. Our collaboration was aided by very similar educational outlooks and instructional philosophies. As with any collaborative venture, however, some minor differences of opinion emerged. For us, these differences centered primarily on issues of timing, selection, use of materials, and activities. But, just as interdisciplinary teams in the schools work together, we also negotiated literacy goals, topics, literature resources, and eventual classroom activities.

Using the multitude of children's books available, we selected specific informational picture books and began to jointly plan literature-based activities for whole-class instruction, cooperative learning groups, and individual reading focusing on activities to involve students in listening, speaking, reading, and writing about the conceptual content (Chamot & O'Malley, 1994). I kept a running record of our planning sessions, typing up our ideas and massaging them into a readable format that took the shape of a calendar of the unit, day by day—ideas, topics to be covered, resources to be used, and language and content activities. All our planning and decisions were a joint effort, and much of the teaching responsibility was as well.

Considering Student Backgrounds

As often as possible, I worked in the class coteaching lessons or interacting with the students solo. The class chosen for implementation of this unit was a self-contained high school ESL class that met for 1 hour daily. These students spent the remainder of the school day in content area classes, some with sheltered instruction but most with no additional assistance. We implemented this unit during the fall semester in an intermediate level ESL class composed of 18 students, sophomore through senior level, with ages ranging from 14 to 19. While the class was leveled according to intermediate English language proficiency, the students reflected a range of ability as to reading, writing, speaking, and listening. Realizing that most of them would not be returning home to their native countries, the students were positive about learning English, understanding its importance to their future. They struggled at times with getting their point across in speaking and writing. In general, the students were positive about school as well, perhaps more so about their ESL class where they shared a common bond with their peers. As to academic level, the class was composed of mainly average students although their grade reports sometimes reflected another reality due to their lack of academic language proficiency for the content classrooms.

Most students had some type of employment after school and on weekends–many times necessitated by the family's economic situation–and this also had an impact on their academic progress and motivation. Students' ethnic backgrounds reflected diverse geographic origins–Vietnam, Mexico, Poland, and Ethiopia–which always added to great comparison/contrast opportunities during class discussions. Additional variety was supplied by the amount of time students had been in the United States. Some were newly arrived, such as a young Polish student whose father worked at the university; others had been in the country for several years, often with sporadic school attendance. Few of the students had a typical home environment; they often lived with older siblings, relatives, or family friends rather than parents.

By the end of the process, the students had accepted me as a natural part of their class.

My experiences provided direct examples of student diversity and literacy instruction in action to share with my preservice students, and the high school students were able to feed their curiosity about the university just around the corner.

How's the Weather?

To introduce the unit, we highlighted various activities for the upcoming weeks. Along with reading and writing using informational picture books as the base of instruction, students would emphasize concrete language and vocabulary by recording weather statistics (e.g., temperature, sun, clouds, precipitation) daily on a class chart and incorporating this new vocabulary into a weather journal, thereby more closely linking ESL with content instruction. The chart and the students' journals served as sources of data for many interdisciplinary activities such as graphing the temperature fluctuation from day to day, again connecting language learning and content exploration. In addition, environmental print from daily weather reports in newspapers to national weather maps and statistics linked the concepts from books we were reading to everyday text that students encountered.

The first 2 weeks' activities furnished an overview of weather. To accomplish this, two informational picture books, *Weather Words and What They Mean* (Gibbons, 1990) and *What Will the Weather Be?* (DeWitt, 1991), were used for read-aloud response. Pre-reading activities included brainstorming for background knowledge (What words associated with weather do you know? Who is responsible for the weather predictions we read in newspapers and see on television?) and prediction strategies (How do we know *What Will the Weather Be* each day? Based on the title, what do you think this book will be about?). Then the class moved through the books together, discussing new ideas and working on vocabulary through the visual-verbal connection-guessing the meaning of new terms from illustrations in the text and developing graphic aids to help remember meanings (Moe, 1989; Neal & Moore, 1992).

An especially useful visual-verbal technique we tested with vocabulary from *Weather Words* was a graphic organizer, the continuum (see Figure 1). Using this technique, students discussed the word meaning and placed new vocabulary items for various kinds of rain (*drizzle, shower, rain, rainstorm, thunderstorm, flood*), snow (*flurry, sleet, snow, snowstorm, blizzard*), and wind (*breeze, gust, wind, gale, tornado, hurricane*) along continuums to denote increasing intensity. Later, they had fun illustrating their continuum with, for example, bolts of lightning or snowflakes—more visual cues to meaning. The students commented that they found this graphic organizer particularly useful in helping them remember the vocabulary words and their meaning. For this exercise, a simple horizontal line showed each end reflecting the extremes (i.e., drizzle, flood). However, students could work with a vertical continuum using font size to differentiate levels of intensity (a technique I learned from one of my own university students).

Figure 1
Possible continuum depicting intensity
of rain words

drizzle
shower
rain
rainstorm
thunderstorm
flood

Whatever the format, I enjoyed using the continuum technique to stress the idea that there are different kinds of rain or wind and, while words can be similar in meaning, not all synonyms can be used interchangeably. Such activities focus students on word choice and the picture they are trying to paint in the reader's mind. We saw the results as students began to incorporate this new vocabulary into their weather journals and class discussions to more precisely describe daily weather conditions.

What Will the Weather Be? proved a rich source of content concepts introducing high and low pressure areas along with warm and cold fronts. The clear presentation of these weather concepts accompanied by great illustrations offered the opportunity to incorporate a discussion of similarities and differences leading to the text structure format of comparison/contrast. To capitalize on this organizational pattern, which is used in picture books and students' content textbooks, we differentiated the two types of fronts, warm and cold, using H-maps or comparison/contrast maps (see Figure 2). The H-map graphic organizer worked well helping students to recognize a specific text pattern, to take notes, and to write summary statements. Consequently, we have incorporated that technique into many other lessons, and students were able to carry this strategy outside the ESL environment to their content classes.

As a review technique, students worked in groups to make a collage of weather words and pictures from environmental print sources. We have learned that somehow you never outgrow your love of cutting and pasting, and these high school students were no exception. The opportunity to browse through magazines and newspapers reinforced their new knowledge, and the evidence that students had mastered the new concepts and vocabulary was apparent from audible cues (Here's a good example of a rainstorm! Look at this tornado and all the damage!) as they excitedly stumbled on photos, key words, and phrases and focused the group's attention on their find. Then, the groups presented their product to the class with a short oral explanation that served as an informal assessment of student comprehension of concepts and use of new vocabulary.

Because there were so many more informational picture books available than we had time to use in the unit, we provided opportunities for students to expand on the information introduced in read-aloud time with other resource books. Many of these supplemental books were organized as browsing books (e.g., *Storms*; Wood, 1990)–busy pages filled with chunks of text, illustrations with captions, and

Figure 2
Student comparison/contrast map of warm and cold fronts

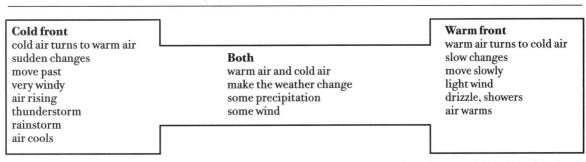

Cold front	Both	Warm front
cold air turns to warm air		warm air turns to cold air
sudden changes	warm air and cold air	slow changes
move past	make the weather change	move slowly
very windy	some precipitation	light wind
air rising	some wind	drizzle, showers
thunderstorm		air warms
rainstorm		
air cools		

fascinating trivia—a format ideally suited for English language learners, nonreaders, and reluctant readers. We knew we were making an impact when students took advantage of free time, turning to these books to explore concepts of special interest.

To engage the class in hands-on language activities, we turned to informational books filled with easy-to-implement experiments. Those from *Be an Expert Weather Forecaster* (Taylor-Cork, 1992) and *Janice VanCleave's Earth Science for Every Kid: One Hundred One Easy Experiments That Really Work* (VanCleave, 1991) helped us to observe how thermometers work, to make raindrops in a jar, and to simulate how tiny water droplets grow into raindrops. While making raindrops in a jar, we explored precipitation, condensation, and evaporation. When we later encountered these terms in an informational picture book depicting the water cycle, students were quick to pick them up, excitedly calling out the vocabulary terms before I finished reading the page aloud and reminding us that we had previously explored this territory (That's precipitation like we saw in the jar activity!). This response added further proof that retention and transfer of concepts were occurring. As a result of these experiments, students truly became better observers, drawing our attention to the natural phenomena around us.

Bring in the Wind, Rain, and Clouds

From the general overview of weather, we moved on to wind, rain, and clouds employing more informational picture books. For read-aloud response, we shared *Feel the Wind* (Dorros, 1989) to lead into our discussion of what makes wind and the force of wind. From the resource *Be an Expert Weather Forecaster*

we explored wind patterns such as the westerlies, doldrums, and trade winds and discovered how wind is measured using the Beaufort Scale. Afterwards, when we recorded the daily weather statistics as a class, students began to add their estimation of the force of the wind with the Beaufort Scale. Then, using *What Makes It Rain?* (Brandt, 1982) as a springboard, we linked the text to a graphic organizer of the rain cycle, and students talked through the process of precipitation, condensation, and evaporation. The cycle graphic organizer of the sequence of events was yet another technique used in both picture books and content texts and a format that students could transfer to other content classes.

Finally, we shared Tomie dePaola's *The Cloud Book* (1975) and examined the excellent illustrations from *Weather* (Smith, 1990) to study various types of clouds. After reading, discussing, and conducting some cloud watching outside—much to the students' joy—the class experimented with the new descriptive vocabulary they had encountered writing concrete poems about clouds, first as a class and then in groups (see Figure 3). DePaola paints some vivid but concrete images of clouds (for instance, comparing cumulus clouds to cauliflower), which helped the students in their artistic renditions.

Beyond introducing specific types of clouds, *The Cloud Book* also uses amusing cartoon-like illustrations to present idioms: "He's in a fog"; "she has her head in the clouds"; "in the morning, mountains [of clouds], in the evening fountains [of rain]." Because figurative language is particularly confusing for students learning another language, these illustrations and related expressions provided a wonderful springboard to a discussion of expressions associated with weather. With the help of their teachers, the class brainstormed additional expressions (e.g., raining cats and dogs), and we searched

Figure 3
Group constructed concrete poem about clouds

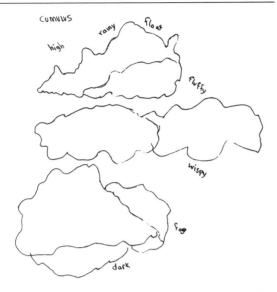

through phrase dictionaries such as *A January Fog Will Freeze a Hog* (Davis, 1977) to extend our knowledge.

Weather for All Seasons

Linking the topic of weather to the seasons was a natural transition, and to assist our study several informational picture books were used. First, *Weather Forecasting* (Gibbons, 1987) presented each season and its associated vocabulary along with weather forecasting and weather maps. From our previous study of warm and cold fronts, we were able to incorporate this information and apply it directly to the weather maps in our local newspapers. The demystification of weather maps and their many symbols was exciting, not only for our students but also for us. With newspapers available in the class each day, students began to pore over the weather maps and share the forecast predictions with us.

Exploring further with the seasons, we scanned resources such as *Autumn Weather* (Mason, 1991), *The Reasons for Seasons* (Gibbons, 1995), *Winter Across America* (Simon, 1994), and *Autumn Across America* (Simon, 1993) for facts and impressions of the seasons. Then, the class brainstormed a semantic map, noting representative weather patterns, colors, activities, clothing, and holidays connected with the four seasons. Students were able to reproduce this map on their own paper to use as a vocabulary bank for future activities related to the seasons (see Figure 4).

This exercise generated some lively discussion and sharing as we talked about the typical American presentation of the seasons. For instance, when brainstorming about winter, students offered terms such as *snow*, *sledding*, and *skiing*. We countered asking if those were really typical of their new home, Texas, or even of their previous home. This led to excellent personal examples from their home countries and also a discussion of how books and the media shape our images and expectations of the seasons. For example, Seymour Simon's books *Autumn Across America* and *Winter Across America* use visual images that are typical representations of the seasons (i.e., snow and ice for winter), but the text notes the wide range of climatic conditions for the seasons according to the different geographic regions.

Using the semantic map as a vocabulary builder and prewriting technique, the students moved to the next step. In groups, they clipped words and phrases from magazines and newspapers to create paste-up poetry (always a popular activity with these English language learners) about the season of their choice. Class members then shared their paste-up poem, and we guessed which season was being described. With all this scaffolding, the ELL were eventually ready to try their hands at some creative writing. So, after we introduced the format for diamante poems and generated one as a class, students worked

Figure 4
Student-generated semantic map on the seasons

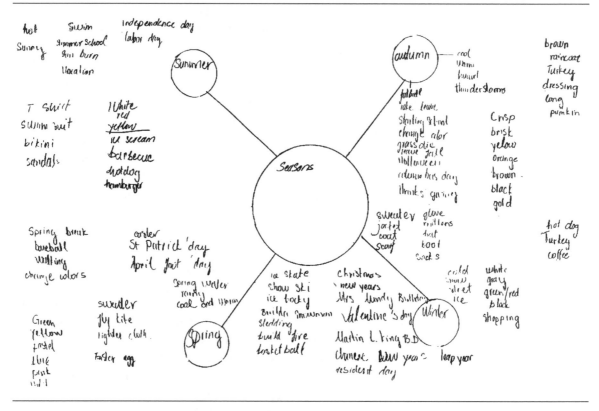

Figure 5
Student-generated bilingual diamante comparing two seasons

fall
briskly crisply
cloudy yellow sleepy
falling changing growing raining
sunny new happy
happily warmly
spring

otoño
ligero seco
nublado amarillo dormir
callendo cambiando naciendo lloviendo
soliado nuevo feliz
feliz caloroso
verano

individually to write a diamante on one season or to create one comparing and contrasting two seasons. Most students created bilingual diamantes (see Figure 5), which we posted around the classroom to highlight the rich diversity of languages and alphabet systems in our midst. For the remainder of the unit, students enjoyed circulating to view the bilingual versions and comparing English and native langauge versions.

Researching Weather Disasters

As a culminating activity for our study of weather across the seasons, the students used informational picture books to research weather-related disasters—floods, hurricanes, and tornadoes—prior to a library visit. For any student, but particularly for these high school ELL, picture books can be a less intimidating, and often more interesting, introduction to research and be a prereading introduction to the typical reference book in the school library. Informational picture books such as the two *Storms* (Simon, 1989; Wood, 1990), *Natural Wonders and Disasters* (Goodman, 1991), *Flood!* (Waters, 1991), *Hurricane!* (Archer, 1991), *Hurricanes: Earth's Mightiest Storms* (Lauber, 1996), *Tornado!* (Archer, 1991), and *Tornado Alert* (Branley, 1988) along with environmental print sources were put to use to discover more about students' topics.

The class worked in cooperative groups, but prior to releasing them to work in groups using the jigsaw method (Peregoy & Boyle, 1997), we brainstormed an example of the research process students would be using. Because tornadoes are common in Texas, we started with that weather phenomenon and generated questions to focus students' search for information. These general questions were extended to all weather disasters under examination as we devised a jot chart format to guide notetaking (see Figure 6). With this structured format, students were to define the disaster; record specific seasons (if any) associated with it; cite causes and effects (to property, people, weather); note famous disasters in each category, interesting facts, and specific geographic zones where each disaster might occur; and suggest any prevention or precaution measures to be taken. Proceeding through three steps, the groups implemented the jigsaw as follows. First, each group chose one member to become an expert on a weather disaster. Next, these experts met and completed the jot chart. Finally, once experts amassed the necessary information, they returned to their original groups to debrief and teach the others about their specific weather disaster.

When this activity was completed, the students moved to the library for more detailed research. By this point, the informational

Figure 6
Jot chart format for research activity

	Floods	Hurricanes	Tornadoes
Define this weather disaster.			
What specific seasons (if any) are associated with this weather disaster?			
What are the causes of this weather disaster?			
What are the effects of this weather disaster on property, people, weather?			
Note some famous disasters for each type of weather disaster (year; location; name, if applicable).			
Cite at least three interesting facts associated with each disaster.			
Note specific geographic regions where each disaster might occur.			
Note any prevention/precaution measures that might be taken for each disaster.			

children's books had provided a prereading framework to help these second-language learners conduct independent research in the library using standard reference materials. For this phase of the study, students researched a famous flood, tornado, or hurricane. They noted when and where (using a map) it occurred, the extent of damage (physical property costs, loss of life, environmental damage), any reconstruction or rebuilding costs, and preventive measures for future occurrences.

For example, intrigued by Patricia Lauber's description of Hurricane Andrew in *Hurricanes: Earth's Mightiest Storms*, one student chose to highlight that storm and its destructive path across south Florida. In reporting their research results, students created a poster presentation about their specific weather disaster. During this culminating activity, we viewed students tackling the regular library materials, and their efforts confirmed that the informational picture books had accomplished their purpose. They had laid the foundation for language growth so that students felt more confident using academically challenging texts.

Reflecting on the Process

One key to successful collaboration is to spend adequate time planning and reflecting along the way. Through this continuous dialogue difficulties or differences emerge and ideas come forth, sometimes with time for modifications in process to be implemented, but certainly with time for suggestions for the future. After all, no matter how smooth the course, there is always room for improvement. Our reflections prompted us to keep track of the many possibilities, so here we share three basic considerations in implementing literature-based units with informational picture books.

First, the use of informational picture books provides a natural connection to the dreaded content textbook because both generally use an expository style of writing. Students struggle with the dry and difficult format of textbooks, so informational books can serve as an instructional bridge to textbooks (Allen, 1994). One suggestion for all teachers using informational picture books is to make specific reference to the external aids as well as the internal structure of the text (Law & Eckes, 1990). We made some initial jaunts into internal text structure territory when we worked with the comparison/contrast structure of warm and cold fronts and when we read about the rain cycle and graphed the process. Yet, while we drew student attention to language patterns, concepts, and vocabulary from the books, we failed to directly walk students through the external aids to comprehension—pictures, maps, italics, boldface print, size and shapes of words to signal relative importance—and then compare these aids and their similarity to the ones used in their content textbooks.

In short, we could have billed informational picture books as an ideal introduction tool for tackling content textbooks, encouraging students to use public library resources and matching those abbreviated conceptual snapshots with their school texts. We realized what an opportunity we had lost because acquiring English is only one of the demanding tasks confronting English language learners; they must also master content concepts and gain an awareness of the skills and strategies needed to become independent learners (Allen, 1994).

Second, the informational picture books we selected were a success with the students, especially the browsing books. The class enjoyed the books' colorful, reader-friendly, and instructive format. Nevertheless, we know that age appropriateness is a key issue in materials selection (Allen, 1994). Based on our experiences, we believe the teachers are pivotal to the success of the process, first in the selection of materials and next in their presentation. As we examine literature options, we always put ourselves in the place of the audience. If we are engaged by the text and its information and not put off by the illustrations or formatting, then the material has passed our first test. We would advocate, for instance, that any of Seymour Simon's books have universal appeal to children and adults. They are well-crafted books with outstanding illustrations. On closer examination, we consider the author's writing style, accuracy of content, and interest level of the text–after all, the idea is to draw students into the process, not put them off. Still, just as crucial as the selection process is the instructional presentation.

Teachers should not use materials if they feel it is necessary to apologize for them; obviously, this need not extend to the many inconsiderate but mandated content textbooks. We approached our unit confident about the materials, and we communicated our enthusiasm about the selected books to the students, likening them to a preparation phase for later reading and writing activities. And indeed, students stepped up to the challenge of library research after the foundation was laid through informational picture books. We also shared our fascination with specific text examples and commented on the new material we were learning through the use of these resources. Indeed, as students spent free time browsing through the classroom library of weather books, we modeled engaged reading, excitedly looking through books and sharing fascinating bits of trivia with each other. For instance, did you know that "the most snow to fall in a year was at Paradise, Mount Rainier, in the winter of 1971. About 1,224 inches fell, enough to reach a third of the way up the Statue of Liberty!" (Wood, 1990, p. 11).

Third, while we made good use of environmental print from newspapers and magazines, we neglected other familiar visual media. A motivational prelude to the unit with video clips of radar screens and weather maps from televised weather reports could pique interest and fold naturally into brainstorming for students' background knowledge and prereading predictions about the specific informational picture books. Moreover, with the increasing availability of the Internet to schools and individual classrooms, students could access a host of Web sites with weather radar updates and forecasts. In addition, with our daily weather data check, we could have confirmed their information by tuning into the Weather Channel on TV or, again, accessing a weather Web site via the Internet.

Another forgotten visual connection was video; the Weather Channel, for example, offers various affordable videos concerning weather phenomena, any one of which would have worked well with the books selected for the jigsaw activity during our final research activity prior to the library phase. For our many visual learners, and for ELL who need the added visual context to support the comprehension of print concepts, connecting print with media just makes sense.

Obviously, there are countless ways to fine-tune an instructional unit. These three points represent just a few of the more important considerations that emerged from our reflections as we moved through this process.

Research Can Inform and Transform

Using the research base on literature-based instruction, we both opened our teaching and our classrooms to incorporate informational picture books with secondary ESL students.

The results were positive; students were actively engaged with text. The short length and visual nature of the picture books helped these English language learners comprehend the concepts presented, and through class discussions and written work related to the unit, we saw an increase in their vocabulary. Also, the students benefited from the cooperative nature of the lessons, practicing listening and speaking skills and learning new concepts and labels for familiar physical phenomena from one another. To demonstrate their comprehension, they wrote about the weather and seasons in journals, poems, and research presentations. In addition, due to the interdisciplinary nature of the unit, links to other areas of the curriculum were made. Even after the unit ended, students were inclined to begin class with a weather report noting the temperature, cloud conditions, and so on.

My class of preservice teachers benefited too. This collaborative effort was a model of teacher research and literature-based instruction. Consequently, my students began to experiment in their field experiences with some of these techniques. Soon after my lecture on using literature across the curriculum, one student shared that she had read Dr. Seuss's *The Lorax* (Geisel, 1971) to a seventh-grade class during a lesson on the environment. I subsequently collaborated with two of my students to plan an Earth Day unit for high school using informational picture books.

What of my public school colleague? We went on to other collaborations and new discoveries because we had realized the power of picture books for students of all ages. In sharing the possibilities with my preservice class, one of my students offered his own personal example of the potential of children's literature. He uses informational picture books to build background knowledge prior to beginning graduate history classes. So, it seems that many of us are already aware that "one way to get an overview of a topic is to consult a picture book" (Freeman, 1991, p. 471).

REFERENCES

Allen, V.G. (1989). Literature as a support to language acquisition. In P. Rigg & V.G. Allen (Eds.), *When they don't all speak English: Integrating the ESL student into the regular classroom* (pp. 55–64). Urbana, IL: National Council of Teachers of English.

Allen, V.G. (1994). Selecting materials for the reading instruction of ESL children. In K. Spangenberg-Urbschat & R. Pritchard (Eds.), *Kids come in all languages: Reading instruction for ESL students* (pp. 108–131). Newark, DE: International Reading Association.

Chamot, A.U., & O'Malley, J.M. (1994). Instructional approaches and teaching procedures. In K. Spangenberg-Urbschat & R. Pritchard (Eds.), *Kids come in all languages: Reading instruction for ESL students* (pp. 82–107). Newark, DE: International Reading Association.

Coonrod, D., & Hughes, S. (1992). Using children's trade books to teach social studies to young children. *Social Studies Texan, 8*, 57–58.

Coonrod, D., & Hughes, S. (1994). Using children's literature to promote language development of minority students. *Journal of Educational Issues of Language Minority Students, 14*, 319–331.

Cullinan, B.E. (1992). Whole language and children's literature. *Language Arts, 69*, 426–430.

Cullinan, B.E. (1993). *Fact and fiction across the curriculum*. Newark, DE: International Reading Association.

Freeman, E.B. (1991). Informational books: Models for student report writing. *Language Arts, 68*, 470–473.

Greenlaw, M.J., Shepperson, G.M., & Nistler, R.J. (1992). A literature approach to teaching about the Middle Ages. *Language Arts, 69*, 200–204.

Guzzeti, B.J., Kowalinski, B.J., & McGowan, T. (1992). Using a literature-based approach to teaching social studies. *Journal of Reading, 36*, 114–122.

Hedgecock, J., & Pucci, S. (1993/1994). Whole language applications to ESL in secondary and higher education. *TESOL Journal, 3*, 22–26.

Krashen, S.D. (1985). *The input hypothesis: Issues and implications*. New York: Longman.

Law, B., & Eckes, M. (1990). *The more-than-just-surviving handbook: ESL for every classroom teacher*. Winnipeg, MB: Peguis.

Maclean, M. (1990). Literature and second language learning. *TESL Talk, 20*, 244–250.

McGee, L.M. (1992). Focus on research: Exploring the literature-based reading revolution. *Language Arts, 69*, 529–537.

Moe, A.J. (1989). Using picture books for reading vocabulary development. In J.W. Stewig & S.L. Sebesta (Eds.), *Using literature in the elementary classroom* (pp. 23–34). Urbana, IL: National Council of Teachers of English.

Neal, J.C., & Moore, K. (1991/1992). The Very Hungry Caterpillar meets Beowulf in secondary classrooms. *Journal of Reading, 35*, 290–296.

Peregoy, S.F., & Boyle, O.F. (1997). *Reading, writing, and learning in ESL: A resource book for K–12 teachers* (2nd ed.). New York: Longman.

Richard-Amato, P.A. (1996). *Making it happen: Interaction in the second language classroom* (2nd ed.). New York: Longman.

Rigg, P., & Allen, V.G. (Eds.). (1989). *When they don't all speak English: Integrating the ESL student into the regular classroom*. Urbana, IL: National Council of Teachers of English.

Roser, N. (1990). Language, literature, and at-risk children. *The Reading Teacher, 43*, 554–559.

Scarcella, R. (1990). *Teaching language minority students in the multicultural classroom*. Upper Saddle River, NJ: Prentice Hall Regents.

Scharer, P., & Detwiler, D.B. (1992). Changing as teachers: Perils and possibilities of literature-based language arts instruction. *Language Arts, 69*, 186–192.

Silverman, A. (1990). Children's literature for ESL adults. *TESL Talk, 20*, 201–207.

Vardell, S.M., & Copeland, K.A. (1992). Reading aloud and responding to nonfiction: Let's talk about it. In E.B. Freeman & D.G. Person (Eds.), *Using nonfiction trade books in the elementary classroom* (pp. 76–85). Urbana, IL: National Council of Teachers of English.

BOOKS CITED

Archer, J. (1991). *Hurricane!* New York: Crestwood House.

Archer, J. (1991). *Tornado!* New York: Crestwood House.

Brandt, K. (1982). *What makes it rain?* Mahwah, NJ: Troll.

Branley, F.M. (1988). *Tornado alert*. New York: Thomas Y. Crowell.

Davis, H. (1977). *A January fog will freeze a hog*. New York: Crown.

dePaola, T. (1975). *The cloud book*. New York: Holiday House.

DeWitt, L. (1991). *What will the weather be?* New York: HarperCollins.

Dorros, A. (1989). *Feel the wind*. New York: Harper & Row.

Geisel, T.S. (1971). *The Lorax*. New York: Random House.

Gibbons, G. (1987). *Weather forecasting*. New York: Four Winds Press.

Gibbons, G. (1990). *Weather words and what they mean*. New York: Holiday House.

Gibbons, G. (1995). *The reasons for seasons*. New York: Scholastic.

Goodman, B. (1991). *Natural wonders and disasters*. Boston: Little, Brown.

Lauber, P. (1996). *Hurricanes: Earth's mightiest storms*. New York: Scholastic.

Mason, J. (1991). *Autumn weather*. New York: The Bookwright Press.

Simon, S. (1989). *Storms*. New York: Morrow Junior Books.

Simon, S. (1993). *Autumn across America*. New York: Hyperion.

Simon, S. (1994). *Winter across America*. New York: Hyperion.

Smith, H.E. (1990). *Weather*. New York: Doubleday.

Taylor-Cork, B. (1992). *Be an expert weather forecaster*. New York: Glouceser Press.

VanCleave, J. (1991). *Janice VanCleave's earth science for every kid: One hundred one easy experiments that really work*. New York: John Wiley & Sons.

Waters, J. (1991). *Flood!* New York: Crestwood House.

Wood, J. (1990). *Storms*. New York: Scholastic.

Nancy Hansen-Krening and Donald T. Mizokawa

Exploring Ethnic-Specific Literature:
A Unity of Parents, Families, and Educators

Americans are diverse in many ways: religiously, linguistically, ethnically, and philosophically. Political responses to such diversity are often contentious; frequently, each end of the political spectrum rises to rhetorical extremes with claims of being the sole arbiters of truth and rational thinking. Literacy educators are not immune from the lengths to which the arguments are carried. For them, the issue of ethnic diversity gives rise to questions such as which piece of United States literature should or should not be included in their curricula and how that literature (fiction and nonfiction) should be chosen. Their quandary is not eased by the rallying calls of "Read my people's literature!" that seem to issue from almost every and any faction, regardless of political leaning.

In view of this controversy, educators from U.S. school districts as well as families served by those school districts are asking for help in collecting a balanced selection of books for the classroom. They seek assistance in identifying both fiction and nonfiction that represent all citizens. In this article, we share our response to requests for help in finding and using such a body of work.

As experienced educators in multiethnic/multicultural education we feel that the question of whose canon is *the* correct canon is a nonissue. We do, however, believe the tra-
ditional canon must be expanded to include worthy literature written by and about people of color. We target ethnic-specific literature because this literature has not received the pervasive visibility it merits. Equally, we believe that U.S. citizens need a deep, unifying, and more respectful knowledge of one another. "Knowledge about ethnic pluralism is a necessary foundation for respecting, appreciating, valuing, and celebrating diversity" (Gay, 1994, p. 20). Reviews of research document that this vast body of literature is either rarely used or undiscovered by classroom teachers (e.g., Aoki, 1981; Hansen-Krening, Mizokawa, & Aoki, 1994; Ostrowski, 1994; Thompson & Meeks, 1990; Tighe, 1994; Vilscek, 1994).

Teachers and librarians are not deliberately and insidiously trying to suppress a canon that represents all writers—authors of color as well as Western European authors. Teachers, librarians, and families simply do not know about the abundance of authors and their books. Writers of whom they are aware comprise a relatively small group: Toni Morrison, Maya Angelou, Ralph Ellison, Amy Tan, and Maxine Hong Kingston for adults; Walter Dean Myers, Mildred Taylor, Virginia Hamilton, Lawrence Yep, and Gary Soto for young adults; and Lucille Clifton, Faith

96

Reprinted From the *Journal of Adolescent & Adult Literacy*, 41(3), 180–189, November 1997.

Ringold, Allen Say, and Arthur Dorros for kindergarten through fifth-grade readers.

Our commitment has been to bring adults, children, and ethnic-specific literature together. We believe that through encounters with ethnic-specific literature, readers see reflections of our broader society. Reading a variety of books from and about an ethnic group, people further learn that each group manifests amazing variety and diversity. Bishop's (1994) clear voice speaks in support of our belief.

> In an important sense, then, children need literature that serves as a window onto lives and experiences different from their own and literature that serves as a mirror reflecting themselves and their cultural values, attitudes, and behaviors. (p. xiv)

Au (1993) joins Bishop in stating "all students, whether of mainstream or diverse backgrounds, learn from multiethnic literature about the diversity and complexity of American society" (p. 177).

Over the past 5 years, school districts have asked us to conduct workshops at their schools on both ethnic-specific literature and response to literature. The audiences have included different combinations of kindergarten through high school inservice and preservice teachers, English as a second language teachers, district and school administrators, public and school librarians, custodians, and sometimes parents. Throughout this time, we have had ample evidence that teachers, librarians, administrators, parents, and other caregivers embrace ethnic-specific stories with spirit and enthusiasm. We have witnessed people discovering that in well-written prose and poetry there is shared experience—some mutual emotion that bridges ethnic and cultural differences. They experience as much interest and feeling for the story as well as appreciation for the craft of the

artist when they read Morrison's *Beloved* (1987) as when they read Fitzgerald's *The Great Gatsby* (1920).

Over and over again we have found that making ethnic-specific literature integral to any literature program enhances a sense of community among teachers, students, and families. By reading one another's stories we not only encounter individual and cultural differences, but we also find the bridges we as human beings experience as we live, have lived, and might live in the U.S.

Ways of Exploring and Reading Ethnic-Specific Literature

Our sessions always begin with a discussion of the language we will use in discussing literature. In the past, terminology for discussing the expanded canon has proven difficult to establish because language can raise as many hackles as it can soothe ruffled feathers (the term "authors of color" is a case in point). By definition, any aggregate of people called a community must share a common vocabulary for clear communication. The terms and definitions and labels that Cai (1992) provides in his doctoral dissertation are easy to understand and helpful in all of our discussions. These are his categories:

- *World literature* comprises stories set in a country other than the United States (e.g., Lawrence Yep's Chinese folktales).

- *Cross-cultural literature* is the work of a European American (usually) author writing about people from another ethnic group (e.g., Scott O'Dell's *Island of the Blue Dolphins*).

- *Ethnic-specific* or *minority literature* is literature about an ethnic group, written by an author who is a member of that ethnic group (e.g., Ken Mochizuki's *Baseball Saved Us*). This category refers

Additional Sources

Asian American Curriculum Project, Inc. publishes a catalogue of materials that may be purchased through their organization. This is a superb resource for readers of all ages. The address is 234 Main Street, PO Box 1587, San Mateo, CA 94401, USA. Telephone +415-874-2242.

Day, F. (Ed.). (1994). *Multicultural voices in contemporary literature*. Portsmouth, NH: Heinemann.

Harris, V. (Ed.). (1992). *Teaching multicultural literature in grades K–8*. Norwood, MA: Christopher-Gordon.

Ruoff, A., & Ward, J., Jr. (Eds.). (1990). *Redefining American literary history*. New York: Modern Language Association of America.

explicitly to authors and characters of color. (We chose the term *ethnic-specific* rather than *minority* literature. This is simply our personal aversion to perpetuating the distancing and marginalizing connotations of the word.)

Cai's categories minimize confusion because people who use them agree to speak from the same conceptual basis. In any community, this kind of shared understanding is essential, if not criterial.

Introducing Cai's categories. We begin our instruction by presenting and providing examples of Cai's categories. Certainly, this gives rise to debate about why literature has to be divided by ethnic membership. People ask, "Why can't we just have U.S. literature? Why do we have to draw lines by ethnic group?" This is indeed our grand goal; however, we start where people are. Research has documented not only the relative paucity of ethnic-specific literature in classrooms but also its sporadic use (see, for example, Flood et al., 1994; Hansen-Krening, 1992; Hansen-

Krening, Mizokawa, & Aoki, 1994). Furthermore, too often the lines between United States literature and texts from other countries are blurred and undifferentiated. Teachers self-report the use of African folktales as examples of African American literature although these are two separate bodies of literature representing two distinct cultures and two distinct periods of time. Establishing categories brings order and organization to what can be a confusing mixture of world, cross-cultural, and ethnic-specific works.

Given enough time, small groups of participants use Cai's categories to sort collections of books. Adults who had used African folktales (e.g., Steptoe's *Mufaro's Beautiful Daughters*, 1987) as central to their African American literature realize that this body of oral tradition falls under the category of *world* literature rather than ethnic-specific literature. They no longer make the mistake of confusing African literature with African American literature, Israeli literature with Jewish American literature, Mexican with Mexican American literature, or any world literature with ethnic-specific literature. The categories provide significant distinctions in identifying and selecting literature.

The explicit discussion of ethnic-specific literature provides a necessary background for engaging adults in talking about their own reading of this literature. Before meeting with us, attendees read a selected novel or autobiography (e.g., Uchida's *Desert Exile*, 1982, or Lee's *China Boy*, 1991) from an ethnic-specific collection of literature. They are asked, as they read, to reflect on their personal responses to the book.

Responding to literature and literature circles. We strive to instill in the adult participants an empathy for the younger readers' experience through connecting their feelings as they read with responses children and young adults might have as they read, as they encounter the powerful effect of ethnic-specific literature. It is essential that all attendees encounter, for themselves, all that we suggest they do with their own children. To sustain this goal, once we gather as a group, everyone becomes part of a literature circle.

We distribute a handout designed to guide a process for use in discussing literature. Questions are posed that move readers and discussants away from vague generalizations (e.g., "This is a good book. I like it.") and the emotional estrangement resulting from merely identifying and critiquing the development of character, plot, setting, style, and tone. The questions arise from our reading of Rosenblatt's (1938/1976) *Literature as Exploration* and our own studies. (These questions are undergoing constant revision as we work with groups and expand our own reading.)

The handouts help readers discover the intimate relationship between their personal lives and their responses to literature. The questions help participants see connections between themselves and the lives of the characters in the stories. There can be no pre-specified amount of time devoted to any single question because the depth of introspection depends entirely on the dynamic of a particular group.

The following represent the more important questions.

1. "What am I thinking (feeling) as I read this story?" (Find the most basic response.)

2. "What is it in me, in my own life, that evokes these thoughts (feelings)?" (Find similarities as well as differences that shade the response.)

3. "What is it that the author actually wrote? Am I reading something into this that isn't there?" (Return to the story and find—or not find—specific passages that trigger the response.)

4. "What role does context play? How significant is that role?" (Shift attention to the historical and social context that either explicitly or implicitly underpins the story.)

5. "How does the author reveal her/his perspective on life?" (Turn to the text to find the subtext.)

6. "What is the dialectic of my cultural group and that of the author?" (Specifically identify and reflect on ethnic group similarities and differences, and the discontinuities or continuities that these may cause.)

7. "How does this influence my cultural assumptions?" (Reflect on or consider personal values and attitudes, as well as the values and attitudes of one's own ethnic group, in relationship to other ethnic groups.)

Literature circles create the context for conversations. Hidden or unexplored cultural or ethnic assumptions emerge from serious attempts to respond to questions such as these. Our goal is for as many participants as possible to discover their own attitudes and the influence these have in their response to literature. As people begin to unearth previously unexplored assumptions they start to see beyond differences to recognize similarities between themselves and the characters in the stories they read.

An additional technique for stimulating thoughtful discussions is dialogue journals, which become written conversations between participants and ourselves or between individuals and chosen journal buddies. To facilitate these interactions, we ask everyone to use the questions to aid their introspection in reading, thinking, and writing. Journal entries often become part of literature circle discussions.

An inevitable result of reading adult literature and of participating in literature circles is the immediate and individual thirst for more books by authors of color. We point out that although we will give participants a bibliography of adult literature as well as a bibliogra-

Additional Ethnic-Specific Literature

Adult

African American

McMillan, T. (1992). *Waiting to exhale*. New York: Viking Penguin.

Morrison, T. (Ed.). (1992). *Race-ing, justice, en-gendering power*. New York: Pantheon.

Naylor, G. (1992). *Bailey's cafe*. New York: Harcourt Brace.

Walker, A. (1992). *Possessing the secret of joy*. Orlando, FL: Harcourt Brace.

Latino/a

Chavez, D. (1986). *The last of the menu girls*. Houston, TX: Arte Publico Press.

Soto, G. (1988). *Living up the street*. San Francisco: Strawberry Hill Press.

Vea, A. (1993). *La maravilla*. New York: Dutton.

Chinese American

Chu, L. (1961). *Eat a bowl of tea*. Secaucus, NJ: Lyle Stuart.

Hong, M. (1977). *The woman warrior*. New York: Vintage Books.

Torres, B. (1994). *The rice room*. New York: Hyperion.

Japanese American

Kadohata, C. (1989). *The floating world*. New York: Viking.

Okada, J. (1977). *No-no boy*. Seattle, WA: Combined Asian American Resources Project.

Sugimoto, E. (1993). *A daughter of the samurai*. Rutland, VT: Charles E. Tuttle.

Korean American

Keller, N.O. (1997). *Comfort woman*. New York: Viking.

Lee, C.-R. (1995). *Native speaker*. New York: Riverhead Books.

Native American

Alexie, S. (1993). *The Lone Ranger and Tonto fistfight in heaven*. New York: HarperCollins.

Wallis, V. (1993). *Two old women*. Seattle, WA: Epicenter Press.

(continued)

phy of K–12 literature, these are finite and, eventually, dated resources. We stress the importance that each member of the group develop the ability—the expertise—for choosing books on his or her own. This statement establishes the need for a set of criteria to use in their search for books that are as authentic, well written, and interesting as possible.

We share in the following segment the compendium of criteria that we use in selecting literature for our work. We add the caveat that a broad variety of genres and authors should be chosen for all ethnic groups. Just as all women and all men are not the same, so do people vary widely within ethnic groups. No individual book can be taken for a prototypical, archetypal, or stereotypical view of any one group.

Criteria for Selecting Books

1. *Is it a good story?* Obviously, books should be well written, and they must engage the reader. Characters should be sufficiently developed and the plot should be dynamic and dramatic enough to keep the attention of the reader. Not so obviously, however, the plot, theme, and resolution do not have to follow the traditional story schema of European American literature. In other words, unlike the latter body of literature, the book might not be about the importance of the individual nor might the story schema include conflict resolution or a dénouement. Nonetheless, it must tell a compelling story.

2. *Has the book engaged the popular support of members of the specific ethnic group guiding the story?* Being a member of the ethnic group portrayed in the story does not ensure the author's accuracy and truthfulness. However, as Sims Bishop (1992) stated, the linguistic patterns, the value structures, and other aspects of the culture revealed are far more likely to be authentic when described by

a member of the ethnic group. Our bibliography offers many print sources for this type of information. One example is *Through Indian Eyes* (Slapin & Seale, 1992), a compendium of reviews of Native American literature for K–12 readers with biographical notes on every author.

3. *Is the author considered to be an authority on the focal ethnic group?* If the author is not a member of the portrayed ethnic group, the work qualifies as cross-cultural, not ethnic-specific, literature. In this case, the background of the author must provide evidence that she or he can write with some authority about the dominant ethnic group. For example, in Japanese American internment literature the author must have some credentials documenting a thorough personal knowledge of this experience. Almost always, this information is provided either on the flyleaf of the book cover or in some kind of epilogue or short biography at the end of the book (for example, see Chin's *When Justice Failed, the Fred Korematsu Story* about a Japanese American by an author who has a Chinese surname).

4. *Does the list comprise a mixture of fiction and nonfiction?* Any body of reading restricted to fiction does not offer sufficient basis to judge the authenticity of historical context and fact. Furthermore, readers often do not have sufficient experience with nonfiction. At one time, for example, the work of Ron Takaki, a well-known Asian American historian, was embraced by the parents, teachers, and librarians with whom we worked, but was not found in any of their school or public libraries.

5. *Do the books provide authentic alternatives to the holiday or folktale approach to multicultural literature?* We have begun to refer to this approach as the "food, festival, and folktale approach." There is nothing inherently wrong with folktales; however, all too frequently they are not tales of Americans set

Additional Ethnic-Specific Literature (continued)

Children's and young adults'

African American

Feelings, T. (1993). *Soul looks back in wonder*. New York: Dial.

Flournoy, V. (1985). *The patchwork quilt*. New York: Dutton.

Myers, W.D. (1988). *Fallen angels*. New York: Scholastic.

Porter, A., & Porter, J. (1991). *Kwanzaa*. Minneapolis, MN: Carolrhoda.

Native American

Banks, S. (1993). *Remember my name*. Niwot, CO: Roberts Rinehart Publishers with the Council for Indian Education.

Begay, S. (1995). *Navajo: Visions and voices across the mesa*. New York: Scholastic.

Bruchac, J. (1993). The first strawberries. New York: Dial.

Diamond, A. (1991). *Smallpox & the American Indian*. San Diego, CA: Lucent.

Japanese American

Hamanaka, S. (1990). *The journey*. New York: Orchard.

Say, A. (1989). *The lost lake*. Boston: Houghton Mifflin.

Uchida, Y. (1993). *The bracelet*. New York: Philomel.

Chinese American

Yee, P. (1989). *Tales from the gold mountain*. New York: Macmillan.

Yee, P., & Chan, H. (1992). *Roses sing on the new snow*. New York: Macmillan.

Yep, L. (1989). *The rainbow people*. New York: Harper & Row.

Yep, L. (1991). *The star fisher*. New York: Morrow.

Korean American

Lee, M. (1992). *Finding my voice*. Boston: Houghton Mifflin.

Latina/o

de Ruiz, C., & Larios, R. (1993). *La causa: The migrant farm workers' story*. Austin, TX: Raintree Steck-Vaughn.

Garza, C. (1990). *Family pictures/cuadros de familia*. San Francisco: Children's Book Press.

Soto, G. (1993). *Local news*. San Diego, CA: Harcourt Brace.

Figure 1
Themes organized by ethnic group

Book titles	Level*	Ethnic group**	Theme
Uncle Jed's Barbershop; *Roll of Thunder, Hear My Cry*; *Grandmothers, Poems, Reminiscences, and Short Stories About the Keepers of Our Traditions*; *Mama Day*	P, El, MS, HS/Adult	AfA	Family love and responsibility
This Land Is My Land; *Native American Book of Wisdom*; *Kinaalda, a Navajo Girl Grows Up*; *Grass Dancer*	P, El, MS, HS/Adult	NaA	Preserving and being proud of the past
Pablo's Tree; *My Name Is Maria Isabel*; *Taking Sides*; *Jesse*; *Bless Me Ultima*	P, El, MS, HS/Adult	Lat	Establishing and keeping your ethnic identity
Yang the Youngest and His Terrible Ear; *Child of the Owl*; *April and the Dragon Lady*; *China Boy*	P, El, MS, HS/Adult	ChA	Family relationships, adjusting to a new environment
Baseball Saved Us; *When Justice Failed, the Fred Korematsu Story*; *Nisei Daughter*; *Desert Exile*	P, El, MS, HS/Adult	JaA	Loss of constitutional rights, living through the internment of Japanese Americans

*P = primary, EL = elementary, MS = middle school, HS = high school
**AfA = African American, ChA = Chinese American, JaA = Japanese American, Lat = Latino/a, NaA = Native American

in the United States. Just as Icelandic eddas or tales of Père Noël would be out of place in U.S. literature, so would the Chinese tale of Moon Maiden be misplaced. Our discussion is of United States literature. Additionally, connecting with diverse contemporary issues, experience, and people provides a more balanced perspective. Values and beliefs presented or implied in folktales may or may not be present in contemporary lives.

6. *Are there themes that bridge a genuine diversity of perspectives?* To understand and to connect with any story there must be something that we as readers can recognize and that makes us care. A human theme, even with cultural variations, draws diverse peoples together in common understanding.

Selecting books by themes can make forays into ethnic-specific literature more manageable and practical. Using this approach, reading levels and abilities can easily be accommodated, and all students and family members can be part of a reading group or lit-

erature circle simply by collecting books centered on a theme. To help get them started, we give them charts that present multiability books that draw on stories within the same ethnic group; collections that combine ethnic groups; and sets of stories that unite traditional, Western European literature with ethnic-specific authors and stories. Figures 1 and 2 are two examples of the charts we present.

Application at Home and at School

Participants in our groups have already learned about and have applied categories and criteria for selecting ethnic-specific literature. They have also become adept at using questions guiding discussions in literature circles. They are now interested in and ready for applications at school and at home. Below we list our suggestions for creating a community of readers in and out of school settings.

1. *Literature circles*. Literature circles are small groups of people gathered together to talk about particular books that they have read independently. Members may focus, for example, on books that share similar themes, several books authored by a single writer, or books presenting different perspectives on the same historical period. Because participants often have wide variations in reading abilities, a thematic approach accommodates all reading levels (see charts for examples). Variability in reading skill is a natural part of the literature circle, particularly when an adult is a member among children.

There is no limit to membership in this reading community. In some schools, parents, librarians, and custodians have joined the literature circles. Family literature circles also include everyone whether they are reading picture books or chapter books.

2. *Read-alouds*. Teachers and families use this special time not only to read aloud but also to engage everyone in a conversation about the story. Sharing a book encourages everyone to think about their perspectives and their personal responses to story. This not only creates and encourages a sense of community, but it also reveals something

Figure 2
Themes unifying ethnic groups with Western European groups

Book titles	Level	Ethnic group*	Theme
The Watsons Go to Birmingham; *Navajo: Visions and Voices Across the Mesa*; *When Justice Failed, the Fred Korematsu Story*; *Going Home*; *The Store That Mama Built*; *Dicey's Song*	Elementary	AfA; NaA; JaA; Lat; JewishA; WhEA	Adjusting to life's demands
The Road to Memphis; *Growing Up Native American*; *Talent Night*; *Jesse*; *Hatchet*	Middle school	AfA; NaA; JaA; Lat; JewishA; WhEA	Adjusting to life's demands
Crossing Over Jordan; *Mean Spirit*; *Desert Exile*; *Bless Me Ultima*; *The Chosen*; *Catcher in the Rye*	High school and adult	AfA; NaA; JaA; Lat; JewishA; WhEA	Adjusting to life's demands
Uncle Jed's Barbershop; *A Boy Becomes a Man*; *Heroes*; *Abuela*; *Sam and the Lucky Money*; *Birthday Presents*; *We Adopted You, Benjamin Koo*	Primary	AfA; NaA; JaA; Lat; ChA; WhEA; KorA	Family love and responsibility
Roll of Thunder, Hear My Cry; *High Elk's Treasure*; *The Happiest Ending*; *Summer on Wheels*; *Yang the Youngest and His Terrible Ear*; *Anastasia Krupnik*	Elementary	AfA; NaA; JaA; Lat; ChA; WhEA	Family love and responsibility
Grandmothers, Poems, Reminiscences and Short Stories About the Keepers of Our Traditions; *The World in Grandfather's Hands*; *The Invisible Thread*; *Taking Sides*; *April and the Dragon Lady*; *Mom, the Wolf Man and Me*	Middle school	AfA; NaA; JaA; Lat; ChA; WhEA	Family love and responsibility
Mama Day; *Tracks*; *Go*; *The Joy Luck Club*; *Native Speaker*; *The Dollmaker*	High school and adult	AfA; NaA; JaA; Lat; ChA; WhEA	Family love and responsibility

*AfA = African American; ChA = Chinese American; JaA = Japanese American; JewishA = Jewish American; KorA = Korean American; Lat = Latino/a; NaA = Native American; WhEA = White European American

about the depth of understanding each person brings to the group. At the same time, able readers are modeling good reading (e.g., reading with expression and fluency, and employing basic skills such as phonics in "sounding out" unfamiliar names or words).

Read-alouds frequently draw everyone into further learning. For example, in one group a parent who was reading *Desert Exile* (Uchida, 1982) to an upper-grade class became so absorbed by the facts of the internment of Japanese Americans (in both the United States and in Canada) during World War II that she decided her own children needed to know more. Using our bibliography, she went to the library and got *Baseball Saved Us* (Mochizuki, 1993) and *Naomi's Road* (Kogawa, 1994), and read these aloud to her children every night. Because the books were geared to the age levels of her children, each family member contributed meaningfully to conversations. When a stage dramatization of *Naomi's Road* came to their city, the entire family attended. The younger children then asked to take their books to school to share with their teachers and classmates.

These experiences spiraled into some classes reading the internment literature as part of social studies. The mother reported that she was amazed at how her family's reading accelerated from the home to the larger school community.

3. *Family literacy training*. Schools can offer literacy training sessions for families. In this instance, ethnic-specific literature is not the focus for community work. Instead, it provides the content used for learning. For example, we were asked to speak to parents of at-risk students so that families could support their children's literacy development at home. Using slides depicting ethnic-specific children's books, we demonstrated ways of reading and talking about stories. For the parents with limited literacy, we included

wordless picture books and we modeled storytelling. The session was held in the evening, and we had encouraged parents to bring their children with them. The result was a comfortable and natural setting, both for creating a community of families and for establishing shared literacies.

After seeing demonstrations of a variety of techniques for sharing stories at home, families were encouraged to practice with one another. Two images were particularly powerful. One was the laughter and sheer pleasure associated with reading as parents practiced the activities we were teaching them. The group was large and it was noisy with literacy experiences.

The second image bore witness to the additional importance of ethnic-specific literature. At the end of the session, a girl–probably 6 or 7 years old–ran to the front of the room where we had our books on display. She grabbed a book and called out, "Look, Mama, here's a little girl who looks like me! I want to read this book." The mother was thrilled that she now had ways to participate in her daughter's developing literacy using books that give visibility to her child. Certainly there are other ways to transform existing literacy curricula and literature selections at home and at school. These are simply examples of the most compelling experiences we have had.

Expanding Perspectives Through Literature

Shared literacies by definition require continued reading and learning by people of all ages. Inherent in this process is the dedication to expanding cultural and ethnic perspectives through literature. The books listed herein are only a tiny sample of the superb ethnic-specific literature available. We do not present our bibliography as any sort of canon, for we think that "canons are capricious human selections among artifacts and are subject to change as the criteria change.... Some texts and writers have greater staying power than others; that is about all we can say" (Purvis, 1993, pp. 112–113). Perhaps that is not quite all we can say. We could add that there is ethnic-specific literature that has greater staying power than too many otherwise literate communities appear to recognize. We can further say that once those communities engage in reading and talking about this enriched body of literature we move closer to a true United States literature, closer to shared literacies, and a unity of parents, families, and educators.

REFERENCES

Aoki, E. (1981). *Turning the page: The appropriate use of Asian American children's literature in the classroom*. Olympia, WA: Washington Office of the State Superintendent of Public Education.

Au, K. (1993). *Literacy instruction in multicultural settings*. New York: Harcourt Brace.

Bishop, R.S. (1992). Multicultural literature for children: Making informed choices. In V. Harris (Ed.), *Teaching multicultural literature in grades K–8* (pp. 39–51). Norwood, MA: Christopher-Gordon.

Bishop, R.S. (Ed.). (1994). *Kaleidoscope*. Urbana, IL: National Council of Teachers of English.

Cai, M. (1992). *Towards a multi-dimensional model for the study of reader response to multicultural literature*. Unpublished doctoral dissertation, The Ohio State University, Columbus.

Flood, J., Lapp, D., Alvarez, D., Romero, A., Ranck-Buhr, W., Moore, M.A., Kabildis, C., & Lungren, L. (1994). *Teacher book clubs: A study of teachers' and student teachers' participation in contemporary multicultural fiction literature discussion groups* (Research Rep. No. 22). Athens, GA & College Park, MD: National Reading Research Center.

Gay, G. (1994). *A synthesis of scholarship in multicultural education*. Washington, DC: Office of Educational Research and Improvement.

Hansen-Krening, N. (1992). Authors of color: A multicultural perspective. *Journal of Reading*, *36*, 124–129.

Hansen-Krening, N., Mizokawa, D., & Aoki, E. (1994). *Teachers as readers of ethnic literature: Initial findings*. Unpublished manuscript.

Ostrowski, S. (1994). *Literature and multiculturalism: The challenge of teaching and learning about literature of diverse cultures*. Washington, DC: Office of Educational Research and Improvement. (ERIC Document Reproduction Service No. 374 427)

Purvis, A. (1993). The ideology of canons and cultural concerns in the literature curriculum. In S. Miller & B. McCaskill (Eds.), *Multicultural literature and literacies: Making space for difference* (pp. 112–113). Albany, NY: State University of New York Press.

Rosenblatt, L. (1938/1976). *Literature as exploration*. New York: Modern Language Association of America.

Sims Bishop, R. (1992). Multicultural literature for children: Making informed choices. In V. Harris (Ed.), *Teaching multicultural literature in grades K–8* (pp. 39–51). Norwood, MA: Christopher-Gordon.

Slapin, B., & Seale, D. (1992). *Through Indian eyes*. Philadelphia: New Society.

Thompson, D.L., & Meeks, J.W. (1990, December). *Assessing teachers' knowledge of multiethnic literature*. Paper presented at the annual meeting of the American Reading Forum, Sarasota, FL. (ERIC Reproduction Service No. ED 328 916)

Tighe, M.A. (1994). *Multicultural literature: What is it and how and why are we teaching it?* Paper presented at the annual spring conference of the National Council of Teachers of English. (ERIC Reproduction Service No. ED 344 454)

Vilscek, E. (1994). *Dialoguing on the interactions between racially/ethnically identifiable characters in children's books*. Paper presented at the annual spring conference of the National Council of Teachers of English. (ERIC Document Reproduction Service No. ED 374 426)

LITERATURE CITED

Ada, A. (1993). *My name is Maria Isabel*. New York: Atheneum.

Anaya, R. (1972). *Bless me, Ultima*. Berkeley, CA: Quinto Sol Publications.

Arnow, H. (1972). *The dollmaker*. New York: Avon.

Brown, L. (1995). *Crossing over Jordan*. New York: Ballantine.

Bunting, E. (1996). *Going home*. New York: Harper-Collins.

Chin, S. (1993). *When justice failed, the Fred Korematsu story*. Austin, TX: Raintree Steck-Vaughn.

Chinn, K. (1995). *Sam and the lucky money*. New York: Lee and Low.

Curtis, C.P. (1995). *The Watsons go to Birmingham–1963*. New York: Delacorte Press.

Dorros, A. (1991). *Abuela*. New York: Dutton.

Erdrich, L. (1988). *Tracks*. New York: Holt.

Fitzgerald, F.S. (1920). *The great Gatsby*. New York: Scribner.

Giovanni, N. (Ed.). (1994). *Grandmothers, poems, reminiscences, and short stories about the keepers of our traditions*. New York: Holt.

Girard, L. (1989). *We adopted you, Benjamin Koo*. Urbana, IL: A. Whitman.

Hogan, L. (1990). *Mean spirit*. New York: Ballantine.

Klein, N. (1972). *Mom, the Wolf Man and me*. New York: Pantheon.

Kogawa, J. (1994). *Naomi's road*. New York: Oxford University Press.

Lee, C.R. (1995). *Native speaker*. New York: Riverhead Books.

Lee, G. (1991). *China boy*. New York: Dutton.

Lehrman, R. (1992). *The store that Mama built*. New York: Simon & Schuster.

Littlechild, G. (1993). *This land is my land*. Hong Kong: Children's Book Press.

Lowry, L. (1979). *Anastasia Krupnik*. Boston: Houghton Mifflin.

Mitchell, M. (1993). *Uncle Jed's barbershop*. New York: Simon & Schuster.

Mochizuki, K. (1993). *Baseball saved us*. New York: Lee and Low.

Mochizuki, K. (1995). *Heroes*. New York: Lee and Low.

Mora, P. (1994). *Pablo's tree*. New York: Simon & Schuster.

Morrison, T. (1987). *Beloved*. New York: Alfred A. Knopf.

Namioka, L. (1992). *Yang the youngest and his terrible ear*. Boston: Little, Brown.

Namioka, L. (1994). *April and the dragon lady*. San Diego, CA: Browndeer Press.

Naylor, G. (1989). *Mama Day*. New York: Vintage Books.

O'Dell, S. (1960). *Island of the blue dolphins*. Boston: Houghton Mifflin.

Okimoto, J. (1995). *Talent night*. New York: Scholastic.

Paulsen, G. (1987). *Hatchet*. New York: Bradbury.

Potok, C. (1985). *The chosen*. New York: Fawcett.

Power, S. (1994). *Grass dancer*. New York: Putnam.

Riley, P. (Ed.). (1995). *Growing up Native American*. New York: Avon.

Roessel, M. (1993). *Kinaalda, a Navajo girl grows up*. Minneapolis, MN: Lerner.

Rylant, C. (1987). *Birthday presents*. New York: Watts.

Salinger, J.D. (1951). *The catcher in the rye*. Boston: Little, Brown.

Sneve, V. (1972). *High Elk's treasure*. New York: Holiday House.

Sone, M. (1979). *Nisei daughter*. Seattle, WA: University of Washington Press.

Soto, G. (1991). *Taking sides*. Minneapolis, MN: Carolrhoda.

Soto, G. (1994). *Jesse*. San Diego, CA: Harcourt Brace.

Soto, G. (1995). *Summer on wheels*. New York: Scholastic.

Steptoe, J. (1987). *Mufaro's beautiful daughters: An African tale*. New York: Lothrop, Lee & Shepard.

Strete, C.K. (1995). *The world in Grandfather's hands*. New York: Clarion.

Tan, A. (1989). *The joy luck club*. New York: Putnam.

Taylor, M. (1976). *Roll of thunder, hear my cry*. New York: Dutton.

Taylor, M. (1990). *The road to Memphis*. New York: Dial.

Uchida, Y. (1982). *Desert exile*. Seattle, WA: University of Washington Press.

Uchida, Y. (1985). *The happiest ending*. New York: Atheneum.

Uchida, Y. (1991). *The invisible thread*. Englewood Cliffs, NJ: J. Messner.

Uyemoto, H. (1995). *Go*. New York: Dutton.

Voigt, C. (1982). *Dicey's song*. New York: Simon & Schuster.

White Deer of Autumn. (1992). *The Native American book of wisdom*. Hillsboro, OR: Beyond Words.

Wood, T., with Wanbli Numpa Afraid of Hawk. (1992). *A boy becomes a man at Wounded Knee*. New York: Walker.

Yep, L. (1977). *Child of the owl*. New York: Harper & Row.

Gary Hopkins and Thomas W. Bean

Vocabulary Learning With the Verbal-Visual Word Association Strategy in a Native American Community

Research on vocabulary learning flourished during the 1980s along with a general interest in classroom exploration of various content area reading strategies. Alvermann and Moore (1991) systematically reviewed much of this work and found that the most promising studies directly involved content teachers in strategy implementation and validation. However, in the 1990s, action research on vocabulary learning in content classrooms languished despite a declining trend in students' vocabulary learning on national assessments (Manzo & Manzo, 1997).

Pearson (1996) noted that our growing unrest with textbooks caused a shift away from direct strategy instruction aimed at teaching students how to read informational texts in the content areas. Pearson cautioned that we need to rethink some of the instructional practices that we may have too hastily abandoned or we run the risk of shortchanging students. He argued that "There comes a time in the lives of students–either when they go to college or enter the world of work–when others expect them to read and understand informational texts" (p. 268).

Sociocultural field studies in content classrooms have contributed to our knowledge of how teachers' beliefs and practices influence instruction (Bean, in press). Alvermann and Moore's (1991) extensive review of research in strategy validation recommended greater attention be paid to exploring the sociocultural context of content classrooms. Research in the 1990s followed this recommendation, but there remains a need to validate many of the content area teaching strategies introduced in methods texts through classroom action research (Bean, 1997).

In this article, we describe classroom action research with the verbal-visual word association strategy. This strategy helps students create personal associations for unfamiliar words. We explored the strategy with a group of junior high and high school students on the Northern Cheyenne Reservation in southeastern Montana, USA, using a teacher-researcher model (see, e.g., Patterson, Santa, Short, & Smith, 1993).

We begin by describing the first author's background. Next, we describe Northern Cheyenne history and culture, the school setting, and Gary Hopkins's move there to teach reading. We then provide an overview of the verbal-visual word association strategy along with some examples. We summarize our action research by sharing interpretive impressions and the results of a vocabulary quiz given to the high school group. Much of the article is in the first-person voice, as Gary takes us into his classroom and highlights his

Reprinted From the *Journal of Adolescent & Adult Literacy*, *42*(4), 274–281, December 1998/January 1999.

107

reflections during this first year of teaching on the reservation.

Gary's Background and the Cheyenne Way

I grew up in the United States in a small, Scandinavian farming community in the Midwest. Born in the early 1950s, I am old enough to remember a time when my oldest relatives spoke Norwegian as fluently as they spoke English. My great-grandparents never spoke English. In contrast, my mother could understand Norwegian but she could not speak it. I can neither understand nor speak Norwegian, in spite of the fact that I was exposed to it frequently as a child. Similarly, the remnants of Scandinavian culture gradually disappeared across the generations. I remember in school consciously choosing to distance myself from my elders' "foreign" culture and to embrace mainstream U.S. culture.

What I experienced as a child, many of my students experience today. They often distance themselves from their traditional language and culture, much to the dismay of their elders. Often, during my first year in Lame Deer, I felt torn between the desire of the Cheyenne elders to educate their children in traditional ways and the desire of many of my students to distance themselves from the Cheyenne Way.

The Cheyenne have shown remarkable cultural variation and adaptation (Pond & McDonald, 1996). The cultural memory of the Cheyenne goes back to a time when they were woodland Indians. Moving west, they became for a short time corn-growing agriculturalists living near the Missouri River. In their next incarnation, they moved out onto the Great Plains, transforming themselves into Plains Indians.

The Cheyenne Way is more like a living organism than a static system of beliefs. Although the Cheyenne Way has many of the characteristics of traditional Plains Indians (e.g., the Sundance), other characteristics of the Cheyenne Way differ subtly from Plains culture. For example, the Cheyenne have a strong reverence for women.

The Northern Cheyenne

The most defining moment in history for the Northern Cheyenne was not the Battle of Little Bighorn and the defeat of General George Armstrong Custer. Rather, the moment was the night of January 8, 1879. Just after their defeat following the short-lived victory at Little Bighorn, the Northern Cheyenne were rounded up and sent to live with their relatives, the Southern Cheyenne in Oklahoma. "For the 1000 Northern Cheyenne living on the reservation in Oklahoma, life was unbearable" (Pond & McDonald, 1996, p. 48). The Cheyenne asked the government's permission to return to the north. Permission was denied. Led by Dull Knife and Little Wolf, 300 Cheyenne men, women, and children set out for home without the government's permission. Hunted unmercifully by the U.S. Army, approximately 100 Cheyenne survived. They were imprisoned in Fort Robinson, Nebraska and told they would be sent back to Oklahoma.

On the night of January 8, 1879, the Cheyenne broke out of their barracks. Men, women, and children were slaughtered by the soldiers. Those who escaped continued their flight north. Appalled by its own brutality, the army asked the government to allow the Cheyenne to stay in the north. The government relented, and permission was granted for the Cheyenne to establish a reservation in Montana. The Cheyenne refused to surrender or be defeated. These beliefs and a remarkable ability to adapt in the face of adversity represent the Cheyenne Way.

Why did I choose to teach in Lame Deer? As a long-time resident of Montana, I had often come in contact with the Cheyenne and developed an affection for them. Their light-heartedness in the face of adversity was inspiring. Only later, after living among the Cheyenne, would I develop a deeper affection for the Cheyenne Way.

Moving to the Northern Cheyenne Reservation

When I finished my master's degree in literacy at the University of Nevada, Las Vegas, I got into my 1991 Honda, with over 300,000 miles on it, and drove to Lame Deer, Montana. I pulled into the Cheyenne reservation, my dented car leaking oil and inspiring pity from the Cheyenne. One student greeted me with disbelief. He asked, "That's your car?"

I walked into the high school and asked the principal for an opportunity to teach in Lame Deer. As luck would have it, a reading position in the high school had just opened up, and I was qualified for it. At this point I really knew relatively little about the Northern Cheyenne public school system or the Cheyenne students I would be teaching.

I returned to Las Vegas to teach a summer class at UNLV, where I spent my spare time in the library. The library had an extensive collection of books on Cheyenne history and culture. I read everything. What I discovered from my readings was that my previous conceptualization of Cheyenne history and culture was overly simplistic.

I finished teaching my summer class on a Friday and reported to Lame Deer the following Monday. Surrounded by steep forested hills and nestled in a bowl-shaped valley,

Lame Deer is one of the prettiest towns in Montana. The high school is a temporary unit of modules and trailers just 3 years old. Lame Deer High School is the only public high school on the Northern Cheyenne Reservation. The State of Montana finally decreed its existence after years of pleading by the tribe. A permanent high school is scheduled to be built in the near future on land donated by the tribe.

Walking through the doors of the school that first morning I felt confident that I had a basic knowledge and understanding of the Cheyenne. My confidence was, of course, mistaken.

Teaching at Lame Deer High School

Despite my summer of reading about the Cheyenne, I began my first day with a number of misconceptions about their literacy and language experiences. For example, I expected to find a number of junior high and high school students at Lame Deer reading at a first- or second-grade level. I found one. Most of my students read at least at a sixth- or seventh-grade level, which initially was cause for delight. However, too many of my high school students had not progressed beyond a sixth- or seventh-grade level. It seemed as though they were satisfied to reach a certain level of proficiency and not pass beyond that ceiling.

Another misconception I had about the Cheyenne was that they were a bilingual culture: Cheyenne and English. I quickly discovered that few of my students were fluent in Cheyenne. Few of their parents spoke Cheyenne, but many of their grandparents were fluent speakers. However, many of my students spoke a dialect with certain similarities to Black English. Like Black English, the

Cheyenne dialect has a tendency to drop final consonants, creating a lilting, musical pattern of speech that effectively excludes outsiders or non-speakers of the dialect.

Richard E. Littlebear, a professor at Dull Knife Memorial College in Lame Deer, is an authority on the Cheyenne language. In a personal interview, Littlebear informed me that the dialect is better compared with the Cheyenne language itself (personal communication, June 1998). Like Cheyenne, the dialect has a tendency to drop final consonants as well as vowels. Vowels are aspirated; spoken so softly as almost to disappear. For example, Billings is the nearest big town, and everyone goes there. In the Cheyenne dialect, the second i in Billings is barely audible. The g disappears altogether and the s almost disappears.

Littlebear further informed me that, contrary to appearances, significant remnants of the Cheyenne language persist in the dialect, even for those speakers who cannot speak or understand Cheyenne. Like the tribe itself, the Cheyenne language endures in the face of adversity.

Interestingly, the dictionary definitions of words did not trouble my students as much as idioms and connotations. For example, one of my students was baffled by a movie poster that asked, "Are you game?"

A final misconception I had about my students was that they would be passionately interested in Native American culture in general, and the Cheyenne Way in particular. In fact, this was true of only a minority of my students. Those students who were passionately interested in the Cheyenne Way were not happy about either reading or discussing Native American literature with a white man.

Most of my students were very interested in hip-hop as television brought the rap community to Lame Deer. While a minority of my students favored fiction and nonfiction books with Native American themes for our regular sustained silent reading, the majority of students preferred more mainstream books. Not surprisingly, their favorite author was R.L. Stine. They read *Beach House* (1992), *Blind Date* (1986), *The Boyfriend* (1990), and *Call Waiting* (1994).

They could also read magazines during sustained silent reading, and their favorites included *Sports Illustrated*, partly because basketball is a passion on the reservation. Pop magazines like *Slam* and *The Source* chronicled the hip-hop nation with everything from basketball to rap. These magazines were very popular with my students.

Thus, while my students engaged in reading, they tended to stay within a comfort zone of magazines and popular novels unlikely to challenge their existing vocabularies. While I knew it was important to value and respect my students' dialect, I also agreed with the view expressed in Corson's (1993) critique of language education that "schools have a major obligation to provide sensitive opportunities and appropriate contexts where non-standard speakers can use the standard variety widely and well" (p. 113).

The Classroom and Vocabulary Development

Although I taught reading in both the junior high and high schools, I was a Title I teacher in the high school but not in the junior high. In the high school, I used a tightly structured lesson plan and an emphasis on direct instruction. In the junior high school, I rarely provided direct instruction; rather, I created an environment where students would enjoy reading and writing in more of a workshop fashion.

While I taught the junior high and high school classes differently, both groups had problems in common. From their Comprehensive Test of Basic Skills (1989) performance and personal observation, I knew that most of my students had limited vocabularies. Talking to my students, I heard a common statement: "When I was in elementary school, I liked to read but now I hate it." I also heard "I hate this class—all we do is read and write!"

I was familiar with work showing the difficulties nonmainstream and indigenous students experience in a classroom oriented toward a mainstream curriculum. For example, Au (1998) noted that "The gap between the school literacy achievement of students of diverse backgrounds and those of mainstream backgrounds is a cause of growing concern, especially given demographic trends" (p. 298).

I knew that when students develop negative attitudes toward reading, these attitudes result in decreased reading engagement and practice with debilitating effects on achievement (McKenna, Kear, & Ellsworth, 1995). In addition, as reading is the major source of vocabulary growth (Nagy, 1989), I knew that lack of reading was one cause of my students' small vocabularies.

Students also struggled with inferences, particularly in terms of using context. Early in the year, to put closure on a unit dealing with inferring meaning from context, we played a vocabulary game patterned after baseball. "Bases" were awarded for a student's ability to infer the meaning of words encountered in a previously read story—"The Skunk Dog" by Patrick McManus (1981). Most of my students struck out repeatedly. From my graduate studies in literacy and the completion of a professional paper on vocabulary learning, I knew that vocabulary acquisition was related to inferential comprehension (see, e.g., Sternberg, 1987). Therefore, my Cheyenne students' struggles with inferring contextual word meanings was a cause for concern.

My students were accustomed to filling out commercial reading guides and fill-in-the-blank pages prior to my arrival. While these provided practice, I wanted to promote more independence in problem solving than their previous experiences offered. These concerns prompted action research with the verbal-visual strategy in collaboration with the second author, one of my former professors at UNLV.

The Verbal-Visual Word Association Strategy

Most reading authorities advocate intensive classroom vocabulary instruction to complement and support a reading program (e.g., Beck & McKeown, 1991). The verbal-visual word association strategy was originally developed a number of years ago to help students move beyond the rote memorization of words and their definitions (Eeds & Cockrum, 1985). It was further refined to include a visual dimension in support of a word's definition and the reader's personal association with the word (Readence, Bean, & Baldwin, 1998).

In my classroom, I modified the original strategy to make it useful for teaching roots and prefixes. The verbal-visual strategy is most often used for helping students learn content words like *trilobite* in science. Figure 1 includes an example from one of my classes.

This same structure was used to teach roots and prefixes. For example, Figure 2 shows Lavonne's (pseudonym) verbal-visual association for the root word *graph*. The personal association with *autograph*, along with the visual signature, helped this high school student remember the meaning of the root word. Vocabulary learning through personal association or analogies becomes relational rather than rote (Glynn, 1994).

Figure 1
Science vocabulary square example

tri – three	Trilobite
A extinct three lobed Marine arthropod of the Paleozoic Era.	

In addition, a word's concreteness, defined by the degree to which a word has a direct sensory referent, also contributes to vocabulary learning (McFalls, Schwanenflugel, & Stahl, 1994). Concrete words call to mind stronger visual images. For example, a word like *cactus* quickly calls to mind a prickly plant, while a word like existentialism is more unwieldy.

Figure 2
Root word vocabulary square example

Root	Defined
Graph	Autograph: A person's own signature or hand writing.
Write	Lavonne
Definition	Drawing

In Figure 2, the target word or root is in the upper left-hand corner with a definition below it. The right-hand squares include a personal association at the top and a visual of this association below. I gave the verbal-visual word association strategy a more straightforward name to use with students: vocabulary square.

Implementing Vocabulary Square

Initially, I planned to use the strategy only with the junior high school students. At the conclusion of this unit, I was so pleased with the results that I did a short 2-week unit with the high school students.

I introduced the strategy by modeling the process for students. I drew a square and divided it into four smaller squares. In the first square I put the prefix. In the next square I put its definition after looking it up in the dictionary. In the third square, after looking through the dictionary for examples of words that used the prefix, I put an example and defined it. In the last square, I drew a picture of the example. I told students that when they began to use the strategy, they could either draw a picture of the prefix or the example of the word using the prefix.

I used a think-aloud procedure to model the strategy. When I finished modeling, I instructed the students to copy this model onto their papers. I informed them that in the future when they entered the classroom, the vocabulary square with a new prefix would be posted every class period. They were to follow this model and complete the vocabulary square.

The next class period I provided guided practice. I helped the students as they began to implement the strategy. In the first couple of class periods students resisted this new approach. They were accustomed to simple worksheets and unaccustomed to independent problem solving. "I don't get it!" and "I don't understand what you want" were common refrains.

One of the things that initially bothered them was that they had to make choices. Which example of the prefix would they use? What should they draw? It was very different from the vocabulary worksheets they were used to where the right answer could be bubbled in on a multiple-choice item. Following a few days of practice, students viewed the vocabulary squares with more enthusiasm.

As they worked, I encouraged them to vocalize their choices and concerns. On the day that we were considering the prefix *fore* someone asked if *foreskin* was an example of a word that used *fore* as a prefix. I said, "Yes, but please don't draw it." Laughter was followed closely by a number of students looking up the definition of the word, then more laughter.

I felt these shared conversations about the prefixes and examples would help the students retain the knowledge more effectively. In addition, students often shared their drawings with one another. They would ask me and their classmates what someone else drew for a particular word. These drawings caused them to conceptualize their knowledge in a concrete and observable form that encouraged collaborative conversation. Figure 3 shows Amber's vocabulary square for the prefix *fore*. Figure 4 shows K.C.'s association for *fore*.

During the course of the unit, I provided instruction about morphological generalization. This is the process of using small units of meaning or morphemes to figure out unknown words (Cunningham, 1995). I informed the students that learning the meaning of individual prefixes and roots was important but that using their knowledge of prefixes to help determine unknown words was the real value of the unit. I was asking them to make inferences, and this step took a good deal of modeling and reviewing.

Figure 3
Amber's prefix vocabulary square example

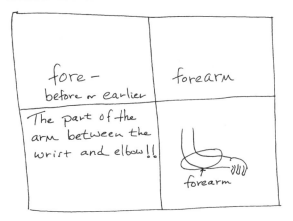

Figure 4
K.C.'s prefix vocabulary square example

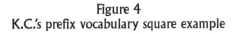

Students' Reaction to the Strategy

One of the problems on the reservation is high absenteeism. It forces teachers to teach and reteach lessons because students are often absent on the day a particular lesson is taught. I quickly discovered that my students would teach other students how to use the strategy. They did this with enthusiasm and without my prompting. This is consistent with Native American learning styles, in which time for reflection and practice in an individual or small-group fashion precedes use of a new skill in a larger setting like the classroom (Stokes, 1997).

The vocabulary square strategy allowed students to use their strengths as well as address their weaknesses. Some students were more comfortable with the sequential, verbal part of the strategy involving definitions and examples. These students had to be encouraged to solve problems in order to decide what they wanted to draw. I made it clear that they were not being graded on their artistic ability. Other students with an interest in artistic creativity had to be encouraged to take the time to look up the definition and find an example. During the course of the unit, no students complained that they were bored with the strategy.

In the junior high setting, students' engagement with the verbal-visual word association strategy suggested its value as a learning experience. In the high school class, I collected additional descriptive data in the form of a quiz that followed the more traditional, structured approach used there. Students were asked to match 10 root words with their respective definitions. For example, therm would be matched to its definition, heat. Most of the students scored 90% or higher on the quiz and demonstrated interest and engagement in the strategy similar to that of the junior high class.

Summing Up

This teacher action research supports the verbal-visual word association strategy as one way of helping secondary students increase their vocabulary knowledge in a fashion they find engaging enough to share with others. Students broke out of their dependence on worksheets and began using independent problem-solving skills more consistent with real-life learning experiences in Native American families (Stokes, 1997). They also benefited from the whole-class conversations in which they wrestled with a new word.

Combining sociocultural knowledge and an interest in experimenting with the promising learning strategies should increase our teaching effectiveness in diverse classrooms.

REFERENCES

Alvermann, D.E., & Moore, D.W. (1991). Secondary school reading. In R. Barr, M.L. Kamil, P. Mosenthal, & P.D. Pearson (Eds.), *Handbook of reading research: Volume II* (pp. 951–981). White Plains, NY: Longman.

Au, K.H. (1998). Social constructivism and the school literacy learning of students of diverse backgrounds. *Journal of Literacy Research, 30*, 297–319.

Bean, T.W. (1997). Preservice teachers' selection and use of content area literacy strategies. *Journal of Educational Research, 90*, 154–163.

Bean, T.W. (in press). Reading in the content areas: Social constructivist dimensions. In M.L. Kamil, P.B. Mosenthal, P.D. Pearson, & R. Barr (Eds.), *Handbook of reading research: Volume III*. Mahwah, NJ: Erlbaum.

Beck, I., & McKeown, M. (1991). Conditions of vocabulary acquisition. In R. Barr, M.L. Kamil, P. Mosenthal, & P.D. Pearson (Eds.), *Handbook of reading research: Volume II* (pp. 789–814). White Plains, NY: Longman.

Corson, D. (1993). *Language, minority education and gender*. Toronto, ON: Ontario Institute for Studies in Education.

Cunningham, P.A. (1995). *Phonics they use: Words for reading and writing*. New York: HarperCollins.

Eeds, M., & Cockrum, W.A. (1985). Teaching word meanings by expanding schemata vs. dictionary work vs. reading in context. *Journal of Reading, 28*, 492–497.

Glynn, S.M. (1994). *Teaching science with analogies: A strategy for teachers and textbook authors* (Reading Research Rep. No. 15). Athens, GA: National Reading Research Center, University of Georgia.

Manzo, A.V., & Manzo, U. (1997). *Content area literacy: Interactive teaching for active learning* (2nd ed.). Columbus, OH: Merrill.

McFalls, E.L., Schwanenflugel, P.J., & Stahl, S.A. (1994). *Influence of word meaning on the acquisition of a reading vocabulary in second grade children* (Reading Research Rep. No. 25).

Athens, GA: National Reading Research Center, University of Georgia.

McKenna, M.C., Kear, D.J., & Ellsworth, R.A. (1995). Children's attitude toward reading: A national survey. *Reading Research Quarterly*, *30*, 934–955.

McManus, P. (1981). The skunk dog. In *They shoot canoes, don't they?* (pp. 18–25). New York: Holt.

Nagy, W.E. (1989). *Teaching vocabulary to improve reading comprehension*. Newark, DE: International Reading Association.

Patterson, L., Santa, C.M., Short, K.G., & Smith, K. (1993). *Teachers are researchers: Reflection and action*. Newark, DE: International Reading Association.

Pearson, P.D. (1996). Reclaiming the center. In M.F. Graves, P. van den Broek, & B.M. Taylor (Eds.), *The first R: Every child's right to read* (p. 274). New York: Teachers College Press.

Pond, D., & McDonald, A.L. (1996). *Cheyenne journey: Morning star, our guiding light*. Santa Ana, CA: Seven Locks Press.

Readence, J.E., Bean, T.W., & Baldwin, R.S. (1998). *Content area literacy: An integrated approach* (6th ed.). Dubuque, IA: Kendall/Hunt.

Sternberg, R.J. (1987). Most vocabulary is learned in context. In M.G. McKeown & M.E. Curtis (Eds.), *The nature of vocabulary acquisition* (pp. 89–105). Hillsdale, NJ: Erlbaum.

Stine, R.L. (1986). *Blind date*. New York: Scholastic.

Stine, R.L. (1990). *The boyfriend*. New York: Scholastic.

Stine, R.L. (1992). *Beach house*. New York: Scholastic.

Stine, R.L. (1994). *Call waiting*. New York: Scholastic.

Stokes, S.M. (1997). Curriculum for Native American students: Using Native American values. *The Reading Teacher*, *50*, 576–584.

Mary E. Blake and Patricia L. Majors

Recycled Words:
Holistic Instruction for LEP Students

Teachers unfamiliar with the process of acquiring a second language often fail to distinguish the real and academically devastating difference between the conversational and academic language proficiencies of students for whom the instructional language is a second language. Research indicates that social proficiency can be achieved in 2 years, while academic proficiency may take 7 or more years (Cummins, 1994).

While there are many approaches to teaching second languages, current ideas about language and literacy development point to the use of holistic strategies as an efficient way to develop and enhance the second language learner's fluency. This approach recognizes the integrated nature of language learning and the importance of combining it with comprehensible, meaningful content (Krashen, 1982).

Integrating language learning with meaningful content is vital for students with limited English proficiency (LEP) to acquire fluency and information simultaneously. Holistic strategies quickly immerse LEP students in real-life uses of the English language (Urzua, 1991).

Integrated language experiences featuring a strong content base provide a rich contextual scaffold to support the learner. The content becomes the medium for learning language (Chamot & O'Malley, 1989; Crandall & Tucker, 1989), which is different from using discrete drills with limited or no context.

Typical holistic lessons used by teachers may include art-based activities such as cartooning one's life and making greeting cards for holidays, composing and decoding song lyrics, creating thematic units, using newspaper-based lessons, using a variety of journals, and building portfolios. In the following sections we describe a broad-based cyclical strategy, Recycled Words, which is intended for intermediate to advanced LEP students. In a multilevel class it may be necessary to provide additional support to beginning LEP students through cooperative learning and individual tutoring.

An Overview

Discrete vocabulary exercises and workbooks are of limited use for LEP students because they need vocabulary words to be embedded in context in order to retain them. The Recycled Words alternative promotes word retention and integration of words into the students' working vocabularies by extracting academic vocabulary from comprehensible, high-interest reading materials. Recycled Words integrates learning through

Reprinted From the *Journal of Adolescent & Adult Literacy*, *39*(2), 132–137, October 1995.

a series of oral and written activities, culminating in a writing workshop. This final segment of the cycle challenges the student to integrate the new vocabulary into meaningful, purposeful text.

The Recycled Words strategy has five stages: prereading activities, oral reading strategies and responses, vocabulary building through focused word study activities, evaluating word knowledge through quizzes or tests, and teachers and students writing together in a writing workshop. This holistic strategy comes full circle when student writing is published and shared, thus recycling the target vocabulary in multiple contexts.

Prereading Activities

Target vocabulary is selected from texts relating to academic and social information needed by the students. According to Krashen (1982), the reading materials should be at a slightly higher level than the student's comfort level. Although the Recycled Words strategy is most appropriate for intermediate and advanced LEP students, adjustments can be made for beginners by using less difficult text and target vocabulary.

Initially, the teacher selects words crucial to understanding the designated text and presents them to the students on an overhead projector, chalkboard, or handout. Words selected may occur frequently in content area classes or may be needed for survival outside the classroom. All words chosen are necessary to the comprehension of the passage.

The teacher then leads the students in a call-response technique that allows students to hear and practice saying the target vocabulary. The teacher says the word, and the students repeat it. Difficult-to-pronounce words should be repeated once or twice before moving on.

The Invisible List activity (Hess, 1993) works nicely as a second-phase prereading activity. Students select five or six words from the master list, and the teacher lists them on the chalkboard. Then the teacher leads the students in reading the list several times, asking them to keep reading the list as s/he erases words one at a time. Students continue "reading" the now invisible words. The Invisible List activity builds recognition and confidence in pronunciation. For small group instruction, words written on index cards can replace the chalkboard; to erase, the teacher simply removes the cards one at a time.

Other activities in the prereading phase of Recycled Words employ vocabulary worksheets and actual text. In one activity students use a worksheet that gives paragraph numbers and definitions of target vocabulary. The instructor asks the students to scan the designated sections of the text to find words that match the definitions. It may be necessary for students to scan the text more than once to find the target word; however, this repetition builds familiarity with the text. Students are also using parts of speech as clues, thus heightening their awareness of grammar. In this way the teacher is able to present vocabulary, stimulate any prior knowledge of the topic, and promote interest in the article. Figure 1 is an example of a scanning worksheet used to preview the article.

A second worksheet option has a multiple-choice format. The students are given a sheet with target vocabulary and possible definitions or synonyms. They are asked to circle the best choice, given their present knowledge; guessing is encouraged. Then they read the text and validate their choices. Figure 2 provides an example of the multiple-choice option for the same article.

Oral Reading and Responses

One of the many ways to conduct oral reading in the classroom is jump-in reading

Figure 1
Sample text excerpt and scanning worksheet

"My mother drank quietly and <u>discreetly</u> in the privacy of her...home.... A woman of curiosity and great intelligence, she read <u>prodigiously</u>, [and] wrote in three languages.... She died last year, in March, of cirrhosis of the liver....

"In our house, the gin and vodka bottles were delivered to the door and left just as seamlessly in the garbage, having been emptied in <u>dignified</u> fashion into large glasses with slices of lime." [Target vocabulary has been underlined here.]

Paragraph/part of speech		Word	Definition
5	adverb	_____	carefully, showing good judgment
5	adverb	_____	enormously, large amount, high quantity and quality
9	adjective	_____	grand, noble, calm and formal

Excerpted with permission from "A Daughter's Plea" by Cynthia Gorney, *Reader's Digest*, November 1993. Originally appeared in *The Washington Post*, April 26, 1993, p. D1, as "A Curtainless Window." Reprinted with the author's permission.

Figure 2
Multiple-choice synonym worksheet

1. *discreetly* (adv.)	A. steadily	B. happily	C. cleverly	D. carefully
2. *prodigiously* (adv.)	A. enormously	B. actively	C. frequently	D. intelligently
3. [omitted here because the excerpted text was not used]				
4. *dignified* (adj.)	A. easy	B. sober	C. grand	D. hurried

Excerpt from worksheet published by the *Reader's Digest* Partners in English Program for "A Daughter's Plea." Reprinted by permission.

(Horn, 1990), an interactive technique that promotes success for students of varied oral reading proficiency. The rules are simple. After the teacher has helped the students activate prior knowledge concerning the topic of the article, one student begins to read aloud and may stop at any time. The longest portion a reader may read aloud is a long paragraph, and the shortest is one word followed by end punctuation, such as "Help!" Readers may stop at commas, dashes, or end punctuation; then another reader jumps in. If more than one reader jumps in, one yields and then reads at the next opportunity.

The teacher may intervene to speed up or slow down the reading, to facilitate a comprehension check, or to call on a reluctant reader. Jump-in reading keeps readers actively involved. Slower, less proficient, or shy readers feel confident enough to read single words or short passages. This technique works especially well in classrooms where students have mixed levels of reading fluency.

Reading materials should be interesting, challenging, and comprehensible. Articles that focus on issues critical to adolescents provide important survival information for middle school and high school LEP students and foster lively discussions and longer journal entries.

During the reading, periodic stops for comprehension remove anxiety. If students know that they can anticipate several stops in a selection, they postpone asking questions, often finding answers within the reading. Pauses are generally brief enough so that overall meaning is not lost. The pauses also allow readers to check their definitions of target words on the worksheets. A quick comment from the teacher–"that was last week's word!"–can recycle vocabulary already studied.

At the conclusion of this segment of the activity, a discussion of the article integrates what students learned with their existing schemata. Students then reflect upon the text in their Literary Response Journals

Focused Word Study

After reading a text, students use individual card activities that help them to focus their attention on specific words. Two options using color-coded index cards provide a systematic way for students to learn new words. Individual study cards have a target word in English, a meaningful sentence using it, and the part of speech on one side. On the reverse side is the definition and, perhaps, the word in the student's first language. By color coding words with their corresponding articles, students are able to recognize groups of words drawn from specific texts, thus linking vocabulary to meaningful context.

For example, words drawn from the article "A Daughter's Plea" are written on yellow index cards that alert students to the particular context from which they come. Words grouped from a subsequent article on fire prevention might be written on pink cards.

Game cards are also popular. Students prepare two cards. One has the target word, sentence, and part of speech; the other contains the definition. Once students have studied their words, the cards are used to play reinforcement games. A caller keeps all the definition cards, dealing the word cards out to other members of the group. The caller then holds up and reads off the definitions, while members of the group match their vocabulary words. The caller gives the definition card to the student who makes the proper match.

In a simpler vocabulary game, all cards are laid face up on a table. Students take turns matching definition cards with word cards. The player with the most pairs wins. If an incorrect response is made, the player must wait for another turn. Our observations indicate that games not only promote word retention but give students an opportunity to practice listening and social skills.

Evaluating Word Knowledge

Word retention can be evaluated in a number of ways. Crossword puzzles, index card quizzes, and numbered lists of definitions projected on an overhead transparency are possible options. The format of quizzes can vary. A typical example is cloze stories with definitions in brackets, a format that recycles the target words in a different context. Figure 3 contains an example.

Writing Workshop

In the last phase of Recycled Words, an alphabetized list of the target vocabulary words (drawn from a series of previous readings) is

---

Figure 3
Excerpts of a cloze quiz using target vocabulary

Directions: Put the numbers 1 through 8 on a sheet of paper. Read the sentences below. Write the missing word beside the correct number on your sheet. Definitions for the missing words are written in brackets [ ].

1. The mother in the story, "A Daughter's Plea," drank ____[carefully]____ so her alcoholism was not obvious to those who knew her.

2. The mother in the story was intelligent and read ____[a large amount]____.

3. The mother drank large amounts of gin and vodka; she poured her drinks into glasses in a ____[grand, noble]_____ fashion with slices of lime.

---

given to the students. After a quick review of the words and their meanings, students set aside the list and focus on copies of a teacher-authored composition that integrates as many of the words as possible. Students follow along as the teacher shares the piece and models appropriate peer editing strategies (Routman, 1991). Learning these techniques is a prerequisite for student participation in their own reader response groups.

After reading her/his manuscript, the teacher asks the students to describe what they liked about the piece. S/he questions them about sections that might be unclear and elicits specific ideas to guide revision, emphasizing that the writing is only a draft. The teacher notes suggestions that can then be attributed to particular students in the final revision. After recording all the comments related to this initial critique, the teacher tells the students how many of the target words appear in each paragraph, challenging the students to find them. This technique helps students see the words in a new context.

The final segment of Recycled Words involves the students in brainstorming, drafting, and revising their own manuscripts. They are encouraged to integrate as many of the target words as possible into their compositions. Class literary magazines and school publications provide acceptable forums for publishing their work.

Another option is the class authors' book, a compendium of showcase manuscripts, autobiographies, and photographs of the student authors mounted in an inexpensive photo album. Sharing of finished pieces both celebrates authors and allows writers and readers to see the target vocabulary in multiple contexts.

We have implemented the Recycled Words strategy for more than 2 years with a variety of LEP students in middle and high schools. It is also currently being piloted in non-LEP classrooms. Figure 4 provides several examples of student work generated during one sequence of Recycled Words.

Articles appropriate for the Recycled Words strategy can be drawn from newspapers and magazines that are slightly above the students' reading level. *Reader's Digest*, for example, provides articles at a variety of reading levels, many of which would be appropriate

---

Figure 4
Student writing samples incorporating recycled words

As I was sitting on my bed.... I found myself alone in the dark surrounded by dead silence. The atmosphere of the small room was so *excessively* silent that I could hear my own breathing and my heart beating *simultaneously*. *Obviously*, I was scared to be alone. Each *infinitesimal* sound *assaulted* my ears.

12th-grade student

After a few months, Jessica *relentlessly waded* around her old home, Lake Laya, *diligently* looking for a gift to give Lisa. *Ultimately*, she found the magic coin again.

6th-grade student

Aunt Larisa, Yan, and I walked to the bus stop and waited for a few minutes until the bus came. The bus was old; it *lurched* along, *belching* black smoke, and *screeched* to a halt.

9th-grade student

George was looking forward to this vacation, but it seemed like everything that we had planned would just *evaporate*. Everyone had a feeling of *despair* because of the news [the eruption of Mt. Pinatubo north of Manila], especially George.

10th-grade student

---

for a multilevel or intermediate class. Articles from *Time* and *Newsweek*, on the other hand, are generally appropriate for advanced LEP students. Selections may be drawn from content area texts and from literature that supports content area topics. More preparation and intensive instruction may be needed if the materials are too difficult. Remember, the primary objective is to provide meaningful, comprehensible input (Krashen, 1982) to promote language learning.

Advantages and Disadvantages

Vocabulary learned through Recycled Words fosters long-term learning rather than short-term retention. Recycled Words provides more repetition and tighter links among vocabulary, reading, writing, listening, and speaking than do skills-based texts and isolated worksheets. Such a holistic format for learning is certainly more motivating than vocabulary workbooks.

Recycled Words also promotes authentic student writing that is purposeful, meaningful, and audience directed. Finally, this strategy can be adapted for small group, ESL class, or regular classroom instruction. Although it works best with small groups, cooperative learning strategies can make Recycled Words workable in a large class.

On the other hand, Recycled Words takes time. Even though many learning objectives may be addressed simultaneously, teachers must be comfortable with the slower, but more thorough, pace of vocabulary acquisition. Teachers pressed to cover a large amount of material may wish to alternate Recycled Words with other types of instruction. This strategy is flexible enough to be a

teacher's primary plan of vocabulary instruction or a periodic unit interspersed with other instruction.

REFERENCES

Chamot, A., & O'Malley, M. (1989). The cognitive academic language learning approach. In P. Rigg & V. Allen (Eds.), *When they don't all speak English: Integrating the ESL student into the regular classroom* (pp. 108-125). Urbana, IL: National Council of Teachers of English.

Crandall, J., & Tucker, R. (1989, April). *Content-based language instruction in second and foreign languages.* Paper presented at the meeting of the RELC Regional Seminar on Language Teaching Methodology for the Nineties, Singapore.

Cummins, J. (1994). The acquisition of English as a second language. In K. Spangenberg-Urbschat & R. Pritchard (Eds.), *Kids come in all languages: Reading instruction for ESL students* (pp. 36-62). Newark, DE: International Reading Association.

Hamayan, E. (1989). *Teaching writing to potentially English proficient students using whole language approaches.* Washington, DC: National Clearinghouse for Bilingual Education (NCBE).

Hess, N. (1993, April). *From meanings to words.* Presentation conducted at International TESOL Conference, Atlanta, GA.

Horn, H. (1990, November). *Constructing & revising meanings.* Presentation conducted at National Council of Teachers of English Conference, Atlanta, GA.

Krashen, S. (1982). *Principles and practices in second language acquisition.* New York: Pergamon Press.

Routman, R. (1991). *Invitations.* Portsmouth, NH: Heinemann.

Urzua, C. (1991). *Thank you, Miss Gladys.* In K. Goodman, L.B. Bird, & Y. Goodman (Eds.), *The whole language catalog* (p. 42). Santa Rosa, CA: American School Publishers.

Yellin, D., & Blake, M. (1994). *Integrating the language arts: A holistic approach.* New York: HarperCollins.

Cynthia Lewis

Rock 'n' Roll and Horror Stories: Students, Teachers, and Popular Culture

Recently, my 13-year-old son was stopped in the hallway by a teacher who questioned whether his T-shirt met the school's dress code. He wore a rock T-shirt depicting the dancing figures of women who would not be considered attractive according to media standards. It seems that the T-shirt's message is in the eye of the beholder. As my son explained it to me, the T-shirt is meant to make a statement about the sexist images on most rock paraphernalia. As the teacher saw it, the T-shirt is disrespectful to women. Yet the meaning of a message is influenced by the context of its production as well.

What if the teacher had known that the rock band was an all-female feminist band? Would that change her interpretation of its message and her interaction with my son? As educators, many of us feel it is our duty to police the popular culture of young people in school—a place where, ironically, we continue to consume our own culture. For instance, in addition to their many other functions, the teachers' lounges in the schools where I have worked have served as centers for sports pools, home decorating tips, soap opera updates, and other signs and symbols of popular culture.

The stances teachers take toward popular culture matter. When we exclude and police, or when we look the other way, we set up limiting dichotomies. We tell our students that some texts are worthy of serious analysis–*Romeo and Juliet*, for example–whereas others are not–TV's *The Simpsons*, perhaps, or other media-related texts. Yet, we dispense even this message inconsistently. After all, certain low-culture media texts, those related to sports, for instance, have always been welcomed and analyzed at school, leading to conversations between teachers and particular groups of students who care about or participate in athletics.

These students can take class time to talk with a teacher about the Final Four (U.S. college basketball championships), whereas students whose interest is, say, rock music receive only the scorn of adults who bemoan the violent and sexual content of MTV. Inadvertently, perhaps, we privilege the particular forms of popular culture that young people share with many adults, especially those forms that male adolescents share with men. The rest, we either fear or trivialize.

Horror Fiction in the Classroom

Here, I'd like to suggest other strategies for responding to the popular culture in our students' lives. Just as an informed response to my son's rock T-shirt would require an aware-

122

Reprinted From the *Journal of Adolescent & Adult Literacy*, *42*(2), 116–120, October 1998.

ness of how teens consume and how artists and corporations produce the T-shirt, an informed response to popular culture in the classroom requires that we consider how our students use it in light of the economics of its production.

The illustrations I'll use are of 11- and 12-year-old boys as they talk with peers in class about a horror series book, *Bobby's Back* (Pickford, 1993), and its relationship to horror films. *Bobby's Back* is the first in a series of books about a young man who seeks murderous revenge on a group of five people (four of them female) who teased him when he was a child. Let's listen in as the boys (not their real names) relate this book to other horror books and movies they all have seen.

Brian: Jason's better than Freddy. Jason kills more people. One movie he kills like 15 people. The most Freddy ever killed was 5, 6.

James: They run from him and they get like a mile away, and then they turn around and he's right there and he's just walking.

Tyler: Who cares who kills more people?

Brian: Jason doesn't even act real.

Mark: The guy is like running away from Jason and he stops and Jason is right in front of him, and he's only walking.

Brian: They're never even scared.

[James makes the sounds from the theme song for the movie *Friday the Thirteenth*.]

Clearly this conversation is not the sort sanctioned in most classrooms. It is, however, in keeping with the masculinist discourse that dominates outside the classroom—language that values violence much as the boys seem to do (Jason is better because he kills more people). The masculinist tenor of the overall discussion is evident, too, in its violence toward females in several of the sections I do not include here. In those sections the boys talk about a girl being hit in the head with a harpoon gun and a mother, who herself was a killer, getting her head chopped off. The boys talk about these events with very little commentary.

Males in horror fiction are of two general types. Either they are violent, dangerous, and vengeful or they are strong, commanding, and protective. No other versions of masculinity are made available to readers of young adult horror fiction. I'd like to suggest, however, that talk about violence and a concern for those who feel fear in the face of violence give the boys a way of examining and questioning such rigid versions of masculinity. At the same time, such talk provides them with an opportunity to resist and challenge the more feminized climate of this classroom, one in which girls' reading and response practices were the expected behaviors.

The meaning of a popular text is shaped, in part, by who is using it, the context in which it is being used, and the purpose it serves. Another look at the boys' discussion of horror books and films will help us to see how these meanings develop and change as the boys interact and respond playfully to one another's comments.

James: Jason's better. He carries a chainsaw.

Tim: It's really scary.

Mark: Not always. He uses anything he can find.

[The conversation turned to a movie about Freddy.]

Tyler: What happened? How does [Freddy] get killed? How does he get killed?

[The boys discuss other movies about Freddy.]

Brian: They conquer him in a video game, like.

Sam: Isn't there a Jason versus Freddy?

[The boys discuss other movies about Freddy and Jason.]

Brian: *Free Willy* scared me.

[laughter]

Tyler: *Free Willy* versus *Jaws*.

Sam: Care Bears scared me.

Tyler: Oh, *Free Willy* versus *Jaws*. Oh!

Brian: The Smurfs versus Jason.

[Several boys repeat the above, laughing as they speak.]

Brian: The Flintstones could bash his face in.

James: Bam Bam Bam Bam.

Sam: Bambi versus the Smurfs.

Tyler: *Free Willy* versus *Jaws*.

Sam: Willy versus Shamu.

James: Tyler versus Mark.

Brian: *Free Willy* versus *Jaws*.

Brian: Mark versus Tyler.

[James is making *Jaws* noises.]

Sam: This dummy on the cover versus *Jaws*.

Sam: We started out talking about *Bobby's Back*. Now we're talking about Bambi versus Spiderman!

As a woman who has been a teacher of one kind or another for all of my adult life my first impulse when I hear students engage in conversations of this sort is to cut them off! However, after reflecting on this literature discussion, I want to make a case for the social work these students are engaged in. First, and this is no small matter, the students who are speaking in this segment (and others in this ½-hour discussion) are all academic outsiders within their classroom; a few are social outsiders as well. Here they are animated, engaged, and participatory; a stance that is highly uncharacteristic for them and one they maintain throughout this literary event.

Second, the language used throughout this excerpt is playful, parodic, and performative in ways that allow the students, in Anne Dyson's words, "to play with each other and with powerful societal images" (1997, p. 283). In this case, and earlier in the conversation as well, the boys bring up the issue of fear. Earlier, we heard Brian say admiringly that the characters in the film were never

even scared. Here, Tim admits that Jason's chainsaw was scary, and soon after that the parodic exchange begins; an exchange that is almost entirely related to fear.

Perhaps this conversation serves as a way for the boys to abstract themselves from the fears they have being members of a culture where they are supposed to be fearless in the face of monstrous opponents. R.W. Connell in *Gender and Power* describes "hegemonic masculinity" as one that aims to dominate femininity as well as other masculinities through "power, authority, aggression, and technology" (1987, p. 187).

It would be scary, I dare say, to take on those attributes, and the boys deal with this condition through parody and performance. They juxtapose something scary with something that's not (*Free Willy* vs. *Jaws*), then something not scary with themselves (Care Bears scare me!), and finally one of them against another–but in play not aggression. The tone is lively, quick, and innovative. The boys are collaborators in performance and in audience. Indeed, being an audience member is to be a part of the performance itself–so entwined are the two. Within the context of this particular classroom, this was a subversive event employing language in opposition to the social discourse of the classroom, yet allowable within it. The boundaries in the classroom culture were permeable enough to allow for this transgression, this sharing of local knowledge among certain members of the classroom culture.

Social Uses of Popular Culture

This discussion occurred among students who were sharing their responses to books they had chosen for "free choice" reading, in a classroom that would be considered student centered. It seems especially important to examine how popular culture is used in just such classrooms because it is in these contexts that students feel empowered to bring into the classroom cultural symbols and materials of the sort that teachers and other adults would rather not legitimize. An assumption underlying the notion of "free choice" is that when students choose their own texts and topics, they are expressing their individual voices and identities. However, given a chance to choose what they want to read, write, and talk about, students often choose subjects that expose group identities—that is, the everyday materials of their lives that constitute "popular" culture.

Indeed, the popular culture of young people is not about individual voices and identities. At the local level, in classrooms and communities, popular culture is related to social and cultural group identities, allegiances, and exclusions. At the global level, popular culture is even more removed from the individual expressions of voice and identity since it is produced largely through multinational corporations and disseminated across a wide range of audiences and geographies. Therein lies one of the many contradictions of popular culture. While its expression can be oppositional and resistant (in that youth subcultures often oppose authoritative cultural norms), it is also co-opted by and reproduced through the very authoritative structures it opposes.

It's an interesting irony, I think, that what we call "free choice" in terms of students choosing the books they want to read is clearly not free of the need for social connection at the local level and the influence of dominant culture at the global level. The substantial investment adolescents place in these symbolic materials is overshadowed by the economic investment corporations make in targeting youth as consumers of popular culture.

One common response that teachers have to popular culture—to worry over its effects on students who are seen as passive consumers—is mistaken given that readers actively revise texts as they read rather than passively consume them (Moss, 1989). While I am arguing that the boys whose conversations I have just shared are doing just that, I don't want to overestimate the control that young people have over the messages promoted by popular culture. The boys' desire for aggression and fearlessness is promoted by popular culture through corporate interests (McRobbie, 1984).

Some theorists argue that popular culture is solely an instrument of capitalism, while others argue that it emerges from marginalized groups (youth, for instance) as the expression of their need to revise social inequities and subvert social norms (Swiss, Sloop, & Herman, 1998). Still others argue for the difficult task of finding a space between these extremes, one that recognizes that while subcultures can be sites of resistance, they are also sustained, and sometimes created, by those who stand to reap economic benefits. So, while the boys we listened in on clearly were engaged in the social work of appropriating popular culture for their own important uses, a steady diet of such conversations would not help them to understand its constitutive process.

I'd like to suggest that school ought to be a place where young people can talk about and use popular culture, at times without teacher input, so that they may challenge authoritative norms. In any case, we have little choice but to try to understand what our students do with popular culture and what it does for them. The 12-year-old female students in one classroom I have in mind chose to read series books by R.L. Stine or Christopher Pike whenever they had a chance to choose a book. In these books, females are often placed in precarious situations, and although they might be involved in extricating themselves from these situations, the male characters ultimately save the day.

The girls talked about these books during free moments at school and often outside of school. One student told me that her friend didn't read these books and was therefore left out of many conversations. The books carried a certain status that resulted in important allegiances and bonds among the girls. When I asked one student, Mackenzie (not her real name), why the girls read Stine and Pike whereas the boys in her class did not, her explanation surprised me:

> Most of the main characters are girls. Like, the girls are the ones that have the problems and they are the ones with the boyfriends that kill them and things like that. So it's basically...it puts boys in a bad position to read about guys killing girls.

From my perspective as a feminist teacher, I was not able to imagine any ways in which "guys killing girls" could be empowering to girls and disempowering to boys. Yet, something about these books allowed Mackenzie to feel in control of male violence and in touch with female perceptions of that violence.

Often, it seems, the contradictory nature of much popular culture is related to its appeal. Males killing females would not seem to place girls in control, yet Mackenzie used what many of us would see as an antifemale storyline to command authority, both in terms of how she was willing to read this text and in terms of how she would interpret the boys' tendency to dismiss these series books. Although males often denigrate females for reading and enjoying series and romance books (and this classroom was no exception), she was able to interrupt this commonplace trivialization of female activity by pointing out that boys don't want to read such books because they don't want to see themselves in a negative light.

I'm suggesting here that the social and political uses of popular culture must be examined, ways in which its use creates allegiances, marking the boundaries of who's in and who's out, and enabling those with less power to make their own tactical use of those who hold more (de Certeau, 1984).

Asking Critical Questions

At times, however, our roles as teachers should include teaching students to probe and resist popular cultural texts in the same way that we ought to teach students to interact with canonized texts (Lewis, in press). Instead of persuading students to revere all that has been deemed "great literature" and forsake the movies, books, and television shows they love, we need to engage students in conversations about the uses they have for a range of texts in their lives. And we adults have to be willing to examine our own consumptions as well. Why do we enjoy watching a soap now and then, listening to our generation's rock music, or entering a sports pool? How do we use these activities? What purposes do they serve?

But to get beyond this inquiry into how and why we consume popular culture, we might also ask students to examine how particular forms of popular culture work on audiences as they do, who is responsible for producing and disseminating popular cultural texts, and whose interests are served by the production and consumption of these texts. For example, while I was encouraged by Mackenzie's response to R.L. Stine because it pointed to ways in which she revised the storyline to protect her own interests, I was not as hopeful about another part of our conversation in which she told me that reading about girls in dangerous situations taught her to be careful. "I read a book where a girl was walking down the street and a guy was chasing her, and so now I'm walking down the street, you know, looking, making sure no one's chasing me."

Had this comment been part of a classroom discussion, I would consider it ripe for what Anne Simpson calls "critical questions" (1996), questions that probe textual ideology by examining such issues as how texts position readers to respond in particular ways and who benefits from such preferred readings. I'd be interested in pursuing these questions in response to Mackenzie's perspective on having learned an important lesson–to be careful–from one of R.L. Stine's books. Who benefits from this lesson? Not Mackenzie, who has learned, in this case, to feel powerless in the face of male violence. How is it that this popular text works to shape Mackenzie as a reader who feels she must protect herself from males as an ordinary part of her day?

As adults and teachers, we may well be put off by images of youth in relation to popular culture. We tend to view young people either as menacing producers of violence and sex, or dupes of advertisers who sell violence and sex. It's no wonder, then, that many educators either prohibit uses of popular culture in their classrooms or resign themselves to its presence and look the other way. Some years ago, a primary teacher I visited tried to enforce a "No Ninja Turtles" rule for writers' workshop, which led to a proliferation of Ninja Rhinoceros stories the likes of which

she never could have imagined. If we choose not to examine the social and political uses of popular culture and not to bring the serious analysis of its forms into the classroom, these expressions of group identities may simply go underground, leading to the disassociation of that which figures most prominently in the everyday lives of our students.

REFERENCES

Connell, R.W. (1987). *Gender and power*. Stanford, CA: Stanford University Press.

de Certeau, M. (1984). *The practice of everyday life*. Berkeley, CA: University of California Press.

Dyson, A.H. (1997). Rewriting for, and by, the children: The social and ideological fate of a media miss in an urban classroom. *Written Communication*, *14*, 275-311.

Lewis, C. (in press). The quality of the question: Probing culture in literature discussion groups. In C. Edelsky (Ed.), *Making justice our project: Critical whole language teachers talk about their work*. Urbana, IL: National Council of Teachers of English.

McRobbie, A. (1984). Dance and social fantasy. In A. McRobbie & M. Nava (Eds.), *Gender and generation* (pp. 130-161). London: Macmillan.

Moss, G. (1989). *Un/Popular fictions*. London: Virago Press.

Pickford, T. (1993). *Bobby's back*. New York: Bantam.

Simpson, A. (1996). Critical questions: Whose questions? *The Reading Teacher*, *50*, 118-126.

Swiss, T., Sloop, J., & Herman, A. (1998). *Mapping the beat: Popular music and contemporary theory*. Malden, MA: Blackwell Press.

Darcy E. Miller

The Literature Project: Using Literature to Improve the Self-Concept of At-Risk Adolescent Females

Of the five factors that contribute to a student's academic risk level (poverty, racial or ethnic minority status, living in a single parent family, a poorly educated mother, and limited proficiency with English) (Davis & McCaul, 1991), it is not uncommon to encounter in schools adolescent females who are attempting to cope with three or four risk factors simultaneously. Adolescent females who are at risk may be facing numerous challenges in their lives, including sexual and physical abuse, suicidal feelings, truancy problems, pregnancy, drug and alcohol abuse, and prostitution (Miller, 1992).

Those at-risk adolescent females come to school with a variety of needs, among them the need to improve their self-concept and perception of themselves. With all of the stresses and problems facing these young women, how can teachers motivate them to read? What types of books, stories, or novels will improve their self-concept and enhance their chances at a more positive future? When traditional reading programs have failed to captivate these adolescents and are seen by these young women as irrelevant, what next?

The Literature Project was developed to assist teachers in addressing these questions. Using novels as the basic reading material, the project is structured to motivate at-risk adolescent females to read and concurrently to improve their self-concepts and perceptions of themselves as women. Literary selections with heroines who are self-reliant, confident, and accomplish goals against difficult circumstances are used. Specially selected literature about women in difficult life situations provides the young women with characters with whom they can identify and from whom they can learn positive attitudes.

The technique of using literature as a psychoeducational intervention tool has been studied extensively and shown to have positive results with a wide range of individuals. Literature has been used to improve the self-concept of learning disabled students (Gerber & Harris, 1983: Lindsey & Frith, 1981) and individuals with cognitive delays (Kantrowitz, 1967). With children in difficult family situations, literature has been used to prevent self-concept problems (Sheridan, Baker, & de Lissovoy, 1984). Literature has also been used to help children cope with abuse (Carla, 1978; Randolph & Gredler, 1985: Watson, 1980) and adults adjust to incarceration (Cellini & Young, 1976).

The use of literature in a classroom setting with at-risk adolescent females has yet to be described, and the literature search I conducted over several years revealed no studies that focused on teaching women's literature to these adolescents. The Literature Project

128

Reprinted From the *Journal of Reading*, *36*(6), 442–448, March 1993.

was developed to meet their needs and fill this void in literature-based instruction. It was hoped that by improving the adolescents' attitudes toward reading, their perceptions of themselves, and their self-concept, the project would help these young women stay in school and therefore face a brighter and more successful future.

Traumatized Young Women

At the time the article was written, 30 adolescent females designated "at risk" by their school systems had participated in two 15-week sessions of the Literature Project (15 adolescents in each session). All of the subjects were enrolled in alternative high school programs in a western, medium-sized U.S. city. The reasons that the adolescents were in the alternative programs were varied but included truancy, drug and alcohol problems, sexual and physical abuse trauma, behavior problems, need and desire for an alternative curriculum, lack of motivation in the traditional high school setting, and pregnancy. The participants' ages ranged from 15-0 to 18-6, with a mean age of 16-2, Their reading achievement grade levels ranged from 4.5 to post high school, with a mean reading grade of 7.2.

The foundation of the Literature Project is novels and stories that have women or girls as the main characters. The curriculum was developed from the adolescents' life experiences, concerns, and interests, using the adolescents themselves as "curricular informants," a practice employed in the whole language approach to reading (Cullinan, 1990).

Before the Literature Project began, the young women were given a reading interest inventory (Warncke & Shipman, 1984) and interviewed by their teachers to obtain information on their reading preferences. This information was used to identify novels from women's literature that were appropriate and

might be beneficial for the participating adolescents to read. The curriculum is not conceptualized as static but adaptable to the needs of any group of adolescents.

Additional criteria that assisted the teachers in choosing the novels included the potential of the selection to: (a) produce a vicarious experience in the adolescents, (b) change the adolescents' self-concepts, future aspirations, or attitudes, (c) provide a story relevant to their lives, and (d) allow them to identify with and learn from the heroines.

When the content of interviews conducted with the adolescents was analyzed, three themes emerged: autonomy/individuation, abuse/coping, and homelessness/abandonment. The novels chosen were based on this interview information and highlighted female heroines who overcame difficult circumstances to become independent and confident.

Ten high school English teachers (5 male and 5 female) were asked to select three novels that would address these themes in an appropriate manner from contemporary literature lists. The three novels cited most often by the teachers were *The Solitary* by Lynn Hall, *The Color Purple* by Alice Walker, and *The Homecoming* by Cynthia Voight. Contemporary and relevant themes with which the adolescents were well acquainted, such as homelessness, physical and sexual abuse, being runaways or throwaways, dysfunctional family relationships, and discrimination were evident in all of the novels identified.

15 Weeks of Instruction

The Literature Project was implemented as a 15-week instructional unit that revolved around *The Color Purple*, *The Solitary*, and *The Homecoming*. The young women met 3 times a week, for 50 minutes per session. Both

Identified literature and themes about women/girls from which the Literature Project selections were drawn

Author/title/publisher	Themes in the book	Author/title/publisher	Themes in the book
Auel, J. (1980). *The Clan of the Cave Bear*. New York: Bantam	Independence, Individualism	George, J. (1972). *Julie of the Wolves*. New York: Harper and Row	Independence, ecology
Blum, A. (1980). *Annapurna: A Woman's Place*. New York: Scribners	Women's achievements	Hall, L. (1986). *The Solitary*. New York: Scribners	Independence, self-reliance
Bridgers, S.E. (1976). *Home Before Dark*. New York: Knopf	Homelessness, loyalty	Hamilton, V. (1976). *Arilla Sun Down*. New York: Greenwillow.	Minorities, identity
Brooks, B. (1987). *Midnight Hour Encores*. New York: Harper and Row	Mother-daughter relations	Levy, M. (1988). *Touching*. Westminster, MD: Ballantine/Fawcett	Family relations, alcoholism
Childress, A. (1981). *Rainbow Jordan*. New York: Putnam	Family, abandonment	McKinley, R. (1982). *The Blue Sword*. New York: Greenwillow	Identity, independence
Cooney, C. (1984). *I'm Not Your Other Half*. New York: Putnam	Identity, self-determination	Voight, C. (1981). *The Homecoming*. Westminster, MD: Ballantine/Fawcett	Homelessness, self-reliance
Dorris, M. (1987). *A Yellow Raft in Blue Water*. New York: Holt	Minorities, identity	Voight, C. (1986). *Izzy, Willy Nilly*. Westminster, MD: Ballantine/Fawcett	Self-understanding, identity
Fleischman, P. (1986). *Rearview Mirrors*. New York: Harper and Row	Identity, family relations	Walker, A. (1982). *The Color Purple*. New York: Washington Square Press	Independence, identity
Fossey, D. (1983). *Gorillas in the Mist*. New York: Putnam	Love of career, ecology		

implementations of the 15-week project were taught by the same English teacher and teaching assistant. Before the project began, the adolescents completed a standardized self-concept scale, The Piers-Harris Children's Self-Concept Scale: The Way I Feel About Myself (1969), to obtain a baseline on their self-concept and their perceptions of themselves.

The adolescents also took the pretest form of a Literature Project Evaluation Form (LPEF) which was designed to solicit infor-

The pre- and posttest Literature Project Evaluation Form (LPEF)

Pretest:

1. Do you like to read? Why or why not?
2. What do you like to read about?
3. Describe yourself, your personality, your likes/dislikes.
4. What do you do well?
5. What do you think women do well?
6. What are some good/bad points about being a woman?
7. What are the best careers or situations for women?
8. What are you going to do when you leave school?
9. What do you think you'll be doing in 5 years? In 10 years?
10. If you could change your personality, what would you change and why?

Posttest:

1. Do you like to read? Why or why not?
2. What do you like to read about?
3. Did reading the novel, _____, change your attitude toward reading? Explain.
4. Did you like reading _____? Explain.
5. Where were your favorite activities and why?
6. Would you like to read more novels like _____? Explain.
7. Describe yourself, your personality, your likes/dislikes.
8. What do you do well?
9. What did you learn about yourself from the novel _____? Explain.
10. What will you do differently because you read _____? Explain.
11. What do you think women do well?
12. What are some good/bad points about being a woman?
13. What are the best careers or situations for women?
14. What did you learn about women from the novel _____? Explain.
15. Do you think differently about women now, after reading _____? Explain.
16. What are you going to do when you leave school?
17. What do you think you will be doing in 5 years? In 10 years?
18. If you could change your personality, what would you change and why?
19. Did reading _____ change your ideas about what you want to do in the future? Explain.
20. What would you like to read about next?

mation about their (a) attitudes toward reading, (b) perceptions of themselves and their abilities, (c) perceptions of women and their abilities, and (d) aspirations for the future.

The sequence of novels to be read was a joint decision, made by the adolescents and their teacher. The first, *The Color Purple*, was divided by the teacher into sections to be read orally each day. The varying levels of reading among the young women necessitated that all of the selections be read aloud by the adolescents, their teacher, and the teaching assistant. Discussion points and questions based on the day's reading were outlined, and daily activities were developed by the teacher to reinforce the salient issues in the passages.

Using art, writing, role playing, drama, music, debate, and discussion the adolescents were encouraged to express their feelings and ideas through the activities about the character, themes, and events in the novels. For example, in one activity, they were asked to draw a picture of Celie (the main character in *The Color Purple*) in the beginning of the story and then again at the end. A discussion ensued as to how Celie changed and grew into an independent woman. All of the Literature Project activities were designed to stimulate the adolescents to discuss, reflect, and relate the situations in the novels to their own lives. (See Miller, 1990, for an in-depth description of Literature Project activities.)

At the completion of the 15-week Literature Project, the adolescents did the self-concept scale again to assess change over the 15-week project. They also completed the posttest form of the Literature Project Evaluation Form (LPEF) which solicited information on (a) their attitudes toward reading, (b) their satisfaction with the novels and the activities in the Literature Project, (c) what they learned from the novels about themselves, (d) what they learned about women, and (e) how the Literature Project affected their aspirations for the future.

Focus on Motivation

The focus of the Literature Project was on increasing the motivation of at-risk adolescent females to read and on improving their self-esteem and self-perceptions. Interviews, interest inventories, and the LPEF provided information on their interests and needs.

The adolescents' self-concept scores significantly improved following the Literature Project. When the pre- and posttest results from the self-concept scale were analyzed using a two-tailed t-test for differences, a significant difference was found between self-concepts before and after the project $(t(15) = 4.251, p < .01)$.

A theme that emerged from the adolescents' initial comments focused on human relations. Over 90% of them indicated that they wanted to read about relationships, including relationships between males and females (e.g., romance novels) and family relationships.

The final LPEF revealed that 95% of the students indicated that they wanted to read more novels about women, while 100% felt that they had improved their reading skills and abilities through the Literature Project. Their comments regarding the novels and activities were very positive and indicated a high level of motivation to participate and reflect on the themes and characters in the novels. In fact, over 70% of the girls indicated that the Literature Project was the best class they had taken in school.

When they were asked "What did you learn about yourself?" in the LPEF, their responses indicated self-learning and growth in the area of independence and maturity: "I think it was great that she could become a businesswoman. Nobody told me we could do that!" and "It makes you see that being alone isn't bad if it's what you want and your [you're] working to get what you want" were two of the typical reactions to the novel *The Solitary*.

Many had comments indicating a changed perception of themselves as women: "I learned alot about what happened to me in a similar way to what happened to Celie. It was a really good feeling to no [know] that women can fight for their rights." "They [women] have to take care of each other." "Women can get what they want out of life if they keep to their goals."

Over 80% of the participants (25) indicated that they had changed their plans for the future as a result of the Literature Project. "I never thought I could be anything. I thought I was going to be a hairdresser like my aunt. Now I have some new ideas." Another participant said, "I am going to explore some new careers. My new ideas about my future are not going to include my old career ideas."

In general, the young women's responses on the LPEF corroborated the statistical finding of improved self-concepts. Their comments showed a wonderful sense of hope and determination: "I think it showed alot of me in the book and how I can turn out if I set myself to it." "I learned that I'm pretty assertive." "I learned that women are shy and need to learn how to fight for themselves." "It taught me to never give up. That if you give up you're giving up on yourself."

Motivation Through Reading

The Literature Project is based on teaching selections from women's literature to at-risk adolescent females. The project motivated these young women in the area of reading and improved their self-concepts and perceptions of themselves. Throughout the project, everyone read aloud, in a group, on a voluntary basis. Even those who had severe reading deficits volunteered to read. The teachers hypothesized that the Literature Project setting was perceived to be warm and personal and therefore appeared to the adolescents to be a safe place to read aloud. Future research should focus on these factors (e.g., warmth, personableness, security) as possible variables in teaching reading to students who are deemed at risk.

From comments on the evaluation forms it was evident that the adolescents identified with the life experiences of the characters in the novels and that they could see how the situations in the novels (both the negative and the positive) related to them. They seemed to develop a true understanding of the characters' hardships and identified with their accomplishments.

The comments made, both on the evaluation forms and spontaneously throughout the project, indicated that the young women developed more independent and assertive attitudes. As a result of the literary characters' fortitude and successes, new feelings of assertiveness, hopefulness, and determination were evident in the adolescents. In fact, most

Activities used in the Literature Project to facilitate reflection, discussion, and problem solving around literature themes

Description of activity	Students involved
Draw a picture of a favorite scene from the novel.	Group or individual
Dramatize a section of the novel.	Group
Write a script with a different ending.	Group or individual
Choose a song that exemplifies main character, scenes from the novel; listen to and analyze the song.	Group and individual
Identify emotions, feelings in novel; cut out or draw pictures that depict those emotions; make collage.	Group or individual
Develop an "I am good enough" chart; add to it when opportunity arises in reading; display it.	Group or individual
Play "the character is missing" by inventing an additional character to write into the novel.	Group or individual
Write a letter to the main character.	Group or individual
Dress like a character in the novel.	Group or individual
Role-play significant scenes, discuss them.	Group

of their favorite parts of the novels included scenes in which the women stood up for themselves, fought back, or were rewarded for their efforts. Perhaps more importantly, the adolescents began to reflect on their roles as young women, and to mentally explore the possibilities of more functional and fulfilling futures.

Despite many of the participants' stressful life problems, they showed a wonderful sense of hope and determination after finishing the Literature Project: "I learned how you can do things in different ways and they're alright." Another adolescent said: "Reading and talking about these things taught me to never give up. I think I can be more assertive in my life now."

Future implementations of the Literature Project should explore the differential effects of a varied selection of novels. Perhaps there are novels with specific themes, settings, or characters that can better facilitate positive changes in these students.

One limitation of the Literature Project is the manner in which change in the adolescents' attitudes and self-concepts was monitored. Future implementations will ask the adolescents to make journal entries regarding their feelings, thoughts, and ideas as the project progresses. The teachers felt that this reflective information would assist both them and the young women in evaluating growth in self-concepts and self-perceptions.

Another limitation on the project as a study is the lack of longitudinal data on the participants in the future. It is hoped that improvement in these adolescents attitudes toward reading, and their self-concepts and perceptions of themselves, will help them stay in school and improve their future outcomes. Collection of longitudinal data in the areas of self-concept, progress in content area studies, graduation, employment, and interpersonal relationships will be sought in the future to evaluate the long term effects of lit-erature-based instruction with at-risk adolescent females.

Providing motivating and interesting reading programs for at-risk young women is a challenge. We found the Literature Project an effective and exciting addition to current curriculum options. A well planned program of literature-based instruction that addresses a variety of contemporary issues through new and old literary classics is a powerful tool in changing the self concept of at-risk adolescent females. Through the readings and activities in the Literature Project, these adolescents began to view themselves as capable and talented young women, an outcome that is hoped will help them realize a brighter future.

REFERENCES

Carla, F.B. (1978). Book therapy for abused children: Briefs. *Language Arts*, *55*, 199–201 .

Cellini, H.R., & Young, O.F. (1976). Bibliotherapy in institutions. *Transactional Analysis Journal*, *6*, 407–409.

Cullinan, B.E. (1990). Why whole language? *Instructor*, May, 46–49.

Davis, W.E., & McCaul, E.J. (1991). *The emerging crisis: Current and projected status of children in the United States*. Orono, ME: Institute for the Study of At-Risk Students.

Gerber, P.J., & Harris, K.B. (1983). Using juvenile literature to develop social skills in learning disabled children. *Pointer*, *27*(4), 29–32.

Kantrowitz, V. (1967). Bibliotherapy with retarded readers. *Journal of Reading*, *11*, 205–212.

Lindsey J.D., & Frith, G.H. (1981). Bibliotherapy and the learning disabled. *Clearing House, 54*, 322–325.

Miller, D. (1990). *Designing curriculum for behaviorally disordered female adolescents: Considerations and processes*. Paper presented at the Council for Exceptional Children 68th Annual International Conference, Toronto, Canada.

Miller, D. (1992, April). *Profiles of adolescents with behavioral/emotional disorders, adolescent of-*

fenders, and adolescents at-risk: Who are they and how do we teach them? Paper presented at the Council for Exceptional Children's 70th Annual Convention, Baltimore, MD.

Randolph, M.K., & Gredler, G.R. (1985). Children of divorce. *Technique*, l, 166–175.

Sheridan, J.T., Baker, S.B., & de Lissovoy, V. (1984). Structured group counseling and explic-it bibliotherapy as in-school strategies for preventing problems in youth of changing families. *School Counselor*, *32*, 134–141.

Watson, J. (1980). Bibliotherapy for abused children. *School Counselor*, *27*, 294–298.

Warncke, E.W., & Shipman, D.A. (1984). *Group assessment in reading: Classroom teachers handbook*. Englewood Cliffs, NJ: Prentice Hall.

SECTION 3
Supporting Classroom Reading

Adolescents who struggle with reading need assistance meeting academic expectations and learning what their high-achieving peers already know about literacy. The articles in this section address ways to accomplish this. They are based on the idea that everyone in a classroom benefits when varied students' insights are pooled and discussed. Working collectively and individually, students can enhance their subject matter and reading competence, and can benefit when teachers teach how to use reading strategies to pursue subject-specific insights.

The authors of the articles in this section present activities that can be used to scaffold reading comprehension in subject-specific study. Some share ideas for helping students glean important information from texts through questioning practices. Others show how to enhance students' vocabulary, a critical need in subject-matter study and in reading development.

James Flood and Diane Lapp

Reading Comprehension Instruction for At-Risk Students: Research-Based Practices That Can Make a Difference

In recent years, much has been written about "state-of-the-art" reading comprehension instructional practices for at-risk students as well as regular students in middle and secondary school (Duffy, Roehler, & Mason, 1983; Durkin, 1978–79; Flood, 1984a, 1984b; Guthrie, 1981; Pearson, 1984; Robinson, Faraone, Hittleman, & Unruh, 1990; Tierney & Cunningham, 1984). Most contemporary educators agree that effective comprehension results from the interaction of four sets of important variables: *reader variables* (age, ability, affect, motivation), *text variables* (genres, type, features, considerateness); *educational context variables* (environment, task, social grouping, purpose); and *teacher variables* (knowledge, experience, attitude and pedagogical approach).

Each of these variables plays a critical role in the successful acquisition of comprehension strategies and each will be discussed as it relates to effective teaching practices for at-risk students. Two major questions will be discussed in this article: (1) What do we know about the ways in which competent comprehenders read texts? (2) What do we know about teaching at-risk students to become competent comprehenders?

Competent Comprehenders

Most educators agree that competent comprehenders exhibit a set of discernible characteristics. Researchers have found that competent readers actively construct meaning through a process in which they "interact" and "transact" with the words on the page, integrating new information with pre-existing knowledge structures (Anderson, Hiebert, Scott, & Wilkinson, 1985; Jensen, 1984; Lapp & Flood, 1986; Paris, 1986; Rosenblatt, 1938, 1982). Further, it has been found that a reader's prior knowledge, experience, attitude, and perspective determine the ways in which information is perceived, understood, valued, and stored (Anderson et al., 1985; Flood, 1984a, 1984b; Holbrook, 1987; Pearson, 1984; Rumelhart, 1981; Squire, 1983).

The competent comprehender: A strategic reader. Good readers are strategic readers who actively construct meaning as they read; they are self-motivated and self-directed (Paris, Lipson, & Wixson, 1983); they monitor their own comprehension by questioning, reviewing, revising, and rereading to enhance their overall comprehension (Baker & Brown, 1984). Good readers have learned that it is the reader in the reading process

138

Reprinted From the *Journal of Reading*, *33*(7), 490–496, April 1990.

who creates meaning, not the text or even the author of the text.

There is some consensus among researchers that competent readers have a plan for comprehending; they use their metacognitive knowledges in an orderly way to implement their plan (Flavell, 1981). While each reader's plan varies for each text and task, the following steps seem to be part of the competent reader's generalized plan for many different kinds of texts:

A PLAN FOR READING

Before reading, the strategic reader:

Previews the text by looking at the title, the pictures, and the print in order to evoke relevant thoughts and memories

Builds background by activating appropriate prior knowledge through self-questioning about what he/she already knows about the topic (or story), the vocabulary and the form in which the topic (or story) is presented

Sets purposes for reading by asking questions about what he/she wants to learn (know) during the reading episode

During reading, the strategic reader:

Checks understanding of the text by paraphrasing the author's words

Monitors comprehension by using context clues to figure out unknown words and by imaging, imagining, inferencing, and predicting

Integrates new concepts with existing knowledge, continually revising purposes for reading

After reading, the strategic reader:

Summarizes what has been read by retelling the plot of the story or the main idea of the text

Evaluates the ideas contained in the text

Makes applications of the ideas in the text to unique situations, extending the ideas to broader perspectives

Teaching At-Risk Students

If the preceding remarks accurately reflect the processes that the competent comprehender engages in, one might wonder: Is there a role for the teacher or does comprehension ability merely occur as a result of practice, of extensive and frequent reading? Are at-risk students at risk because they have not been taught how to comprehend or because they do not practice reading?

Can comprehension be taught? Although some educators have suggested that the controversial question "Can comprehension be taught?" is no longer a burning, lingering issue (Pearson, 1984; Tierney & Cunningham, 1984) it seems to have been re-ignited recently in both its old form and in a newer form. Carver (1987) in his article entitled "Should Reading Comprehension Skills Be Taught?" argues that the evidence for teaching comprehension is "weak, nonexistent, or directly counter (to the data)." He states:

> The evidence presented to support the case for teachers spending more time teaching reading comprehension skills is frail at best. Too often the Easiness Principle and the Reading Time Principle are not accounted for in research, and there is no solid evidence that gains due to the Reading Practice Principle will transfer to reading ability in general. It makes more sense to regard comprehension skills as study skills in disguise, and teaching them to unskilled readers is a questionable practice.

However, Haller, Child, and Walberg (1988) in their article entitled "Can Comprehension Be Taught? A Quantitative Synthesis of Metacognitive Studies" examined the results of 20 seminal studies (that included 1,553 students) on the effects of "metacognitive instruction" on reading comprehension performance. Although the exact nature of metacognition is still being debated, it was defined in their study as three mental activities that constitute metacognition: being aware, monitoring, and regulating in order to aid faltering understanding.

Their results strongly suggest that comprehension can be taught. They found that there was ample evidence to encourage teachers to instruct students in reading comprehension from a series of research studies that were rigorously conducted. Three specific findings were highlighted in their analysis: (1) there were age effects especially for seventh/eighth grade and second-grade at-risk students; (2) reinforcement was the single most effective part of reading comprehension instruction; and (3) the more instructional features involved in the learning episode, the more significant the results.

It seems that the real answer to this question must be a qualified one in which definition and purpose are clearly explained. In asking the question "Can comprehension be taught?" one has to be careful to add "Comprehension of what, by whom, under what conditions, and for what purposes?"

Although one has to attend to the possibility that the question is still open, there is ample and ever increasing evidence that comprehension instruction has been effective for many at-risk students. The purpose of this article is to review representative samples of these studies to determine elements of comprehension instruction that seem general and useful for teachers working with at-risk students at various grade levels in various settings. Naturally not all relevant studies can be included in this paper; rather only a modest number will be included as illustrations of what we currently know about comprehension instruction for this population.

An instructional approach: Constructivism in practice. In recent years it has been argued that students develop comprehension skills and strategies most successfully through a process approach that emphasizes the under-

lying cognitive and linguistic skills that are prerequisites for understanding and appreciating texts. Just as has been the case for some time in writing instruction, reading instruction is undergoing a profound change in its theoretical orientation and ensuing pedagogy. Educators are moving away from fragmented component skills approaches in which reading is taught as a series of subskills to a holistic approach in which comprehension is viewed as a generative process (Robinson et al., 1990).

As a result, contemporary comprehension instruction for at-risk students needs to be based on constructivist principles that acknowledge the student's role as the meaning-maker in the reading act. Constructivism calls for an understanding and implementation of the notion that the student takes ownership for learning and the teacher provides appropriate direction and support. It requires a form of collaboration between teachers and students in which teachers and students work together to ensure that students internalize rules and strategies for making meaning.

Seven practices that foster constructivist principles. There are many teaching and learning activities that foster constructivist notions and lead to the development of comprehension abilities. These activities are based on the premise that comprehension is constructive; that it is a gradual, emerging process in which students grow in comprehension abilities by processing texts in a generative manner, building on their own experiences, knowledges, and values.

Seven practices that have been proven to be successful in helping at-risk students develop their comprehension abilities will be discussed. These include: (1) preparing for reading practices, (2) reciprocal teaching practices, (3) understanding and using knowledge of text structure practices, (4) questioning practices, (5) information processing practices, (6) summarizing practices, and (7) voluntary/recreational reading practices.

(1) Preparing for Reading Practices

Two activities that help at-risk students ready themselves for reading are PReP and Previewing.

Prereading Plan (PReP). Langer (1982, 1984) proposed an activity that prepares students for reading by activating their prior knowledge through a series of prompt questions. There are three stages to PReP: (1) initial associations; (2) reflections about initial associations; and (3) reformulation of knowledge.

In the initial association stage, the teacher selects a word, phrase, or picture about the key concept in the text and initiates a discussion to induce concept-related associations. For example, in teaching a lesson about the American Revolution, the teacher might ask "What comes to mind when you hear the words 'Revolutionary War'?"

During the reflection stage students are asked to explain their associations, e.g., "Why do those ideas come to mind?" Langer (1984) found that the social context of this activity advanced students' understanding–they expanded or revised their knowledge through listening to and interacting with their peers.

In the final stage, reformulation of knowledge, students might be asked "Have you gained any new information about the Revolutionary War?" She found that students' knowledge was expanded through the generative processes in which they were engaged. She found that students' responses changed from remotely related personal experiences to an understanding of relations between pieces of knowledge.

Previewing. Many researchers and educators have used previewing as an effective technique. Graves, Prenn, and Cooke (1985) tested a specific procedure in which students listened to a lengthy preview of an assigned text.

The preview was prepared by the teacher and its purpose was to motivate students. It had three parts: (1) the activation of prior personal experiences that were relevant to the text; (2) the building of necessary background knowledge for the text; and (3) the establishment of an organizational framework for the text that was consistent with the framework the author used to present information.

Students who listened to the previews before reading the text significantly outperformed students who did not have previews on multiple measures of comprehension.

(2) Reciprocal Teaching Practices

Palincsar and Brown (1985) and Palincsar (1984) have developed a paradigm that has been effective for developing constructivist, process-oriented reading comprehension abilities. In their methodology, students take turns assuming the role of the teacher through a structured dialogue.

The teacher models four distinct comprehension strategies and the students have opportunities to practice these strategies. Students are asked to (1) summarize in a simple sentence the paragraph that was read, (2) generate a question about the paragraph that was read to ask a fellow student, (3) ask for clarity (or resolution) of anything in the text that was unclear, and (4) make a prediction about what will happen next in the text.

In their studies, students were shown how to do this by teacher modeling. Adult support was withdrawn gradually as students exhibited their ability to perform the task independently. Palincsar (1984) reported gains of 35% and more on comprehension assessments after 20 days of instruction.

Palincsar and Brown's original formulation was based on Vygotsky's (1978) notions about the zone of proximal development which he described as:

> The distance between the actual developmental level as determined by independent problem solving and the level of potential development as determined through problem solving under adult guidance or in collaboration with more capable peers.

Reciprocal teaching is highly dependent upon discussions between students and teachers. Alvermann, Dillon, and O'Brien (1987), Duffy and Roehler (1987), and Palincsar (1986) explain that discussion is a critical component of effective comprehension instruction because it is through discussion that the teacher learns what is in the students' minds, and thereby can restructure the situation to aid the student in understanding.

(3) Understanding and Using Knowledge of Text Structure Practices

Narrative texts. Some researchers argue that explicit instruction of story structure is unnecessary because students will automatically acquire this knowledge indirectly as a by-product of story listening/viewing (Moffett, 1983). Schmitt and O'Brien (1986) argued against instruction in narrative structure, suggesting that this form of instruction was both unnecessary and counterproductive; it emphasized only one piece of a story and deemphasized story content.

However, there are other researchers who have found that instruction in narrative

structure positively affects student reading (Fitzgerald & Spiegel, 1983). Further, Buss, Ratliff, and Irion (1985) found that students who had little knowledge of story structure benefited considerably from direct instruction in text organization, specifically in story grammars.

Information/expository texts. Many researchers have reported that students at all grade levels can be taught the structures that underlie expository texts (Berkowitz, 1986; Peabody, 1984; Slater, Graves, & Piche, 1985; Taylor & Beach, 1984) and that the consistent use of this knowledge enhances recall and comprehension (Armbruster, Anderson, & Ostertag, 1987; Baumann, 1984). Further, students who had the knowledge but did not use it were more negatively affected when reading texts with unfamiliar material than texts with familiar material (Meyer, Brandt, & Bluth, 1980; Taylor & Beach, 1984).

At-risk students particularly benefit from instruction in text structure because it becomes a useful aid when the content is unfamiliar (Palincsar & Brown, 1985).

(4) Questioning Practices

Question/Answer Relationships (QARs). In several studies, Raphael (1982, 1986) demonstrated that at-risk as well as regular students were capable of generating and answering questions that enhanced their comprehension and led to independent processing. She designed four types of QARs: (1) text-based QARs in which the answers are "right there," i.e., explicitly stated in the text; (2) text-based QARs in which the student has to "think and search" for relevant information throughout the text; (3) knowledge-based QARs in which the reader has to read the text to understand the question, but the answer is not in the text; and (4) knowledge-based QARs in which the student can answer the question without reading the text.

In the beginning stage of this process, the teacher accepts total responsibility for the five key elements of the activity: (1) assigning the text, (2) generating the questions, (3) providing answers, (4) identifying the QAR, and (5) providing a justification for the QAR identified. Eventually, control is released to the student after guided practice is offered to the student.

Students who were trained in the QAR activity demonstrated significant gains in comprehension.

(5) Information Processing Practices

KWL: What we know, what we want to find out, what we learn and still need to learn. The KWL procedure, developed by Ogle (1986), rests upon constructivist principles: it is the reader who ultimately must seek and find meaning. Initially, the student is shown how to use the guide–this is followed by the teacher's question "How do you know that?" which reminds the student to seek evidence from the text or from previous knowledge. This procedure is intended to activate, review, and develop background knowledge and to set useful purposes that will enable the student to be an active, independent learner.

Concept-Task-Application (C-T-A). Wang and Au (1985) found that the asking of focused prereading discussion questions about critical concepts contained in the text enhanced students' background knowledge before reading. During this first phase, students set purposes for reading and the goals of the questions were twofold-to find out what students already knew about a topic and to determine what they still needed to know.

During the second stage, the task stage, the teacher asked cueing questions that focused the students' attention to important sections of the text, directing them to formulate satisfactory answers to the questions. When the students' answers indicated that comprehension was inaccurate or incomplete, the teacher asked questions that enabled the students to realize they had a need for more information (which was frequently only available from an outside source) in order to "fix" their comprehension.

The third stage, application, occurred through a summarization process in which the teacher repeated the initial questions and the student summarized all the information that had been discussed throughout the teaching/learning episode.

Analogies. Several researchers have demonstrated the effectiveness of using analogies to enhance comprehension (Hayes & Tierney, 1982; Peabody, 1984). Bean, Singer, and Cowen (1985) developed an Analogical Study Guide to help students in biology understand the concepts that they were learning. In their study, they used the analogy of a functioning factory to understand the working of cells in the human body. Students who were given the analogical guide significantly outperformed students who wore taught the information in more traditional ways.

(6) Summarizing Practices

Summary writing. A renewed interest in summarization as a means for improving reading comprehension for at-risk students has occurred during the past few years (Bean & Steenwyk, 1984; Hidi & Anderson, 1986). Much of this contemporary interest has been a result of Kintsch and Van Dijk's (1978) work that tied summarization ability to reading comprehension.

The antecedents to this contemporary work can be found in a series of research studies conducted in the 1920s and 1930s. In 1934, after conducting several studies on summarizing, Salisbury found that students who were made aware of important points in the texts before reading and asked to summarize (list) the central ideas in the text had increased comprehension scores.

However, in its more recent development, summary writing has been difficult to describe because the summary itself has no universally accepted definition. Therefore, appropriate instruction that results in informal summaries is often very difficult to describe. However, even with that caveat, summary writing in its various forms still seems to be one of the best vehicles available for implementing a constructivist, process-oriented approach to teaching reading comprehension.

Annis (1985) noted that three traditionally accepted cognitive/linguistic requirements for comprehending prose form the basis for summary writing: (1) orientation of attention toward the task; (2) recording the information in the text into one's own words; and (3) making connections between the new material and one's prior knowledge.

As readers work through these three requirements, they are retelling the text. Retellings serve as a potent instructional technique for enhancing summarizing abilities as well as overall comprehension (Gambrell, Pfeiffer, & Wilson, 1985).

(7) Voluntary / Recreational Reading Practices

Several studies have indicated that few children or adults choose reading as a source of information or as a recreational activity (Anderson, Wilson, & Fielding, 1988; Greaney & Hegarty, 1987; Morrow & Weinstein, 1982). Greaney and Hegarty's 1987 statistics on how many fifth graders read were alarming–almost one fourth of the students in his study said that they did no leisure reading.

Conversely, several studies have revealed convincing data that suggests students who engage in voluntary reading significantly outperform students who do not on many different measures of comprehension (Irving, 1980; Long & Henderson, 1973; Morrow, 1983; Morrow & Weinstein, 1982).

One contemporary approach to addressing the problems associated with aliteracy (those who can read but do not) has been the use of voluntary reading programs within and outside school. These programs forward the tenets of a constructivist approach to developing reading comprehension because they foster self-selection by the student which, in turn, encourages personal meaning making. When students select their own literature, they are taking a first step toward being responsible for their own comprehension development.

Several studies that examined the effectiveness of voluntary literature programs where classrooms were filled with high quality trade books reported success in overall reading comprehension and improved attitudes toward reading (Anderson, Wilson, & Fielding, 1988; Ingham, 1981).

A Final Note

Effective instructional practices for developing successful comprehenders are available to teachers of at-risk students. Not every practice will work with every student, but the practices that have been described in this article have a research base that argues strongly for their use. Each practice is deeply rooted in the belief that reading is a constructive process in which the student is the meaning maker. Ultimately, it must be the reader who creates meaning, not the text or the teacher.

REFERENCES

Alvermann, D., Dillon, D., & O'Brien, D. (1987). *Using discussion to promote reading comprehension*. Newark, DE: International Reading Association.

Anderson, R.C., Hiebert, E.H., Scott, J.A., & Wilkinson, I.A. (1985). *Becoming a nation of readers: The report of the commission on reading* (Contract No. 400-83-0057). Washington, DC: National Institute of Education

Anderson, R.C., Wilson, P., & Fielding, L. (1988). Growth in reading and how children spend their time outside of school. *Reading Research Quarterly*, *23*, 285-303.

Annis, L.F. (1985). Student-generated paragraph summaries and the information-processing theory of prose learning. *Journal of Experimental Education*, *54*, 4-10.

Armbruster, B.B., Anderson, T.H., & Ostertag, J. (1987). Does text structure/summarization instruction facilitate learning from expository text? *Reading Research Quarterly*, *21*(3), 331-346.

Baker, L., & Brown, A.L. (1984). Metacognitive skills and reading. In P.D. Pearson (Ed.), *Handbook of reading research*. New York: Longman.

Baumann, J.F. (1984). The effectiveness of a direct instruction paradigm for teaching main idea comprehension. *Reading Research Quarterly* *20*(1), 93-115.

Bean, T.W., Singer, H., & Cowen, S. (1985). Acquisition of a topic schema in high school biology through an analogical study guide. In J.A. Niles & R.V Lalik (Eds.), *Issues in literacy: A research perspective*, Thirty-fourth Yearbook of the National Reading Conference. Rochester, NY: National Reading Conference.

Bean, T.W., & Steenwyk, F.L. (1984). The effect of three forms of summarization instruction on sixth graders' summary writing and comprehension. *Journal of Reading Behavior*, *16*, 297-306.

Berkowitz, S.J. (1986). Effects of instruction in text organization on sixth grade students' memory for expository reading. *Reading Research Quarterly*, *21*(2), 161-178

Buss, R.R., Ratliff, J.L., & Irion, J.C. (1985). Effects of instruction on the use of story starters in composition of narrative discourse. In J.A. Niles & R.V. Lalik (Eds.), *Issues in literacy: A research perspective* (pp. 55-58). Rochester, NY: National Reading Conference.

Carver, R. (1987). Should reading comprehension skills be taught? In J.E. Readence & R.S. Baldwin (Eds.), *Research in literacy: Merging perspectives*, Thirty-sixth Yearbook of the National Reading Conference (pp. 115-126). Rochester, NY: National Reading Conference.

Duffy, G.G., & Roehler, L.R. (1987, December). *Characteristics of responsive elaboration which promote the mental processing associated with strategy use*. Paper presented at annual meeting, National Reading Conference, St. Petersburg Beach, FL.

Duffy, G., Roehler, L., & Mason, J. (Eds.). (1983). *Comprehension instruction*. New York: Longman.

Durkin, D. (1978-79). What classroom observations reveal about reading comprehension instruction. *Reading Research Quarterly*, *14*, 481-533.

Fitzgerald, J., & Spiegel, D. (1983). Enhancing children's reading comprehension through instruction in narrative structure. *Journal of Reading Behavior*, *12*, 1-17.

Flavell, J.H. (1981). Cognitive monitoring. In W.P. Dickson (Ed.), *Children's oral communication skills*. New York: Academic Press.

Flood, J. (Ed.). (1984a). *Promoting reading comprehension*. Newark, DE: International Reading Association.

Flood, J. (Ed.). (1984b). *Understanding reading comprehension*. Newark, DE: International Reading Association.

Gambrell, L., Pfeiffer, W., & Wilson, R. (1985, March/April). The effects of retelling upon reading comprehension and recall of text information. *Journal of Educational Research*, *78*, 216-220.

Greaney, V., & Hegarty, M. (1987). Correlates of leisure-time reading. *Journal of Research in Reading*, *10*, 3-20.

Graves, M.F., Prenn, M.C., & Cooke, C.L. (1985). The coming attraction: Previewing short stories. *Journal of Reading*, *28*, 594-598.

Guthrie, J. (Ed.). (1981). *Comprehension and teaching: Research views*. Newark, DE: International Reading Association.

Haller, E.P., Child, D.A., & Walberg, H.J. (1988). Can comprehension be taught? A quantitative synthesis of "metacognitive" studies. *Educational Researcher*, *17*, 5-8.

Hayes, D.A., & Tierney, R.J. (1982). Developing readers' knowledge through analogy. *Reading Research Quarterly*, *17*, 256-280.

Hidi, S., & Anderson, V. (1986). Producing written summaries: Task demands, cognitive operations, and implications for instruction. *Review of Educational Research*, *56*, 473-493.

Holbrook, H.T. (1987). Reader response in the classroom. *Journal of Reading*, *30*, 556-559.

Ingham, J.L. (1981). *Books and reading development: The Bradford books flood experiment*. Exeter, NH: Heinemann.

Irving, A. (1980). *Promoting voluntary reading far children and young people*. Paris: UNESCO.

Jensen, J.M. (1984). Introduction. In J. Jensen (Ed.), *Composing and comprehending* (pp. 1-4). Urbana, IL: ERIC Clearinghouse Document No. ED 243 139

Kintsch, W., & Van Dijk, T.A. (1978). Toward a model of text comprehension and production. *Psychological Review*, *85*, 363-394.

Langer, J.A. (1982). Facilitating text processing: The elaboration of prior knowledge. In J.A. Langer & M.T. Smith-Burke (Eds.), *Reader meets author/bridging the gap: A psycholinguistic and sociolinguistic perspective* (pp. 149-162). Newark, DE: International Reading Association.

Langer, J.A. (1984). Examining background knowledge and text comprehension. *Reading Research Quarterly*, *19*, 468-481.

Lapp, D., & Flood, J. (1986). *Teaching students to read*. New York: Macmillan.

Long, H., & Henderson, E.H. (1973). Children's uses of time: Some personal and social correlates. *Elementary School Journal*, *73*, 193-199.

Meyer, B.J.F., Brandt, D.H., & Bluth, G.J. (1980). Use of author's textual schema: Key for ninth graders' comprehension. *Reading Research Quarterly*, *16*, 72-103.

Moffett, J. (1983). *Teaching the universe of discourse*. Boston: Houghton Mifflin.

Morrow, L.M. (1983). Home and school correlates of early interest in literature. *Journal of Educational Research*, *76*, 221-230.

Morrow, L.M., & Weinstein, C.S. (1982). Increasing children's use of literature through program and physical design changes. *Elementary School Journal*, *83*, 131-137.

Ogle, D. (1986). K-W-L: A teaching model that develops active reading of expository text. *The Reading Teacher*, *39*, 564-570.

Paris, S.G. (1986). Teaching children to guide their reading and learning. In T.E. Raphael (Ed.), *The contexts of school-based literacy* (pp. 115-130). New York: Random House.

Paris, S.G., Lipson, M.Y., & Wixson, K.K. (1983). Becoming a strategic reader. *Contemporary Educational Psychology*, *8*, 293-316.

Palincsar, A.S. (1984). Reciprocal teaching of comprehension fostering and comprehension monitoring activities. *Cognition and Instruction*, *2*, 117-175.

Palincsar, A.S. (1986). The role of dialogue in providing scaffolded instruction. *Educational Psychologist*, *21*(1-2), 73-98.

Palincsar, A.S., & Brown, A.L. (1985). Reciprocal teaching activities to promote reading with your mind. In E.J. Cooper (Ed.), *Reading, thinking and concept development: Interactive strategies for the class*. New York: The College Board.

Peabody, M.B. (1984). *The effect of concrete examples on transitional and formal students in the instruction of chemical bonding*. Unpublished doctoral dissertation, Northern Arizona University.

Pearson, P.D. (Ed.). (1984). *Handbook of reading research*. New York: Longman.

Raphael, T. (1982). Question-answering strategies for children. *The Reading Teacher*, *36*, 186-190.

Raphael, T. (1986). Teaching question answer relationships, revisited. *The Reading Teacher*, *39*, 516-522.

Robinson, H.A., Faraone, V., Hittleman, D., & Unruh, E. (1990). In J. Fitzgerald (Ed.), *Reading comprehension instruction, 1783-1987. A review of trends and research*. Newark, DE: International Reading Association.

Rosenblatt, L.M. (1938). *Literature as exploration*. New York: Noble & Noble.

Rosenblatt, L.M. (1982). The literacy transaction: Evocation and response. *Theory into Practice*, *21*, 268–277.

Rumelhart, D.E. (1981). Schemata: The building blocks of cognition. In J.T. Guthrie (Ed.), *Comprehension and teaching: Research reviews* (pp. 3–26). Newark, DE: International Reading Association.

Salisbury, R. (1934). A study of the transfer effects of training in logical organization. *Journal of Educational Research*, *38*, 241–254.

Schmitt, M.C., & O'Brien, D. (1986). Story grammars: Some cautions about the translation of research into practice. *Reading Research and Instruction*, *26*(1), 1–8.

Slater, W.H., Graves, M.F., & Piche, G.L. (1985). Effects of structural organizers on ninth grade students' comprehension and recall of four patterns of expository text. *Reading Research Quarterly*, *20*, 189–202.

Squire, J.R. (1983). Composing and comprehending: Two sides of the same basic process. *Language Arts*, *60*, 581–589.

Taylor, B.M., & Beach, R.W. (1984). The effects of text structure instruction on middle grade students' comprehension and production of expository text. *Reading Research Quarterly*, *19*, 134–146.

Tierney, R.J., & Cunningham, J. (1984). Research on teaching reading comprehension. In P.D. Pearson (Ed.), *Handbook of reading research* (pp. 609–656). New York: Longman.

Vygotsky, L.S. (1978). *Mind in society: The development of higher psychological processes* (M. Cole, V. John-Steiner, S. Scribner, & E. Souberman, Eds. and Trans.). Cambridge, MA: Harvard University Press.

Wang, J.A., & Au, K.H. (1985). The concept-text application approach: Helping elementary students comprehend expository text. *The Reading Teacher*, *38*, 612–618.

Sally Sue Rothenberg and Susan M. Watts

Students With Learning Difficulties Meet Shakespeare: Using a Scaffolded Reading Experience

As students enter the middle and secondary grades, they enter a new domain of literate activity. For most, developmental reading instruction has ceased and their encounters with literature focus heavily on the study of literary styles, genres, and universal themes, as well as appreciation. However, many English teachers find their students unable to independently comprehend literature selections, a necessary prerequisite for study and appreciation. The challenge for these teachers is providing appropriate support for reading the literature without giving up the time necessary for study and appreciation. This article describes an approach to teaching *Macbeth* to a group of eighth and ninth graders with learning difficulties that blends elements of interdisciplinary instruction with elements of a Scaffolded Reading Experience (Graves & Graves, 1994).

Sally Rothenberg teaches students with learning difficulties in a self-contained setting. Her students are of average or above-average intelligence, but they do not perform, academically, at a level commensurate with their ability. Specifically, they experience difficulties in reading fluency, spelling, and writing fluency.

The year before last, Sally exposed her students to Shakespeare's *Macbeth*. She had never before "taught Shakespeare," so the number of hours she spent studying scholars' interpretations of *Macbeth* was exceeded only by the number of hours she spent planning lessons designed to convey these interpretations to her students. Like many English literature teachers, Sally focused on the content to be taught rather than the students. While her investment in the unit may have been misdirected, it was nonetheless strong. Her students, on the other hand, invested very little in the experience. Consequently, they took very little away from it.

Upon completion of the unit, the general consensus of the class was evident when one student's remark—"Thank God, no more Shakespeare"—met with unanimous agreement from his peers. Sally felt that the unit had been a failure and attributed that to the fact that her students, though intelligent, were young and unable to learn as easily as others their age. She decided that they simply couldn't handle Shakespeare and that she would not teach it in the future.

Therefore, Sally was apprehensive when, in the spring of the following year, her class expressed a desire to read *Macbeth*. Their interest in the play was based on their assumption that mainstream students would be familiar with it and that they would be mainstreamed within the next few years. Realizing that motivation is critical to learning, Sally

Reprinted From the *Journal of Adolescent & Adult Literacy*, *40*(7), 532–539, April 1997.

decided to make a second attempt at teaching Shakespeare. In so doing, she rethought her instructional methods and goals.

Sally decided that the challenge in teaching *Macbeth* would be to sufficiently facilitate the reading so that her students would be successful in their tasks and, consequently, gain an appreciation of the play and its playwright. Graves and Graves (1994) describe a Scaffolded Reading Experience (SRE) as "a set of prereading, during-reading, and postreading activities specifically designed to assist a particular group of students in successfully reading, understanding, learning from, and enjoying a particular selection" (p. 5). The role of the teacher as a decision-maker is paramount in the implementation of an SRE since the teacher determines the specific prereading, during-reading, and postreading activities on the basis of characteristics of the readers and the reading selection and the instructional purposes for reading the text.

The SRE model is based on Pearson and Gallagher's (1983) model of explicit instruction, as extrapolated from the work of Campione (1981), and Vygotsky's (1978) concept of the zone of proximal development. Both bodies of work emphasize the importance of supporting or scaffolding students as they move from one level of competence to the next. The model of explicit instruction, as discussed by Pearson and Gallagher (1983), suggests that early reading experiences of any type must be modeled and explained by the teacher, after which students can assume increasingly large amounts of responsibility for their own learning as they engage in guided practice. As students become more adept at particular reading experiences, they can assume almost total responsibility for their own learning. This movement from teacher to student responsibility in the learning process is referred to as a gradual release of responsibility.

According to Vygotsky (1978), cognitive development exists on a continuum. The first range of the continuum represents the zone within which students can function independently. The second range represents the zone within which students can learn only if they are provided with assistance. The final range represents a zone within which students cannot function, even with assistance. This support, or scaffolding, closes the gap between what students already know or can do and what they can learn–the zone of proximal development.

An SRE consists of prereading, during-reading, and postreading activities. It differs from Betts's Directed Reading Activity (1946) and Stauffer's Directed Reading-Thinking Activity (DR-TA, 1969a, 1969b) in its flexibility. Like the DR-TA, the SRE approach rests on the assumption that reading involves thinking, examining, judging, and applying. However, it is not a fixed template used with all texts. Rather, the SRE provides a menu of options from which the teacher may select those activities suitable for the teaching situation. Further, it is appropriate for a range of text types, unlike the DR-TA, which was originally designed for use with basal readers (Stauffer, 1969b).

Another advantage of the SRE is that it is fully designed by the teacher rather than someone outside of the instructional setting. The teacher is guided by three variables as s/he designs the prereading, during-reading, and postreading activities: the needs of her/his students, the characteristics of the text the students will read, and her/his purposes for instruction. The students are at the center of the plan, and the role of the teacher as a guide is critical to its success. This aspect of the SRE is important to the teaching of students with learning difficulties, as they need instructional support in many areas but also possess learning strengths upon which to build. The SRE options appear in Table 1.

Table 1
Possible components of a scaffolded reading experience

Prereading activities
  Motivating
  Relating the reading to students' lives
  Activating background knowledge
  Building text-specific knowledge
  Preteaching vocabulary
  Preteaching concepts
  Prequestioning
  Predicting
  Direction setting
  Suggesting strategies

During-reading activities
  Silent reading
  Reading to students
  Guided reading
  Oral reading by students
  Modifying the text

Postreading activities
  Questioning
  Discussion
  Writing
  Drama
  Artistic, graphic, and nonverbal activities
  Application and outreach activities
  Reteaching

From *Scaffolded Reading Experiences: Designs for Student Success* by Michael Graves and Bonnie Graves. Reprinted by permission of Christopher-Gordon Publishers.

In Sally's class, a 10-day scaffolded reading experience made *Macbeth* accessible to a group of students who otherwise would have found it too difficult. In this case, the students were one female and three males reading below grade level and experiencing difficulties with writing and spelling. One-hour literature and writing classes were combined to form a 2-hour literacy block during which the unit took place.

We begin with a brief description of the planning needed to design an SRE, followed by an overview of the SRE designed for this particular group of students reading *Macbeth*. The remainder of the article describes, in more detail, the prereading, during-reading, and postreading activities that constituted this particular SRE.

Planning Phase

The SRE described here was used in conjunction with an interdisciplinary approach to instruction. This approach allowed for a holistic experience in which students were actively involved in directing their own learning. Prior to the study of *Macbeth*, 2 months were spent studying mythology of African, Indian, Greek, and Roman origin. The interdisciplinary approach to Greek mythology involved discussions of Greek culture, philosophy, literature, and warfare. During the study of Greek literature, the concept of literary tragedy was introduced. When students expressed an interest in *Macbeth*, Sally returned to this concept of literary tragedy to lay the foundation for the introduction of the play.

In order to design an appropriate SRE, Sally considered characteristics of the reading material, the instructional goals, and characteristics of the students. She decided that the readability of *Macbeth* would be enhanced by its predictable nature, relative to other Shakespearean plays, and its themes of violence and lack of moral character, which are not uncommon in television and films viewed by adolescents. The instructional goals resulted from a cooperative effort between Sally and her students. They were to (a) learn why Shakespeare is considered to be a great writer and (b) gain an in-depth understanding of literary tragedy. A third goal, on Sally's part, was to guide her students through reading strategies that would facilitate meeting the first two goals.

The students' needs were somewhat unique. While they read slowly and laboriously compared to others their age, their word-by-word reading belied relatively strong reading comprehension. They were also of average to above-average intelligence with an advanced breadth and depth of general knowledge for their age, yet they lacked specific knowledge related to Shakespeare and

Macbeth. Sally wanted to challenge her students' thinking abilities without exceeding their reading and writing abilities. Thus, it was important to use scaffolding to build additional schema, to model and provide explicit instruction, to guide students through the reading, and to gradually release the responsibility for learning to the students at a pace that would allow for success.

Initially, the K-W-L (Ogle, 1986) strategy was used to serve three purposes: (a) to determine whether students' (lack of) background knowledge warranted an SRE, (b) to get an idea of what types of activities should be included in the SRE, and (c) to help shape the instructional goals of the unit. Students were asked "What do you know?" and "What do you want to know?" about Shakespeare, *Macbeth*, and literary tragedy. Two instructional goals emerged from their responses: to learn why Shakespeare is considered to be a great writer and to learn what literary tragedy is.

Implementation Phase

The remainder of this article describes the application of the SRE model to a 10-day unit on *Macbeth*. Although Sally had 2-hour blocks of time with her students each day, the activities could be implemented in shorter time blocks over a longer period. General prereading activities occurred during the first 3 days. Reading and during-reading activities occurred on days 4 through 8. The last 2 days of the unit were devoted to general postreading activities. An overview of the entire unit appears in Table 2. As students read the play, on days 4 through 8, specific prereading, during-reading, and postreading activities were implemented for each act.

Table 2
Overview of *Macbeth* unit

Days 1–3: General prereading activities

Activate prior knowledge.	Review relevant information in Greek mythology unit (previously taught).
Build text-specific knowledge.	Use manipulatives and discussion to learn about the history of Scotland.
Preteach concepts and relate reading to students' lives.	Discuss modern-day examples of a tragic hero, provide handout with list of characters, and discuss and answer questions about the play.

Days 4–8 General during-reading activities

Prereading	*During-reading*	*Postreading*
Review journal writing.	Read aloud.	Journal–Redirect students to key aspects of guided reading.
Discuss homework.	Guide reading with questions and comments.	Writing–Students respond to question posed by teacher.
Make predictions.		

Days 9–10: General postreading activities

Discuss the play.	Use color coding of journal entries to facilitate discussion.
Summarize the play.	Do journal activity.
Apply new knowledge.	Do in-class project using *New York Times* articles.
View film version of *Macbeth*.	Discuss ways the film influences students' perception of the play.

General Prereading Activities

Graves and Graves (1994) suggest 10 prereading activities from which to choose those most appropriate for the particular set of students involved in the reading task, the reading selection, and the instructional goals (see Table 1). Since Sally's students had already expressed an interest in reading *Macbeth*, motivating students was not a selected prereading strategy. And although the play contains difficult vocabulary, the modern version used in this class included specific words and definitions on each page, allowing students to learn word meanings independently. Thus, Sally decided not to preteach vocabulary at this point. However, students' surface-level prior knowledge, as revealed during the K-W-L exercise, led to the selection of relating the reading to students' lives, activating background knowledge, and building text-specific knowledge as activities that would be included. Concepts were taught prior to reading to facilitate the reading process.

Day 1—Activating Prior Knowledge

During the study of Greek mythology that had occurred earlier in the year, students read a story version of *The Oresteia*. Activating prior knowledge consisted of having students summarize what they knew about this Greek trilogy and its author, Aeschylus. Based on their recollections, students developed a working definition of tragedy that focused on the concept of fate.

Day 2—Building Text-Specific Knowledge

Students were taught about the history and culture of Scotland in the year 1050 in order to provide a sense of the setting of the play. There was a lively discussion of the clothing of the period, castles and other dwellings, warfare, and religion. A map of Scotland was posted in the classroom and students discussed the country's geographical features. Like the events of Day 1, these activities relied heavily on an interdisciplinary approach to instruction. Further, this phase of the preparation for reading *Macbeth* was structured as an extension of the multisensory activities students had used throughout the year.

Day 3—Preteaching Concepts and Relating the Reading to Students' Lives

At this point, students' general concept of tragedy was expanded upon to create a definition of literary tragedy. Using elements of Frayer, Frederick, and Klausmeier's (1969) model of concept development, this included a presentation of what literary tragedy is and what it is not as well as the presentation of examples and nonexamples of the concept. The definition used with Sally's students consisted of (a) showing human misery at its worst and human grandeur at its greatest and (b) the monumental struggle of human will against inescapable destiny. Students had difficulty differentiating between the slaughter of innocents, typical of the Greek pathos, and the tragic hero. Sally presented an example that addressed this difference and also served to relate the reading to students' lives. The example came from the contemporary film and book trilogy, *Star Wars*. Students had read modified versions of the book trilogy earlier in the year.

Darth Vader, the *Star Wars* figure comparable to the character Macbeth, started as a great Jedi warrior. Unfortunately, and ultimately fatally, he was instructed in Jedi traditions by Obi-Wan Kenobi rather than Yoda, who was considered the wisest Jedi warrior and who normally trained Jedi. When Darth Vader was at a particularly vulnerable stage in his mastery of "the Force," he fell prey to the Emperor, who turned him to the "dark side of the Force." This was portrayed as inevitable.

Darth Vader's actions demonstrated an evil comparable to Macbeth's. Darth Vader went on a killing spree much like Macbeth. The lack of remorse in both characters was a consistent plot element until the end, when both accepted their destiny. In *Star Wars*, this occurred when Darth Vader watched his son, Luke Skywalker, fighting the Emperor. Darth Vader saved his son by killing the Emperor, and in the process was killed himself. This example illustrated for the students a human at his darkest hour and at the height of grandeur, as well as the concepts of inescapable destiny and the tragic hero.

During-Reading Activities

After providing a foundation for the play in its entirety, students began to read one act of the play each day for the next 5 days. Each day, students were led through a set of prereading, during-reading, and postreading activities. Prereading activities included reviewing responses to a question posed by Sally at the end of the preceding day, verifying teacher and student understandings through discussing, questioning and making predictions. On the first day of reading, there was also a minilesson on the structure of the play as a form of literature.

During-reading activities consisted of reading aloud from a modern English version of the play, with each student assuming a part and with the teacher interjecting a key question or statement to guide students' reading. Journal writing, either in class or for homework, and responding to a teacher-posed question for homework were the postreading activities. The following sections describe the specific prereading, during-reading, and postreading activities for Acts I and V of the play.

Day 4—Act I

Prereading minilesson: The structure of the play as literature. Sally discussed the structure of a play, the format of character development, and the format for the development of themes. Students were encouraged to think about the differences between performing a play and reading a play in class and came to an understanding that interaction is present when role-playing in the classroom, but the vital elements of action and setting are missing. Sally then suggested that the students use a comprehension strategy taught earlier in the year, visualization, to aid in reading the play.

During-reading questions and comments to guide reading. Sally reminded the students that, by the definition of tragedy, "we know that Macbeth is a heroic figure. Pay close attention to lines reflecting this. What is the atmosphere or feeling established in the beginning of the play? Watch to see if it changes."

Postreading writing. Students were instructed to keep a journal of their reactions and reflections on the reading, especially in areas discussed before the reading. Students were told that journal entries could be written in diary format and that they should refer to exact page and line numbers as frequently as possible in order to facilitate daily discussions and to aid in the organization of thoughts at the end when students would be summarizing the play as a whole. Sally's students understood that, as with other response journals kept throughout the year, spelling and form would not be corrected. The purpose of the journals was to record ideas and extend thinking related to the reading.

Postreading question for homework. "How would you respond if you were Macbeth after hearing the witches' prophecy, particularly after one unlikely prophecy immediately comes true?"

Day 8—Act V

Prediction. Students were asked, "What do you suppose the witches' prophecy will do to Macbeth's ability to think clearly? Do people believe what they want to believe?"

Questions and comments to guide reading. Sally had students recall the definition of literary tragedy. After a brief discussion, the students realized that the positive side of Macbeth had yet to reemerge. Students were instructed to watch for the change in Macbeth and the reemergence of the great man that he was at the beginning of the play.

Writing. Students wrote their responses to the final act with an emphasis on the change in Macbeth's character.

Question/Guide for summarization. Students were asked to reread their journal entries for each of the five acts and to look for major themes. They were instructed to write a conclusion about the play based on their comprehensive personal reactions.

Postreading Activities

The postreading activities selected for use at the end of the entire play were discussion, writing, and application. These took place on the 9th and 10th days of the unit. Sally designed discussion, writing, and application activities that would simultaneously serve to enhance students' understandings and responses to *Macbeth* and as ways to assess these understandings. With a focus on the construction of

meaning through interaction with the text and through collaboration, Sally's postreading activities reflect current conceptions of literacy assessment (Calfee & Hiebert, 1991; Valencia, Hiebert, & Afflerbach, 1994).

Day 9

To facilitate a discussion of the play, students color coded their journal entries. Statements pertaining to Macbeth before the murders were coded in yellow, during the murders in pink, and at the end in blue. Green was used to highlight entries pertaining to events in the play illustrating nature's revolt. Students then discussed the results of this analysis by comparing and contrasting their entries. In fulfillment of a writing assignment, each student summarized the play in his/her journal by focusing on one of the four categories that were color coded.

For an in-class project, students worked in pairs on an application activity involving a statement made in the *New York Times* regarding former U.S. President Richard Nixon's death. A Conservative Member of Parliament in England referred to the former president as "a Shakespearean hero of tragic proportion." Students were to use their understanding of tragedy and the coverage of Nixon's death in numerous articles in the *New York Times* to defend or refute this assertion. Each pair was assigned a position in the debate. Using their new knowledge of literary tragedy, students scanned the relevant section of the newspaper for words and phrases associated with this concept to identify articles that might help them prepare for the debate. They color coded passages as they built their cases, then presented their findings to the class. Afterward, personal opinions were discussed.

Day 10

On the final day of the unit, students watched a film version of *Macbeth*. For homework, students were assigned to think about ways in which the movie changed or affirmed their summary of the play. They rewrote their summaries accordingly and described their new perspective and its origin.

Final Remarks

Perhaps the most essential factor contributing to the success of this unit was the enthusiasm of the students. They formed a partnership with Sally at the very beginning of the project. Student projects created as part of the unit on Greek mythology contributed to a sense of ownership in the following unit on *Macbeth*. Student evaluations of their experiences with the *Macbeth* unit were high. Yet enthusiasm was not the only factor leading to success.

The SRE model provided Sally with a structure for thinking about her instruction so that reading instruction and literature study could be integrated. The fact that the model focuses on dimensions for instructional decision-making allows teachers and students to capitalize on their strengths and the strengths of the reading material while addressing students' current limitations as well as the limitations of the text. In this case, the SRE worked particularly well in conjunction with a holistic, interdisciplinary approach to literacy development. Further, students who were experiencing difficulty in reading were given access to and participated in higher order literacy experiences related to reading.

Rather than constricting her students' experiences with *Macbeth*, Sally provided support that facilitated an expansive range of responses throughout the reading of the play. Students disagreed with one another and changed their own opinions about the events of the play during the unit. For example, there were multiple explanations for Macbeth's downfall including the control of supernatural forces, the power of inescapable destiny, and manipulation by Lady Macbeth. Students' comments during discussions reflected what has been described as metaliteracy or critical literacy (Calfee, 1996). They did not reflect the kind of literacy often expected of students with learning difficulties.

All of the students were delighted with the outcome of the unit. They particularly enjoyed the hands-on activities, relating the lesson to their own lives, and the encouragement to develop a personal interpretation of the story. One student in particular, who had had difficulty with abstract thinking throughout the school year, thrived when she was given the opportunity to make connections between what she was learning and what she had already learned and experienced in her own life. At the end of the unit, she developed one of the most novel interpretations of *Macbeth* in the class, which focused on the influence of Lady Macbeth's motivations on the chain of events in the play.

At the beginning of the project, Sally's students did not believe they could be successful with Shakespeare, despite their strong desire to attempt it. One student stated that it was for "really smart kids." As a result of this project, the students learned about Shakespeare, about reading, and about themselves. Contrary to breathing a collective sigh of relief at the end of the unit, the students asked whether they could write their own tragedies. And they did.

REFERENCES

Betts, E. (1946). *Foundations of reading instruction*. New York: American Book.

Calfee, R.C. (1996). Assessing critical literacy: Tools and techniques. In M.F. Graves, P. van den Broek, & B.M. Taylor (Eds.), *The first R: Every child's right to read* (pp. 224–249). New York: Teachers College Press.

Calfee, R.C., & Hiebert, E.H. (1991). Classroom assessment of literacy. In R. Barr, M. Kamil, P. Mosenthal, & P.D. Pearson (Eds.), *Handbook of reading research* (Vol. 2, pp. 281–309). White Plains, NY: Longman.

Campione, J. (1981, April). *Learning, academic achievement, and instruction.* Paper presented at the second annual Conference on Reading Research of the Center for the Study of Reading, New Orleans, LA.

Frayer, D.A., Frederick, W.D., & Klausmeier, H.J. (1969). *A schema for testing the level of concept mastery* (Working Paper No. 16). Madison, WI: Wisconsin Research and Development Center for Cognitive Learning.

Graves, M.F., & Graves, B.B. (1994). *Scaffolding reading experiences: Designs for student success.* Norwood, MA: Christopher-Gordon.

Ogle, D. (1986). K-W-L: A teaching model that develops active reading of expository text. *The Reading Teacher, 39*, 564–570.

Pearson, P.D., & Gallagher, M.C. (1983). The instruction of reading comprehension. *Contemporary Educational Psychology, 8*, 317–344.

Stauffer, R.G. (1969a). *Directing reading maturity as a cognitive process.* New York: Harper & Row.

Stauffer, R.G. (1969b). *Teaching reading as a thinking process.* New York: Harper & Row.

Valencia, S.W., Hiebert, E.H., & Afflerbach, P.P. (1994). *Authentic reading assessment: Practices and possibilities.* Newark, DE: International Reading Association.

Vygotsky, L.S. (1978). *Mind in society.* Cambridge, MA: Harvard University Press.

Carol Weir

Using Embedded Questions to Jump-Start Metacognition in Middle School Remedial Readers

When I returned to the classroom as a middle school reading teacher after a 12-year leave, I turned to professional journals to see what was new in the field of reading. I discovered that there had been a sea change in discourse about literacy. During the information blackout I experienced while immersed in diapers and storybooks, a new notion about the reading process had emerged–metacognition (Cross & Paris, 1988; Vygotsky, 1978). I was fascinated with the idea of "the monitoring and redirection of one's activities during the course of reading to reach the desired goals" (Cross & Paris, 1988, p. 131). This is the story of my struggle to put this idea into practice in my classroom.

It was the internal dialogue of metacognition, I recognized intuitively, that my seventh- and eighth-grade remedial students were missing. Reading for them was a passive experience of running eyes over print, then hoping that they'd "got it," only to find, when faced with comprehension questions after reading, that they had not. I realized that the notions that skilled readers are often confused, must reread, and wonder about things as they read, were foreign to my students. In their view, either you were a good reader and "got it" all at once, or you didn't.

Indeed, research shows that poor comprehenders use metacognitive strategies with much lower frequency than skilled comprehenders do (Duffy, Roehler, & Hermann, 1988; Garner, 1980; Myers & Paris, 1981). Furthermore, there is evidence that (a) poor readers improve their comprehension to a greater extent with metacognitive instruction than good readers do (Nolan, 1991) and that (b) metacognitive awareness grows developmentally (Cross & Paris, 1988). I became intrigued with the promise of programs like SAIL (Bergman & Schuder, 1993; Pressley, Bergman, & El-Dinary, 1992) and the "How Readers and Reporters Are Alike" model investigated by Baumann, Jones, and Seifert-Kessell (1993), which teach thinking aloud and other comprehension strategies. I began to struggle with the implications of these new ideas for my students. How could I interrupt their passive stance and engender more thinking? How might students come to internalize the metacognitive dialogue?

Opportunity Knocks

A serendipitous opportunity presented itself in my school district at about this time, one that cemented my interest in metacognition and forced me to specify very clearly what I wanted students to learn about being self-regulating readers. Our assistant superinten-

Reprinted From the *Journal of Adolescent & Adult Literacy*, *41*(6), 458–467, March 1998.

dent, Kathleen Buckley, arranged for researchers Lois Hetland and Chris Unger of Harvard University's Project Zero, to train volunteer teachers in the teaching framework promulgated by David N. Perkins in *Smart Schools: From Training Memories to Educating Minds* (1992).

The Teaching for Understanding (TfU) framework emphasizes deep understanding developed through carefully sequenced, performance-based, guided learning experiences as opposed to rushing to cover a curriculum heavy on skills or facts and light on understanding. It further meshed with my own philosophy in advocating instructional units centered around themes, or generative topics, that would be motivating to students.

Ongoing authentic assessment and an emphasis on reflective practice were two more aspects of TfU that set it apart from the status quo. Assessment, especially self-assessment, is carefully attended to in the TfU framework, and not just as regards product. There is a distinct metacognitive component of self-assessment in a TfU classroom that directs students and teachers alike to examine process and how they are managing it. Perkins posits that the highest level of metacognitive thinkers are "reflective learners" who "reflect on their thinking-in-progress, ponder their strategies, and revise them" (p. 102). (For a more complete description of the TfU framework, see Perkins, 1992, and Perkins & Blythe, 1994.)

The TfU framework encouraged me to think about metacognition not as just another skill, but as a fundamental understanding about literacy. I expressed this understanding as inquiry questions, known as "throughlines" in TfU terminology. I wrote out these questions and posted them prominently in the classroom:

- How can we know if we understand what we read?

- What can we do to make sure we understand what we read?

The throughline questions became an explicit agenda for every lesson, and class discussion frequently returned to them.

In posing these fundamental questions, I was compelled to carefully specify the understandings and strategies that they addressed. I wanted students to understand that skillful, effective readers use a variety of strategies to make sure that they understand what they read. These strategies are

- self-monitoring for understanding;
- making, confirming, or disproving predictions;
- formulating and answering questions;
- rereading, retelling, or mentally replaying a story;
- employing sensory imagery;
- noticing organizational patterns of text; and
- making connections between story features and personal experience.

Embedded Questions

As I set about designing classroom performances to guide my students toward these understandings, I returned to my original dilemma of how to get kids thinking in process, *during* reading. In explaining the problem to a colleague, I heard myself repeatedly speaking of needing to interrupt the students' ineffective passive process. Of course! I'd do just that–interrupt them. I sat down with scissors, markers, and glue and began literally cutting stories apart.

What resulted was a series of stories on a common theme (friendship) with questions embedded in the text, complete with blank lines where students could write or draw their answers. The questions occurred at points

Excerpt from "The Boy With Yellow Eyes"
by Gloria Gonzalez*

Only a handful of the residents of Preston Heights recall the actual events. And even then, years and conflicting accounts have clouded the facts.

Still, in some quarters, and especially during the relentless winters unique to the hillside village, the incident is spoken of with pride and awe.

1. What is the setting? (name and description)

Preston Heights, hillside village.

2. The author has mentioned something but hasn't explained it. Write a question to keep in mind as you continue reading.

What incident is spoken?

Till today, if you get a couple of old-timers in the same room, a heated debate will erupt over the mundane detail of whether <u>Norman</u> was ten or going on <u>thirteen</u>. They'll also argue whether he lost one shoe or both in the scuffle.

What the parties do agree on is that it happened in Preston Heights and it involved Norman and his next-door neighbor <u>Willie</u>, whose age for some reason is never questioned–<u>thirteen</u>.

3. Underline the names of the two characters and their ages.

*From *Visions* by Donald R. Gallo, Editor. Copyright ©1987 by Donald R. Gallo. Used by permission of Dell Books, a division of Bantam Doubleday Dell Publishing Group, Inc.

that I identified as being crucial to understanding subsequent developments in the story. For instance, questions embedded at the beginning of a story drew readers' attention to noticing details of setting and character to lay the foundation for understanding succeeding plot development. In this fashion, students could build meaning incrementally as they proceeded through a story. They arrived at page 2 with the crucial understandings from page 1 in place.

Figure 1 shows a completed page from "The Boy With Yellow Eyes" by Gloria Gonzalez (1987). This story begins with a reference to the setting and to an "incident" that townspeople have been discussing for many years. A competent reader would notice that the author gives no explication of what this "incident" refers to, and would formulate a mental question or purpose to discover what the incident was as reading proceeds. The embedded question directs the student to (a) identify what the author has mentioned but not explained, and (b) formulate a question about it. The reader now has a mental framework–determining what this incident was–in which subsequent details may be situated and made meaningful. Confusion and noncomprehension are replaced with an attitude of inquiry and purpose.

In preparing embedded questions for the stories, I tried to simulate the metacognitive strategies that skillful readers employ. Therefore, opportunities to summarize, self-question, and predict were frequent. Another category of questions directs readers to the fundamental literal and inferential elements of the story. Others focus on characteristics of text that function as roadblocks to comprehension for less able readers such as unreferenced pronouns, time shifts, untagged dialogue, and figurative language. Some guidelines for determining when to insert questions are found in Figure 2.

Why not read the story together and stop to discuss it, as in the Reciprocal Teaching method pioneered by Palincsar and Brown (1984)? In keeping with the TfU model, I wanted the students to use many modalities and intelligences, so I felt the drawing and writing were important, yet not intimidating, because each question was brief with a limited number of blank lines to fill. I also wanted students to gain experience in annotating text—underlining, and writing margin notes and questions. The physical manipulation of the text itself seemed important. I wanted each student to literally make his or her mark on the story. Finally, I felt that working as an individual with the text would foster independence and internalization of the metacognitive process, which is, in fact, a solitary experience.

However, talk was very important to the students in developing their understanding. To guide students in coping with this novel format, and to assist them with the high readability of the stories, we completed the first few pages of each story together. I read the story aloud, and the students collaborated on answers to the embedded questions. Thus, as they gradually built familiarity and comfort with the format, they moved from completing

---

Figure 2
Guidelines for writing embedded questions

When to embed a question

Draw attention to (especially at the beginning of a story):
    -details of setting;
    -character descriptions, relationships, and reactions;
    -features of the text, like italics or breaks in the print, that indicate time shifts;
    -unreferenced events (i.e., the reader is expected to make sense of it as details are revealed in subsequent text);
    -conclusions that are implied, not stated directly.

Include several prediction points:
    -when conflict begins to develop;
    -just before the climax;
    -just before the resolution.

Ask students to pose questions about and identify:
    -unclear pronoun reference;
    -cultural references that may be unfamiliar (e.g., Morse code, bootleggers);
    -figurative language;
    -the most confusing section of the story, and tell how they resolved their confusion;
    -speakers in dialogue with no tag lines.

Have students highlight:
    -evidence and clues to support answers to inferential questions;
    -unfamiliar vocabulary;
    -words that establish tone or mood.

Ask students to paraphrase long, difficult sentences or retell incidents.

Typical embedded questions
What do you think will happen next? Make a prediction.
What are you wondering about at this point? Write a question.
Underline the quality about character X that the author emphasized.
Stop and visualize X. Draw a sketch of your visualization.
What was the most confusing part of this story? How did you handle it?

---

the stories in a teacher-led group, to working with a partner, to working alone.

This laid the foundation in comprehension for the students to then participate in a substantive discussion of the story. Because they had worked through the important literal elements of the story, they were well prepared to discuss higher level issues of interpretation and application. Their opinions were vociferous, and they spontaneously turned to the text to support their ideas. Students designated as "concrete thinkers" began to articulate theme statements for the stories that were anything but concrete.

After three cycles of completing stories with embedded questions, I asked students to get all their work from the unit out on the table for analysis. I asked them to list in their journals all the different types of questions and activities they had been asked to complete thus far that had helped them to understand what they read. Some were succinct, like Brian, who wrote, "your are tring to get us to ask ourselfs questions while we read–creat thiryes [theories] basted on infomation–to help us know what information to look for." Others took up the quantitative challenge, like Brandon, who listed no less than 21 strategies (Figure 3), my favorite being "notice your confusion." I concluded that these students were developing metacognitive awareness of strategies that they could use to improve their reading comprehension.

Outcomes

Given their own clear articulation of the various strategies available to them, I felt that my readers were beginning to sense that they could be in charge of their own understanding. I decided that they were ready to fly on their own and deal with "uncut" text. I designed a final project that required the students to read a short story independently,

annotate it with predictions and questions, and highlight characters' features and unfamiliar words.

After a second reading, the project wrapped up with oral presentations. Each student created and displayed a collage-style graphic organizer, retold the story in an organized way, and included an interpretation of the theme backed up with passages read aloud from the text. I encouraged students to organize their graphic in a way that reflected the structural organization of the story and to focus on an object in the story as a central symbol.

Take Stefanie's poster for an example of understanding (Figure 4). She read "On The Bridge" by Todd Strasser, a story of a teen's poor choice of role model. After a poorly considered incident involving a cigarette, the main character, Seth, is scapegoated and abandoned by Adam, the tough "friend" he emulates. Because of Adam's betrayal, Seth endures a beating by even tougher strangers. Stefanie has illustrated the contrast between the two characters by dividing the page with a giant cigarette. Seth's qualities of being "decent, brave, and stubborn" are on the right. On the left is Adam, "dangerous, selfish, and rude." A figure representing Seth is stepping tentatively into the territory of the cigarette, trying out a lifestyle that he is ultimately uncomfortable with.

Stefanie's theme statement focuses on the cowardly actions of the antagonist: "If you do something wrong 'fess up don't have anyone else take the blame For you!" She has made high level meaning from the literary elements in the story and illustrated them in a sophisticated way. Of note is the theme of betrayal causing friendship to "go up in smoke," that is suggested in the cloud of smoke above the cigarette with the word *friendship* prominently in the center. Although she has not articulated this theme verbally, this piece of art is credible evidence

① list some adjectives about main character.

② Make a prediction.

③ Who is in the story?

④ What's the setting?

⑤ Write a question so that you know you are understanding.

⑥ Am I getting this?

⑦ Tell about the characters attitude.

⑧ Circle vocab words.

⑨ Identify the characters.

⑩ Ask questions

⑪ actions for characters

⑫ explain sentences and phrases.

⑬ Define vocab words.

⑭ why did this happen?

⑮ what's there attitude?

⑯ How are there emotions?

⑰ what is the tone or mood

⑱ What is the plot?

⑲ what is the theeme?

⑳ Is there a conflict, if so what is it?

㉑ Notice your confusion.

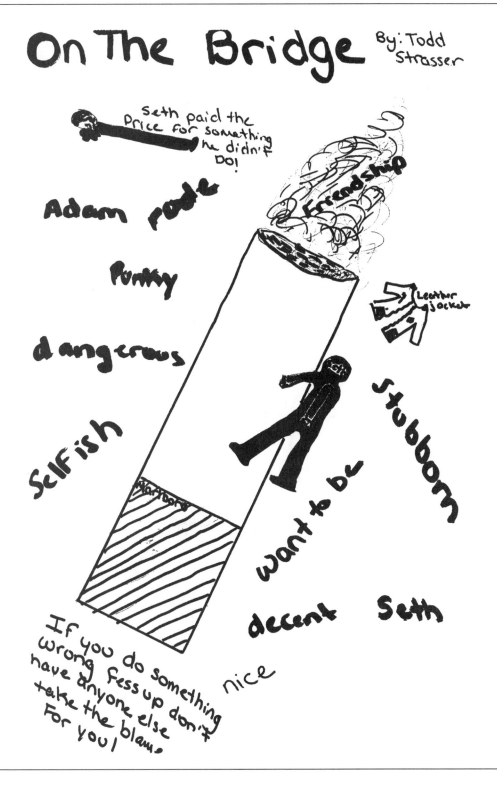

Figure 5
Drawing in response to embedded questions in "St. Agnes Sends the Golden Boy" by Cin Forshay-Lunsford, drawn by Atsushi, Grade 8

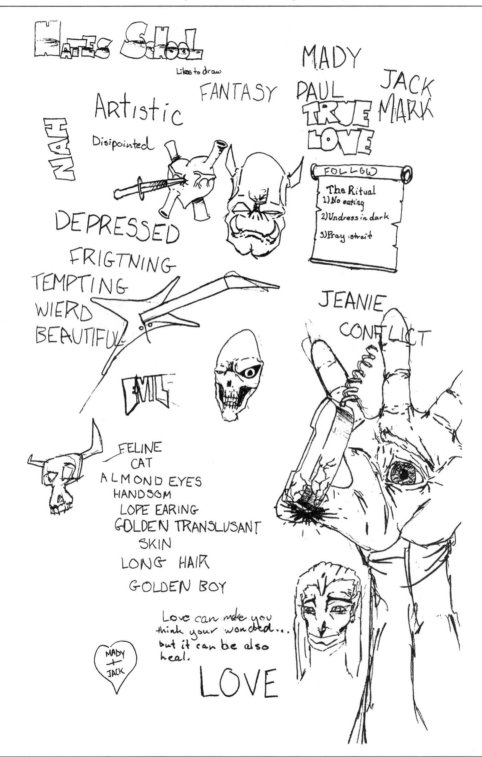

that Stefanie understands this interpretation of the story very well.

A second example of high level understanding can be found in Atsushi's poster (Figure 5), a response to the story "St. Agnes Sends the Golden Boy" by Cin Forshay-Lunsford (1987), a tale of misplaced and refound love. His drawing includes the salient features of the characters, graphic suggestions of plot elements, visualizations of characters, and a theme statement, "love can make you think your [sic] wounded...but it can also heal." This reader has done a lot of thinking on a high level to arrive at this abstraction. Atsushi also expresses other story themes through his artwork. The cracked telephone, held by a hand with an eye in the palm, evokes the "eye opening" experience of the main character during a fateful telephone call with her misplaced love object.

Examining the annotations students made on their stories gave quite clear insight into the students' metacognitive process as well. Students emulated the embedded questions they had experienced in previous stories by asking many questions of their own while reading. Like Stefanie, Brian chose to read "On the Bridge," and became very involved in annotating the story as he read. He was methodical, stopping to make 42 separate annotations on the first reading and 27 on the second reading.

I categorized Brian's notations and found that the predominant type was a predictive question such as "Is Adam lying?" or "Will Adam fall apart?" (17 occurrences). The next most numerous category was questions of clarification (15 occurrences). Seven questions of clarification began with "why," primarily questioning Seth's reasons for wanting to imitate Adam when "that's not even his pirnisaty [personality]." Eight other questions of clarification were efforts to resolve some confusion, "When was this written?"; "Who started the fight?"; or, to clarify character motivation, "Is Adam trying to impress Seth?"

Brian underlined six unfamiliar vocabulary words and wrote statements that summarized or retold an incident four times, "He is lying," "Adam is just using him." Fully one third of the total number of notations deal with character motivation, an indication that Brian was indeed struggling to make meaning around the central issue in this story. His annotations provided a clear window into his mind, a view that displayed the steady, mindful pursuit and construction of meaning.

Validation

Did stories with embedded questions in the context of a carefully sequenced, guided series of activities really help my students to become metacognitive? I thought so. The students thought so also, expressing clear awareness of metacognitive strategies in a videotaped interview.

Interviewer (I):	Did you learn anything about how to understand what you're reading?
Tracy:	Making predictions...it helps you to think ahead.
I:	If you got a story where the first two pages were boring and confusing, what would you do?
Tracy:	Ask questions. Why all the peoples talking about that? [sic]
I:	Would you give up? Would you say to yourself, "I'm a bad reader" and throw it away?
Atsushi:	No, I'd reread it or something like that. If I understood what they were trying to get across, I'd keep going, but if I didn't understand it that way I'd go back.

I: Do you think about your thinking while you read? Has your "in your brain" habit changed any from the kind of reader you were?

Annie: Now, when I read, I try to go into it more like what is he trying to tell us? Why is he writing this book? But before, I just read it. I didn't really care. Now I can go into it more deeper. I can ask myself questions and see if I understand the book. I can question myself and see how I understand it.

Atsushi: Back then it was like, boring...now you can picture what's going on. It seems interesting when you understand it.

Predicting, self-questioning, self-monitoring, rereading, visualizing–these essential metacognitive strategies were now clearly owned by Tracy, Atsushi, and Annie. Their metacognition had been jump-started, and they were moving through text unaided, understanding it, and enjoying it.

Test results also validated gains in reading competency for many of the 15 students. The test I administered in October and June was the Stanford Diagnostic Reading Test, Forms G and H, Reading Comprehension subtest. Pretest percentiles ranged from 14 to 52 for reading comprehension in a school population whose average is within the sixth stanine. Posttest percentiles ranged from 11 to 99. The mean change in grade equivalent was 1.7 years. The mean increase in National Curve Equivalent scores was 20.35. Not only did students improve, but they showed far greater than expected growth. (Delta NCE = 0 represents 1 year's expected growth.) Several showed jumps of 2 or more grade equivalent units. One (Brian) even achieved a perfect score on the posttest, up from the 37th percentile.

Back to the Research

Encouraged by these results, I went back to the research looking for empirical support for the embedded question technique as a comprehension remediation. Two studies–Walczyk and Hall, (1989) and Salomon, Globerson, and Guterman, (1989)–found positive effects on metacognitive behavior and reading comprehension from using embedded questions. Salomon et al. (1989) reported that social discourse about metacognition may have a stronger effect on learners' performance than the embedded questions themselves.

This confirmed my belief that talking to one another is important for adolescent learners and gave me insight into the value of our small group discussions in reinforcing the utility of the strategies modeled by the embedded questions. Embedded questions combined with lots of classroom talk are an effective way to help students acquire and internalize metacognitive strategies for reading comprehension.

I see now that my students were not the only ones who received a metacognitive jump-start. Just as embedded questions guided my students to become more metacognitive readers, so reading professional research has prompted me to examine my teaching and seek innovation. As Pressley has asserted, "the most compelling comprehension strategies instruction probably is being designed in schools by people who have both knowledge of the research and theoretical literature and the realities of classrooms" (Pressley et al., 1995, p. 211). Embedded questions in a Teaching for Understanding context have proven to be just such a powerful strategy, one that can jump-start metacognition and transform a passive reader into a reader who is really in the driver's seat.

REFERENCES

Baumann, J., Jones, L., & Seifert-Kessell, N. (1993, Summer). *Monitoring reading comprehension by thinking aloud* (Instructional Resource No. 1). Athens, GA: National Reading Research Center.

Bergman, J., & Schuder, T. (1993). Teaching at-risk students to read strategically. *Educational Leadership, 50* (4), 19-23.

Cross, R., & Paris, S.G. (1988). Developmental and instructional analysis of children's metacognition and reading comprehension. *Journal of Educational Psychology, 80*, 131-142.

Duffy, G., Roehler, L., & Hermann, B. (1988). Modeling mental processes helps poor readers become strategic readers. *The Reading Teacher, 41*, 762-767.

Forshay-Lunsford, C. (1987). Saint Agnes sends the golden boy. In D. Gallo, (Ed.). *Visions: Nineteen short stories by outstanding writers for young adults* (pp. 11-21). New York: Dell.

Garner, R. (1980). Monitoring understanding: An investigation of good and poor readers' awareness of induced miscomprehension of text. *Journal of Reading Behavior, 12* (1), 55-63.

Gonzalez, G. (1987). The boy with yellow eyes. In D. Gallo (Ed.), *Visions: Nineteen short stories by outstanding writers for young adults* (pp. 204-211). New York: Dell.

Myers, M., & Paris, S. (1981). Comprehension monitoring, memory and study strategies of good and poor readers. *Journal of Reading Behavior, 13* (1), 5-22.

Nolan, T. (1991). Self questioning and prediction: Combining metacognition strategies. *Journal of Reading, 35*, 132-138.

Palincsar, A.S., & Brown, A.L. (1984). Reciprocal teaching of comprehension-fostering and monitoring activities. *Cognition and Instruction, 1* (2), 117-175.

Perkins, D. (1992). *Smart schools: From training memories to educating minds*. New York: The Free Press.

Perkins, D., & Blythe, T. (1994). Putting understanding up front. *Educational Leadership, 51* (5), 4-7.

Pressley, M., El-Dinary, P., Brown, R., Schuder, T., Bergman, J., York, M., Gaskins, I., & Faculties and Administration of Benchmark School and the Montgomery County, MD, SAIL/SIA Programs. (1995). A transactional strategies instruction Christmas Carol. In A. McKeough, J. Lupart, & A. Marini (Eds.), *Teaching for transfer* (pp. 177-213). Mahwah, NJ: Erlbaum.

Pressley, M., SAIL Faculty and Administration, Bergman, J.L., & El-Dinary, P.B. (1992). A researcher-educator collaborator interview study of transactional strategies instruction. *Journal of Educational Psychology, 84*, 231-249.

Salomon, G., Globerson, T., & Guterman, E. (1989). The computer as a zone of proximal development: Internalizing reading-related metacognitions from a reading partner. *Journal of Educational Psychology, 81*, 620-627.

Strasser, T. (1987). On the bridge. In D. Gallo (Ed.), *Visions: Nineteen short stories by outstanding writers for young adults* (pp. 122-128). New York: Dell.

Vygotsky, L.S. (1978). *Mind in society*. Cambridge, MA: Harvard University Press.

Walczyk, J., & Hall, V. (1989). Effects of examples and embedded questions on the accuracy of comprehension self-assessments. *Journal of Educational Psychology, 81*, 435-437

Larry Crapse

Helping Students Construct Meaning Through Their Own Questions

Chris, a reluctant reader in a 10th-grade English class, is called upon to read a portion of Gary Snyder's poem "Above Pate Valley." With effort, he does so, but upon completion he emphatically states "This don't make no sense!"

Comments like Chris's are not meant to belittle the author or embarrass the teacher. They are honest expressions of readers' confusion, which may stem from a number of sources. The vocabulary may be unfamiliar, the context in which the writing was produced may be unclear or unknown to the reader, or the reader's experiences may be so disconnected from those of the writer that no understanding occurs.

We know from both research and experience what can be done before the student reads a selection to lay the foundation for comprehension: predictions can be made about the subject and content of the work, background on the author's life and experiences can be discussed, expressive writing can be assigned as a lead-in to the reading, and so on. Teachers also have methods to stimulate responses soon after the reading: journals, logs, freewriting, and related strategies.

I have found that the best way for me to help students construct meaning, and therefore comprehend literature, is through questioning of a nontraditional sort. Instead of directing questions to the students and having them give me answers, I have them develop their own questions for discourse in groups.

I decided long ago that I would never stand before a class and insist on one interpretation of a literary piece. As a student, I had had too many teachers who dispensed gems of insight from old college notes and would not allow me to form my own opinions and responses. As a teacher, I came to believe in the integrity of the reader's interaction with the text and in the importance of conversations with other readers about it, so I began requiring my students to become active readers and respondents.

I ask my students to jot down questions about the piece of literature under consideration. These must not be questions for which the answers are obvious and therefore easily determined—no "who was the author" or "in what year was the poem written." Instead, students must write questions for which they do not have immediate answers and in which they are genuinely interested, honest ones that can be pursued and discussed by both teacher and students. While students are writing, I am also writing, because I want them to see me not as an authority with all the answers but as a fellow learner. I want them to avoid playing "Guess What's in the Teacher's Head."

Reprinted From the *Journal of Reading*, *38*(5), 389–390, February 1995.

At the conclusion of the writing, which may take as long as 10 minutes or as few as 3, I use one of two methods for helping students shape meaning from the text.

1. As students call out questions from their papers, I make a jot list on the chalkboard or overhead projector. I try to elicit a sampling from different parts of the room to keep everyone alert and involved. Along the way, I throw in some of my own questions. If my questions overlap with some of the students' questions, this is positive because the class is seeing me as a learner.

When the master list is finished, I stand back from it to get the gestalt of the ideas expressed. We then select the most interesting questions for our discussions. We might vote, or students may call out the numbers of the ones they want, or I may arbitrarily mark the ones that will be the focus of our attention. Next, I put the students into groups of four or five and tell them to pursue possible answers until I call time. Discussion takes about 20 minutes.

While they are talking, I walk among the groups or sit with them to listen or participate. I also make notes on my clipboard for later reference. At the end of group discussion time, we have closure with a summary of the most salient points brought out in the groups. I always involve individuals here either by calling on them or asking for volunteers to share some thoughts.

2. I ask students to form groups of four or five and I give each group some chart paper, colored markers, and tape. The paper is taped to the wall near each group; a recorder must list questions called out by group members. A leader then helps the group select the most interesting questions while the recorder marks the ones that will be discussed. The leader must next guide the group in pursuit of possible answers. Every effort must be made to see that all members respond.

I rotate among the groups, observing and making notes. The recorder jots on another sheet of paper some of the most interesting points emerging from discussion. After time is called, we follow the procedures for closure previously mentioned, with students doing most of the talking.

The day after the group discussions, I spend about 10 minutes at the beginning of the period pointing out certain interesting points from the notes I made on my clipboard. Often, this generates other questions and responses that may need immediate elaboration. If we are on a tight schedule, though, I note the students' concerns and tell them that we will schedule a time later for additional discussion, perhaps as part of a unit review. I always make it a point to share with the class my observations about how they responded in groups and what they need to work on in terms of participation.

Usually, the students find the group discussion of honest or genuine questions to be helpful. They are able to investigate problems in a text and to share impressions about the literary content and author's craft. They are also able, in most cases, to reason through the issues involved in particular works and reach meaningful conclusions about them. When they get stuck, I am reminded that it is my job to get them unstuck. So, without pontificating, I might share my own insights and responses as a way of generating more connections between the students and the texts. I also ask questions that could not possibly be in a manual or lesson plan because they are so context specific. From there, I am usually able to get dialogues going in ways that lead to greater understanding.

Through the experience of honest questioning, I have observed students celebrating their own insights and solutions to problems posed by texts that might have seemed difficult at first. I have also seen students making close connections between their own feelings and those of characters and authors. Louise Rosenblatt (1938/1976, in *Literature as Exploration*) said "Once there has been a lived through evocation of the text, students can be led toward increasingly self-critical and sound interpretation" (p. 394). The sound interpretation, it seems to me, is that which is most genuine to the reader, that which vibrates the strings of both the intellect and the affect and makes them resonate with satisfaction. When students are trusted to construct meanings from texts individually and cooperatively, they say "This does make sense!"

Marguerite Green

Rapid Retrieval of Information:
Reading Aloud With a Purpose

As a middle school reading teacher, I often have experienced the problem of my students wanting to read aloud in class as a routine way of dealing with content area reading assignments. These assignments are both difficult and boring for them, and their instinctive palliative approach to the chore is wanting to read the material aloud. I have found that they have all been exposed at some time or another to the round-robin routine of oral reading in their classrooms, with several negative results. Students' comprehension is severely compromised because poor readers are not effective oral readers. Students are often concerned only with the sections that they will be assigned to read aloud, and therefore do not listen to or concentrate on the other readings. Some students are nervous and uncomfortable about reading aloud. Most importantly, they do not learn that adult reading for comprehension is silent reading.

With these negative effects so prevalent, I needed to find a way to satisfy my students' desire to read aloud, achieve a purposeful result from oral reading, and at the same time teach adult silent reading patterns. I began to use a technique I call RRI–Rapid Retrieval of Information. The underlying principle is not a new idea. RRI focuses on the strategy of oral rereading to answer a question, prove a point, or provide an example from the text after silent reading.

We know that reading aloud in the middle school should serve a purpose and should follow silent reading, not replace it. Reading aloud becomes a worthwhile activity in the intermediate and upper grades when it provides an alternative method for assessing comprehension of silent reading at various levels. For example, oral rereading can be used occasionally in lieu of answering the standard end-of-the-chapter questions. RRI works as such an alternative. What makes this strategy a little different is that it becomes almost a game.

I prepare a list of tasks that the students listen and respond to one by one. These tasks zero in on locating and reading aloud anything from one word to several paragraphs from the assigned text. Students first silently read the text in class right before the RRI activity begins. When they have completed the silent reading, we begin the RRI phase of the lesson. I present the tasks orally one by one; each task is repeated as often as necessary. Students listen to each task, decide on the part(s) of the text they need to locate, and then read aloud to the whole class. All this is done fairly rapidly to keep the rhythm of the activity going, although the emphasis is certainly on thinking and accuracy.

Reprinted From the *Journal of Adolescent & Adult Literacy*, *41*(4), 306–307, December 1997/January 1998.

The tasks I present involve more than simple literal recall and subsequent location of the information in the text. After listening to each task, students first need to use higher level thinking skills to decide what information they want to retrieve; they use critical thinking strategies such as drawing inferences, evaluating, and analyzing, as well as knowledge of synonyms, antonyms, and parts of speech. Next, they skim the already-familiar text to find the words or paragraphs they will read aloud to complete the task. If the text being used for the lesson is longer than one page, I usually inform the students which specific page we will focus on for any particular RRI task.

I always begin each RRI activity by calling on volunteers, but as we warm up and move through several tasks, I encourage participation of all students by calling on nonvolunteers as well. My goal is for all students to try to do all tasks, and for each student to be called on at least once during the activity. With the importance of higher level thinking skills today, students need to think critically as much as possible in a natural way in all subject area classrooms.

Although I find the oral presentation of tasks most effective because it encourages the development of listening skills and produces a high level of concentration in the room, I have on occasion presented RRI tasks in writing, after students have completed a silent reading assignment. I have asked them individually or in pairs to write out their responses. Later they read these responses aloud. This becomes a very different kind of activity: It is productive and effective, but not nearly as motivating or spontaneous as the oral RRI.

Recently I used the RRI technique with my seventh-grade students, who had silently read a selection on slavery in the original U.S. colonies. To respond to the following tasks, the students needed to use higher level think-ing strategies. By appropriately choosing and then reading aloud the substantiating words, phrases, or passages, many students clearly demonstrated that they had successfully employed the critical thinking process. No further analysis or explanation of their read-aloud choices took place at this point. However, if it was apparent to the class and to me that a response was not on target, we stopped to discuss it and elicit new responses. Here are some examples of RRI tasks I used for this lesson.

- Read aloud one slave law that seems to be harsher than the others.
- Find proof that even attempted suicide wasn't the answer to escaping slavery.
- Read aloud as much as you need to prove your point.
- Read aloud any paragraphs that support the idea that slavery in Africa was different from slavery in the New World.
- Read aloud at least two paragraphs that suggest that younger slaves were treated far better than older ones.
- Find a phrase of four words from the text that can be substituted for the word *indentured*.
- Read aloud the one law that would discourage a slave from even attempting to become Christian.
- Read aloud a section of this text that you feel gives the overall summary of the whole text.
- Read aloud any parts of the text that suggest that more severe slave laws might be added to the original ones.
- Read aloud four sentences that sound more hopeful than the others.

The combination of using higher level thinking skills, scanning information, and reading aloud highly motivates most of my students. Careful preparation of tasks dramatically improves the quality of the procedure. There is an exciting atmosphere in the room. The students are actively engaged in content area reading, which is by far their least favorite kind of reading. Completion of tasks may be timed to add a competitive component to the lesson. Students now have a purpose for reading silently, which seems to replace, at least for a while, their desire for oral round-robin reading.

As a bonus, this whole procedure becomes an additional informal diagnostic tool for the classroom teacher or reading teacher. In addition to assessing the various comprehension skills, the oral reading becomes a good vehicle for evaluating decoding skills, fluency, and the ability to skim and scan information. The final result is that the students feel they have accomplished something, and so do I. We seem to have hit upon a happy compromise.

Janis M. Harmon

Vocabulary Teaching and Learning in a Seventh-Grade Literature-Based Classroom

Vocabulary is an important area of concern for teachers, because children who know many words are more likely to be competent readers than those with limited vocabularies. As children approach the middle grades and become more proficient in decoding and recognizing known words, vocabulary acquisition focuses more on meaning than recognition (Chall, 1987). From then on, children learn new words for known concepts and new words for new concepts in various content areas and in more sophisticated literature books. The need for a rich vocabulary base becomes even more important during the ensuing middle and secondary school years.

Word learning is a complex task that occurs in many settings. These settings range from incidental occurrences in oral and written contexts to direct instruction. Nagy and Anderson (1984) estimated that the average student in the middle grades and beyond must acquire approximately 3,000 new words yearly in order to stay current with each succeeding grade level. As a result, many vocabulary experts assert that learning from context plays a significant part in the student's yearly acquisition of such a large volume of words. Incidental word learning from oral and written contexts seems to occur incrementally over a long period of time with multiple exposures to words (Jenkins, Stein, & Wysocki, 1984; Nagy, 1988; Nagy,

Anderson, & Herman, 1987; Nagy, Herman, & Anderson, 1985).

Direct instruction is also an important aspect of vocabulary acquisition. Studies have shown that direct instruction informs reading comprehension when children can integrate new words with other conceptual knowledge, are exposed to multiple encounters with the new word in natural print environments, and can process the new word in a meaningful manner (Beck & McKeown, 1991; Beck, McKeown, & Omanson, 1987; Nagy, 1988; Stahl & Fairbanks, 1986).

Because many curricular frameworks emphasize a literature-based approach for language instruction, questions arise as to how such programs facilitate vocabulary development. What components in a literature-based program foster vocabulary growth? How are these components implemented? How do teacher beliefs and perspectives about vocabulary influence the word learning opportunities in this type of reading program?

As a way to answer these questions, I studied the literature-based program of one seventh-grade teacher, with a focus on vocabulary teaching and learning. In this article, I will explain the shared components of vocabulary development and literature-based programs and then describe different word learning opportunities that emerged in this program.

174

Reprinted From the *Journal of Adolescent & Adult Literacy*, *41*(7), 518–529, April 1998.

Shared Components of Vocabulary Development and Literature-Based Programs

Literature-based programs use trade books as major instructional materials for enhancing reading development (Hiebert & Colt, 1989; Scharer, 1992; Zarrillo, 1989). Differing interpretations have created some "diversity among teachers' philosophical stances" (Zarrillo, 1989, p. 23) as well as variation in the degree to which specific components and patterns of literature-based instruction are emphasized (Hiebert & Colt, 1989). Nevertheless, the following characteristics consistently appear in different studies as descriptors for literature-based classrooms (Eeds & Wells, 1989; Hiebert & Colt, 1989; Huck, 1992; Huck, Hepler, & Hickman, 1993; McGee, 1992; Peterson & Eeds, 1990):

- Use of trade books as the primary material source
- Student response to literature in diversified ways
- Individualized reading time with self-pacing and self-selection of literature
- In-depth discussion groups
- Read-alouds
- Group projects
- Informal assessment/conferences
- Teacher-student interaction–whole class, group, and individual
- Direct instruction of strategies
- Literacy for authentic reasons

Important overlapping issues indicate how well these literature-based reading programs can inform vocabulary development. Three major components are described as (a) instruction or learning episodes that expand knowledge schemas, (b) social interactions and interventions, and (c) wide reading (see Table 1).

Learning episodes include those activities involving direct instruction of reading strategies, specifically independent word learning strategies for vocabulary development. Other situations arise in authentic, purposeful reading that call for direct instruction of specific word meanings. As students respond to literature in diverse ways, they should also develop awareness and appreciation for learning new words and for eventually using them in oral and written discourse across a variety of learning tasks. In this way we enhance procedural knowledge by teaching independent word learning strategies, declarative knowledge by emphasizing specific word meanings, and conditional knowledge by cultivating an awareness of and appreciation for learning new words (Paris, Lipson, & Wixson, 1994).

The second component stresses the importance of social interactions and interventions in the classroom community. Grand conversations (Peterson & Eeds, 1990) about shared readings of literature can include rich discussions about new words that students select themselves. Group projects enable students to work collaboratively in exploring their responses to the literature and in satisfying their curiosity about unfamiliar words. Furthermore, informal assessment procedures can also facilitate teacher interventions in helping individual students learn about new words.

Wide reading is repeatedly included as one important quality of effective vocabulary instruction (Blachowicz & Lee, 1991; Nagy, 1988) and is discussed in reports on literature-based programs (Galda, 1988). We know that time spent engaged in independent reading can have positive effects upon children's reading proficiency. It promotes incidental learning of words through written contexts and provides meaningful practice for acquiring higher levels of word mastery in diverse settings. This active engagement with words also enhances lexical access and automaticity.

Table 1
Parallel and shared components of vocabulary development and literature-based reading programs

Vocabulary development	Literature-based programs
Learning episodes/instruction expanding knowledge schemas	
Direct instruction of independent word learning strategies	Direct instruction of strategies
Direct instruction of specific word meanings	Literacy for authentic reasons
Cultivation of an awareness, appreciation, and understanding for learning new words and using them in oral and written discourse	Student response to literature in diverse ways
Social interactions and interventions	
Rich discussions about new words	In-depth discussion groups (Grand Conversations)
Informal assessment and teacher intervention	Informal assessment
Teacher-student interactions fostering responses about important words	Teacher-student interactions—whole class, group, individual
Group projects	Group projects
Wide reading	
Promotion of incidental learning of words	Use of trade books as the primary material source
Practice for acquiring higher levels of word mastery in diverse settings (active engagement with words)	Independent reading time with self-pacing and self-selection
Promotion of lexical access (automaticity)	Read-alouds

What we know about word meaning acquisition through direct instruction and incidental learning from context can inform the types of reading programs we offer middle school learners. It appears that these overlapping issues of learning episodes, the social climate of the classroom, and wide reading of literature hold important implications for how literature-based reading programs are fruitful grounds for promoting vocabulary development.

Purpose and Description of the Study

This article describes a study that explored vocabulary learning opportunities in a seventh-grade literature-based reading program. The purpose of the study was to closely examine the explicit and implicit actions of the teacher as well as student responses to vocabulary teaching and learning events. This report provides information concerning word learning engagements embedded within a literature-based framework and how these opportunities paralleled the shared components.

I conducted the study at Katherine Stinson Middle School in San Antonio, Texas, USA. The principal, Debbie Sonnen, recommended one teacher, Denise Staton, because of her talent and excellent reputation in teaching reading. After Denise agreed to participate, I observed her and her students during every class meeting for approximately 6 months, from August until the end of February. My role as an investigator can be described as passive participant or complete observer, as I maintained an unobtrusive stance during my visits (Bogdan & Biklen, 1992). This stance was important because I wanted to observe explicit as well as implicit messages about vocabulary that may have been part of the classroom discourse. As this was a qualitative study, data collection occurred across multiple sources. Through interviews, prolonged observations, and taped transcriptions of classroom interactions, guiding questions and responses produced important information concerning vocabulary teaching and learning (Bogdan & Biklen, 1992; Patton, 1990).

Teacher Beliefs About Reading and Vocabulary

Denise described her reading program as literature-based because trade books were the "textbooks of the program." She believed in allowing students time to read self-selected books at their own pace and for their own enjoyment. Her program emphasized the pleasure and satisfaction gained from reading. Denise's major focus for her program was critical thinking and problem solving, with little emphasis on segmented skills-based activities. She expressed her view about reading and the use of literature in the following manner:

> All of our work comes out of the literature—the vocabulary, the study skills, the research—everything has its origin in whatever books the students are reading. To me that's what a literature-based approach means. We don't use a basal reader and we don't do drills and study sheets. Our approach is broad where we are looking more at the thinking skills of the students. We really want them to look at what happens when they are reading; we want them

to think about their own thinking. We want to find out what is going on in their minds, and we cannot do that with true-false statements and multiple-choice questions.

Denise's beliefs about vocabulary teaching and learning were situated within the broader purpose of promoting critical reading and reasoning. She felt that vocabulary was important even though it was not a major aspect of her reading program. She believed that students could not increase their vocabulary effectively from contrived lists of unrelated words. Rather, she asserted that words are more readily learned when students make connections to related ideas and other words. She also advocated the use of an individualized approach where students find words to study from their personal readings.

The Reading Program

Major components of Denise's program were Sustained Silent Reading (SSR) in which students read self-selected trade books, specific activities with teacher-selected readings and discussions that focused on critical thinking, book discussion groups, and integrated instructional episodes addressing literary elements and related writing events. Classes met three times a week for 75 minutes per session. SSR lasted for approximately 20–30 minutes during each class meeting. The rest of the class time was devoted to the other literacy activities. Embedded within each program component were word learning opportunities as illustrated in Table 2.

These levels included whole-class teacher-directed lessons, student-directed group sessions in which one group member served as a "vocabulary enricher" (Daniels, 1994), and opportunities for word learning during independent reading with self-selected books. During whole-class sessions, Denise selected

Table 2
Reading program

Components of the program	Word learning opportunities
Whole-class activities	**Whole-class activities**
Teacher-directed lessons	Social interactions between teacher and students to promote word knowledge acquisition
Teacher-selected short stories, excerpts, and poems related to a common theme	Text clarification
Integrated instructional episodes addressing literary elements and related writing events	Exposure to implicit modeling of ways to define words
	Opportunities to use words in speaking and writing events
Group activities	**Group activities**
Student-directed group sessions	Mobilization of independent word learning strategies
Self-selected books from a required list	Self-generated meaning constructions
	Shared meaning constructions
	Exposure to peer-selected words in expressive and receptive language
	Active word learning opportunities
Independent reading	**Independent reading**
Sustained Silent Reading	Mobilization of independent word learning strategies
Self-selected readings	Self-generated meaning constructions
	Active word learning opportunities

words from short stories to discuss as a pre-reading activity. With the book discussion groups, learners who served as "vocabulary enrichers" were responsible for selecting words to discuss in their groups. These reflections about new words were springboards for critical discussions about important concepts and literary elements in the readings.

Outcomes of vocabulary learning during teacher-directed instructional episodes focused on text clarification and exposure to teacher-selected words that were central to the story. When students engaged in more learner-centered activities, such as book discussion groups and independent reading, learning behaviors and outcomes shifted. In group sessions where students participated as vocabulary enrichers and group members, learning outcomes resulted in the mobilization of independent word learning strategies, self-generated and shared meaning constructions, and exposure to peer-selected words.

Students had a vested interest in their own learning and that of the group, because they were responsible for creating specific opportunities to learn new concepts and ideas. Independent reading during Sustained Silent Reading provided another word learning opportunity for them. Learning outcomes during this time included the mobilization of independent word learning strategies and opportunities for active word learning through incidental encounters with unfamiliar words.

Whole-Class Instructional Episodes

Teacher actions. Vocabulary instructional episodes were embedded within class discussions about stories. Denise's actions became major components in the process of vocabulary teaching and learning. During teacher-directed discussions, she related, explained, and questioned students about specific terminology. Students, in turn, reacted by activating their prior knowledge and past experiences, by making connections, and by asking questions about targeted words and related concepts. Outcomes in terms of vocabulary learning and meaning construction pivoted around the teacher's personal store of words, her beliefs about vocabulary instruction and acquisition, and her responses to students' inherent curiosity about words. She was a major vocabulary source and stimulus for students.

During these instructional episodes with vocabulary, Denise consistently tried to establish common references and links to what students knew. She sometimes generalized actions on a personal level to help students identify with new ideas. She also guided students back to the context in which the words were used. She would even tell students when context was not helpful in figuring out meanings, such as with the word restitution used in this sentence: "He specializes in requiring public acts of contrition and *restitution*." Denise related the word to something students would understand by stating, "*Restitution* is repayment. For example, if you steal something from someone and you have to make *restitution*, what would you have to do?" Such statements blended the use of synonyms and familiar scenarios to help learners understand the meaning of the word.

Denise used a variety of techniques to clarify word meanings through explanation. These techniques included the use of synonyms, brief descriptions, examples and nonexamples, rephrasing, repetition, associations, and unique expressions. Similar to direct questioning, these loosely woven categories represented Denise's way of clarifying terms that were central to the targeted readings.

Because Denise preferred to let students fashion their own definitions of words instead of using what they found in dictionaries, she frequently modeled definitions by using synonyms. Every vocabulary instructional episode contained examples of synonyms. Some included "compete" for *contend*, "winding and twisting" for *sinuous*, and "urges" for *exhorts*. She also explained word meanings with short, descriptive phrases, such as "army camp supplies" for *commissary stores* and "a machine in human form" for *android*. With each short definition, however, Denise elaborated, extended, and clarified meanings to make sure students had ample opportunity to make connections with the words. When words confused students, Denise offered important examples to describe meanings, as in the following excerpt:

> Have you ever seen an elderly person who has arthritis and their hands are all twisted? That's *gnarled*. Or have you ever seen a tree trunk that the trunk itself is twisted? That's *gnarled*.

When Denise used a certain word in her explanations, she often followed with an elaboration for the benefit of those who were uncertain of the word's meaning. Because of the frequent use of this technique, rephrasing was an intrinsic component of Denise's perceptions of how to explain concepts to students. The following decontextualized excerpts illustrate Denise's use of rephrasing.

> Let's start recounting the events of the story. *We will tell about the beginning, middle, and end.*
> This is an *excerpt—one tiny piece.*

In extended class discussions, Denise repeated general utility words frequently. Whether done purposefully or incidentally, such repetitions served to help students internalize word meanings. Denise also clarified word meanings through associations instead of definitions. In reference to the word *contend*, she asked students if they ever *contended in athletic events, academic events, and even poker games*. For the word *humble*, she asked the question: "If you have a *humble* home, is it like a castle?"

These teacher-directed discussions about words were a natural part of the classroom dialogue about the selected readings and occurred frequently as prereading activities. Apparently, Denise's beliefs concerning the importance of word knowledge in enhancing comprehension informed her decision to pursue these discussions. The ways in which she framed her questions and used familiar situations to help learners make connections proved essential in making this a worthwhile learning engagement. While focusing on specific word meanings, she also inadvertently modeled specific ways to define words. Students, in turn, used these methods to explain word meanings during other classroom episodes.

Student engagement. Because learners took their cues from the teacher, their responses were directly influenced by class discussions of required readings and specific writing assignments. A close examination of student responses during these episodes revealed several cognitive processes in use. Overall, they demonstrated engagement in activating prior knowledge when they used words recently discussed in class. They made connections by defining terms in their own words, using examples to define words, relating words to other languages, and engaging in word play. Furthermore, students asked questions about certain words when they were confused about the meaning. They used words mentioned in previous class events, unsolicited words described as general utility words used by mature language users, domain-specific words, and school-related words.

One segment of the program was a unit on heroes that lasted for 12 weeks. The six short stories selected by Denise depicted heroes from different cultures. Denise deliberately chose these stories so that students could reflect upon different perspectives about heroism. The focal point of this unit was a hero characteristics chart, which emerged from class discussions about each hero. Descriptive words listed on the chart were continually referred to in discussions across all six required readings. Furthermore, each successive reading of a story brought forth more words. Table 3 illustrates a segment of this chart.

As a result, students frequently used these words in both their talking and writing. Words such as *confidence*, *determination*, *self-reliance*, *achievement*, *loyalty*, and related derivations were used freely by students because they had been highlighted repeatedly across all hero stories. This repetition and continual referral to all descriptors on the heroes chart offered students rich opportunities through multiple exposures to use the terms in meaningful and functional ways. In addition, students had to think critically about what these words meant in different situations. For example, in a discussion about Harriet Tubman, one student rationalized that she was intelligent but not in the sense of "like school," but rather that she "was intelligent because she knew which way to go."

The use of these terms extended into their writing. At the end of the unit, they wrote an essay describing a personal hero. The following excerpts are representative samples of how students used descriptive words previously discussed in class.

> I think a hero is someone who's caring and also shows leadership in whatever he or she tries to conquer. A hero is also *persistent* in his or her task. Some of the characteristics that I value in a hero is the leadership and skill that a hero shows. I also value the *persistency* or the refusing to give up until he or she conquers the task. (David)

Table 3
Hero characteristics chart

Traits	Yudhisthir	Siegfried	Scarface	Luke Skywalker	Harriet Tubman	Judge
Skillful	x	x	x		x	
Intelligent	x	x			x	x
Physically strong	x	x	x	x	x	
Mentally strong	x	x			x	
Brave					x	
Loyal			x	x		
Confident				x		
Determined	x	x	x	x	x	x
Respectful		x	x		x	x
Persistent					x	
Honorable						x
Responsible						x
Patient						x
Good judgment						x
Positive						x
Open mind						x

Harriet Tubman was a very smart person. She was very skillful. She was not always *obedient* to others. What makes her so *admirable* is that she led so many people out of slavery. She is strong, loyal, and *confident*. (Amy)

My hero is my dad. Both his parents were dead when he was 17 so he had to learn *self-reliance* and *responsibility* at a very young age. My dad and the heroes share other character traits such as *honesty*, *confidence*, and *dedication* and the ability to stay cool under pressure. There would be no *inspirations* and no dreams without heroes. (Mary Ann)

Students experienced multiple exposures of words describing heroes. The use of these terms in their writing appeared to be a natural progression from previous opportunities to listen, speak, and read about words that described different people from different cultures. This integrated approach enhanced and reinforced students' word knowledge.

During an instructional episode with "The Pledge of Allegiance," a discussion about the meaning of the word *justice* enabled students to make interesting connections.

Teacher:	All right, boys and girls. Steven wants to talk about *justice*.
Steven:	It's laws.
Heath:	*Justice* is like what you deserve. If somebody kills another person, then they deserve to pay the penalty for it. If like somebody hurts you, then you know they should pay the consequences.
Joanie:	It's like fairness for everybody. So everybody will have equal rights.
Teacher:	Fairness for everybody. At school through all the years I've been teaching, I've had students say that some teachers are not fair. I try to be fair but what does *fair* mean? Steven?
Steven:	Like equal, the same thing.
Teacher:	Can you treat every person exactly the same?

Whole class:	No.
Chad:	I think *justice* is in the eye of the beholder.
Teacher:	I know what you're saying. The person who is making the judgment and saying whether it's fair or unfair, it's in their eyes. Janine?
Janine:	I was going to say what you were saying about fair and equal being the same thing. But it wouldn't be really fair if like somebody who murders somebody got the exact same punishment as somebody who stole a piece of gum.
Teacher:	Okay. So should the punishment fit the crime?
Whole Class:	Yes.
Teacher:	Someone this morning said that in some countries the penalty for theft is to cut your hand off. They used to do that a long time ago.
Heath:	They still do in Iran and Iraq.
Teacher:	Where did you hear that?
Heath:	Because my uncle was in Desert Storm and he went to Saudi Arabia and he told us that's true.
Teacher:	That's pretty severe punishment, but will it keep them from stealing again? In our country that's cruel and unusual punishment. Jill?
Jill:	In social studies last year, like in the early years...[pause]
Teacher:	Medieval times?
Jill:	Yes. The punishment would be exactly what you did to them. Like if you killed a person, then you get killed.

This excerpt illustrates how students made important connections about the concept of *justice* in terms of what they already knew about fairness and equality for all. They tapped into schemas about universal sayings ("eye for an eye"), stories from relatives, and lessons from past history classes. They used their knowledge to contribute to the group effort of exploring the meaning of *justice*. Resulting social interactions among the teacher and students provided fertile ground for the enhancement of word learning through relevant and meaningful connections with prior knowledge and past experiences.

When students mobilized their conceptual knowledge and accompanying vocabulary about certain topics, they sometimes made inaccurate connections. For instance, Michael always thought that the Underground Railroad was the forerunner of today's *subway*. Quite often, however, their connections showed originality and insights. For example, Stephanie made connections to another language when she stated that *Negro* meant black in Spanish.

As they activated, connected, and questioned vocabulary during the course of class discussions, students also experienced those serendipitous moments when they played with words. One student caught the attention of others when he used the word *wiseness* instead of wisdom. Subsequent chuckles and smiles indicated that students appreciated and liked this word. These episodes heightened their attention and promoted inquiry about new words.

Book Discussion Groups

As part of a 12-week multicultural unit, students became participants in specific book discussion groups with books including *Bearstone* by Will Hobbs (1989), *Children of the River* by Linda Crew (1991), *Dragonwings* by Lawrence Yep (1993), *Jemmy* by Jon Hassler (1988), and *Roll of Thunder, Hear My Cry* by Mildred D. Taylor (1976). Table 4

Table 4
Student engagement during book discussion groups

Student actions

Selected	**Activated**	**Related**
general utility words	background knowledge	sentence context
foreign words	prior knowledge	passage context
proper names		real-life experiences
domain-specific words		multiple sources
		multiple attempts

Modeled	**Explained**	**Questioned**
teacher actions	dictionary definitions	themselves
independent word-	synonyms	other students
learning strategies	brief phrases	

outlines student engagement in these book discussion groups.

Denise used the idea of literature circles as described by Daniels (1994). She defined and discussed the roles of discussion director, literary luminary, connector, summarizer, vocabulary enricher, and process checker. The vocabulary enricher was responsible for selecting interesting or unfamiliar words in the readings and for conducting group discussions about these words. Once again, vocabulary was only one aspect of this activity, as learners engaged in discussing literary elements, making personal connections, and summarizing important events.

The following actions represent a variety of tactics students employed based upon their own interpretation of the role of vocabulary enricher:

- Some vocabulary enrichers defined words before the group sessions by using their own knowledge or by referring to the dictionary.
- Some vocabulary enrichers relied on the group to provide the definitions.
- Several vocabulary enrichers read their definitions to the group.
- A few vocabulary enrichers explained the words to the group.

- Some vocabulary enrichers either read aloud the passage containing the targeted words or asked other group members to read.

Students equated this role of vocabulary enricher in ways that parallel teacher actions. They targeted, defined, read, and explained words to the group. They even questioned the group's background knowledge about the words. For example, one student prepared herself for the group session by consulting a dictionary for meanings of her targeted words. During group discussion time, she presented each word by reading the sentence. Then she asked if anyone wanted to comment about the word. After listening to these comments, she read her definition. These actions were evident when the group discussed the word *expounding* in the following passage from *Roll of Thunder, Hear My Cry*:

> "See, fellows, there's a system to getting out of work," T.J. was *expounding* as I sat down.
> "Jus' don't be 'round when it's got to be done. See, you should do like me." (p. 72)

Lynette, the vocabulary enricher, pronounced the word *expounding* and then read the sentence to the group. This discussion followed:

Lynette:	Okay. Do y'all like have any guesses to what it means?
Sam:	Wait. Where is it again?
Janelle:	I'll guess what it means.
Jill:	Well, what is it?
Janelle:	His ego is boasting and he knows exactly how to get out of working.
Lynette:	Well, the definition I found was he did it with explaining. That's the definition I found. It says "state, interpret, or explain." So I thought explain was like the best one.

Discussions about other words followed this same pattern. Lynette was prepared with definitions and took the time to clarify these meanings in reference to the text. Members of this group were willing to take risks in constructing word meanings and sharing these constructions with the group. The ways in which words were described were similar to the way Denise defined words. Students used synonyms and brief phrases based upon dictionary definitions.

In other sessions, vocabulary enrichers found words but did not search for meanings. Rather, they chose to rely on group members to generate word meanings. In these episodes, some definitions remained at a general level of description. Examples include the word *Ute* defined as "an Indian group" and the word *irrigate* as "water your crops." Group members were satisfied with these general meanings and did not engage in any further discussion.

In general, vocabulary enrichers relied on the dictionary as well as their peers as sources of word knowledge. Some students adopted a "teacher" stance as they provided information to their groups. Others simply provided words and depended upon group members for definitions. As group members, students followed the lead of the vocabulary enricher in terms of the amount of discussion that emerged. When the vocabulary enricher asked for comments, students offered their ideas about targeted words as they interpreted and clarified points for others. When they interacted with one another, students generated word meanings in the form of synonyms, brief phrases, and examples. Again, these definitions were similar to the teacher's way of explaining words.

When Marian was vocabulary enricher, she initially shared her meaning of a word and then asked others to share their interpretations. For example, for the word *housemother* from *Bearstone* by Will Hobbs, the group members elicited descriptions, such as "a director like the main person in orphanages," "a matron," "a foster mother," and "a person in charge of a group home." As sources of knowledge, students used their own background knowledge about *housemother* to express these meanings. As a result, the various configurations for the word reinforced and expanded their own schemas. Furthermore, the social interaction among group members stimulated discussions that produced these variations in the meaning of the word.

On several occasions, students defined words in a syntactically correct fashion. For example, when Heath looked up *precipice* in the dictionary, he was quick to use a phrase from the definition as a substitute for the word. He told group members that the word meant "a very steep or overhanging place; a hazardous situation." Then he read the sentence containing *precipice* in the following manner:

> Cloyd put the smooth stone in his pocket and started back across the very steep overhanging place. (Hobbs, 1989, p. 16)

Group members agreed that the meaning fit the context of the sentence. This pattern of word meaning construction occurred across several book discussion groups.

On other occasions students used multiple sources and multiple attempts to construct word meanings that satisfied the group. For example, when Katherine served as vocabulary enricher, she targeted the word *erratically* in this passage:

> The saw didn't want to start. After dozens of attempts Cloyd made it idle *erratically*, but it cut out as soon as he tried the throttle. (Hobbs, 1989, p. 55)

Because the word was challenging to the group, students elicited several meaning attempts simultaneously. After David read the sentence, he used arm motions to demonstrate what he thought *erratically* meant, while Terry commented that it could mean "faster." Tom thought that it could mean "odd." Katherine then offered her dictionary definition of "deviating from what is ordinary or standard." With these four attempts, group members were satisfied that they understood what the word meant. They also talked about how some words, like *erratically*, were difficult to define, because it was hard to articulate a clear meaning without using examples or physical motions.

Overall, students worked collaboratively in these group sessions to construct word meanings when the vocabulary enricher assumed a role of group facilitator rather than "teacher director." They shared their opinions and interpretations of words and listened to the ideas of others. By focusing on these student-targeted words, they had the opportunity to engage in authentic word learning experiences where they modeled their own personal strategies for their peers. Denise's role during these book discussion groups was that of facilitator. She visited each group, offering clarification when needed, informally assessing student actions, and monitoring group progress.

Independent Reading

Sustained Silent Reading presented opportunities for students to learn new words. This context enabled them to self-select texts and to engage in personal reading for at least 20–30 minutes during each class session. As an avenue for word learning, independent reading time allowed learners to actively use their strategies as they encountered unfamiliar words. It also offered opportunities for multiple exposures to new words. Students also kept personal logs where they recorded information about new words they encountered during reading.

Insights About Vocabulary Teaching and Learning

As participants in a literature-based reading program, these students engaged in a variety of literacy tasks with a focus on critical reading and problem solving. Word learning opportunities were situated within this broad context and provided different engagements for the students. Denise emphasized knowledge of specific words in prereading discussions about stories. Students in turn used these words in subsequent writing assignments. Learners also benefited from activities where individual word learning strategies were highlighted. Specifically, students practiced these strategies in book discussion groups and in personal reading during Sustained Silent Reading.

Learners openly displayed their independent word learning strategies as they participated in book discussion groups. The roles of vocabulary enricher as well as group members served as ways for learners to use their word learning strategies to construct meaning and to contribute to group discussions. These social events enabled learners to actively engage in specific word learning and to observe the word learning strategies of their peers. The impact of Denise's instructional patterns was evident in how learners interpreted their role as vocabulary enricher. They emulated teacher approaches as they highlighted and defined new words for their groups. Members in the groups became actively involved in word meaning construction when the vocabulary enricher assumed a facilitative stance similar to Denise's actions during the multicultural unit.

Another aspect of vocabulary development in this literature-based reading program occurred in whole-class events, where students listened while the teacher talked about targeted words related to a required reading. Outcomes of these teacher-directed instructional episodes were attainment of specific word knowledge as well as exposure to implicit modeling of ways to define words. Conversely, the outcome of book discussion groups and independent reading, where students took a more active stance, was the enhancement of independent word learning strategies. These events resulted in opportunities where learners mobilized word learning strategies and constructed self-generated and shared meanings of unfamiliar words. In addition, they received exposure to the ideas and strategies of their peers, and, above all, a chance to develop a deeper awareness of individual word learning strategies. Related research (cited in Baumann & Kameenui, 1991; Beck et al., 1987) also indicates the value of active student engagement in word learning opportunities and the need to help learners develop a stronger awareness and appreciation of words. Thus, word learning episodes in this literature-based program promoted acquisition of word knowledge and activation of independent word learning strategies.

Although literature-based programs are defined and implemented in different ways by different teachers, the configuration of this program supported vocabulary teaching and learning both explicitly and implicitly. The program resembled Burke and Short's description of "curriculum as activity" (cited in Heald-Taylor, 1996). Within this paradigm, the teacher made decisions about selections and activities, students read the same texts during a large portion of the time, discussions promoted higher level thinking, and the teacher guided meaning construction. She pulled stories from anthologies for the whole class to read and also presented a list of novels from which students could select a book. Thus, students read self-selected books during Sustained Silent Reading, teacher-selected short stories for whole-class activities, and self-selected books from a required list for small book discussion groups.

In sum, the reading program and observed student engagement paralleled and supported current research in regard to vocabulary learning. Like many other middle school teachers, this teacher wrestled with formulating a program that bridged different paradigms of teaching and learning. Her actions vacillated between objectivist and constructivist stances as she conscientiously sought to provide an effective reading program for students. As a result, the program encompassed a variety of important teaching and learning events where the teacher offered clarification about new words and learners practiced their existing repertoire of independent word learning strategies. The teacher demonstrated how a literature-based program could inform vocabulary through overlapping components of instructional learning episodes, wide reading of student-selected and teacher-selected books, and social interaction in peer groups and whole-class settings. A balance in varying classroom configurations provided learning opportunities that promoted vocabulary development in different ways. These engagements both expanded word knowledge and enhanced word learning abilities, as learners engaged in meaningful literacy events.

Literature-based reading programs can be fruitful grounds for vocabulary teaching and learning at the middle school level. Although vocabulary was not a major focus in this program, students still engaged in activities that supported word learning while enhancing overall reading proficiency. For example, through rich discussions and responses about words describing heroes, this teacher actually highlighted critical reading and reasoning as learners analyzed character traits. Her major goal of promoting critical reading and problem solving was embedded within these contextualized encounters with words as learners used their knowledge to make sense of text. Thus, vocabulary teaching and learning was an important aspect of the literacy experiences in this literature-based program.

REFERENCES

Baumann, J.F., & Kameenui, E.J. (1991). Research on vocabulary instruction: Ode to Voltaire. In J. Flood, J.M. Jensen, D. Lapp, & J.R. Squire (Eds.), *Handbook on teaching the English language arts* (pp. 602-632). New York: Macmillan.

Beck, I., & McKeown, M.G. (1991). Conditions of vocabulary acquisition. In R. Barr, M.L. Kamil, P. Mosenthal, & P.D. Pearson (Eds.), *Handbook of reading research: Vol. II* (pp. 789-814). White Plains, NY: Longman.

Beck, I., McKeown, M.G., & Omanson, R.C. (1987). The effects and uses of diverse vocabulary instructional techniques. In M.G. McKeown & M.E. Curtis (Eds.), *The nature of vocabulary acquisition* (pp. 147-163). Hillsdale, NJ: Erlbaum.

Blachowicz, C., & Lee, J. (1991). Vocabulary development in the whole literacy classroom. *The Reading Teacher, 45*, 188-195.

Bogdan, R.C., & Biklen, S.K. (1992). *Qualitative research for education: An introduction to theory and methods* (2nd ed.). Boston: Allyn & Bacon.

Chall, J. (1987). Two vocabularies for reading: Recognition and meaning. In M.G. McKeown & M.E. Curtis (Eds.), *The nature of vocabulary acquisition* (pp. 7-17). Hillsdale, NJ: Erlbaum.

Crew, L. (1991). *Children of the river*. New York: Dell.

Daniels, H. (1994). *Literature circles: Voice and choice in the student-centered classroom*. York, ME: Stenhouse.

Eeds, M., & Wells, D. (1989). Grand conversations: An exploration of meaning construction in literature study groups. *Research in the Teaching of English, 23*(1), 4-29.

Galda, L. (1988). Readers, texts, contexts: A response-based view of literature in the classroom. *The New Advocate, 1*, 92-102.

Hassler, J. (1988). *Jemmy*. Westminster, MD: Fawcett.

Heald-Taylor, B.G. (1996). Three paradigms for literature instruction in Grades 3 to 6. *The Reading Teacher, 49*, 456-466.

Hiebert, E.H., & Colt, J. (1989). Patterns of literature-based reading instruction. *The Reading Teacher, 43*, 14-20.

Hobbs, W. (1989). *Bearstone*. New York: Atheneum.

Huck, C. (1992). Literacy and literature. *Language Arts, 69*, 520-526.

Huck, C., Hepler, S., & Hickman, J. (1993). *Children's literature in the elementary school* (5th ed.). Fort Worth, TX: Harcourt Brace.

Jenkins, J.R., Stein, M., & Wysocki, K. (1984). Learning vocabulary through reading. *Educational Research Journal, 21*, 767-787.

McGee, L.M. (1992). Focus on research: Exploring the literature-based reading revolution. *Language Arts, 69*, 529-537.

Nagy, W. (1988). *Teaching vocabulary to improve reading comprehension*. Urbana, IL: National Council of Teachers of English.

Nagy, W., & Anderson, R. (1984). How many words are there in printed school English? *Reading Research Quarterly, 19*, 303-330.

Nagy, W., Anderson, R., & Herman, P. (1987). Learning word meanings from context during normal reading. *American Educational Research Journal, 24*, 237-270.

Nagy, W., Herman, P., & Anderson, R. (1985). Learning words from context. *Reading Research Quarterly, 20*, 233-253.

Paris S., Lipson, M., & Wixson, K. (1994). Becoming a strategic reader. In R.B. Ruddell, M. Ruddell, & H. Singer (Eds.), *Theoretical models and processes of reading* (4th ed., pp. 788-810). Newark, DE: International Reading Association.

Patton, M.Q. (1990). *Qualitative evaluation and research methods* (2nd ed.). Newbury Park, CA: Sage.

Peterson, R., & Eeds, M. (1990). *Grand conversations: Literature groups in action*. New York: Scholastic.

Scharer, P. (1992). Teachers in transition: An exploration of changes in teachers and classrooms during implementation of literature-based reading instruction. *Research in the Teaching of English*, *26*, 408–445.

Stahl, S., & Fairbanks, M. (1986). The effects of vocabulary instruction: A model-based meta-analysis. *Review of Educational Research*, *56*, 721–810.

Taylor, M. (1976). *Roll of thunder, hear my cry*. New York: Dial.

Yep, L. (1993). *Dragonwings*. New York: Harper-Collins.

Zarrillo, J. (1989). Teachers' interpretations of literature-based reading. *The Reading Teacher*, *43*, 22–28.

Nancy K. Lewkowicz

On the Question of Teaching Decoding Skills to Older Students

Making a serious effort to teach word attack skills to older students who lack them has not been in fashion in recent years. While the relevance of word attack skills to reading in the primary grades is widely accepted (Anderson et al., 1985), the prevailing view toward upgrading such skills in students past the middle grades seems to be that the effort is impractical at best and perhaps even pernicious. Accordingly, research journals rarely offer reports on the decoding skills of students in the 7th–12th grades, and journals on teaching reading probably contain more admonitions against teaching decoding to this group than recommendations for better ways to do it.

In my judgment, this widespread anti-remedial-word-attack consensus is based on too narrow a view of the role of decoding in developing reading competence and on untested or un-thought-out assumptions about older students with decoding problems. This article will raise questions about some of these assumptions.

Six arguments against teaching word attack skills to older students, all of which I have encountered repeatedly either in print or at conferences on reading, are presented below. Following each are comments on its logic, farsightedness, or factual basis. It is my hope that these comments will motivate both researchers and teachers to reexamine the role of decoding skills in reading in the upper grades and beyond.

Perhaps it is not really necessary to preface a defense of decoding training with an avowal of my belief that reading is above all a meaning getting process and that comprehension training is an essential component of teaching reading. However, given "the false dichotomy between phonics and meaning that has dominated the field for so many years" (Anderson et al., 1985), it is probably prudent to emphasize at the start that I do view meaning as the reader's goal, and that I regard decoding skills as valuable chiefly because they can be an efficient route to that goal. With this orientation in mind, let us consider some of the common antidecoding arguments.

Questionable assumption 1: *"If a student has not mastered decoding skills by grade 8 (or grade X), s/he never will."*

This pessimistic attitude is extremely widespread, and is frequently rooted in discouraging personal experience. Some who voice it cite the incompetence or lack of motivation of students; others blame the inadequacy of traditional syllabication rules when applied to the polysyllabic vocabulary typical of content area reading. All of these complaints reduce to the same thing: The students can't make the rules work.

Reprinted From the *Journal of Reading*, *31*(1), 50–57, October 1987.

Figure 1
Relationships between reading skills implied by Assumption 2

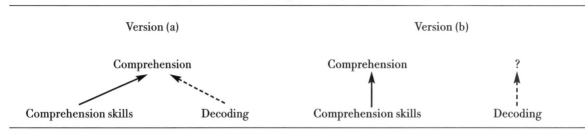

I agree that the traditional techniques for getting pronunciation via syllabication are of little value. But the problem is not, as is often assumed, the irregularity and unpredictability of English spelling. In fact, the pronunciation of most English polysyllables is highly predictable, as modern linguists have shown (Chomsky & Halle, 1968; Schane, 1979). Rather, the problem is that the traditional rules fail to take advantage of this predictability.

It is perfectly possible to create rules which do utilize this predictability and do enable students to achieve smooth, accurate pronunciations (Lewkowicz, 1985). Now that these radically different techniques are available, older assumptions about the incapacity of disabled readers to acquire effective decoding skills must be reconsidered.

Questionable assumption 2: *"Besides the relatively few students with decoding difficulties, remedial classes are full of students who can sound out words effectively but can't comprehend what they read. Remediating word attack problems will merely move students from the former group into the latter; they will still have comprehension problems, so teaching decoding is a waste of time and effort."*

This argument is the upper grades version of the false dichotomy mentioned above. It treats decoding either as (a) an alternative, less effective route to comprehension or (b) as an irrelevancy.

The relationship between skills implied by this argument can be diagrammed as in Figure 1. (The arrows mean something like "makes a contribution toward.")

I consider the view of relationships between reading skills that is represented in Figure 1 to be seriously distorted and untenable. A far more plausible view of these relationships, in my opinion, is shown in Figure 2. Perhaps the most important clarification provided by Figure 2 is that *decoding is a comprehension skill*, which contributes to comprehension not only at the word level, but also at the sentence, paragraph, and whole-text levels.

There is no need to elaborate here on the relationships shown in Figure 2 between word comprehension and "higher level" comprehension skills. Abundant testimony to the importance of word knowledge in text comprehension can be found in the *Journal of Reading*'s April 1986 issue on vocabulary, which includes this blunt summation of research findings: "Vocabulary knowledge *is* critical to comprehension. If you don't know the words, you're not going to understand the passage" (Johnson & Johnson, 1986, p. 624, quoting from Johnson, Toms-Bronowski, & Buss, 1983). But the relationships in the other direction, between word comprehension and its component subskills, particularly decoding, are more complex than Figure 2 might suggest and require further comment. In particular, it should be emphasized that decoding,

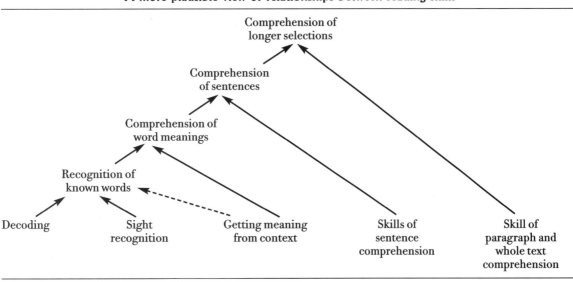

for the not-yet-skilled reader, can contribute to word and text comprehension not only in a direct and immediate fashion, but also in a couple of indirect and long-range ways.

The direct contribution of decoding skill is that it enables students to recognize words that are in their oral vocabulary but not yet a part of sight vocabulary. Just as vocabulary knowledge is critical to comprehension, so word recognition is critical to accessing vocabulary meaning, and decoding can be critical to word recognition in the absence of sight recognition. Decoding can also, of course, be used in tandem with shaky sight recognition or word recognition.

But when we shift focus from the ongoing reading process to reading acquisition and improvement, at least two other contributions of decoding skill to word and text comprehension become apparent. One relates to use of the context in vocabulary building, and will be described under Assumption 3. The other long term contribution involves the elevation of words to sight word status, and works as follows.

Sight recognition, though depicted in Figure 2 as one of a triad of word recognition skills, might better be regarded as a type of prior knowledge. (Prior knowledge, a key factor in comprehension, was for the most part excluded from the above diagrams of relations between skills.) That is, sight recognition is really not so much a technique that one applies as it is an association "already there" or an event that "just happens" because of a history of previous encounters with a word.

Aside from the handful of words directly taught by teachers, every sight word was once *not* a sight word; at least once its identity had to be figured out through some combination of decoding and context skills. Probably on several subsequent encounters decoding plus context use facilitated increasingly rapid recognition, as the word gradually developed sight word status. Thus development of an adequate sight vocabulary, permitting rapid access to the word meanings important to higher levels of comprehension, is greatly facilitated by adequate decoding.

In short, improving decoding skills and improving "comprehension" skills should not be regarded as competing approaches. Comprehension will suffer if the student lacks either decoding skills or techniques for seeing how the author's ideas are related. Thus, remediation should be provided for either deficiency and for both if necessary. The fact that most older students do *not* have decoding problems does not mean that decoding training is not an essential part of an effective program for those who do have such problems.

Questionable assumption 3: *"Decoding ability is no longer very important after the middle grades, because there is an increasing load of unfamiliar vocabulary, especially in content area reading. Thus it is better to emphasize getting meaning from the context rather than decoding."*

Here we need to separate the well grounded claims from the shaky ones. Deriving meaning from context is clearly an important strategy for ongoing comprehension, and also for vocabulary building (Nagy, Herman, & Anderson, 1985), and should be cultivated to the fullest extent. But use of context should not be regarded as a substitute for decoding skills at any age. Even with well developed context skills and passages containing much new vocabulary, decoding remains important.

To begin with, words in the text that are in the student's vocabulary but are not recognized at sight may be important both in their own right and as part of the context that explains new vocabulary. Nor can context be trusted to supply the meaning of these known but unrecognized words, since "many, probably most, contexts in normal text give little information about word meanings" (Nagy et al., 1985, p. 235).

Secondly, with regard to new words which are not in the student's oral vocabulary, I think a strong case can be made that students benefit from being able to assign a pronunciation even when the meaning of the word must be sought through other strategies. The student has two goals in such encounters: to grasp the meaning of the passage at hand but also to build vocabulary to aid future comprehension. And without successful application of decoding skills, little vocabulary growth is likely to take place, for two reasons.

First, any reader who can't recognize many of the words s/he has known for a long time is obviously going to have at least equal difficulty recognizing recent vocabulary, no matter how clearly the meaning was understood on first encounter. And, without repeated recognition of the new word in subsequent reading, there will be little opportunity for rehearsal and strengthening of associations of form and meaning.

In addition (and this is the third important contribution of decoding to comprehension), the fact that meaning is often not completely clear on first encounter puts the decoding disabled student at a special disadvantage, even if s/he is sensitive to context clues. According to Deighton (1959), "vocabulary growth through context revelation is a gradual matter...of building meaning into a word over a period of years" (p. 3). Similarly, Nagy et al. (1985) propose that while "incidental learning from context is the major mode of vocabulary acquisition during the school years" (p. 234), "incidental learning from context proceeds in terms of small increments" (p. 236).

If these authors are correct, then a prerequisite for vocabulary growth is that students realize on each encounter that they are dealing with the same word, and that they not misidentify it as some more familiar word. For example, they should be able to say "Oh, there's that word 'original' again—now, what did it mean?" Otherwise they may never build up a clear idea of what *original* means. And they must not assume from its first two letters and its length that *original* is *ordinary*, or they may never discover that there *is* a word *original*.

Questionable assumption 4: *"It's not important for students to pronounce a word correctly as long as they know its meaning when they see it in print."*

This argument overlooks the fact that correct pronunciation can be critical to recognition of nonsight words which are already in oral vocabulary. Nevertheless, an element of common experience in this argument can make it seem convincing. It is perfectly true that one can go on mentally mispronouncing a particular word for years, and still have it a functioning part of one's print vocabulary. And such mispronunciations do not constitute a reading problem.

However, for an individual with serious word attack problems, it is not simply a matter of incorrect pronunciations. It is more likely a case of no pronunciation at all, or assigning the pronunciation of a known word to a new word, or assigning a different pronunciation on each encounter. In all of these cases, the student fails to create a *consistent* phonological form for the word, to serve as one element of a three-way association between pronunciation, graphic form, and meaning. And this *does* constitute a reading problem, because it hinders vocabulary acquisition.

One of the things that competent decoders are able to do is to assign a phonological form to an unfamiliar word, store this name for the word in memory along with whatever meaning has been garnered, and then reconstruct the same phonological form on next exposure to the word, thereby activating the stored pronunciation/meaning association. This process does not necessarily require correct pronunciation, but it does require consistent pronunciation, which is something that the decoding disabled student cannot supply.

At this point some readers may be inclined to ask whether a phonological component is really essential to the vocabulary acquisition process. Are not two-way associations between print and meaning sufficient? Can't the reader just attach meanings to strings of letters, like *ordinary* and *original*, as if they were written 96487265 and 96818723, or %&($?¢&# and %&$)$?¢@, without assigning any phonological values?

Whether anybody can build an extensive vocabulary this way is an intriguing question for which no definitive answers are available. (Note this is not the same question as whether mature readers habitually go directly from print to meaning when reading familiar vocabulary.) But clearly such a method does not work for decoding disabled students. Their problem is not merely inability to pronounce; it is inability to recognize words and link them with meanings, and confusion between visually similar words. Furthermore, we teachers have no system to offer them for improving direct visual recognition. On the other hand, we do have rules for pronunciation which can be taught and can mediate word recognition until familiarity brings sight recognition.

Questionable assumption 5: *"Focusing on the isolated skill of decoding, or any other isolated skill, is pedagogically unsound."*

The widespread denunciation of teaching isolated skills rests on yet another false dichotomy. The underlying premise is that reading teachers must choose between teaching everything as isolated skills or teaching nothing as an isolated skill. But there is no reason for excluding the middle ground between these two extremes. It may be that some or most reading skills are best taught in the context of extended passages, while a few skills are best taught by focusing on them in isolation.

The most likely candidate for successful teaching in isolation would be a skill that meets the following criteria: (a) it has a fairly complex internal structure, requiring considerable initial concentration for mastery; thus it cannot be combined with reading a text for meaning without seriously disrupting ongoing comprehension or hindering mastery of the skill; (b) application of the skill, at least in pure form, utilizes information from only a small segment of text (e.g., a word); (c) its importance and its application in getting meaning are well understood by the students. (According to Moore and Readence, 1985, the main drawback in teaching skills in isolation is that students see little purpose for them and have difficulty transferring them to other settings.)

For the decoding disabled older students with whom this article is concerned, the skill of decoding qualifies for teaching in isolation on all three counts: (a) it has its own complex set of rules; (b) though it can profitably be applied in conjunction with context analysis, it relies on a separate set of clues found within the word; (c) older students who need it are usually acutely aware of that need.

When we also consider that generally only a few students in a class need help with this skill, and that it is best taught in a small group to permit individual practice and avoid embarrassment, I believe we have a strong case for teaching word attack primarily as an isolated skill, outside the regular classroom, to those few older students who need it.

Questionable assumption 6: *"Older students dislike word attack training."*

None of us enjoys activities that accomplish nothing and make us feel stupid and helpless—a fair description of what has often resulted when teachers have tried to teach older students the traditional but ineffectual syllabication rules for pronouncing polysyllabic words. There may indeed be students who will dislike word attack training in any form, but this should not be assumed until they have been exposed to a method that results in actual word recognition. Success can be enormously motivating.

Granted, older students may be reluctant, except in private and nonthreatening surroundings, to concede that they have a word attack problem. However, when such students are offered a credible hope of getting free of this embarrassing handicap, in the company only of similarly afflicted students and a sympathetic teacher, their apparent indifference or hostility can be abruptly converted to relief, gratitude, and a singleminded concentration on the task at hand, to the extent of begging to continue the lesson after the bell. Obviously, the motivation was there all the time, waiting to be tapped.

My experience is that this kind of motivation is *not* effectively tapped by training in getting meaning from the context—perhaps because context training, valuable and well designed though it may be, does not alleviate the longstanding pain of being unable to do something that most classmates do effortlessly. Occasionally I witness or hear about students requesting word attack help from their teacher and being glibly told that word attack skill is not important and that they should concentrate on using the context—and I find it regrettable that well meaning teachers are attempting to extinguish this powerful motivation instead of putting it to good use.

To explain to such students that word attack is not their only problem is one thing; to try to persuade them that incompetence in decoding is not really a problem is something very different.

One qualification: I am not recommending that every decoding disabled older student should be plunged immediately into a remedial word attack program. The students need at least some minimal level of sight vocabulary and reading fluency, and should have had the experience of reading easy materials with comprehension.

For extremely disabled readers who lack even this foundation, it may well be appropriate to defer decoding training for a while. Individuals like those described by Eldridge (1985) and Rigg and Kazemek (1985) may have so little experience of reading for meaning, and be so thoroughly demoralized, that remediation should begin by concentrating on building fluency and morale through much repetition of very meaningful text. Eventually, however, unless these individuals have managed to infer decoding principles on their own they are likely to need some decoding training in order to become independent readers.

A final note: The comments in this section have been based primarily on my own experience; obviously I have no assurance that all students in all situations will prove as easy to motivate as mine have been, even if they have reached comparable reading levels. While I have often wished that my students' academic calendar allowed for a longer period of practice to help consolidate the gains made, Perfetti (1985) suggests that "This problem, the need for extended practice, is unfortunately coupled with the problem of motivation" (p. 248). On the other hand, Perfetti asserts that "this is a solvable problem where there is a will to solve it." I heartily agree with Perfetti's suggestion that incorporating practice into computer games (similar to those described in Frederiksen et al., 1985), holds great potential for maintaining motivation. Well designed, entertaining, and commercially available computer programs for improving older students' decoding skills would be a most welcome development.

Recommendations

It has been my goal, in examining and responding to these six anti-remedial decoding arguments, to take a step toward rehabilitating the practice of providing decoding train-
ing for older students. I hope it is clear that I do not view such training as a cure-all for reading problems. I believe what is needed, along with recognition of the complexity of reading and learning to read, is a greater recognition of multiple sources of reading disability, necessitating multiple kinds of remediation. Here, in brief, are the changes that I would like to see:

(a) Wider recognition of the fact that lack of decoding skills is a serious handicap for some older students, and of the importance of decoding as a readiness skill for vocabulary building.

(b) Greater acceptance by teachers of their responsibility for identifying older students who have serious decoding problems, and for providing help.

(c) Greater effort by both teachers and researchers to create better ways to explain decoding principles (as in Lewkowicz, 1985), and to make the decoding process faster and more efficient (as in Frederiksen et al., 1985).

REFERENCES

Anderson, R.C., Hiebert, E.H., Scott, J.A., & Wilkinson, I.A.G. (1985). *Becoming a nation of readers: The report of the Commission on Reading*. Champaign, IL: Center for the Study of Reading.

Chomsky, N., & Halle, M. (1968). *The sound pattern of English*. New York: Harper & Row.

Deighton, L. (1959). *Vocabulary development in the classroom*. New York: Teachers College.

Eldridge, B.H. (1985). Reading in context: An alternative approach for the adolescent disabled reader. *Journal of Reading, 29,* 9–17.

Frederiksen, J.R., Warren, B.M., & Rosebery, A.S. (1985). A componential approach to training reading skills: Part 2. Decoding and use of context. *Cognition and Instruction, 2*(3–4), 271–388.

Johnson, D.D., & van Hoff Johnson, B. (1986). Highlighting vocabulary in inferential comprehension instruction. *Journal of Reading, 29,* 622–625.

Johnson, D.D., Toms-Bronowski, S., & Buss, R.R. (1983). A critique of Frederick B. Davis's study: Fundamental factors of comprehension in reading. In L.M. Gentile, M.L. Kamil, & J.S. Blanchard (Eds.), *Reading research revisited*. Columbus, OH: Charles E. Merrill.

Lewkowicz, N.K. (1985). Attacking longer words: Don't begin at the beginning. *Journal of Reading*, *29*, 226-237.

Moore, D.W., & Readence, J.E. (1985). Approaches to content area reading instruction. In W.J. Harker (Ed.), *Classroom strategies for secondary reading* (2nd ed.). Newark, DE: International Reading Association.

Nagy, W.E., Herman, P.A., & Anderson, R.C. (1985). Learning words from context. *Reading Research Quarterly*, *20*(2), 233-253.

Perfetti, C.A. (1985). *Reading ability*. New York: Oxford University Press.

Rigg, P., & Kazemek, F.E. (1985). For adults only: Reading materials for adult literacy students *Journal of Reading*, *28*, 726-731.

Schane, S. (1979, September). The rhythmic nature of English word accentuation. *Language*, 55, 559-662.

Stevenson, H.W. (1984, May). Orthography and reading disabilities. *Journal of Learning Disabilities*, *17*, 296-301.

SECTION 4
Supporting Classroom Writing and Inquiry

Most adults probably can remember a teacher who made life a bit easier for them as adolescents by being cognizant of their need to feel supported, whether in matters of academic work or in trying social situations that arose from time to time. Nowhere is this support more keenly needed than in classrooms where teachers routinely require students to demonstrate at least a modicum of independence in writing and inquiry-oriented assignments. Guiding student reflection through writing that is done in connection with classroom inquiry is both an art and a science. Teachers who recognize the symbiotic nature of the two processes are quick to find ways of blending the affective and the cognitive, and they are also facile at showing students how inquiry writing is a skill that is very much alive and needed in life outside of school.

The authors of the articles in this section offer practical suggestions for helping students become independent writers and inquirers. They do so through describing strategies they have developed or tried in their own classrooms. We think the special insights of these authors provide clear and relevant guidelines for the complexities of classroom inquiry. These articles are especially convincing in their argument for making inquiry writing an activity for which adolescents see both a need and a purpose.

Sally N. Randall

Information Charts: A Strategy for Organizing Student Research

As a teacher of eighth-grade language arts and the mother of three daughters who struggled with research papers, I began to search for a way to help my students learn the skills used in the research process. I wanted this learning to carry over and serve my students throughout their high school careers. Organized notetaking (McKenzie, 1979) with a critical thinking component (Ennis, 1987) became the major focus of my search because those two areas seemed to be difficult for most students. I also wanted a process that would build heavily on students' prior knowledge (Symons & Pressley, 1993) and increase their metacognitive awareness (Baker & Brown, 1984; Wade & Reynolds, 1989).

As in many middle schools, my classes are all heterogeneously grouped. Students have varying abilities in critical thinking, organization, and reading and various levels of motivation. They needed a method of notetaking that would help those who needed external structure and pacing but would also benefit those who had had prior successes with research. I wanted to avoid the common pitfalls of students copying pages of unorganized facts out of encyclopedias and find an alternative to the notecard system for students who have difficulty staying organized. My students needed to learn to select the most rele-

vant information from a lengthy text, organize that information in a systematic way, and interpret contradictory information from multiple sources.

My search led me to an article by Hoffman (1992), in which he proposed the use of an inquiry chart (I-Chart) as a structure for elementary teachers to guide their classes through an exploration of key ideas related to a particular topic. The chart offered a method for organizing information from several sources. Hoffman's proposed I-Chart was one large piece of paper divided into a grid. Key questions about the subject were listed at the top of each column and the different reference materials were written at the beginning of each row. Hoffman envisioned the elementary teacher selecting the topics, sources, and the questions; guiding the whole class through the reading and recording of multiple answers; and finally leading a discussion focusing on a comparison of sources and a summation.

Hoffman developed the I-Chart as a strategy for direct instruction of critical thinking skills through literacy. His work is based on McKenzie's (1979) data charts or comparison charts and Ogle's (1986) K–W–L model for active reading. According to McKenzie, adolescents need explicit instruction in just what a

Reprinted From the *Journal of Adolescent & Adult Literacy*, *39*(7), 536–542, April 1996.

report or research project is. They need to understand why several sources are used, know how to recognize basic principles, and compare and synthesize what they learn from different sources. They should be able to "abstract question-relevant information from a source" and subordinate "different kinds of elaborative or qualifying material" (p. 784). McKenzie suggested that a controlled and systematic use of charts in the early grades may allow for flexible adaptations by older students.

Hoffman (1992) briefly discussed modifications of the I-Chart, including its potential for independent research. This was exactly what I was looking for. I extensively adapted his idea and have used this modified I-Chart in my classroom for 2 years with excellent results.

Step By Step Through the I-Chart

These steps represent a synthesis of what I learned as I went through the process with my students during the last 2 years. Both times the students researched a topic for an interdisciplinary unit on the wilderness or the environment. Like Hoffman (1992), I found that the process of using I-Charts involved three components: the preparation of the charts, research and notetaking using the charts, and the completion of a final product using the information organized within the charts. My eighth graders were actively involved at all three stages and were able to work more independently than elementary students. I have included Melanie's I-Chart (see Figure on the following page) to illustrate how one student used the strategy.

Preparation for Research

Teaching background skills. The wilderness unit was introduced in both science and language arts. Students spent their time in science class studying topics related to the unit. They brainstormed areas of interest and began deciding what their individual research topics might be. In language arts class, students spent some time learning skills they would need for research and reading fiction selections related to wilderness survival. Specific language arts skills included letter writing, paraphrasing, interviewing, library skills, and bibliography format.

Writing topic proposals. Students wrote proposals explaining their interest in their chosen topic, listing what they already knew about the topic, adding what they wanted to learn, and detailing where they planned to find information. The purpose of the proposal was to encourage students to narrow their topics, to begin to hunt for resources in the community, to consider what knowledge they already had about the topic, and to reflect on what else they really wanted to know. Student topics included edible wildflowers, deer calls, wilderness survival techniques, wolf communications, composting, and the effects of acid rain. Melanie decided to research the destruction of the rain forest because she views this destruction as a major environmental problem that affects animals, weather, resources, and people.

Brainstorming questions. Next, students generated specific questions they would like to have answered about their own topics that could not be answered by a simple yes or no. The students then turned these questions into subtopics that would direct their research. Among other questions, Melanie wanted to know more about endangered animals in the rain forest.

Setting up I-Charts. I provided each student with a copy of the I-Chart. Some took them home for parents to photocopy; others hand-copied them so they had 10 charts. Each

Name: Melanie   **Topic:** Rainforest Destruction

Subtopic: What animals live in the Rainforest?

What I already know: There are a lot of birds an other animals big and small. Some of the animals living in rainforests are going extinct.

Bibliography #:	
1	colorful birds, chattering monkeys, butterflies
2	Monkeys, squirrels, birds, jaguar, giant armadillo, plants: giant water lilies, stilt-roots, strangler, and buttresses, an aerial roots, palm. Anaconda, geometric moth, poison arrow frog, Matamata turtle, Kinkajou.
3	Keel-billed toucan, rare butterflies, howler monkeys, the 3-toed sloth, tamandua (related to the anteater). jaguar, the ruby-topaz humming bird, genus Denodraba, a bird eating spider, leaf cutter ants, and the red brocket deer.

Interesting related facts: 6% of the earth's land surface is covered by Rain forests which are a home to over half the planets species. ⅓ of earth's species are beleived to live in this rainforest, only a fraction of them have been given scientific names.

Key words: biodeversity

New questions to research: What types of tree species live in the rain forest?

chart was the size of notebook paper and could be stored in folders or notebooks.

Students wrote one subtopic/question at the top of each I-Chart. They then reflected on what they already knew about each topic; they wrote this prior knowledge in the section on the I-Chart labeled "What I Already Know," as shown in the Figure. Melanie knew only general information about rain forest animals that reflected her concern about their possible extinction. Some students had picked topics about which they knew little and wrote either "Nothing" or made a guess about what they might learn. Others picked topics about which they already had personal knowledge. These students jotted down what they knew and made plans to confirm, correct, or add to that knowledge base as they researched their topics.

Simulating research. Before the students began their own research, we did a class simulation of researching and completing I-Charts. I had reproduced enlarged charts identical to theirs on poster board and had chosen a topic related to the unit of study. The students brainstormed questions to research, and we recorded a subtopic at the top of each large chart. Then I gave students a variety of reference materials. As they found information related to one of the subtopics, they came to the front of the room and entered the information on the appropriate chart. We discussed the use of all sections of the chart and filled in appropriate information.

Research and Notetaking

Finding resources. When students began their research, we spent the entire class period every day for a week in the school library. I monitored the students to make sure they were using the charts correctly and adding each new source to their bibliography. Students then had to make time for research

and find resources on their own. Some used community resources such as the county library, the county extension office, a nearby university library, friends or parents who had relevant expertise, and personnel at the state Department of Natural Resources. Others used independent work time at school in the school library. Melanie used both magazines and encyclopedias that were available to her at home. We also took a field trip to the county library where the students were given time for individual research. We spent class time generating interview questions for experts in their fields and writing letters to agencies that might have information to share.

Answering research questions. The I-Chart provided the structure for the students' search for information as well as for their notetaking. I encouraged students to have all of their I-Charts in front of them as they worked and to first skim a new source to determine if it would be helpful to their research. As they read, students paraphrased the information they learned about each subtopic in the righthand section of the corresponding chart. As they read from one source, they would pull the chart with the subtopic that matched the information they were reading and record the information. As they read a new piece of information, they would pull out the corresponding I-Chart. This enabled students to think critically about the relevance of each piece of information to their subtopics and eliminated random copying of unorganized data. As students moved to additional resources, they continued taking their notes on the I-Chart with the appropriate subtopic. Even with this structure, Melanie sometimes slipped and included names of plants under the subtopic of animals of the rain forest, as can be seen in her I-Chart.

Recording bibliographic information. After students completed taking notes on all the available information from one source, they drew a line across the I-Charts under the last recorded facts indicating the end of the information from that particular source. On a separate sheet of paper headed "References," the students wrote a complete bibliographic reference for the resource. Each new resource was added and numbered in order of use. Then students jotted down only the corresponding number in the lefthand column of each I-Chart to indicate the source for those particular pieces of information. This prevented needless repetition of the complete bibliographic information on each chart.

Completing the I-Chart. As students encountered *interesting related facts* that did not really answer one of the research questions but were of interest to them, they recorded them at the bottom of any I-Chart. Melanie used her interesting related facts in the introduction of her paper.

As they came across *key words*, students also recorded them. Key words were words students didn't know and would look up later to define, or they were words that might act as entry words in the search for further information. *Biodiversity* was a new word to Melanie, as can be seen on her I-Chart. She later looked up the meaning and used the term in her final paper.

As students came across information that they had not anticipated finding, they recorded it as *new questions to research* to remind them to set up an additional I-Chart. Melanie realized that plants, particularly tree species, were also found in great variety and could constitute a separate subtopic. She eventually set up an additional I-Chart on plant species and learned about the medicines that are derived from rain forest plants.

Critically evaluating research findings. Evaluation was an ongoing process with the I-Chart strategy. Some students found that they were unable to find information on one of their subtopics. If they could not find an expert in the field to interview, they had to abandon that I-Chart. For the research paper, this inability to find an answer to a question led to a discussion of unanswered questions and possible further research. Like Melanie, many students also found information they had not anticipated learning, so they set up new charts midway through the research process.

Students were constantly evaluating whether they had adequately answered the question behind any one subtopic. They knew their research was not over until they had learned what they wanted to know about every subtopic or had exhausted the available information. Because Melanie's major focus was the destruction of the rain forest, the purpose of her subtopic on animal life was to show the diversity of life rather than find complete information on each species. Therefore, she made the decision to stop researching this subtopic with the amount of information shown and move to other important subtopics.

Students also had to deal with conflicting information from various sources. They learned to reach their own conclusions by checking an additional source, checking the date of the publication, or evaluating the expertise of the author/publisher. My goal for them was to view conflicting information as an interesting challenge rather than as a problem.

Completion of Final Product

Writing a research paper. The first year the final product was a research paper. Each student finished the research process with information on 8 to 10 subtopics. I used the organization of the I-Charts to teach the students outlining. As they outlined their individual information, each subtopic on the I-Charts became a Roman numeral. Important facts and details found within the I-Charts filled out the rest of the outline. Some students found that subtopics needed to be divided when they were too broad or combined when they were too closely related. The I-Charts provided the organization for the outline and consequently the final paper.

Creating a visual display. The second year the final product was a visual display for a wilderness convention much like the typical science fair. Students used the information they had learned to create a display of maps, charts, listings of facts, pictures, graphs, and timelines. They created a visual display and a pamphlet informing the public of their expertise. These were showcased at an evening program to which we invited parents, experts who had been interviewed, and county librarians who had provided research assistance. I also eventually taught students the skill of outlining from their I-Charts. Even though outlining wasn't necessary to their visual displays, the opportunity was too good to pass up.

Student Assessment of I-Charts

During the second year of using I-Charts, I surveyed student opinions about the I-Charts at three stages. The results convinced me that the strategy is useful to a significant number of students during both guided and independent research projects.

First, during one of five written weekly reflections on their progress through the wilderness project, I asked the following open-ended question: "What is the most helpful thing you have learned so far about doing research?" At this point the students had finished all of their notetaking and were ready to work on their final products. Of 38 respondents, 16 students spontaneously mentioned the usefulness of the I-Charts.

Second, as a part of their last written reflection, when the final product was complet-

ed, I asked, "How would you evaluate the usefulness of the I-Chart as a research tool?" Of the 38 respondents, 28 or 74% rated the I-Chart positively. They wrote many narrative comments that were great testimonials. "I rate the I-Charts a 10!" "I thought it was easy to find what you wanted in the subtopic with the I-Chart." "The I-Charts helped a lot. They were a life-saver!" Negative comments such as "I felt more secure taking notes on a regular sheet of paper" were written by 5 students, about 13%. Neutral or mixed comments were recorded by another 5 students. Typical of the mixed comments was, "I hated them & they were a waste of time, but they did get info organized & easy to refer back to."

Finally, during the spring following the required use of I-Charts for the wilderness project, students were assigned an independent research paper on World War II. This was a joint social studies/language arts project. They were required to take notes organized by subtopic but were given the choice of using I-Charts or notecards. After they had finished outlining and writing their papers, I asked them to write about which notetaking strategy they had used and why, and how it had worked for them.

The results of that survey tell me that the I-Charts provided a helpful structure for the majority of the students. Twenty out of 44, or 45% of the students, chose to use notecards and were satisfied with their choice. The following comments are typical of their explanations for their choice of notecards. "They are easier for me to keep up with." "I wanted to try something different." "I could use my own system with the notecards." "The I-Charts were too specific on format."

Interestingly, 7 out of 44 or 16% chose to use notecards but reported that they would go back to I-Charts for their next research project. "I chose to use notecards cause [sic] I thought it would be easier to use them instead of

I-Charts but then it turns out that I like I-Charts better cause [sic] there [sic] more organized." "I used notecards because I tried to use something different. But the next time I will use I-Charts because they are much easier to write a paper after you did your research."

Finally, 17 out of 44 or 39% decided that I-Charts were the best strategy for them. "They have more room to put the facts than on note-cards." "I also chose them because you could stick them in your notebook and they weren't so small that you lost them." "I liked the subtopics because they helped me know what I needed to look up." "They keep your stuff straight and in order."

The students' ability to adapt and modify the charts to fit their needs provided proof of the strategy's flexibility. Some students used them to research and organize material on subjects with conflicting information. Others decided to do group projects and assigned each member different subtopics; individuals set up different I-Charts and then shared information at the end of the research process. Students worked together to fill in "What I Already Know," significantly increasing the available background knowledge.

Students' comments on the last evaluation helped me realize I must do even more to encourage the students to adapt the charts to fit their needs and styles.

Critical Thinking, Prior Knowledge, and Metacognitive Awareness

To my knowledge there is no published research that provides evidence of the usefulness of the I-Chart. However, the strategy is well grounded in theory and research on critical thinking, the importance of prior knowledge, and metacognitive awareness.

Critical thinking is a skill that must be taught explicitly to many students. Ennis (1987) defined critical thinking as "reasonable reflective thinking that is focused on deciding what to believe or do" (p. 10) and suggested that the teaching of critical thinking must be integrated into the teaching of all curricular areas. Some of the component abilities of critical thinking that he outlined include identifying or formulating a question, seeing similarities and differences, identifying and handling irrelevancies, summarizing, and asking and answering questions of clarification (p. 12). All of these skills are integral to the use of the I-Charts.

The I-Chart has an important prior knowledge component similar to Ogle's (1986) K–W–L model for active reading. Both build on what students already know and questions they want answered or addressed. In fact, Symons and Pressley (1993) found that the level of prior knowledge influenced students' abilities to locate relevant information in text.

Young readers and poor readers have particular difficulty monitoring their own cognitive processes as they read (Baker & Brown, 1984; Wade & Reynolds, 1989). They tend to attribute importance to facts that are personally relevant rather than those that are relevant to the assigned learning task. Wade and Reynolds suggest that students must develop a metacognitive awareness that includes three components. The I-Chart process helps students identify what it is that they want to know (task awareness), provides a flexible strategy for organizing what is read (strategy awareness), and contains an evaluation process to determine if the material has been learned (performance awareness).

Visualize, Organize, Evaluate

This action research has convinced me that the guided use of this modified I-Chart can provide middle school students with an important research strategy. After structured experiences, students can modify the technique in ways that suit individual learning styles and specific assignments. The charts help students visualize the task before them, provide a strategy for organizing formal research, and guide students through a continuous evaluation of their progress.

The students in my classroom who seemed to benefit most from the structure of the I-Chart were those with no previous research practice and those reading below grade level. One student in particular struggled with many reading tasks. He chose to research wolves, which would have been too broad a topic for a more advanced reader. However, this student wanted to know some very basic facts about habitat, diet, communication, reproduction, and threats to the wolf. The I-Charts helped him sift through massive amounts of material and focus on what he wanted to know. He was delighted with his success when the charts helped him visualize the organization of an outline and the structure of his final paper.

I will continue to use this modified I-Chart to help my students as they learn to do formal research. Their evaluations have convinced me of the value of the strategy for many of them. I believe it also has potential for modifications that might make it useful to high school students as well.

REFERENCES

Baker, L., & Brown, A.L. (1984). Metacognitive skills and reading. In P.D. Pearson (Ed.), *Handbook of reading research* (pp. 353-394). New York: Longman.

Ennis, R.H. (1987). A taxonomy of critical thinking dispositions and abilities. In J. Baron & R. Sternberg (Eds.), *Teaching thinking skills: Theory and practice*. New York: W.H. Freeman.

Hoffman, J.V. (1992). Critical reading/thinking across the curriculum: Using I-Charts to support learning. *Language Arts*, *69*, 121-127.

McKenzie, G.R. (1979). Data charts: A crutch for helping pupils organize reports. *Language Arts*, *56*, 784-788.

Ogle, D.M. (1986). K-W-L: A teaching model that develops active reading of expository text. *The Reading Teacher*, *39*, 564-570.

Symons, S., & Pressley, M. (1993). Prior knowledge affects text search success and extraction of information. *Reading Research Quarterly*, *28*, 251-259.

Wade, S.E., & Reynolds, R.E. (1989). Developing metacognitive awareness. *Journal of Reading*, *33*, 6-14.

Lu Huntley-Johnston, Sherri Phillips Merritt, and Lois E. Huffman

How to Do How-To Books:
Real-Life Writing in the Classroom

The questions high school students ask about writing in the classroom often reveal what they think is important. When teachers assign writing, for example, it is not unusual for some students to ask, "How much does this count?" "How long does this have to be?" "Does this have to be typed?" Questions like these reduce the process of writing to concerns about grading or format. If students complete the work and ask the teacher, "Do you want this?" it suggests that they may have invested very little of themselves in the process or the final product and implies that they have a narrow view of literacy as something disconnected from their lives. Perpetuating the idea that writing is something students produce for teachers removes students from positions of responsibility for their written literacy development, thus missing the point "that there are real, human reasons to write" (Calkins, 1994).

The complexities in understanding writing require knowledge of how writing is inextricably connected to thinking; for teachers this demands examination of and knowledge about different writing forms and attendant thinking involved in the production of these forms (Langer & Applebee, 1987). The dilemma for teachers is how to design instruction that attains desired curricular objectives while also engaging students in writing that they perceive as relevant. Significant changes in the teaching of writing over the last 20 years have centered on the shift from traditional views to the "process paradigm" (Zemelman & Daniels, 1988); yet adopting a process approach does not, in itself, guarantee that students will see authentic purposes for the writing they produce in school.

If our goal is for student work to be significant, meaningful, and useful, we may need to envision alternative assignments and be mindful about structuring a pedagogy that invites authentic learning. One alternative that is proving successful at the secondary level is writing how-to books. In this article we define this genre, present one teacher's success with a how-to book project, and close with an analysis of the project in connection to authentic instruction and literacy development.

Definition and Rationale For The How-To Genre

In basic terms, how-to books "describe a process and explain how to perform such activities as playing chess, conducting science experiments, folding paper artistically, cooking, repairing cars, and making music" (Moore, Moore, Cunningham, & Cunningham, 1994, p. 38). Although Moore et al. maintain that the

Reprinted From the *Journal of Adolescent & Adult Literacy*, *41*(3), 172–179, November 1997.

how-to genre applies only to a few content areas such as science, mathematics, and vocational studies, Donelson and Nilsen (1989) argue that topics for these books are unlimited and may range from the simple to the complex. Likewise, a variety of rhetorical forms of persuasion (e.g., parody) may be employed to gain attention and communicate with readers (Huntley-Johnston, Huffman, & Merritt, 1995). How-to writing, a genre with which most secondary students would be familiar, has appeal, utility, and challenge for both students and teachers.

Appeal. Students are attracted to the how-to genre because explaining how to do things makes sense to them, while they may fail to see other reasons to write (Moffett, 1981). "[S]tudents…[are] eager to read each other's directions, both to learn to do what others can do and to find out what others know how to do" (Moffett, 1981, p. 115). When they write in this genre, adolescents see how they fit into the world (Donelson & Nilsen, 1989). The motivational element inherent in this genre and its developmental appropriateness also make it appealing to teachers.

Utility. Students may be unaccustomed to thinking about their school work as having a purpose or use beyond the classroom. Writing how-to books invites students to think differently about the written work they will produce; this project engages students in research for a real reason. Both writing and reading processes assist in achieving the desired ends—in this case, how-to books. Additionally, producing how-to books forces students to consider the concept of audience in ways different from most school writing assignments and leads to written products that can serve the needs of people of all ages.

The utility of how-to books is that teachers can create a context for students to develop authority as writers. When we delve into a genre study, we "create conditions that encourage our students to live like poets or journalists or short story writers" (Calkins, 1994, p. 365). In the case of the how-to genre, we invite students to live like researchers.

Challenge. Researching and writing how-to books challenges students and teachers because they can engage in "authentic tasks that accomplish goals at the same time as [they are] teaching [and learning] academic skills" (Damon, 1995, p. 212). We talk about the importance of these challenging authentic tasks for literacy development in the next section that tells about a how-to project that we designed. Sherri, the second author and a classroom teacher, implemented the how-to book-writing project with her students. Our story maps out how we invited students to engage more authentically in literacy and inquiry.

Our How-To Book Project

We conducted the how-to book-writing project with four heterogeneous English classes, two at Grade 9 and two at Grade 11. The project lasted approximately 10 weeks and ran simultaneously with literature study. Specific class periods were set aside for work on the project, but students also worked on it outside of class.

In its first run, the how-to book project was successful in that it engendered an authenticity unlike traditional, format-oriented research projects. By the time the project ended, we realized it was much more than creating an authentic context for inquiry, as we were forced to make our philosophy about authentic instruction and classroom practice come together in new ways. The story that follows and the eight key points that emerge from our reflections and those of the students represent a convergence of philosophy and practice, thus providing a foundation of understanding upon which to build further.

To begin the project, we were sensitive to the idea of establishing community (O'Flahavan &

Tierney, 1996). We wanted to initiate the project and introduce students to the how-to genre in ways that would invite involvement. To generate interest and have students share in decisions that would influence directions, we started by having a book-sharing day when students brought in at least one how-to book on a topic of interest. In small groups, students previewed and evaluated the books. As they conducted their reviews, they commented on both content and style. One student, Elliott, noted that a book about learning tennis in one weekend contained too much information for the reader; Kristin and Kirby tried out the instructions in books about origami and drawing to see if the steps were clear; Gray explained why one book's use of humor made it particularly interesting and helpful.

Exploring interests and needs. To generate further interest in topics, we asked students to complete two activities. One activity required them to ask three people who knew them well to respond to the following three questions about the student: (a) What would you say seem to be my main interests based on what you know about me? (b) What do you think I'm good at doing? (c) What are some things you think I might be interested in or do well if I had the chance?

Students, who sometimes had trouble identifying their own interests and talents, seemed to enjoy the feedback they received. When students returned to class with their completed sheets, we shared responses and tried to identify answers that surprised us. Carrie was astonished when someone suggested she would be good with electrical things. However, that comment encouraged her to tackle a topic that interested her: how to install a car stereo.

The second activity required students to consider their interests and talents in light of possible audiences and eventual outlets for their books. Most students easily generated a topic, but some struggled with identifying a

location to place their books for others to use. The students who had ideas for distribution were those who had already noted a need. For example, on the second day of the project Linda asked if she could create a book on basic soccer skills for a summer soccer camp. A few days later, Mike said that he and a coworker at a laser game room had noticed that new customers were confused when they first arrived and probably would benefit from a how-to manual. Other students gradually began to see ways that their interests and community needs could mesh.

Creating a support system for research. We realized that students would need support to tackle the research and writing stages. This support took many forms and included establishing peer groups, providing minilessons, having conferences with individual students, and creating opportunities for teacher responses. One particularly effective strategy to encourage student reflection and teacher response was the "Brain Dump and Pump" reflection sheets (see Figure 1). This activity helped students see where they had been and where they were going.

We also introduced the idea of a mentor. Because the term *mentor* has been used broadly in many contexts, we chose to call this person a *Yoda*. As expected, most students knew Yoda as the mentor of Luke Skywalker in the movie *The Empire Strikes Back*. After showing a brief excerpt from the movie, we discussed the qualities that made him an effective support person for Luke.

Students then brainstormed the names of prospective Yodas, narrowed their selection to one person, and contacted this individual. Students' Yodas included parents, coaches, older siblings, friends, and people knowledgeable about their particular topic. Only one student needed help in finding a Yoda. Students worked with the Yoda to determine how he or she could be of assistance and cre-

Figure 1
Brain dump and pump reflection sheet

Purpose: To figure out what you already know and decide what you need to do next.

1. List the things you know so far about your topic.

2. What do you need to know more about? What questions do you have about your topic?

3. What are the next steps in the process for you? What questions do you have about the process?

4. Describe what has been happening in your peer group since the last brain dump.

5. Describe what has been happening with your Yoda since the last brain dump.

6. Are there any places where you are stuck and need help?

---

ate a timeline for completing the project. The Yoda was asked to "sign off" to indicate support for the student's plans.

Preparing for research. As students began to create their proposals, it was time for the next step, preparing to do research. We wanted students to combine their knowledge with what had already been done on the subject. We began with a typical research day in the library during which students were instructed to "see what's out there" on their topic. Interest was high because they were excited about their topics. Some students were thrilled to find sources they could use for their project; others were concerned when they could not find anything on their topic. We used both situations to further address the need for the book they wanted to write.

We also spent several days exploring alternative research methods because students were required to use at least one method that did not involve getting information from a text. Such methods included conducting interviews, distributing surveys, and using electronic sources. We created handouts on how to conduct an interview, individually coached students on creating questions for their surveys, and helped students locate people they could interview or survey.

Widening the research community. We also began contacting potential guest speakers, and soon added to our research community a freelance writer, a technical writer, and a pro-

fessional illustrator. The freelance writer spoke to each class twice, once near the beginning of the project when students were beginning their research and later when they had written their rough drafts and had questions about style and content. During the first visit she introduced her own method of research, which involved collecting questions in a notebook and using different research methods to answer them. A number of students adopted her method. When the freelance writer visited a second time, she helped students troubleshoot weak introductions, gave them real-world advice on common editing mistakes, and guided them in thinking through the organization of their books.

The technical writer brought in applications of how-to writing from his company and stressed the need for clarity, accuracy, and completeness in written directions. The illustrator showed samples of interesting ways to integrate text and graphics. Because students were required to draw their own illustrations or create them using a camera or computer, she also offered specific suggestions for designing effective visuals.

Revisiting our book-sharing lesson. Once students were firmly involved in the research and writing stages, we revisited the book-sharing lesson to assist us in creating a rubric for the project. We spent two class periods brainstorming and debating various requirements to include. Two ground rules for the

How to Do How-To Books: Real-Life Writing in the Classroom   209 project guided students: (a) create a how-to book with illustrations, involving a minimum of two types of research (e.g., getting information from a text and conducting an interview), and (b) make use of standard parenthetical documentation form. Students reviewed their notes on the how-to books they had evaluated and were encouraged to use these in developing our rubric.

There was heated discussion on several issues. For example, some students were uncomfortable including author information on the book jacket, while others felt they owed it to the reader to give such information. After much debate, students agreed that everyone would provide a brief biographical sketch, but they could choose whether to include a picture of themselves. Questions also arose about the need for parenthetical documentation. Brian noted that he had not seen citations in any of the how-to books his group evaluated. We finally concluded that using documentation would give the students' voices more authority since they were not yet established experts on their topics.

Drawing on the suggestions from each class, a rubric that included subtopics, a description of requirements, and point values was created. This rubric was then presented to each class for reactions and revisions (see Figure 2).

Entering into final stages. Near the end of the project, we scheduled lab time for students needing access to school computers. Students with home computers spent this time writing and getting feedback from classmates. Each class then conducted an in-house review (peer swap) of their drafts. Students were encouraged to have an out-of-house review by someone with superior editorial skills or considerable content knowledge. At this point, students also returned a signed contract, finalizing placement arrangements for their books.

The day arrived for final books to be collected. There was obvious relief as students handed in this project. We should note that every student from these classes submitted a book, even students who had not turned in assignments for the literature study. This degree of participation, along with students' reflections on their process, suggests that the project was meaningful for the students. After books were graded and returned, students placed them in the contracted locations.

Project Reflections

For an inquiry project like this to truly meet its potential, we would emphasize eight points that best reflect what the students taught us as we immersed ourselves in the how-to book-writing project. Brief explanations follow each point to emphasize dimensions of authenticity inherent in this form of inquiry.

1. *Be flexible and take advantage of the unexpected.* Jenn, for example, had planned to write her book about backstage work in the drama department, but halfway through the project her home was destroyed by fire. This disaster prompted her to create a book on fire prevention that was used by all of the first-grade teachers in her brother's school.

It was also necessary to be flexible about the form of the book. Angel, for example, chose to write a how-to parody entitled *How to Survive Your Mother*, and several students wrote books to be used by children. Therefore, we had to collaborate to determine how they could use these alternative forms and still work within the ground rules of the assignment.

2. *Engage and motivate students by inviting authentic choices and power in the research process.* This proved especially challenging as we created the rubric. It was somewhat frustrating when students did not want to include

Figure 2
How-to book project evaluation rubric

Checklist for how-to book project	In-house	Out-of-house	Final
Parts of the book (20%)	Peer suggestions:		
Front cover	_____	_____	_____
Title page	_____	_____	_____
Acknowledgements and/or dedication	_____	_____	_____
Table of contents	_____	_____	_____
Foreword and/or introduction	_____	_____	_____
Textual content and illustrations	_____	_____	_____
Bibliography	_____	_____	_____
Author information (biographical information; photo optional but encouraged)	_____	_____	_____
Brief description of book on back cover (illustration optional)	_____	_____	_____
Optional additions: Glossary, Index, Appendix, List of recommended readings	_____	_____	_____
Format (10%)			
Use of page numbers	_____	_____	_____
Use of chapters or subheadings	_____	_____	_____
Use of captions for illustrations (or numbering system within text)	_____	_____	_____
One-sided pages or thick paper	_____	_____	_____
Parenthetical documentation of sources within text	_____	_____	_____
Professional-looking pages	_____	_____	_____
Binding	_____	_____	_____
Textual content (40%)			
Use of research and personal experience (minimum two different types of sources)	_____	_____	_____
Clear and understandable writing	_____	_____	_____
Topic effectively covered	_____	_____	_____
Information grouped in ways that make sense	_____	_____	_____
Text interesting to read	_____	_____	_____
Text well edited	_____	_____	_____
Illustrations (15%)			
Support the text	_____	_____	_____
Clear and easy to follow	_____	_____	_____
Accurate	_____	_____	_____
Well placed within text	_____	_____	_____
Audience (15%)			
Content builds on audience knowledge	_____	_____	_____
Appropriate to audience reading level	_____	_____	_____
Book placed where it can be read by audience	_____	_____	_____

something we believed was essential. We had to evaluate why something was so important to us if it had little apparent meaning for the students. However, allowing students control over content and process helped them realize their own strengths. As one student observed, "I am surprised at how much I actually know. I didn't know I had so much knowledge. My personal experiences really helped."

3. *Provide and arrange for individual support throughout all phases of the project.* After we were well into the project, we discovered that many students were confused about the role of the Yoda; therefore, many of the Yodas did not know how they could be of assistance. In the future we will collaborate as a class to determine what tasks the Yodas could perform that would be helpful during the research project. In effect, together we will write a *How to Be a Yoda* book. One part of this book will contain guidelines for creating a contract that will specify what each will do to accomplish the project goals.

4. *Offer many well-timed minilessons.* We found that students need much in-class coaching and practice on real-life research, writing, and production. A series of how-to lessons could include how to write a project proposal, plan a timeline, conduct interviews, create surveys, edit writing, and budget money and supplies. Because students are so accustomed to teachers making content and process decisions for them, they are often unprepared for this responsibility. Interestingly, the most frequent complaint about the project, by students and by some parents, was that some students spent too much money on the final version of the book. Although some students budgeted resources and found creative ways of making their books look professional, others needed assistance with finding low- or no-cost ways to make their books look good.

Many of the minilessons did help students broaden their vision of what counts as "research." For example, Kevin, who wrote his book on water-skiing, was initially skeptical about his ability to conduct an interview. Later Kevin remarked that, "The interviews were absolutely astonishing. My neighbor and a guy at the lake were more than willing to give help or advice or anything."

5. *Require that the books be placed where they will be used.* Books ended up in waiting rooms, at sports camps, in church libraries, on store counters, in classrooms, and even in company break rooms. Jenny's book on how to survive high school was well received in the guidance office of a local middle school, Kristin's book on cheerleading techniques was popular at a cheerleading camp, and the high school librarian continues to refer teachers to Geoffrey's book on how to untangle the Internet.

Many students, however, were initially uncomfortable with making contacts in the community and thinking about the prospect of the books actually being read. This presents another learning opportunity: There is no way that the teacher, as the sole reader of the text, can give students the good feeling they had when someone mentioned having seen their book in public. One student came in to tell us that her friend's mother saw her book at a local retail store. Another showed his increased understanding of audience when he proudly exclaimed, "My introduction and back cover could hook you on the book. It could sell it." Another student had an actual buyer for her book. These students saw a tangible audience, beyond the teacher, who would read or even buy their books. A local librarian was so excited when she saw one of the books that she created a display at the public library using 23 student books.

6. *Include reflection as an ongoing part of the process.* Throughout the project, we re-

flected on it through our journals, e-mail, and conversations. This allowed us to think through instructional processes and identify stressful phases of the project. Students periodically completed the Brain Dump and Pump reflections to keep us abreast of their progress and to provide a route for personal feedback. In the future we plan to use learning logs as a central component of the project because authentic inquiry calls for students to struggle with some big issues; the logs would provide a safe place for them to ask questions and think through problems.

7. *Require students to use multiple methods of research*. Students experienced research as more than just copying down someone else's information. They had to identify possible sources and determine how to use them. Forrest, for example, could not find a skydiving instructor to interview, but he called a local radio personality who had recently completed a jump on a dare from her listeners. He interviewed her on how it felt to jump.

Chris, who was writing a book about how to win a certain video game, had his friends play the game repeatedly so he could observe them and determine the most common mistakes people make and how they learn from them. These students experienced meaningful and personal inquiry.

8. *Allow the project to evolve*. As educators who like to plan ahead, we were challenged when the project began to unfold in unexpected ways. When students were struggling with part of the project, we had to figure out what lesson, activity, or guidance would help them work out problems. Some of the things we had planned were not reasonable given practical restraints. The students also confronted the uncertainties and fluid nature of the project, but providing time to think, work, and discuss in class helped everyone move with the project rather than against it.

Authentic Instruction and Literacy Development

Too often when students are engaged in traditional school-based writing assignments they do not see themselves as real authors; hence, they never come to know themselves as writers. This may happen if the process seems too unfamiliar or if genres with little connection to the world beyond school—like the traditional research paper, five-paragraph themes, or teacher-based essays—continue to proliferate (Bomer, 1995). Because the only audience for the final paper is usually the teacher, it may seem as though the writing is done in a vacuum. As Kutz and Roskelly (1991) observe, "[W]riting is seldom self-motivated and is seldom seen as a tool of inquiry or learning" (p. 161). At a time when students should be developing a writing identity, writing assignments may create setbacks rather than move them forward. Therefore, as we envision alternatives to conventional written assignments, we would be wise to consider the learners' areas of interest, expertise, and quest.

Shifting our stance from focus upon remote written assignments to attention toward students' interests may lead to more authentic contexts for student research. Direct connections are then present between our students' lives and their literacy development. Consistent with authentic instruction, Newmann and Wehlage (1993) would have "students (1) construct meaning and produce knowledge, (2) use disciplined inquiry to construct meaning, and (3) aim their work toward production of discourse, products, and performances that have value or meaning beyond success in school" (p. 157) to attain "authentic student achievement."

Writing how-to books is a form of authentic instruction, linking literacy development to student achievement based upon learning that transcends the schoolroom walls. This story of our experience with a how-to book writing project illustrates an effective inquiry assignment, paving the way for others who want to embrace more authentic instruction, purposeful research, and meaningful learning.

REFERENCES

Bomer, R. (1995). *A time for meaning: Crafting literate lives in middle and high school.* Portsmouth, NH: Heinemann.

Calkins, L. (1994). *The art of teaching writing.* Portsmouth, NH: Heinemann.

Damon, W. (1995). *Greater expectations: Overcoming the culture of indulgence in America's homes and schools.* New York: Free Press.

Donelson, K.L., & Nilsen, A.P. (1989). *Literature for today's young adults* (3rd ed.). Glenview, IL: Scott, Foresman.

Huntley-Johnston, L., Huffman, L.E., & Merritt, S.P. (1995, November). *Writing how-to books: An alternative to research papers in secondary content classes.* Paper presented at the Combined International Reading Association Regional Conference, Nashville, TN.

Kutz, E., & Roskelly, H. (1991). *An unquiet pedagogy: Transforming practice in the English classroom.* Portsmouth, NH: Heinemann.

Langer, J.A., & Applebee, A.N. (1987). *How writing shapes thinking: A study of teaching and learning.* Urbana, IL: National Council of Teachers of English.

Moffett, J. (1981). *Active voice: A writing program across the curriculum.* Montclair, NJ: Boynton/Cook.

Moore, D.W., Moore, S.A., Cunningham, P.M., & Cunningham, J.W. (1994). *Developing readers and writers in the content areas K–12* (2nd ed.). New York: Longman.

Newmann, F.M., & Wehlage, G.G. (1993). Five standards of authentic instruction. *Educational Leadership, 50,* 157–160.

O'Flahavan, J.F., & Tierney, R.J. (1996). Moving beyond reading and writing in the content areas to discipline-based inquiry. In D. Lapp, J. Flood, & N. Farnan (Eds.), *Content area reading and learning instructional strategies* (2nd ed., pp. 339–351). Boston: Allyn & Bacon.

Zemelman, S., & Daniels, H. (1988). *A community of writers: Teaching writing in the junior and senior high school.* Portsmouth, NH: Heinemann.

Beth Broder Epstein

Creating Skinny Books Helps Students Learn About Difficult Topics

When students create "skinny books" through researching minitopics they want to explore, they feel a real sense of ownership in their learning. What is a skinny book? It is a collection—an anthology—of photocopied articles compiled from newspapers, magazines, microfiche, and books relating to a topic a student wants to learn more about (see D. Watson in *Whole Language Strategies for Secondary Students*, Richard C. Owen, 1988, p. 33).

As students go through the steps of their project, they learn research strategies, first by asking narrow, answerable questions. They use the question starters Who? What? Where? When? Why? How? Causes? Consequences? Gathering answers, they learn the parts, placement, and function of books as they construct and bind their own. Their product is a whole text we call a skinny book.

Students learn to include both primary and secondary material and both objective and subjective sources. They collect material from both short and long works. As they collect and photocopy selections, they begin to organize their materials into "chapters," learning how to divide and classify, moving from broad to narrow subject, playing the role of research editor as they work. They learn to analyze and synthesize as they accumulate information. They decide what to include and exclude on the basis of repetition, writing quality, currency, or relevance to their minitopic. They document their sources in a list that appears in their book.

As they create their anthology, they also highlight the vocabulary from the articles that they believe their audience needs to know to understand their topics. They include these words in a glossary at the end of their books. As they read, they identify related subtopics that appear in several of the articles to create an index.

To construct their books, they use their sources as models. Skinny books contain a title page, copyright page, dedication page, table of contents, list of works cited, glossary, and index. Students learn standard forms as well as research and reporting strategies and book parts and uses.

Seventh graders can use skinny books in a unit on the Holocaust because material is easily accessible through books, television, newspapers, and magazines, as well as from members of their grandparents' generation. This material raises so many issues to investigate that students should have no problem narrowing a topic. On the other hand, the issues of moral choice, civic responsibility, and human behavior raised by Holocaust study make the period a challenge for teachers who may often feel their own knowledge base is in-

Reprinted From the *Journal of Adolescent & Adult Literacy*, *39*(6), 496–497, March 1996.

adequate. But when students create skinny books, the teacher poses not as the expert on the topic but as an information resource and advisor. The teacher coaches students about how and where to find answers for questions, pointing out relationships and celebrating accomplishments. Making skinny books is a way to help students learn more and overcome a teacher's own sense of being overwhelmed by a subject.

I anchor my seventh-grade unit on the Holocaust to novels, poetry, and memoirs of World War II. Good literature has always posed the important questions about human nature, and good authors have never assumed that the answers are easy. It also shows readers that more knowledge helps us to ask well-framed questions of ourselves and our society.

All of my students read *Daniel's Story* (Carol Matas, Scholastic, 1993), but students can also select other books and form natural cooperative reading groups according to their selections. The historical base gives students a chronological framework and allows them to use background knowledge about the war. Students can also make associations between what they know about World War II from recent 50th anniversary commemorations, what they learn from grandparents, other relatives, and neighbors through oral history interviews, and information they find skimming newspapers and magazines. Inevitably, their reading and oral history interviews lead students to develop their own questions. When they do, they naturally assume the roles of research editors.

For example, one student who had heard about Yevgeny Yevtushenko's poem "Babbi Yar" (translated in *Twentieth Century Russian Poetry, Silver and Steel: An Anthology*, Doubleday, 1994) asked what happened at Babi Yar. Another wanted to know about Kristallnacht (Night of the Broken Glass) because he was intrigued by the sound and translation of that term. Another, having seen the movie *Schindler's List* with her family, wanted to know more about rescuers and then narrowed this large topic to Raoul Wallenberg's activities in Budapest. Each of these interests led to a different skinny book.

As students play the role of editor in selecting and laying out material, they learn about their topic, they consider the needs of their audience, and they satisfy their own purposes in answering questions important to them. When they are finished, they have a complete product—a bound book—that they can share with great pride in a whole-class symposium. Students use their skinny books to teach others about their topics because they have become the experts. Constructing a vision of the whole subject by seeing each skinny book as a piece of the puzzle, we acknowledge the limitations of what we have learned as well as celebrate our growth. We know what we know—and what we might continue exploring.

Creating skinny books brings home to students the need to be lifelong learners. Our books contain an average of 15 to 25 articles, portions of articles, and illustrations. We realize that there is more to know, even as we celebrate having created a minilibrary. We also recognize that finding, organizing, and sharing information is a hallmark of becoming an educated adult and a good citizen.

Sharon E. Andrews

Writing to Learn in Content Area Reading Class

Overwhelming support exists in the literature for using writing to learn in all content areas, from math to science to social studies. Most of the preservice teachers I work with in a content area reading class equate writing to learn with only one format, journal writing. Most students recall a freewriting that did not target course content. Typically, these writing-to-learn experiences were limited to their English classrooms.

I have long advocated using writing as a tool to promote learning and have employed learning logs as an assessment tool. Learning logs allowed students to become engaged in writing, facilitated their involvement with course content, and served as a powerful model of writing to learn. Unfortunately, my announcement that we would be writing in learning logs was often met with groans of disappointment and protests that "We've been journaled to death!" Perhaps the overuse and sometimes misuse of journal writing, in the name of writing to learn, has caused students to develop negative attitudes toward this format. Based upon their prior experiences with journal writing, students felt that there was no inherent purpose and did not feel that it was time well spent.

I still advocate the use of learning logs, based upon my positive experiences in using them and the tremendous amount of feedback related to the course I received through them. However, I took on the challenge of responding to my students' protests and began to consider how I could use alternative writing-to-learn strategies.

After experimenting, I have come to feel most comfortable with the following writing-to-learn strategies: admit/exit slips, looping, cinquains/progressive cinquains, and What I Know/What I Want to Know/What I Learned (K-W-L). Although I still yearn for the familiarity and comfort of learning logs, implementing a variety of strategies has made me a more effective role model and advocate for writing to learn. The likelihood of my students using writing to learn in their own classrooms will be greater.

Admit/Exit Slips

Admit/exit slips are among the most versatile writing-to-learn strategies. Perhaps the most attractive feature of this strategy is its brevity. This makes it a favorite among my students, and many imagine that they could and will use admit/exit slips in their future classrooms.

Upon arrival to class, students are given an index card and asked to respond to a question, such as "What was the most important

Reprinted From the *Journal of Adolescent & Adult Literacy*, *41*(2), 141–142, October 1997.

aspect of your assigned reading?" or "What questions do you have about the assignment?" or "What aspect of today's lesson are you most interested in discussing?" Students complete their admit slip as a "ticket" into class. Discussion of their responses provides the springboard into the topic area. The slips also provide a nice model of activating students' schema and allow the class to have a voice in the direction of the day's lesson.

Conversely, exit slips provide an effective way to bring closure to a day's lesson. Students are asked to reflect upon the day's lesson and respond on an index card to questions like "What did you learn today?" or "What do you want to learn more about?" or "What is still confusing you?" The information I receive on exit slips can assist in determining what topics need additional time and can provide ideas for extending the learning experience.

Another attractive feature of admit/exit slips is that students are not asked to sign their names; thus, it is a safe place for students to voice their concerns regarding course content.

Looping

I also use looping, another writing-to-learn strategy, when we are beginning to explore a new concept or topic area. Students are asked to turn to a clean page in their notebooks and write whatever comes to mind about a particular idea or concept, for a set period of time, usually from 3 to 5 minutes. I ask them to keep writing for the entire, time even if they can only jot down words or phrases, as long as it is related to their understanding of the topic. At the end of the time period, students are asked to stop writing, read what they have written, and summarize it into one succinct sentence.

When they have completed their sentences, students fold their papers so only their sentences are showing. They pass their papers to their neighbors, who are asked to read the sentence written by their classmate and continue writing about the topic area, using their classmate's sentence as a beginning point. Students again write for a set period and repeat the process of freewriting, rereading, and writing one sentence. This process is repeated as many times as needed.

Throughout the process of freewriting and summarizing, students are exploring, in writing, their understanding of the topic area and responding to their classmates' perspectives. At the conclusion of the looping exercise, students return the papers to their originators, and the final sentences are shared and provide the basis for a rich discussion of the topic. I typically use this exercise when we first begin discussing the area of metacognition. It has worked well to bring out students' thoughts and ideas.

Cinquains / Progressive Cinquains

Cinquains and progressive cinquains are another writing-to-learn strategy that I have successfully employed. A cinquain is just one version of patterned poetry writing (you may be familiar with biopoems or story frames). A cinquain is a five-line poem in which each line represents a particular aspect of the topic. The first line is one word, a noun, that could be the topic itself or a word that is synonymous with the topic. The second line is a two-word description of the topic. The third line is made up of three -*ing* words that convey the action of the topic. The fourth line is a four-word phrase describing the topic and showing feeling. The fifth line is a single synonym that restates the essence of the topic.

When students have created their individual cinquains, they can be shared and displayed, or the activity could continue by employing progressive cinquains. With progressive cinquains, students pair up and create a collaborative cinquain by using bits and pieces of their individual cinquains or together create an entirely new cinquain. Pairs then form quads and the process of negotiating and collaborating to create yet another cinquain is repeated. Groups then share their cinquains by reading them aloud and/or putting them on the board. Groups also explain the process they went through to arrive at their final cinquain.

I have used cinquains after we have studied schema theory. As students collaborate and negotiate word choices, their understanding of schema theory is strengthened, and they agree that this writing-to-learn strategy caused them to think and reflect about their understanding of the topic.

Following are examples of schema cinquains created during a recent semester:

Schema
Background Knowledge
Activating, Anticipating, Analyzing
Linking New to Old
Learning

Schema
Prior Information
Thinking, Organizing, Remembering
Making Connections and Associations
Knowledge

Schema
Personal Understanding
Connecting, Associating, Remembering
Broadening One's Own Understanding
Wisdom

K-W-L

I use K-W-L (What I Know, What I Want to Know, and What I Learned) often and in a variety of ways. K-W-L was originated by Donna Ogle (see "K-W-L: A Teaching Method That Develops Active Reading of Expository Text"

in *The Reading Teacher*, 1986, pp. 564–570). I typically use this strategy early in my course as a way to get students thinking about the major topics we will study throughout the semester. Topics typically include transactional philosophy of teaching and learning, instructional frameworks, the process of learning, schema theory, metacognition, writing to learn, teaching skills in context, alternative and authentic assessment, thematic units, and planning instruction for students with special needs.

K-W-L becomes a writing-to-learn strategy as students circulate around the room, writing what they know and what they want to know on posterboards devoted to different topic areas. As students read one another's contributions, it activates their own schema about topic areas and they are able to add to the K-W-L posters. I have also arranged the desks in a circle and rotated sheets around the circle for students to write on. The size of my class usually dictates which format I use.

As students complete the What I Want to Know portion of the K-W-L posters or sheets, the activity provides me with direction in planning future class meetings. I also refer back to the students' contributions upon each new topic area's introduction to the course and often read some aloud as a way to activate students' thinking about a new topic area before they attempt an assigned reading.

At the last class meeting, I bring out the original K-W-L posters or sheets for students to complete the What I Learned portion. This provides students with an effective review as they prepare to write their final essay exam.

Writing to learn provides a format for students to demonstrate their personal understanding of course content. Use of writing-to-learn strategies in our own teaching can encourage preservice teachers to incorporate writing to learn in their future content area classrooms.

Lois E. Huffman

Spotlighting Specifics by Combining Focus Questions With K-W-L

K-W-L is a well-known, simple strategy for developing comprehension by helping students relate what they know to what they read, hear, or view. Originated by Donna Ogle (see "KWL: A Teaching Model that Develops Active Reading with Expository Text" in *The Reading Teacher*, 1986, pp. 564–570), K-W-L is an acronym for the three steps of the procedure: activating what we Know, determining what we Want to learn, and assessing what we Learned. To begin the process, students write ideas for Steps K and W; at the end of the lesson, they complete Step L. Typically, information is recorded in a three-column chart.

Many variants of K-W-L have been suggested. Arne Sippola's "K-W-L-S" (see *The Reading Teacher*, 1995, pp. 542–543) emphasizes metacognition and further inquiry by including a separate column for "What I still need to learn." Utilization of multiple sources of information is likewise encouraged in K-W-L charts that provide a column for "How we will find out" (see Ogle's "Study Techniques That Ensure Content Success" in *Content Area Reading and Learning* edited by Diane Lapp, Jim Flood, and Nancy Farnan, Boston: Allyn & Bacon, 1996). "K-W-L Plus" developed by Eileen Carr and Donna Ogle (*Journal of Reading*, 1987, pp. 626–631) adds mapping and summarizing

to the three principal components to promote reorganization and consolidation of information. In their adaptation of the K-W-L activity, Judy Richardson and Raymond Morgan (*Reading to Learn in the Content Areas*, Belmont, CA: Wadsworth, 1997) acknowledge the importance of affect in learning by also asking students to indicate how they feel about the reading.

K-W-L can be further enhanced by incorporating focus questions into the basic procedure. Focus questions direct attention toward important aspects of a topic and encourage in-depth examination of subject matter. When a lesson includes a considerable amount of content or students possess extensive background knowledge, spotlighting specifics with questions may make learning more manageable and meaningful.

Generating focus questions is a relatively simple task. The instructor might select from questions that are often provided at the beginning or end of a reading selection, choosing those that are thoughtful and targeted toward important concepts. S/he can also modify existing questions to match students' needs and curricular goals. Another option is to develop a set of focus questions that mirrors the major content objectives of the lesson.

For some topics and groups, still another possibility is to simply ask Who? What? When?

Reprinted From the *Journal of Adolescent & Adult Literacy*, *41*(6), 470–472, March 1998.

Where? Why? and How? (as relevant to lesson content). Focusing on the 5 Ws and How during each step of K-W-L ensures that students will not overlook essential facts. These generic questions, like more specific ones, provide a useful framework for organizing and storing information in print and memory.

K-W-L can be implemented at all levels with almost any subject matter. In the content reading methods class that I teach, I combined focus questions with K-W-L in a lesson on "Learning With Visuals." Because of previous coursework in art, design, technology, and computers as well as everyday experience in our visually oriented world, many of the prospective teachers in the class already knew a great deal about graphic aids. Much of their prior knowledge was applicable to the lesson. To help them key into the most pertinent ideas and issues, I posed the following questions at the outset of the lesson: "What are visuals/graphics?" "What is the relationship between visuals and text?" "What is visual literacy?" "Why is visual literacy important?" "How can teachers help students read visu-

als effectively?" "What are some ways educators can assist students in generating useful visuals?" These questions were written at the top of a large K-W-L chart that was posted in the classroom (see Figure).

The class used the questions to maintain focus throughout the K-W-L activity. During Step K, the students jotted down ideas on the chart under each question. The questions enabled them to quickly identify areas of inconsistency or deficiency in their pooled knowledge. For example, students brainstormed numerous ideas and examples in relation to the questions "What are visuals/graphics?" "What is visual literacy?" and "Why is visual literacy important?" Their responses to the other focus questions were limited. In fact, some of the preservice teachers were not able to answer the question, "How can teachers help students read visuals effectively?" They admitted that they usually ignored textbook graphic aids and did not recall receiving instruction in how to utilize visuals in content texts.

Chart used for combining focus questions with K-W-L

	What are visuals/ graphics?	What is the relationship between visuals and texts?	What is visual literacy?	Why is visual literacy important?	How can teachers help students read visuals effectively?	What are some ways educators can assist students in generating useful visuals?
K						
W						
L						

In Step W, class members listed their individual concerns related to the focus questions introduced in Step K. For example, in response to the question, "How can teachers help students read visuals effectively?" they wrote that they wanted to learn such things as "creative ways to get kids to pay attention to tables" and "what I can do to help my students get something out of pictures." For homework, I asked them to read two journal articles on the lesson topic. Their interactions with the texts were guided by both the focus questions and the concerns we generated in Step W.

During the postreading phase of the lesson, the focus questions served as a guide for discussing the articles. Interwoven in the discussion were several activities that applied and extended information in the readings. To conclude Step L, the students amended the K-W-L chart to show their new understandings. The bulk of their ideas pertained to the focus questions about which they initially knew little or had many concerns.

Throughout the activity, there was a high level of student interest and engagement. In reflecting on the lesson, many of the teacher education students recognized the scaffolding that the questions offered. Some compared the questions to "cues" and "hints."

One young woman, who had been required to use the K-W-L format for journal entries in another education course, said that with focus questions, she "didn't feel that [her] thoughts were so scattered."

The focus questions also seemed to influence performance on the final exam. In responding to an essay item on visual literacy, many students organized their answers in a manner that was reminiscent of the focus questions. In general, their explanations of visual literacy teaching techniques were also more detailed than those of students from the previous semester who had studied the same topic using only the basic K-W-L procedure.

While questions can help learners at all levels manage large amounts of material, they may be particularly beneficial to students with attention, learning, or language difficulties. These students may not yet be ready, sufficiently confident, or capable of activating and constructing knowledge through the standard steps of K-W-L. They may require teacher guidance to stay on task, analyze a topic, and structure information. Focusing the K-W-L procedure with questions may provide the additional direction and physical involvement that these learners need, increasing both the efficiency and effectiveness of this versatile instructional strategy.

Leslie Anne Oja

Using Story Frames to Develop Reading Comprehension

In the last decade comprehension research has encouraged teachers to give their students opportunities to become more engaged in literature. Repeated readings, story retellings, and dramatic reenactments allow students to become more aware of stories and more familiar with their structure. This article provides an overview of another type of comprehension strategy: the story frame.

The term *story frame* can refer to a number of methods for looking at a story's structure. For my purposes, the story frame is a cloze procedure. However, instead of only one word being left out of a sentence, key phrases or clauses are left out of a paragraph that summarizes the story or highlights some important aspect of it.

Using story frames along with the basic elements of story grammar directs both students' and teachers' attention to the actual structure of the story and how the content fits that structure. The strategy is particularly useful with middle school students, who are developing summarizing skills and other basic analytic approaches to literature.

Story frames can be used with basal stories as well as trade books. However, because not all the elements in a specific story frame are present in all stories, it may be necessary to develop more than one story frame or change previously used story frames to fit the passage. For example, you may start with "This story begins when…" and add "and then." Following this you may add words that appropriately follow the sequence of events such as "next," "following that," or "the problem is solved when…."

Students' ability to monitor their comprehension may be enhanced by using story frames. Students have an opportunity to review the main idea of the story, clarify parts they may not have understood, and decide on the author's purpose for writing the story. (See Gerald L. Fowler, "Developing Comprehension Skills in Primary Students Through the Use of Story Frames," *The Reading Teacher*, vol. 36, 1982, pp. 176–179.)

Figure 1 shows five types of story frames that may be appropriate for all types of stories; however, you will probably find that one or two of them will fit your style or purpose more readily. I suggest you first introduce students to one of the simpler types of frames after they have completed reading a story. Initially, the whole class may complete the cloze activity posed by the story frame. Story frames also lend themselves to cooperative group work or a reading partner format. After students become more adept at using each type of story frame, they may use frames as advance organizers to monitor their own comprehension as they read.

Reprinted From the *Journal of Adolescent & Adult Literacy*, 40(2), 129–130, October 1996.

Figure 1
Types of story frames

Story summary with one character

Our story is about _____.
_____ is an important
character in our story. _____
tried to _____.
The story ends when _____.

Important idea or plot

In this story, the problem starts when _____.
After that, _____. Next, _____.
Then, _____.
The problem is finally solved when _____.
The story ends _____.

Setting

The story takes place _____.
I know this because the author uses the words " _____
_____."
Other clues that show when the story takes place are __
_____.

Character analysis

_____ is an important
character in this story. _____ is
important because _____
Once, he/she _____
Another time, _____.
I think that _____(character's name)_____ is _____(character's trait)_____ because _____.

Character comparison

_____ and _____ are
two characters in this story. _____(character's name)_____ is
_____(character's trait)_____ while _____(other character's name)_____ is _____(character's trait)_____.
For instance, _____ tries to _____.
_____ learns a lesson when _____
_____
_____.

Figure 2 shows two middle school students' story frames.

The following questions can help you create your own story frame: (a) Is there a problem? (b) If so, why is it a problem? (c) Is there a relevant sequence of events that leads to a solution of the problem? (d) If so, what is the sequence? (e) How is the problem resolved? (f) How does the story end? After answering these questions, look over the basic frame to make sure it will fit the cloze procedure. If

Figure 2
Sample student story frames

not, often the addition or deletion of a few words will correct the problem.

When introducing story frames, tell the students that when they complete a frame they will have a summary or a short way of retelling the story that they have just read. You may want to begin with half-page frames because they are less intimidating to students learning this process (see Karen Wood, "Probable Passages: A Writing Strategy," *The Reading Teacher*, vol. 37, 1984, pp. 496–499).

The main purpose of the story frame is to encourage students to rethink some aspect of the story. They can refer back to the passage if necessary as they complete the frame. As with any reading activity, the more engaged and enthusiastic your students are about the content, the more effective the strategy will be.

SECTION 5

Varying Texts to Meet Students' Interests and Needs

Finding reading material that appeals to adolescents who struggle with reading sometimes is difficult. Textbooks can seem like inaccessible tomes. Literary texts written for younger children can seem offensive, even though they might be easier to understand. More complex chapter books might look uninviting even though they contain interesting, even exciting stories that might encourage reading. Informational books written for adolescents who struggle with reading can be difficult to acquire.

The articles in this section describe many ways to overcome these obstacles. The authors share useful hints for using a variety of print with adolescents to develop literacy skills, to help with subject-area study, and to support family literacy. They present practices for stimulating reading and for establishing personal identities as readers. Several articles in this section list useful book titles, and they present ways to regularly add titles to your own lists.

Jo Worthy

"On Every Page Someone Gets Killed!" Book Conversations You Don't Hear in School

While eating ice cream outside on a warm spring night, my sixth-grade son, Jared, and his friend, Chase, began talking about books they had recently read and books they were planning to read. They weren't talking to me, but I asked them to hold their thoughts while I ran to the car to get my tape recorder. After some self-conscious giggling and posturing, they continued their conversation, with Chase taking the lead.

> Chase: I just read *Cycle of the Werewolf* (King, 1983). It was only 120 pages, and most of Stephen King's books are like 500 pages. And the thing about it is, it's so gripping. On every page someone gets killed.
>
> Jared: Yeah! But I mean it's really, really descriptive, and the pictures are amazing—they look like real photographs. And it's a really good book.
>
> Chase: Yeah! The only thing I don't understand is how he became a werewolf.
>
> Jared: It said that he went to a graveyard and got flowers and the flowers like withered and died and shot some spores at him and made him like a werewolf.
>
> Chase: Oh yeah! Cool!

In my experience as a classroom teacher in middle and elementary school, a reading specialist, and a school-based preservice and inservice teacher educator, I have rarely heard a conversation like this take place in a classroom. Jared and Chase's conversation was spontaneous, informal, self-directed, and similar to a conversation about a book adults might have in the coffee room at work or over the dinner table. Books in which someone gets killed on every page are not the usual school fare, and, to be honest, I am uncomfortable that my son and his friend were so obviously thrilled by this genre. However, after hearing many times from teachers that Jared was not an engaged reader and from him that he hated reading class, I was pleasantly shocked that he would spend his own time voluntarily talking about books.

My sense of the importance of the conversation between Chase and Jared was heightened by my interest in students who are labeled "reluctant readers" and by the fact that the excitement they demonstrated is so rare in school "book talk," particularly beyond the elementary grades. Through my work and interviews with students who say they don't like to read, I have found the reluctant reader label to be ambiguous because what appears to be reluctance may stem from a variety of complex and individual factors (Worthy & McKool, 1996). Jared and Chase

Reprinted From the *Journal of Adolescent & Adult Literacy*, *41*(7), 508–517, April 1998.

were both considered disengaged readers in their language arts classes, but, like other so-called reluctant readers that I've talked to, they were passionate about reading self-selected materials outside of school. Their perspectives, presented here, suggest that we may need to rethink how reading is presented in school if we are to reach preadolescent and older students.

Reluctant Readers and School Reading

Research about reading attitudes and voluntary reading shows that, in general, both show a steady decline as students progress through school and that negative attitudes become especially prevalent in the middle and high school years (Cline & Kretke, 1980; McKenna, Ellsworth, & Kear, 1995; Shapiro & White, 1991). Despite this grim portrayal, however, researchers have noted that some adolescents read more than educators think they do, even if they do not appear to enjoy reading in school (Alvermann, Young, Green, & Wisenbaker, 1996; Bintz, 1993; Worthy & McKool, 1996). Through interviews with high school students fitting the reluctant reader profile, Bintz concluded that some students "lose interest in school reading as they progress through school but do not lose interest in reading per se" and that one major reason for resistance to school reading is that students "are forced to read materials that they have no voice in selecting" (p. 612).

Perhaps another reason for students' resistance to school reading is their perceived or real lack of control in classroom book talk. Recent research has focused on the desirability of moving from teacher-controlled recitation, in which student participation and interaction are minimal, to discussion or open forum (Alpert, 1987; Alvermann,

O'Brien, & Dillon, 1990; Cazden, 1988; Mehan, 1979). Discussion implies active student participation and collaborative construction of meaning, rather than passive answering of teachers' questions. Participating in discussions has potential cognitive, social, and affective benefits (Almasi, 1997). Teacher-led discussions, however, sometimes tend to slip back to the old recitation mode, with the teacher controlling the tone and direction of the conversations, determining turn-taking, and emphasizing specific skills or curricular goals (McMahon, 1997).

Book discussions led by students rather than teachers can allow students to "engage in exploratory thinking, resulting in more extended and more elaborate mental representations and higher level analytical thinking" (Gambrell, 1997, p. 31) as well as to improve communication skills and attitudes toward reading (Almasi, 1997). Researchers and practitioners point out that as long as students are provided instruction and modeling in effective group process (Au, 1993) and have interaction guidelines, topics to discuss, and tasks to complete (Purves, Rogers, & Soter, 1990), student-led discussions can be quite productive.

Jared and Chase's conversation takes student-led discussions a step further. It is student initiated, and there *are* no guidelines, no preset topics to discuss, no tasks to complete, no requirements to cover particular issues or skills, and no teacher or designated leader to make sure the participants stay on task. Because of the informal context and the rather illicit (for school) books they discussed, I have dubbed their conversation a "renegade" book discussion.

In this article, I examine the renegade book conversation of two middle school reluctant readers, provide background information on the participants and on related research, and explore through interviews the participants' perspectives and attitudes toward reading both at the time of the initial conversation and 2 years later. Their perspectives hold implications for educators who are interested in improving students' engagement with reading in school.

Exploring Reading with Renegade Readers

At the time of the book conversation and first interview, Jared and Chase were in sixth grade in a middle school in central Texas, USA, with homogeneously grouped language arts classes. They were in the same basic language arts class in which they kept B averages. Both Chase and Jared had followed a typical course of development in all academic and social areas and had been average to above-average students during their earlier school years. Each had grown up in homes in which literacy was valued and reading materials were abundant, and in which they had rich access to books, magazines, and comics of their choice. Both had enjoyed reading in their preschool and primary years, and both had begun to resist school reading in their upper elementary years and continued to do so. Although they were more likely to spend their free time playing video games, playing sports, or "hanging out" with their friends, they both read regularly from self-selected materials at home. Neither read standard fiction or nonfiction at home except for what was required to complete school assignments. Both Jared and Chase had discovered less conventional materials, such as comics, drawing books, and magazines in elementary school, and had begun before middle school to read horror and suspense books mainly written for adults.

According to Nieto (1994), students' voices are often missing in discussions of education-al practice. In consideration of the importance of including students' perspectives, the data examined for this study consist of Jared's and Chase's own words gathered through their renegade book conversation and interviews. In the renegade conversation, I was an observer and participant on the fringe, asking occasional questions to clarify issues that arose but letting the boys do most of the talking. Within a week after the initial conversation, I conducted individual follow-up interviews with both boys in which I inquired about school and home reading and asked them to help me understand better some of the issues brought up in their conversations.

During the 2 years that elapsed between Jared and Chase's renegade conversation and follow-up interviews, I analyzed the transcripts and my notes several times and wrote reflections. Following procedures recommended for constant comparative analysis (Erlandson, Harris, Skipper, & Allen, 1993; Strauss & Corbin, 1990), I first unitized the data into meaningful segments (phrases, sentences, or paragraphs), wrote summaries and reactions to each unit, and made an exhaustive list of issues and topics that emerged. I shared these with a colleague, who offered advice and new insights. I then grouped the list of issues and topics into broader categories and asked a different peer to comment. I further refined the categories and evaluated my analysis in terms of previous research results, wrote a first draft of the paper, and formulated questions for the follow-up interview (Miles & Huberman, 1994). Two years later, I showed both boys a draft of this article, and we read and discussed it together. They gave feedback on my descriptions and analysis and updated me on their current ideas about reading both in and out of school.

My analysis of Jared and Chase's conversations and interviews is presented in the following sections. I begin with discoveries about their reading habits both in and out of school and follow with their recommendations to teachers for making school reading more engaging for students.

Discoveries About Renegade Readers

While analyzing the initial renegade book conversation and subsequent interviews, I found three salient themes. Chase and Jared's conversation illustrates that they understood and were engaged in the books they discussed. Their preferences were ardent and discriminating. Chase and Jared expressed general indifference and sometimes distaste toward reading in school.

Demonstrating understanding and engagement through conversation. Following their *Cycle of the Werewolf* discussion, Chase continued the conversation by talking about another book both boys had recently read. They collaboratively summarized and evaluated the book and clarified plot details. As in the first excerpt, their engagement and understanding were readily apparent. They understood the plot at both literal and inferential levels, and when events were unclear, Jared asked a question about a plot point (italicized) and Chase clarified.

> Chase: Oh and I just got done reading *Congo* (Crichton, 1980), too.
> Jared: Oh, yeah!
> Chase: Like it's really sick at the beginning. It's like he steps on this, he thought it was like this...
> Jared: Berries.
> Chase: Yeah, berries. And it was an eyeball. It was like a human eyeball and it was like, squishing.
> Jared: They were throwing eyeballs at him, the monkeys.

> Chase: And they had, they had like a submarine going underwater searching for the lost city, Congo.... And at the end they find the place Congo but it's like all shredded up and it's really disgusting how they describe it.
> Jared: Isn't in *Congo*, isn't it like the monkeys beat people with paddles or something?
> Chase: Yeah.
> Jared: *How do they stop 'em at the end?*
> Chase: They like set this bomb up to stop all the monkeys and it like makes a big explosion....

As the conversation continued, Jared and Chase talked more about *Congo* and *Cycle of the Werewolf*. They had recently seen movie versions of both after having read the books. The movie and book talk included thoughtful evaluations of the similarities, noting differences in plot, character, and detail. Later they both discussed books that they had recently read, giving concise summaries and either recommending or panning the books. Jared discussed and highly recommended John Grisham's books, and Chase had mixed reviews of books by Christopher Pike and Lois Duncan that he had just read. The remainder of the conversation was dedicated to talk about personal preferences and how they chose books.

Even the short segments of the renegade book conversation shown in this article include elements that researchers and teachers find important in book discussion. The boys used and understood vocabulary from the books, and their talk was full of "book language." They compared, synthesized, evaluated, responded personally, and supported their opinions with examples (Rosenblatt, 1983; Zarillo & Cox, 1992). Names of authors were bandied about, and the boys made intertextual and experiential connections (Zarillo & Cox, 1992). They both actively participated, collaboratively constructed meaning (Alpert, 1987; Alvermann, O'Brien, & Dillon, 1990), and clarified and questioned when necessary. Their talk had an authentic "real reader" quality that teacher-led discussions and even book club meetings usually don't have, because Chase and Jared's talk was unstructured and decidedly informal, and there was no agenda. It seems clear that such talk has led and will continue to lead the boys toward more books.

Book preferences: "What's the big deal About R.L. Stine?" Popular materials don't suit everyone. General preferences for reading materials seem to go in cycles. At any given time there are materials that are wildly popular among most students. However, educators caution that general preferences do not apply to everyone (Monson & Sebesta, 1991). As Howes (1963) pointed out: "Each child is himself no matter what the generalizations about the reading patterns and interests for his age may be" (p. 492). Jared and Chase's conversation underscored these cautions. A major theme of the book discussion and individual interviews was the boys' ardent personal, individualized preferences. They liked many of the same books (especially suspense and horror), but they also had some different personal tastes (Chase liked sports and didn't like fantasy at all, while Jared liked fantasy, science fiction, and suspense novels but only particular authors, such as Piers Anthony and John Grisham).

The boys emphasized that because certain books or genres are generally popular, it doesn't mean that they are universally liked. At the time of the book conversations and interviews, Goosebumps (Stine) were the most popular books among late elementary to middle school students (Worthy & Turner, 1997). Although horror was Jared's and Chase's favorite genre, they didn't like the "childish horror" of Goosebumps or R.L.

Stine. Chase spoke with disdain about Stine's popularity among other students in the school by saying "I don't know what's the big deal about R.L. Stine." Jared agreed: "He's a freak! He writes like a book every week." Jared went on to explain that "[R.L. Stine's] books are really childish," they have the "corniest titles," and "they're not really scary." He insisted that he "wouldn't even have liked them in second grade." This disdain for popular books did not seem to be overgeneralized, though. While both boys were quick to reject books that did not immediately grab their attention, they were open to recommendations from peers, parents, and teachers. Jared and his father often read and discussed John Grisham's books, and Chase's father had introduced him to Stephen King's novels. Parent recommendations weren't always successful, though. Chase shared a recent memory of attempting to read a book his mother highly recommended.

> One book I cannot get into. My mom requested it [from the library] and I started to read it: *Gone With the Wind* (Mitchell, 1939). I got 200 pages into it and I fell asleep (laughter). 'Cause all it was was just romance. Like, this guy, at the very beginning he gets home, and they marry, and they start in on the romance. And the next page—romance. Ten pages later—romance. It's like nonstop romance. They could have declared me legally dead, I was so bored.

Chase explained that after that experience he always went to the library and bookstore with his mother "'cause she doesn't really choose good books."

"Chase usually recommends it": Deciding what to read. I asked the boys to talk about how they decided what books to read. Consistent with the results of previous studies (Burgess, 1985; Wendelin & Zinck, 1983), Jared and Chase considered the genre, author, title, summary, and physical features

of the book, including length, cover illustration, and back cover summary when they chose books. As other researchers have found (Wendelin & Zinck, 1983; Worthy & Turner, 1997), peer recommendations have become increasingly important to Jared and Chase over the years.

Jared: Well, Chase usually recommends it. How do you decide about the books?

Chase: OK, well, I'll tell you. Usually what I do is I go to the bookstore, I go straight to the section I like—suspense—'cause I can get into that. Uh, let's see, drama is dull. Romance—sleep. I don't like Tom Clancy 'cause his books are too much of the cop and CIA type stuff; I don't get into that. Let's see, I'm not into J.R.R. Tolkein; I don't like that fantasy stuff.

Jared: Fantasy's OK. It depends on who the author is.

Chase: Yeah. But, like I said, I go to the bookstore, I pick up the book. If the author I know is recognizable, it grips my attention. The title sometimes gets me and then the cover.

Jo: What kinds of covers and titles do you look for?

Jared: The suspenseful titles, good titles...

Chase: I got *Cujo* (King, 1981). You see the claw and he's like making a big scratch and it's cool...

Jared: A bloody scratch...

Chase: Yeah, and...I always read the back before I buy something, too, and that's basically it.

Jared: You usually recommend them to me.

Chase: Yeah, I usually recommend books to Jared. And I just got done reading *Gone But Not Forgotten*. It's a book by Philip Margolin (1993). It's about this, like this really smart killer who leaves, all he leaves after the killing is just an envelope and a rose on it that says "gone but not forgotten." And at the end they like shoot him. It's so stu-

pid but like they have this rose gun, it's like a gun with a rose on it (laughter). It's so stupid (laughter from both boys).

Jared: I'm gonna read *Gone But Not Forgotten*.

Chase: I have it, do you want to borrow it?

The last segment of conversation above illustrates the power of peer book recommendations for Jared. If not for his talks with Chase, Jared might not have discovered *Gone But Not Forgotten*, a book that he went on to read later. In fact, Jared's reading was often dependent upon a confluence of having the right materials at the right time and "nothing else to do." In the next segment of the renegade conversation, Chase and Jared talked about another book that Chase had recommended.

"There was nothing else I wanted to read right then." After he struggled with reading in his early elementary years, Jared's attitude toward school reading was quite negative by the late elementary years. He had developed intense, personal interests in reading materials that were not typically found in school, and his decision to read or not to read was dependent on the availability of those specific materials. When he had his sights set on a particular book or comic (usually the result of a peer recommendation), a different publication even in the same genre or by the same author wouldn't satisfy him. His self-selected books and comics are still on his shelves, and he revisits them frequently.

Jared and Chase again brought up *Cycle of the Werewolf*, and Jared's sister, who was 7 at the time of the conversation, recalled Jared's exhaustive search for it.

Jenna: Jared liked that book so much he went to three or four bookstores to get it.

Jared: I went to like five or six bookstores, and they didn't have it anywhere.

Jo: So why didn't you just get another book?

Jared: See, 'cause I really, really wanted to read it, and there was nothing else I wanted to read right then. And [after I got it] I read it in like 2 hours.

In the individual interviews, the boys explored the topic of school reading. Their perspectives on assigned reading were quite different from their voluntary reading and gave me some insight into why they were at best indifferent to reading in school.

School reading. I asked both boys to talk generally about their perspectives and enjoyment of reading in school and probed with additional questions about time for reading and materials available. According to the boys, reading that was done in school was largely teacher selected, teacher directed, and skills focused.

In many classrooms, time allotted for sustained reading is relatively rare, even during instructional periods (Allington, 1994; Morrow, 1991; Ysseldyke & Algozzine, 1982–1983). Jared's and Chase's perspectives of their classrooms were consistent with patterns identified in earlier studies. Jared and Chase said that there was rarely a planned reading time in their classes; that most such times took place serendipitously. Thus, students didn't always have their personal books with them to use during free reading times. In fact, Jared took a personal book to school for a week but found only a few occasional minutes to read it. When the opportunity for free reading finally came, he didn't have his book with him, and he had to read one of his teacher's "booooring" books.

The books they read as assignments, Jared explained, were from a variety of genres ("just not horror"), with a focus on "things like biographical fiction," chosen to follow the school's curriculum. Both boys read the books they were assigned in school, and both had enjoyed some of them but "hated" most. While the teacher's library contained "a couple of good books," according to the boys, "lots of people have already read 'em," and most of the other books are "not very good." According to Chase, a few of the books "look good but you don't have time to read 'em anyway." Thus, their time and opportunities to get involved in books during school were limited.

The boys said that they rarely had time to talk to their peers about books in class, but that they often talked about and recommended books to each other during lunch. Jared said, "Chase really likes horror books and so I usually listen to him and he usually has good books that he recommends." I was encouraged that these boys, who had been labeled reluctant readers by their teachers, were so excited about their own reading that the subject regularly came up at lunch and outside of school.

Eighth-grade update: "I haven't read my own book in like a year." Two years after the initial book conversation, Jared, Chase, and I met to listen to the first tape and to read the first draft of this article together, so they could comment and update me on their current in-school and out-of-school reading attitudes and habits. Even beyond their shrill sixth-grade voices, which had deepened considerably in the 2 years, they insisted that they had changed greatly since the earlier conversation ("I don't know how I could have said that"; "I was an idiot back then"). After the laughter and embarrassment died down, I asked them if they still read a lot outside of school.

Jared: No!

Chase: Absolutely not. I haven't read my own book in like a year. I used to be like a reader in sixth grade. I read all the Stephen King books. I know he has all these new books, but I haven't read them.

Jared: I'm more active. I have more stuff to do now. I actually have friends to play with.

Both added that they were interested in girls now, and that reading time has been displaced by talking on the phone. Despite their protests to the contrary, however, it became clear that they *do* still read outside of school, but that their reading interests have changed. Neither reads books often, but both read parts of the newspaper and subscribe to magazines (Chase to *Sports Illustrated* and Jared to *GamePro* and *Entertainment Weekly*) and read them regularly. In fact, during our meeting, Jared couldn't put down an *Entertainment Weekly* that had just arrived in the mail.

Chase's move in his eighth grade year from basic language arts to advanced had brought some changes in the books read, but he insisted that it was still boring and that "it's still easy but we actually read good books every once in awhile now." He mentioned *The Hobbit* (Tolkein, 1966) and *Alas, Babylon* (Frank, 1959) as examples. Jared reported that in his basic language arts class, the books were mainly "boring and stupid." A case in point was a teacher-chosen book, *Summer of My German Soldier* (Greene, 1973), which both the advanced and basic classes had read. According to Jared, "nobody liked it except a few girls," and Chase labeled it "pointless." Both admitted rather proudly that they had been "getting away" with not doing assigned reading while still receiving adequate grades. Jared's and Chase's apathy about school reading had apparently continued to grow, causing me to wonder: Why can't reading in school engage these boys as much as they obviously have the potential to be engaged? Why is reading in school a turnoff for so many students? Can the enthusiasm found in renegade discussions be transferred to school settings?

Advice for Teachers From Renegade Readers

I asked the boys if there was anything they could suggest to their teachers that would promote reading engagement and enjoyment in school for students who, like they, are not avid school readers. The suggestions that they offered are not new to the literature on voluntary reading. However, according to Jared and Chase, and affirmed by previous research (Worthy, Moorman, & Turner, 1997), this advice is not regularly followed in many language arts classes. Thus, these suggestions warrant repeating and developing.

"Let us choose the books we read for class." Student choice and control in reading material and instruction play an important role in involvement with and enjoyment of reading and in fostering voluntary reading (Bintz, 1993; Turner, 1995). When students are not permitted to exercise choice, they may avoid teacher-selected books as a matter of principle. Thus, when students say they hate the books they read in school, part of this opinion may be due to their perceived lack of voice in the school curriculum. Especially in the upper grades, then, teachers should consider "negotiating the curriculum with their pupils and making their purposes in teaching specific books more explicit" (Thomson, 1987, p. 24). Jared and Chase stated that opportunities for choice were infrequent and that students were given minimal voice in the curriculum or in the selection of instructional materials. Jared's suggestion was modest: "Like she could pick three books and ask the class which they want to read." Chase wanted the choice to be more individualized: "Just have everyone read their own book and like do a project for that book...so they can read the book they want to read."

"Let us talk to our friends about what we like to read." Jared and Chase couldn't stop

laughing when I asked them if they had opportunities to talk with their friends about books in school: "Talk to our friends? In class?" "Oh yeah, right." As Bintz (1993) contends, "We need to value and legitimate what students do outside of school rather than bemoan what they are not reading in school" (p. 614). Jared and Chase requested the opportunity to spend "just a couple of minutes" in school talking to their friends about books and magazines they read outside of school. While discussions based on teacher-chosen books are an important part of the curriculum, enjoyable, social exchanges and self-initiated interactions with books have been found to be important in the development of reading motivation (Morrow & Weinstein, 1986). In addition, such talk opens the door to peer recommendations that, for adolescents, may be the most important motivator for voluntary reading (Shore, 1968; Wendelin & Zinck, 1983; Worthy & Turner, 1997). Providing a few unstructured minutes for renegade book conversations in class may make an impact on students' attitudes in class as well as on their out-of-school reading habits.

"Get some good books and other stuff to read in the classroom." Thomson (1987) concluded from surveys of the reading habits of British teenagers that "as students progress through secondary school, the gap between what they choose to read and what the school provides and recommends becomes increasingly wider" (pp. 32–33). Jared and Chase also found few materials that they enjoyed in school. Surveys and interviews of U.S. middle school students, librarians, and teachers affirm that most school and classroom libraries have limited numbers of student-preferred materials (Worthy, 1996; Worthy & Turner, 1997). In interviews with middle school librarians and teachers, my colleagues and I found that many are open to the idea of students reading nontraditional materials of interest to them, but that schools don't typically provide money for teachers to buy materials that are not obviously relevant to the school's curriculum. Most teachers who have such materials in their rooms have to solicit donations or use their own money to purchase them (Worthy, 1996; Worthy, Moorman, & Turner, 1997). Until schools offer some support for teachers to buy student-preferred materials, many students will not have access to them.

Discussion

Because student-preferred reading materials often include materials that have been traditionally seen as inappropriate for school, such as light fiction, series books, magazines, comics, horror, and satire, there is ample potential for disapproval of student choice from parents, administrators, and community members. I offer two ideas for educators who have concerns about using students' preferred materials in school.

First, I believe that instruction using high-quality, critically accepted literature is the most essential component of a language arts program and that the major place of student-preferred materials is in free-choice reading, which should supplement rather than replace the instructional curriculum. Even so, educators will find the need to proactively head off complaints that are likely to accompany the addition of such materials. Fortunately, there is ample research evidence of the academic and affective benefits of listening to students' opinions. Encouraging student choice leads to better attitudes toward reading and learning. Many times students' chosen materials are more complex than teacher-chosen materials, and even light materials promote fluent reading and vocabulary development and help to develop the linguistic competence, confidence, and motivation necessary for reading more sophisticated materials (Carlsen & Sherrill, 1988; Dorrell & Carroll, 1981; Mathabane, 1986; Parrish & Atwood, 1985).

Second, research suggests that students' personal interests need not be static and that teachers can stretch students' topic interests through instructional approaches and materials that are motivating (Schiefele, 1991). Educators can also be encouraged by evidence that personal preferences are not necessarily static and that they can be simultaneously encouraged and broadened. For example, elementary and middle school students value their teachers' recommendations and help in choosing books if the teacher shows genuine interest in the materials (Csikszentmihalyi & McCormack, 1986; Roettger, 1980; Worthy & Turner, 1997). In addition, the transition from light materials to more complex texts can be hastened by providing student-preferred materials for free-choice reading, using more sophisticated works on similar topics for instruction and read-alouds, and encouraging students to adopt a critical stance in comparing the texts.

Coda

Jared and Chase have almost given up on school reading, perhaps due to what they see as limited choice and control in school and the widening gulf between the books they read in school and their personal preferences. According to them, they are "absolutely not" avid readers, yet on closer examination they both admit to reading out of school frequently. Perhaps this incongruity comes from the fact that the materials they read are magazines and not books, and thus perhaps not regarded as "real reading." In many ways, Jared and Chase fit Bintz's (1993) description of adolescents who are reluctant *school* readers but avid *out-of-school* readers.

As did the teenagers in Bintz's study, Jared and Chase think of most school reading as "an imposition, inconvenience, and interference with current reading interests" (p. 612). Fortunately, they are still interested in self-selected reading. Yet there are many students who have similarly negative feelings toward school reading and also do not read outside of school. For these students, Jared's and Chase's suggestions may be vital. Time spent reading is tied to reading and writing competence (Greaney, 1980; Mullis, Campbell, & Farstrup, 1993; Wilson, 1981), and many students who do not read in their free time eventually lose academic ground, even if they are not initially remedial readers (Anderson, Wilson, & Fielding, 1988; Mikulecky, 1990; Stanovich, 1986). Beyond mere time, however, "involvement in reading remains the most potent factor in the development of reading processes" (Allington, 1994, p. 21).

REFERENCES

Allington, R.L. (1994). The schools we have. The schools we need. *The Reading Teacher*, *48*, 14-29.

Almasi, J.F. (1997). A new view of discussion. In L.B. Gambrell & J.F. Almasi (Eds.), *Lively discussions! Fostering engaged reading* (pp. 2-24). Newark, DE: International Reading Association.

Alpert, B.R. (1987). Active, silent, and controlled discussions: Explaining variations in classroom conversation. *Teaching and Teacher Education*, *3*(1), 29-40.

Alvermann, D.E., O'Brien, D.G., & Dillon, D.R. (1990). What teachers do when they say they're having discussions of content area reading assignments: A qualitative analysis. *Reading Research Quarterly*, *25*, 296-332.

Alvermann, D.E., Young, J.P., Green, C., & Wisenbaker, J. (1996, December). *Adolescents read when they want to and that's more often than we thought*. Paper presented at the National Reading Conference annual meeting, Charleston, SC.

Anderson, R., Wilson, P., & Fielding, L. (1988). Growth in reading and how children spend their time outside of school. *Reading Research Quarterly*, *23*, 285–303.

Au, K.H. (1993). *Literacy instruction in multicultural settings*. New York: Harcourt Brace Jovanovich.

Bintz, W.P. (1993). Resistant readers in secondary education: Some insights and implications. *Journal of Reading*, *36*, 604–615.

Burgess, S.A. (1985, January). Reading but not literate: The Child Read survey. *School Library Journal*, *31*, 27–30.

Carlsen, R., & Sherrill, A. (1988). *Voices of readers: How we come to love books*. Urbana, IL: National Council of Teachers of English.

Cazden, C.B. (1988). *Classroom discourse*. Portsmouth, NH: Heinemann.

Cline, R.K.J., & Kretke, G.L. (1980). An evaluation of long-term SSR in the junior high school. *Journal of Reading*, *23*, 502–506.

Crichton, M. (1980). *Congo*. New York: Knopf.

Csikszenthmihalyi, M., & McCormack, J. (1986). The influence of teachers. *Phi Delta Kappan*, *67*, 415–419.

Dorrell, L., & Carroll, E. (1981). Spider-Man at the library. *School Library Journal*, *27*, 17–19.

Erlandson, D.A., Harris, E.L., Skipper, B.L., & Allen, S.D. (1993). *Doing naturalistic inquiry*. Newbury Park, CA: Sage.

Frank, P. (1959). *Alas, Babylon*. Philadelphia: Lippincott.

Gambrell, L.B. (1997). What research reveals about discussion. In L.B. Gambrell & J.F. Almasi (Eds.), *Lively discussions! Fostering engaged reading* (pp. 25–38). Newark, DE: International Reading Association.

Greaney, V. (1980). Factors related to the amount and type of leisure-time reading. *Reading Research Quarterly*, *15*, 337–357.

Greene, B. (1973). *Summer of my German soldier*. New York: Dial.

Howes, V. (1963). Children's interests—a key note for teaching reading. *Education*, *8*, 491–496.

King, S. (1981). *Cujo*. New York: Viking.

King, S. (1983). *Cycle of the werewolf*. Westland, MI: Land of Enchantment.

Krashen, S.D. (1992). *The power of reading*. Englewood, CO: Libraries Unlimited.

Margolin, P. (1993). *Gone but not forgotten*. New York: Doubleday.

Mathabane, M. (1986). *Kaffir boy*. New York: Plume.

McKenna, M., Ellsworth, R.A., & Kear, D. (1995). Children's attitudes toward reading: A national survey. *Reading Research Quarterly*, *30*, 934–957.

McMahon, S.I. (1997). Guiding student-led discussion groups. In L.B. Gambrell & J.F. Almasi (Eds.), *Lively discussions! Fostering engaged reading* (pp. 224–247). Newark, DE: International Reading Association.

Mehan, H. (1979). *Learning lessons*. Cambridge, MA: Harvard University Press.

Mikulecky, L.J. (1990). Stopping summer learning loss among at-risk youth. *Journal of Reading*, *33*, 516–521.

Miles, M.B., & Huberman, A.M. (1994). *Qualitative data analysis* (2nd ed.). Thousand Oaks, CA: Sage.

Mitchell, M. (1939). *Gone with the wind*. New York: E.B. Greenstone.

Monson, D.L., & Sebesta, S. (1991). Reading preferences. In J. Flood, J.M. Jensen, D. Lapp, & J.R. Squire (Eds.), *Handbook of research on teaching the English language arts* (pp. 664–673). New York: Macmillan.

Morrow, L.M. (1991). Promoting voluntary reading. In J. Flood, J.M. Jensen, D. Lapp, & J.R. Squire (Eds.), *Handbook of research on teaching the English language arts* (pp. 681–690). New York: Macmillan.

Morrow, L.M., & Weinstein, C.S. (1986). Encouraging voluntary reading. The impact of a literature program on children's use of library centers. *Reading Research Quarterly*, *21*, 330–346.

Mullis, I., Campbell, J., & Farstrup, A. (1993). NAEP 1992: *Reading report card for the nation and the states*. Washington, DC: U.S. Department of Education.

Nieto, S. (1994). Lessons from students on creating a chance to dream. *Harvard Educational Review*, *64*, 392–426.

Parrish, B., & Atwood, K. (1985). Enticing readers: The teen romance craze. *California Reader*, *18*, 22–27.

Purves, A.C., Rogers, T., & Soter, A.O. (1990). *How porcupines make love II: Teaching a response-centered literature curriculum*. White Plains, NY: Longman.

Roettger, D. (1980). Elementary students' attitudes toward reading. *The Reading Teacher*, *33*, 451-454.

Rosenblatt, L.M. (1983). *Literature as exploration* (3rd ed.). New York: Noble & Noble.

Schiefele, U. (1991). Interest, learning, and motivation. *Educational Psychologist*, *26*, 299-323.

Shapiro, J., & White, W. (1991). Reading attitudes and perceptions in traditional and nontraditional reading programs. *Reading Research and Instruction*, *30*, 52-66.

Shore, R.B. (1968). Perceived influence of peers, parents, and teachers on fifth and ninth graders' preferences of reading material. *Dissertation Abstracts International*, *47*, 051, No. 86-16, 829.

Stanovich, K. (1986). Matthew effects in reading: Some consequences of individual differences in the acquisition of literacy. *Reading Research Quarterly*, *21*, 360-406.

Strauss, A.L., & Corbin, J. (1990). *Basics of qualitative research: Grounded theory procedures and techniques*. Newbury Park, CA: Sage.

Thomson, J.L. (1987). *Understanding teenagers' reading: Reading processes and the teaching of literature*. New York: Nichols.

Tolkein, J.R.R. (1966). *The hobbit*. Cambridge, MA: Houghton Mifflin.

Turner, J.C. (1995). The influence of classroom contexts on young children's motivation for literacy. *Reading Research Quarterly*, *30*, 410-441.

Wendelin, K.H., & Zinck, R.A. (1983). How students make book choices. *Reading Horizons*, *23*, 84-88.

Wilson, R.M. (1981). Any way you read it, illiteracy is a problem. *Presstime*, *3*, 4-8.

Worthy, J. (1996). Removing barriers to voluntary reading: The role of school and classroom libraries. *Language Arts*, *73*, 483-492.

Worthy, J., & McKool, S.S. (1996). Students who say they hate to read: The importance of opportunity, choice, and access. In D.J. Leu, C.K. Kinzer, & K.A. Hinchman (Eds.), *Literacies for the 21st century: Research and practice* (pp. 245-256). Chicago: National Reading Conference.

Worthy, J., Moorman, M., & Turner, M. (1997, March). *Can the teacher make a difference in students' attitudes toward reading?* Paper presented at the American Educational Research Association meeting, Chicago.

Worthy, J., & Turner, M. (1997, February). *Motivating students to read: Ideas from 6th grade students and their language arts teachers*. Paper presented at the Southwest Regional conference of the International Reading Association, Fort Worth, TX.

Ysseldyke, J.E., & Algozzine, R. (1982–1983). Where to begin in diagnosing reading problems. *Topics in Learning and Reading Disorders*, *2*, 60-68.

Zarillo, J., & Cox, C. (1992). Efferent and aesthetic teaching. In J.E. Many & C. Cox (Eds.), *Reader stance and literary understanding* (pp. 235-249). Norwood, NJ: Ablex.

Joseph Sanacore

Creating the Lifetime Reading Habit in Social Studies

When was the last time a former student said "I'm reading a historical book for pleasure"? What a fantastic feeling to know that something the social studies teacher did in class motivated the lifetime reading habit. Unfortunately, students commenting on their longterm love of historical books are a rarity. Social studies teachers and their content area colleagues must share the blame for this negative outcome because many of them still believe that using class time to encourage reading for pleasure is not their responsibility.

To the contrary, social studies teachers must share a role in promoting longterm literacy. Many language activities occur during social studies lessons, including reading textbooks, discussing ideas, making speeches, writing essays, and studying notes. These activities represent a natural literacy context for supporting pleasurable reading.

Positive efforts by social studies teachers may not only encourage students to read for pleasure but also challenge content area colleagues to use class time for attaining this important goal. The ultimate thrust is to create schoolwide efforts so that virtually all teachers are motivating students' independent reading (Sanacore, 1988).

What, then, can social studies teachers do to promote the lifetime reading habit? The following suggestions are not comprehensive, but they do provide instructional direction.

Suggestions for the Classroom

- Include literature as part of the instructional program.

Historical fiction, biography, autobiography, and diary help readers to personalize history. According to Wilson (1988, p. 313), "Students can experience history through literature more dramatically, and can often have a more indepth transaction with the subject, when it deals with characters 'who were there.'" This process supports students' appreciation for an author's historical perspective and imaginary power.

Literary works selected for social studies classrooms should be interesting, and factual content should be blended smoothly with the narration. After selecting sources, the teacher may approach literature by covering recurring themes in history and by motivating students' reading of related titles.

For example, the theme "in quest of freedom" can be linked to Dickinson's *The Dancing Bear* (Byzantium, 6th century), Haugaard's *Hakon of Rogen's Saga* (Viking times), Collier and Collier's *Jump Ship to*

Reprinted From the *Journal of Readomg*, *33*(6), 414–418, March 1990.

Freedom (U.S., 1780s), and Holm's *North to Freedom* (Europe, 1940s).

These and other themes and related literary titles are provided by Huck, Hepler, and Hickman (1987), and the books themselves are especially useful to young readers because they provide insight for problems of the past as well as today. In addition to themes or topics, the teacher may decide to cover certain historical periods or events and to include appropriate literature. If the American Revolution is the focus of study, then Forbes's *Johnny Tremain*, Avi's *The Fighting Ground*, and Clapp's *I'm Deborah Sampson: A Soldier in the War of the Revolution* are inspirational stories reflecting a variety of perspectives. If World War II is being covered, then *Anne Frank: The Diary of a Young Girl* and Greene's *The Summer of My German Soldier* are excellent literary sources revealing poignant aspects of the War.

Regardless of the approach taken, using literature in social studies classes increases the potential for enjoying reading and for considering it as a lifetime activity. Students also gain important values from literary activities, and teachers should therefore encourage them as a major complement to the instructional program.

• Use a wide variety of materials during class time.

In addition to historical literary works, potential lifetime readers need exposure to a variety of resources. Textbooks, anthologies, paperbacks, magazines, and newspapers provide sufficient diversity for accommodating students' interests.

Interestingly, although newspapers are not used often, they have their greatest impact in social studies classrooms because of their current events value. They are inexpensive owing to reduced cost for students, and they provide readers with a direct sense of ownership. Kossack (1986, p. 769) believes that they support lifelong learning:

> The newspaper is one way to assure application of the tools we teach (decoding, comprehension, study skills) in a resource that helps students in many ways: economically (through used merchandise sales, locating a job), socially (upcoming civic, social, cultural events), and intellectually (current inventions, concerns, politics, books, trends). Best of all, the daily newspaper is a way to ensure lifelong reading, learning, and self renewal.

Newspapers and other materials can support the curricular standards of social studies and simultaneously promote the lifetime reading habit. These resources serve as a mini-classroom library that nurtures instructional lessons and units. For example, if the focus of study is the American Civil War, materials concerning the following areas should be available: slavery, abolitionism, Jefferson Davis, Abraham Lincoln, General Robert E. Lee, General Ulysses S. Grant, the Confederacy, the Union, the Battle of Bull Run, and Fort Sumter.

If the supportive resources reflect a variety of reading levels and consist of different formats and lengths, students are more likely to read them with pleasure (Sanacore, 1989). Even current events materials can be effective, provided they reveal updated information or present new perspectives concerning the topic.

When the classroom minilibrary has been established, the teacher has options for covering the instructional unit. An ambitious approach would involve all the students in sustained silent reading every day until the unit is completed. During this activity, the teacher models the appropriate behavior by reading silently at his or her desk. (No clerical tasks are performed during silent reading.) Occasionally, the teacher varies the routine by discussing interesting books, holding individual or small group conferences, and encouraging students to share insights gained from their books.

Sharing insights takes on special meaning because social interaction is as necessary in the classroom as it is in the cafeteria and at home. Carlson and Sherrill (1988) provide autobiographies or self-reports of individuals who are lifetime readers, and many of them consider reading both a social and a solitary phenomenon.

If time does not permit such an ambitious approach, the teacher may consider a plan that engages students in silent reading for about the last 15 minutes of each class period. Thus, traditional instruction is provided for the bulk of the lesson, while silent reading is used in a supportive fashion. Again, teacher modeling is essential during silent reading.

For both approaches to work effectively, students must have opportunities to select their own materials. This process builds students' self-esteem and independence, which are necessary for creating the lifetime reading habit. In addition, the teacher does not have to be anxious about students' ability to select appropriate resources since those who gain experience reading for pleasure tend to choose suitable materials (Nell, 1988).

• Read aloud to students regularly.

Reading to students frequently is an excellent strategy for motivating them to read. Materials selected for reading aloud should be linked to students' interests and experiences as well as to the social studies curriculum. These resources may be short, appealing magazine articles to be read in their entirety or longer selections of which only segments will be read aloud. Such activities expand students' awareness of the wide diversity of available materials and also tease or motivate individuals to read similar resources on their own.

According to Matthews (1987), reading aloud should reflect the same intimate atmosphere of a parent or teacher cuddling a child during the reading of a favorite story. The teacher does not have to place the older child on his or her lap, but intimate aspects of lap reading can be recreated. In this warm, trusting context, the teacher selects and reads powerful passages that provoke students into listening and responding to the ideas presented.

In social studies, potentially controversial passages are appropriate. Then, the teacher guides students' responses toward critical thinking by asking questions, such as "Why did you not like the treatment?" or "What would have strengthened the author's case?" (Matthews, 1987, p. 411). This type of questioning improves the listeners' attending ability while it builds their interest in the reading material. The books named here (see display) do not represent a sacrosanct list, but they do contain passages that can be read aloud effectively during social studies lessons.

The social studies teacher may consider these and other materials for reading aloud to students. Choices will probably reflect a number of factors, including the students' abilities and interests, the teacher's flexibility, curricular demands, and time constraints. The important thing to remember is that reading aloud is a vital activity for reinforcing the joy of reading and that it is especially needed today since many students are not reading on their own.

• Avoid conditions that dissuade students from reading.

With the best of intentions, teachers sometimes discourage students' reading by requiring book reports. In discussing their findings concerning lifetime readers, Carlson and Sherrill (1988, p. 154) state: "Book reports were almost universally disliked by the respondents. Book reports did more to kill the young people's interest in reading than to promote it."

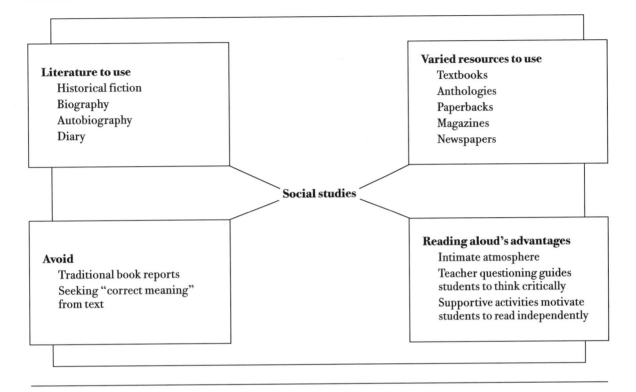

Literature to use
Historical fiction
Biography
Autobiography
Diary

Varied resources to use
Textbooks
Anthologies
Paperbacks
Magazines
Newspapers

Social studies

Avoid
Traditional book reports
Seeking "correct meaning"
from text

Reading aloud's advantages
Intimate atmosphere
Teacher questioning guides
students to think critically
Supportive activities motivate
students to read independently

To avoid the drudgery of traditional book reports, Criscuolo (1977) suggests creative alternatives. These include:

Computerized dating—Students attempt to have a date with a book. Volunteers complete a dating application that includes their name, age, hobbies, favorite TV program, last book they read, and types of books they enjoy. This information reveals personal characteristics, and it helps others be aware of potential books to recommend. The applications are posted so that classmates have opportunities to read them and to match the right book with the "right" friend.

Book a trip—The teacher motivates students to read materials concerning travel by asking: "If you had a chance to take a trip, where would you go?" When travel materials are read, volunteers make oral presentations using photographs, pictures from magazines, postcards, and slides. Those making presentations can secure appropriate resources (probably free of charge) from travel agencies.

Criscuolo believes that activities such as these will lead to "enthusiastic results because they double the student's joy and satisfaction in a most pleasurable experience—reading" (p. 895).

Focusing on Process

In addition to book reports, another condition that can discourage students' reading is the teacher's insistence on finding the "correct meaning" of the text (Carlson & Sherrill, 1988). This rigid approach tends to frustrate students because the interpretation of certain books becomes unreachable or incomprehensible.

Books for reading aloud in social studies classes

Amos Fortune, Free Man by Elizabeth Yates

Beloved by Toni Morrison

Beyond the Divide by Kathryn Lasky

Eleanor Roosevelt, First Lady of the New World by Doris Faber

The Faraway Lurs by Harry Behn

The Good Earth by Pearl S. Buck

John Treegate's Musket by Leonard Wibberly

The Light in the Forest by Conrad Richter

Love and Rivalry: Three Exceptional Pairs of Sisters by Doris Faber

The Memory String by Chester Osborne

Mumbet, The Story of Elizabeth Freeman by Harold Felton

Old Yeller by Fred Gipson

On the Frontier with Mr. Audubon by Barbara Brenner

Sounder by William Armstrong

The Upstairs Room by Johanna Reiss

The challenge to teachers is to support students' attempts in constructing meaning based on their prior knowledge, which involves cognitive factors as well as affective aspects such as feelings, personal awareness, and experiences (Bartlett, 1932).

Thus, the comprehension act is viewed as a process involving the interaction of reader and text rather than as an activity focusing on locating the "correct meaning" embedded in text (Rauch, 1985). Although this reader response view of comprehension demonstrates much respect for the reader's role, it raises serious questions concerning substantive versus shallow interpretation of text (Sanacore, 1983, 1985).

One way of dealing with this problem is to use a response heuristic to help set appropriate standards for interpretation (Bleich, 1978). For example, students write about their understanding of text as they blend aspects of their personality and also of the world as they understand it. Then, individuals are encouraged to engage in a critical discussion that can lead them to analyze their readings as well as the process that informs them (Bartholomae & Petrosky, 1981).

Good responses to literature include clear retellings of the passage, specific connections between personal associations and comprehension of the passage, and generalizations from the discussion. On the other hand, poor responses are sketchy, not focused, narrow, and limited in description and explanation as they relate to the individuals' prior personal knowledge (Petrosky, 1982).

Although using a response heuristic is an important strategy for maintaining standards, excessive use of this strategy (as with required book reports) could negate the joy of reading.

The Teacher's Role

Students will not become lifetime readers unless they frequently experience reading as a pleasurable activity. By providing class time for reading self-selected resources, the social studies teacher increases the potential for generating the longterm reading habit. In-class reading not only supports the importance of reading for pleasure, but also gives students opportunities to realize that social studies materials provide both valuable information and much enjoyment.

The teacher's basic roles include encouraging the use of literature, using a variety of materials, reading aloud, and avoiding conditions that discourage reading. Although these roles are recommended for social studies teachers, they can be applied to virtually every content area. The important consideration here is to send a message to all that developing the lifetime reading habit is a major activity. With no naiveté intended, this message and its backup activities may lead to a former student saying "Thanks to your support, I continue to read historical materials for pleasure!"

REFERENCES

Bartholomae, D., & Petrosky, A.R. (1981). Facts, artifacts, and counterfacts: A basic reading and writing course for the college curriculum. In M. Sternglass & D. Butturff (Eds.), *Building the bridges between reading and writing*. Akron, OH: Land S Books.

Bartlett, F.C. (1932). *Remembering*. London: Cambridge University Press.

Bleich, D. (1978). *Subjective criticism*. Baltimore, MD: Johns Hopkins University Press.

Carlsen, G.R., & Sherrill, A. (1988). *Voices of readers: How we come to love books*. Urbana, IL: National Council of Teachers of English.

Criscuolo, N.P. (1977). Book reports: Twelve creative alternatives. *The Reading Teacher, 30*, 893-895.

Huck, C.S., Hepler, S., & Hickman, J. (1987). *Children's literature in the elementary school* (4th ed.). New York: Holt, Rinehart & Winston.

Kossack, S. (1986). Realism: The newspaper and the older learner. *Journal of Reading, 29*, 768-769.

Matthews, C.E. (1987). Lap reading for teenagers. *Journal of Reading, 30*, 410-413.

Nell, V. (1988). *Lost in a book: The psychology of reading for pleasure*. New Haven, CT: Yale University Press.

Petrosky, A.R. (1982). From story to essay: Reading and writing. *College Composition and Communication, 33*, 19-36.

Ranch, S.J. (1985). What the volunteer tutor should know about reading instruction. In S.J. Ranch & J. Sanacore (Eds.), *Handbook for the volunteer tutor* (2nd ed.) (pp. 1-9). Newark, DE: International Reading Association.

Sanacore, J. (1983). Improving reading through prior knowledge and writing. *Journal of Reading, 26*, 714-720.

Sanacore, J. (1989). *Linking vocabulary and comprehension through independent reading: Considerations for teacher modeling*. Unpublished manuscript, Hofstra University, Department of Reading, Language, & Cognition, Hempstead, NY.

Sanacore, J. (1985). New ways of thinking about reading instruction. In S.J. Ranch & J. Sanacore (Eds.), *Handbook for the volunteer tutor* (2nd ed.) (pp. 84-106). Newark, DE: International Reading Association.

Sanacore, J. (1988). Schoolwide independent reading: The principal can help. *Journal of Reading, 31*, 346-353.

Wilson, M. (1988). How can we teach reading in the content areas. In C. Weaver (Ed.), *Reading process and practice: From socio-psycholinguistics to whole language* (pp. 280-320). Portsmouth, NH: Heinemann.

Terry Miller

The Place of Picture Books in Middle-Level Classrooms

The picture books and short, illustrated books, so prevalent in primary grade classrooms, have generally not been found in intermediate grades and middle school classrooms. The traditional wisdom is that as the average reading ability level of students increases, the class library and class reading activities need to be limited to reading materials at "instructional level." For Grades 5 through 8, this tends to mean "no picture books."

However, the last 25 years have seen the emergence of more sophisticated picture books and short, illustrated books, and these books are beginning to appear in middle-level classrooms. This article will present arguments for using picture books in middle-level classrooms and give some specific examples of genres and books that can be used in various curricular and interdisciplinary areas.

What Is a Picture Book?

Technically, the term "picture book" refers specifically to a book whose story can be understood only with the illustrations supplementing the written text (the words cannot stand alone). A short story or nonfiction work with illustrations is referred to as an "illustrated book." However, in common usage, we use the term "picture book" for a short story or nonfiction work whose words could stand alone, but whose artwork is integral to the experience of the book (Brown & Tomlinson, 1993). This is the sense in which this article will refer to picture books.

Why Use Picture Books in Middle-Level Grades?

• *Enjoyment.* A common, and perhaps surprising, experience of middle-level teachers introducing quality picture books in their classrooms is the delight of many of their early adolescent students (10–14 years old). The combination of stimulating artwork, accessible language, and shortness of text can be very appealing to this age group. Part of the appeal, too, is probably to that side of middle-level students that is not quite ready to completely give up childhood experiences.

• *Independent reading options.* Picture books can be an attractive option for independent reading time and for free time when class work is done. Once established as "acceptable" (without embarrassment) independent reading for all students, picture books can provide needed reading practice with text at the reading level of some of the struggling readers in every classroom. These books can be very useful motivators for getting reluc-

244

Reprinted From the *Journal of Adolescent & Adult Literacy*, *41*(5), 376–381, February 1998.

tant readers to experience the pleasure of reading (Clary, 1991).

• *A culturally diverse classroom.* Quality picture books include a rich variety of stories and artwork from diverse cultures around the world. The beauty of the artistic characterizations of people from all ethnic and racial backgrounds provides a strong visible statement of valuing diversity, which is an especially important message for early adolescents (Bacharach & Miller, 1996). These books can be used to integrate multicultural content in all subject areas, and their visible presence in the class library helps create an inclusive classroom atmosphere.

• *Vocabulary development.* Even though the text may be relatively short in picture books, the vocabulary can be fairly advanced. By the middle grades, most new vocabulary is learned through reading, rather than through verbal communication, and multiple exposures to each new word are needed before the word becomes familiar (Anderson & Freebody, 1981). Vocabulary-rich picture books can provide an enjoyable source of exposure to more sophisticated language.

• *Introduction to abstract topics.* Fiction and nonfiction picture books can also provide a very concrete and motivating introduction to the study of an abstract subject in science, technology, math, history, or geography. Whole-class reading, group reading, or individual reading of a "concept-related" picture book can be an excellent way to activate background knowledge and stimulate curiosity about the subject to be studied (Irvin, 1990).

• *Research project sources.* An important part of the curriculum in all middle-level classrooms is the research process. Students need practice and guidance in researching all subject areas, both to deepen their knowledge in the core subjects and to improve their reading, writing, and thinking abilities

(Maxwell, 1996). Quality picture books in science, history, geography, and other subject areas can be used both for whole-class modeling and practice of the research process and for source options for research projects.

Using Picture Books in All Subject Areas

In the following sections, some examples are given of quality picture books (see Sidebar for a complete list) that may be used effectively in various content and interdisciplinary areas. These are just a few of the many quality works that exist—many new and excellent books are published every year.

Literature units: Traditional Tales unit. English or language arts teachers can use quality picture books as whole-class, group, and individual reading options as part of both theme units (e.g., Survival) and genre units (e.g., Traditional Tales). Generally, in a theme or genre unit, the whole class reads a particular book to establish the common themes and issues for the unit. Then students choose books to read in groups or individually, complete response activities to the reading, and finish the unit by completing a project. Picture books can provide excellent options for all of these types of reading activities.

A Traditional Tales unit (including myths, legends, fables, folk tales) can be an English/language arts genre unit, and can also be part of an interdisciplinary World Cultures unit. Rich traditional tales from all parts of the world demonstrate the common stories and values with which all human beings attempt to make sense of the natural and spiritual worlds, and these originally oral stories are the foundation for all written human literature (Russell, 1994). This literature provides an incredibly fertile source of inspiration for artistic elaboration on the stories.

Quality Picture Books

Traditional tales

Aardema, Verna. *Why mosquitoes buzz in people's ears*. Pied Piper, 1978.

Bryan, Ashley. *The ox of the wonderful horns and other African folktales*. Atheneum, 1971.

Delacre, Lulu. *Myths, legends, and folktales from Latin America*. Scholastic, 1996.

Ehrlich, Amy. *Cinderella*. Dial, 1985.

Hamilton, Virginia. *The people could fly*. Knopf, 1985.

Ingpen, Robert. *Folktales and fables of the Middle East and Africa*. Chelsea House, 1994.

Medlicott, Mary. *The river that went to the sky: Twelve tales by African storytellers*. Kingfisher, 1995.

Rhee, Naomi. *Magic spring*. Whitebird, 1993.

San Souci, Robert. *Sukey and the mermaid*. Four Winds, 1992.

Taylor, C.J. *Bones in the basket: Native stories of the origin of people*. Tundra, 1994.

Uchida, Yoshiko. *The magic purse*. Margaret K. McElderry, 1993.

Wilson, Barbara. *Wishbones: A folktale from China*. Bradbury, 1993.

Vocabulary development

Base, Graeme. *Animalia*. Harry Abrams, 1984.

Carle, Eric. *All about Arthur (An absolutely absurd ape)*. Franklin Watts, 1974.

Cox, Lynn. *Crazy alphabet*. Orchard, 1990.

Jonas, Ann. *Aardvarks, disembark!* Greenwillow, 1990.

Kellogg, Steven. *Aster Aardvark's alphabet adventures*. Morrow, 1987.

Linscott, Jody. *Once upon A to Z: An alphabet odyssey*. Doubleday, 1991.

Provensen, Alice, & Provensen, Martin. *A peaceable kingdom: The Shaker abecedarius*. Viking/Penguin, 1978.

Van Allsburg, Chris. *The Z was zapped*. Houghton Mifflin, 1987.

(continued)

For example, recurring in the world's traditional literature is the story of the young person who suffers in an unhappy family situation, and who is exploited or neglected, in spite of having very admirable moral and spiritual qualities. However, in the end these moral virtues are rewarded with great good fortune that comes from some magical source. To pursue this theme, students can read (as a whole class, in groups, or individually) the French story of *Cinderella* by Amy Ehrlich, the Chinese story of *Wishbones: A Folktale from China* by Barbara Wilson, the African story of *The Ox of the Wonderful Horns* by Ashley Bryan, and the African American story *Sukey and the Mermaid* by Robert San Souci.

All of these stories inspire admiration and sympathy for the protagonist, and there is a feeling of satisfaction when virtue is finally rewarded. Although the theme and plots are very similar, each picture book has its own style of art and language that reflects the culture from which the story emerged. A discussion of these stylistic differences can help prepare students to create their own versions of this universal story.

Vocabulary development activities. Vocabulary-rich picture books can add to the enjoyment of playing with words. For whole-class activities, they can be used to reinforce vocabulary-learning strategies (Miller, 1994). While reading the book aloud to the class, the teacher can model good strategies for figuring out difficult words and lead the class in further guided practice of these strategies. Having a number of vocabulary-rich picture books in the classroom library can also provide a source of new words for the students' individual vocabulary lists.

The reading of an alphabet picture book such as *Animalia* by Graeme Base can provide a rich source of words for these kinds of whole-class and individual activities. For example, one page from *Animalia* reads "Meticulous Mice Monitoring Mysterious Mathematical Messages." The full-page picture shows eight mice busy at computers in a laboratory full of objects beginning with the letter *m*. Using this page (perhaps on the overhead), a discussion can be held about the word and picture context clues to what the word *meticulous* might mean. Students could be asked to come up with their own alliterative phrases and pictures using *meticulous*. Then students could choose their own difficult words from other pages in *Animalia* to create their own page for an alphabet book.

Creative writing prompts. Students in the middle grades need practice in the prewriting skill of brainstorming ideas for their creative writing. The illustrations and language in picture books can be stimulating prompts to the imagination for creative writing assignments. Unusual characters, settings, or plot devices can provide models for students to follow in developing their own creative writing. Highly imaginative and provocative picture books (or single pages from these books) can also be part of a Creative Writing Center for independent writing activities. Students can create stories from illustrations alone, change the endings, add new characters to the stories, or create new stories with a similar plot device.

A classic example of such a book is Chris Van Allsburg's *The Mysteries of Harris Burdick*, in which each page presents a mysterious setting with just one picture and one phrase. One page is titled "Oscar and Alphonse" and reads "She knew it was time to send them back. The caterpillars softly wriggled in her hand, spelling out 'goodbye.'" The opposite page is a black-and-white illustration of a girl looking pensively at two caterpillars on her hand. A creative writing assignment using this page as a prompt could be to build a story around these caterpillar

Quality Picture Books *(continued)*

Creative writing prompts

Base, Graeme. *Jabberwocky*. Harry Abrams, 1984.

    The eleventh hour. Harry Abrams, 1993.

Demi. *Demi's secret garden*. Henry Holt, 1993.

Lobel, Arnold. *Fables*. Harper & Row, 1980.

Macaulay, David. *Black and white*. Houghton Mifflin, 1990.

Scieszka, Jon. *The book that Jack wrote*. Viking, 1994.

    The true story of the Three Little Pigs. Viking, 1989.

Van Allsburg, Chris. *Bad day at Riverbend*. Houghton Mifflin, 1995.

    Two bad ants. Houghton Mifflin, 1988.

    The mysteries of Harris Burdick. Houghton Mifflin, 1984.

    The wretched stone. Houghton Mifflin, 1991.

    The wreck of the Zephyr. Houghton Mifflin, 1983.

Weisner, David. *Free fall*. Lothrop, Lee & Shepard, 1988.

Math/science/technology

Anno, Masaichiro, & Anno, Mitsumasa. *Anno's mysterious multiplying jar*. Philomel, 1983.

Brown, David J. *How they were built*. Barnes & Noble, 1996.

Butterfield, Moira. *Richard Orr's nature cross-sections*. Dorling Kindersley, 1995.

Demi. *One grain of rice: A mathematical folktale*. Henry Holt, 1997.

Jones, Charyn (Ed.). *Eyewitness science: Electricity*. Dorling Kindersley, 1992.

Macaulay, David. *The way things work*. Houghton Mifflin, 1988.

    Ship. Houghton Mifflin, 1993.

    Mill. Houghton Mifflin, 1983.

Parker, Steve. *How nature works*. Barnes & Noble, 1996.

(continued)

Quality Picture Books (continued)

Porter, Alison, & Davies, Eryl (Eds.). *How things work*. Walden Owen, 1996.

Scieszka, Jon. *Math curse*. Penguin, 1995.

Simon, Seymour. *Our solar system*. William Morrow, 1992.

Spiders (Eyes on Nature Series). Kids Books, 1996.

Ecology

Base, Graeme. *The sign of the seahorse: A tale of greed and high adventure in two acts*. Harry Abrams, 1992.

Bunting, Eve. *Someday a tree*. Clarion, 1993.

Cherry, Lynne. *The great kapok tree: A tale of the Amazon Rain Forest*. Harcourt Brace Jovanovich, 1990.

Geisel, Theodor Seuss. *The Lorax*. Random House, 1971.

Jeffers, Susan. *Brother Eagle, Sister Sky: A message from Chief Seattle*. Scholastic, 1992.

Luenn, Nancy. *The song for the ancient forest*. Atheneum, 1993.

Wildsmith, Brian. *Professor Noah's spaceship*. Oxford University Press, 1980.

Effects of war

Breckler, Rosemary. *Sweet dried apples: A Vietnamese wartime childhood*. Houghton Mifflin, 1996.

Bunting, Eve. *The wall*. Clarion, 1990.
The blue and the gray. Scholastic, 1996.

Coerr, Eleanor. *Sadako*. Putnam, 1993.

Hamanaka, Sheila. *The journey: Japanese Americans, racism and renewal*. Orchard, 1990.

Heide, Florence, & Gilliland, Judith Heide. *Sami and the time of the troubles*. Clarion, 1992.

Hoestlandt, Jo. *Star of fear, star of hope*. Walker, 1995.

Maruki, Toshi. *Hiroshima no pika*. Lothrop, Lee & Shepard, 1980.

(continued)

creatures, explaining where they came from and what their mission was on earth.

Math, science, technology: Concept-related readings. Abstract concepts in science, technology, and mathematics can be given more concrete and visual connections to students' experiences by using the visual examples, models, and diagrams in a picture book on the topic being presented. A popular example is David Macaulay's *The Way Things Work*, which uses fascinating drawings and simple explanations for everything from simple machines to nuclear power. Each page in this book could be used as a whole-class, concept-related introduction to the topic, both to provide a simple visual foundation on which to build more abstract ideas, and to provide motivation for studying those ideas.

Science and mathematics picture books are also useful for presenting mathematical problems and puzzles, and scientific investigations and experiments. For example, both *Anno's Mysterious Multiplying Jar* by Masaichiro and Mitsumasa Anno and *One Grain of Rice: A Mathematical Folktale* by Demi lead readers through seemingly simple progressions and end up with an example of a factorial number. Students can create their own versions of these stories to demonstrate the power of factorial numbers.

Science/technology issues: Ecology. There are a number of quality picture books in both fiction and nonfiction format that present social issues related to science and technology. Stories with an ecology theme can stimulate concern for the dangers to our environment, provoke debate on solutions to environmental problems, and arouse curiosity to discover more information on this topic. These books may also provide examples for an ecology unit final project option of creating your own picture book with an ecology message.

A powerful introductory book is *Brother Eagle, Sister Sky: A Message From Chief*

Seattle. This book retells the words of Chief Seattle responding to the U.S. government offer to buy "his land." His arguments are not simply practical, but have a deep spiritual message as well: "We do not weave the web of life, we are merely a strand in it. Whatever we do to the web, we do to ourselves." Each set of facing pages is illustrated with lightly colored paintings of Native American people living in harmony with nature. The last pages depict a deforested land and a contemporary family replanting the trees. After a whole-class reading and discussion of this book, students can create their own graphic "webs," connecting the products and resources that they all use daily.

Social studies topics: Effects of war. History and geography topics tend to be removed from students' familiar experiences and perspectives. Quality picture books, both fiction and nonfiction, can make historical periods and faraway lands come alive for students. Use them for both whole-class reading and discussion, and for reading choice options. Students will relate to the lifelike characters in the fiction stories, and to the concrete visuals in the nonfiction books, and form a reference point for understanding the more abstract historical and geographical concepts.

For example, the study of a historical period involving a war can be made more meaningful and complete by using stories of the effects of war on real people (and other living things). The book *Faithful Elephants: A True Story of Animals, People and War* by Yukio Tsuchiya tells the story of three elephants living at the Ueno Zoo in Tokyo near the end of World War II. Due to the daily bombing raids on the city, the authorities were afraid that wild animals would escape the zoo and attack people in the city. The keepers were ordered to kill all of the dangerous animals, including these three elephants.

Quality Picture Books (continued)

Polacco, Patricia. *Pink and Say*. Philomel, 1994.

Tsuchiya, Yukio. *Faithful elephants: A true story of animals, people and war*. Houghton Mifflin, 1988.

Uchida, Yoshiko. *The bracelet*. Philomel, 1993.

Death and loss

Clifton, Lucille. *Everett Anderson's goodbye*. Holt, Rinehart & Winston, 1983.

Cohn, Janice. *I had a friend named Peter*. Morrow, 1987.

Goble, Paul. *Beyond the ridge*. Bradbury, 1989.

Mathis, Sharon Bell. *The hundred penny box*. Viking, 1975.

Miles, Miska. *Annie and the old one*. Little, Brown, 1971.

Turner, Barbara. *A little bit of Rob*. Albert Whitman, 1996.

Walker, Alice. *To hell with dying*. Harcourt Brace Jovanovich, 1988.

The anguish of both the animals and their human keepers is movingly portrayed in both words and highly realistic illustrations. After reading and discussing this powerful story, students can brainstorm their own ideas about what to do with the animals in a similar situation.

Health/family life science topics: Death and loss unit. Important but sensitive topics such as death, family changes, addictions, or domestic violence can be approached in a more nonthreatening manner using quality literature, both novels and short illustrated stories. Characters in well-written fiction can provide role models for how young people might cope with difficult life situations. The experience of reading (or listening to) these stories can give a more empathetic perspective to all students, and give a sense of "not being along" to those students who have actually experienced the life crisis being discussed (Allen, 1995).

For a death and loss unit, *A Little Bit of Rob* by Barbara Turner is an example of a picture book short enough to be read in one class period, but serious enough to stimulate a discussion on the feelings and issues around the death and dying of a loved one. In this story, a young girl and her parents are going out on the ocean on their crabbing boat. It is the first time they have gone out since her teenaged brother, Rob, died a month before. They are all trying not to think about Rob, and trying not to cry. The young girl finds her brother's old sweatshirt and puts it on, and this begins a process of grieving and acceptance. Reading and discussing this short story can set the stage for the reading of longer works dealing with the same issues of grief, denial, and acceptance of the death of a loved one.

One final project option for a health or family life theme unit, such as death and loss, is for students to create their own picture book designed to present the topic to younger students. This is also an opportunity for collaboration with the art and family life teachers. The art teachers can guide the type of artwork used for illustrations, and the family life teachers can advise on the appropriate content and techniques for presentation to younger students.

Universal Appeal

Picture books, such as the examples mentioned in this article, can make invaluable contributions to any middle-level classroom. They can be used specifically for academic purposes, and they can provide popular options for free reading. In a sense, all early adolescents begin their academic careers with their early picture book experiences. It is entirely appropriate to continue to use this rich source of learning and enjoyment as long as the appeal remains. In the case of quality picture books such as the ones mentioned in this article, the appeal and the inherent learning value remain not only for early adolescents, but for people of all ages.

REFERENCES

Allen, J. (1995). *It's never too late: Leading adolescents to lifelong literacy*. Portsmouth, NH: Heinemann.

Anderson, R.C., & Freebody, P. (1981). Vocabulary knowledge. In J.T. Guthrie (Ed.), *Comprehension and teaching: Research reviews* (pp. 77-117). Newark, DE: International Reading Association.

Bacharach, N., & Miller, T. (1996). Integrating African American fiction into the middle school curriculum. *Middle School Journal*, *27*(4), 36-40.

Brown, C.L., & Tomlinson, C.M. (1993). *Essentials of children's literature*. Boston: Allyn & Bacon.

Clary, L. (1991). Getting adolescents to read. *Journal of Reading*, *34*, 340-345.

Irvin, J. (1990). *Reading and the middle school student*. Boston: Allyn & Bacon.

Maxwell, R.J. (1996). *Writing across the curriculum*. Boston: Allyn & Bacon.

Miller, T. (1994). Improving the schoolwide language arts program: A priority for all middle school teachers. *Middle School Journal*, *25*(4), 26-29.

Russell, D.L. (1994). *Literature for children: A short introduction*. New York: Longman.

Judith K. Cassady

Wordless Books: No-Risk Tools for Inclusive Middle-Grade Classrooms

Although the genre of wordless books is over 50 years old, some of the most beautiful and intricate books have been published in the last 10 years. All are just recently beginning to achieve the recognition they are due. The 1992 Caldecott Medal winner, *Tuesday* by David Wiesner, is evidence of this.

Wiesner commented in an interview (Caroff & Moje, 1992) that he has received numerous letters from students in drama classes, English as a Second Language classes, and creative writing classes who have used his wordless picture book, *Tuesday*. Wiesner identifies one of the most valuable characteristics of wordless books—the endless possibilities for creative interpretations. (For *Tuesday* and all wordless books cited, see Sidebar.)

Educators have recognized the value of wordless books for many years (Larrick, 1976). Virtually every objective in the language arts curriculum at every grade level can be developed and enhanced through the use of wordless books. But too often we think wordless books are only for preschool and kindergarten. In fact their greatest asset seems to be that they ensure successful reading experiences because there are no "right" words.

Wordless books enhance creativity, vocabulary, and language development for readers of all ages, at all stages of cognitive development, and in all content areas. Along with teacher guidance, wordless books can especially benefit linguistically or culturally different readers and struggling readers and writers, as well as the more experienced ones in the middle or junior high school years. Those are crucial years in the development of lifelong readers.

Struggling and Reluctant Readers

To struggle, or to not easily meet with success, makes anyone reluctant to do something. Struggling and reluctant readers come in all ages and all stages. They usually are caught in the downward spiral of failure that produces dislike and mistrust. This leads to an avoidance of practice that leads to a lack of development, to further failure, and so on. In order to end this downward spiral and turn it upwards toward success, which leads to pleasure, trust, and further practice, at least one truly successful activity needs to occur. Introducing a wordless book to struggling readers is sometimes a shock to their understanding of what reading is. When these students come to realize that they can "read" a book, even though it has no words of its own, they begin to realize what reading is—and that they can do it!

Reprinted From the *Journal of Adolescent & Adult Literacy*, *41*(6), 428–433, March 1998.

Wordless Books Cited

Briggs, R. (1978). *The snowman*. Random House/Scholastic. The video (26 minutes) by SONY was an Academy Award Nominee in the U.S. and is available through Scholastic Books.

DePaola, T. (1978). *Pancakes for breakfast*. Harcourt.

Goodall, J.S. (1978). *An Edwardian Christmas*. Atheneum.

Goodall, J.S. (1976). *An Edwardian summer*. Atheneum.

Goodall, J.S. (1975). *Creepy castle*. Atheneum.

Goodall, J.S. (1988). *Little Red Riding Hood*. Margaret K. McElderry.

Goodall, J.S. (1986). *The story of a castle*. Margaret K. McElderry.

Karlin, B. (1991). *Meow*. Simon & Schuster.

Krahn, F. (1977). *The mystery of the giant footprints*. E.P. Dutton.

Krahn, F. (1974). *The self-made snowman*. Lippincott.

Turkle, B. (1976). *Deep in the forest*. E.P. Dutton.

Romann, E. (1994). *Time flies*. Random House.

Wiesner, D. (1992). *Tuesday*. Clarion/Houghton Mifflin.

One such student was Robert, a nonreading 12-year-old, whose mother did not read or write. Robert was shown a wordless book and, after looking at it for a few minutes, was asked his opinion of the story. He sat expressionless until his teacher modeled how she would read the first few pages. Suddenly Robert spoke up, disagreed with the teacher's interpretation, and provided excellent reasons for his own. Encouraging him to finish reading the story was then a very natural act.

Robert was next asked to read the story into a tape recorder at the publishing table (as suggested by Lindauer, 1988). His story was then typed on the word processor by a volunteer teacher's aide as Robert watched. Robert enjoyed cutting the sentences into strips and pasting them on photocopies of each page of the story. After adding some color to the photocopied pages, he put a cover on his book and bound the pages with a plastic spiral.

Robert proudly read his book to his mother and any classmate or relative who would listen. In fact, he read it so many times to so many different people that he easily developed automaticity with the over-200-word vocabulary of his story and easily transferred this knowledge to other books during the school year. But most important, Robert now saw himself as a reader and an author. His remarkable success is not an isolated incident.

McGee and Tompkins (1983) described a successful program using wordless books to emphasize prediction strategies and assist readers with word and phrase recognition. Wordless books chosen for this program had structured stories (ones with intricate illustrations to emphasize the story) that would encourage students to create longer, detailed, and more organized stories. Although McGee and Tompkins described a group of younger students, the creativity stimulated by wordless books encourages older students to look more closely at story details, to carefully consider all story elements, and to more clearly understand how text is organized so that a story develops. The plots of wordless books can be mapped, the characters examined and compared, and the settings analyzed for their significance to the plot or action.

The use of wordless books can encourage reluctant and struggling readers in middle school and junior high to read, develop vocabulary, and make the connection between written and spoken language. Older readers seem to respond to wordless books because they are so visually appealing and because they often involve cleverly developed plots. But best of all, these books seem to counter struggling readers' tendency to focus on the words to a degree that interferes with their being able to make sense of the story and predict outcomes.

Linguistically and Culturally Different Readers

Wordless books are equally valuable for ESL readers or struggling readers of any age simply because lack of print lends them to any language. The learner can "read" the book in his or her native tongue as a foundation for creativity.

Wordless books seem to act as story frames (Fowler, 1982) for assisting linguistically and culturally different readers to process concepts and for guiding them through the structure of the plot. In addition, the pictures provide students with something to speak, read, and write about. As one teacher has described it, "The pictures stimulate the students to tell the stories in their own words" (Gitelman, 1990, p. 525). In five lessons, Gitelman's class discussed a book, wrote their version of the story, read their own text, illustrated it, and recorded their story on audiotape. Gitelman concluded that wordless books "stimulate oral communication and foster literacy" (p. 525).

Creating their own book not only provides diverse language learners with the language skills they desperately need, but also gives them a sense of accomplishment that is so essential to continuing successful literacy development.

One snowy morning not long ago, in an inner-city, multiracial sixth-grade classroom, the teacher shared *The Snowman* by Raymond Briggs. She introduced the story as one man's memory of a time it snowed when he was a little boy. She used an opaque projector to show students the beautiful, dream-like pictures and began by describing what she saw in each frame. After only a couple of pages, she asked if anyone would like to read the next page. Students eagerly volunteered to read each page of the remainder of the book.

The teacher then asked students to work with a friend to write the story as they saw it, and she distributed five paperback copies of the book to be shared. Students worked on their stories for two more class periods, and they kept her busy asking for advice about what to call something they saw in the pictures or what she thought the characters were doing in a particular frame, to settle a dispute between partners. The teacher witnessed students working together, developing their vocabulary and writing skills, and enjoying the story.

Later in the week, students edited and shared their stories. They were surprised to see how the others' stories differed—some students included dialogue, some saw the story as a dream, others as a real event—and all took pride in their products, even though some were not entirely complete. As a culminating experience, the teacher showed the video of *The Snowman* (also wordless—see Sidebar) and displayed the students' stories in a notebook on the reading table. Later a companion story, The *Self-Made Snowman* by Fernando Krahn, was made available for students who wanted to prolong this successful experience.

Using partners or the buddy system (Swan, 1992) during in-class reading time is a recommended procedure, especially if there are culturally or linguistically different students in the group. Even in bilingual programs, both languages can be developed with the use of wordless books. Pairs of students can discuss and alternately write the story for each page. The teacher should then assist each pair in editing their story. Finally each pair should be encouraged to share their story with the class, in either or both languages, using their sentences taped to photocopied pages, or they might record their text on audiotape for their classmates to hear as they look through the book.

This activity builds social relationships, cooperative learning skills, and expands students' literacy experiences. An excellent follow-up to such a lesson might include allowing students to respond creatively to the book in whatever way they wish—in writing, art, or music. At the conclusion of this process, students will have been exposed to both spoken and written standard English in a nonthreatening way that's also fun (Flatley & Rutland, 1986).

Cross-Age Tutoring

Wordless books can also be fun and helpful in cross-age tutoring programs. Ellis and Preston (1984) described a cross-age tutoring program in which fifth graders worked with first graders using wordless books. In a similar program at a local junior high school, eighth graders were paired with first and second graders to provide one-to-one literacy experiences. In years past, the older student had created "Big Books" and helped the younger students to write the text and illustrate their books. This past year, the eighth graders selected wordless books to share with their young partners. The purpose was to encourage the younger readers to create their own stories using complete sentences and to develop their understanding of sequence and content.

This program produced positive academic results for everyone involved. Regardless of the skill or developmental level of the older student, every first and second grader benefited from the individual attention, demonstrating increased competence and confidence; but just as important, the eighth graders developed a greater understanding of the literacy strategies they were teaching and proved themselves to be very dedicated and responsible.

Wordless books used in this way, involving younger children, should have simple story lines, such as *Meow* by Bernie Karlin, *The Mystery of the Giant Footprints* by Krahn, or Tomie DePaola's *Pancakes for Breakfast*. These simple but beautiful little stories, and others like them, will ensure success for everyone.

Theme Units and Content Areas

Theme units have been found to be most successful with younger readers when wordless books were included in the book choices. But in middle and upper grades, the advantages of wordless books have been virtually overlooked. However, sharing and discussing a wordless book might enhance or even introduce a unit.

A seventh-grade social studies teacher, for example, recently introduced a unit on the Middle Ages by sharing John S. Goodall's *The Story of a Castle*. The vivid half-page illustrations beautifully display the evolution of lifestyles as well as living quarters, the impact of religion, the ingenuity and hard work of the people, and social relationships during this fascinating period in Europe. Students were instantly hooked into the flavor and fascination of the unit. A companion book by Goodall, *Creepy Castle*, a whimsical look at the daily workings of a castle, also became a part of this unit, along with many other books at varying levels of reading difficulty. Other books by Goodall, such as *An Edwardian Christmas* and *An Edwardian Summer*, lend themselves equally well to other historical units.

Similarly, a unit on prehistoric times might involve the use of *Time Flies* by Eric Romann, the picture story of a fly who ventures from (or through) a museum of history into the real thing. A unit on comparing fairy tales should include Brinton Turkle's *Deep in the Forest*, a new twist to the "Three Bears" story, as well as Goodall's *Little Red Riding Hood*, a vivid rendition of the original tale in the artist's famous half-page style. Wordless books can beautifully enhance many theme units.

Recently, an eighth-grade English/reading class was introduced to a thematic unit on "The Hows and Whys of Humor," which the teacher had developed to entice her most reluctant readers and writers. Almost desperate to help her students recognize the significance of plot, characters, and setting, the teacher brought to class a box of wordless books, carefully selected for their clever plots, interesting characters, and recognizable settings, and all depicting humorous situations, events, or characters. She passed them out randomly and simply asked students to look through them to see if they would like to read and study them during their next unit on humor. After a time, the teacher asked her students to trade books until they had each seen two or three different ones.

At first several students voiced complaints: How are we supposed to read them? These stupid books don't have any words! But soon everyone was chuckling and telling one another which one was "the best!" The teacher then asked if anyone would like to tell the class about his or her favorite book. One girl, Jessica, whose voice had not been heard in class before, stood and read (or retold) Turkle's *Deep in the Forest* about a little bear who wanders into a house in the woods, eats the soup on the table, tries out the chairs, and so on. Jessica easily and simply compared it to the Goldilocks tale as she showed and explained each page. Everyone was so impressed with her performance that spontaneous applause followed her reading.

The discussion of whether or not this story was "humorous," what humor was, and how authors create humor (through plot, characters, and setting) was more animated than any discussion this class had ever had; everyone seemed to have something to contribute. All agreed that these books were worthy of study and should definitely be a part of their unit on humor.

The Teacher's Role

When introducing wordless books, the teacher must often model how the pictures tell a story. The teacher takes on the role of coach and collaborator, observing, listening, sometimes interacting with students, and sometimes prompting them with an appropriate question when needed. It is important that the teacher allow the wordless book experience to be nonthreatening. This means allowing students to speak in their natural language without correcting them, and not suggesting what to see or to look for in the stories. Lindauer (1988) wrote,

> It is important to allow the child's language to remain intact. It may be tempting to correct such things as grammar and sentence structure as the child invents her story, but resist! Children learn oral language in safe and supportive situations, not when they fear failure or are inhibited by continual corrections....The use of wordless books should be a nonthreatening experience designed by accepting teachers to be successful for all children. (p. 140)

Most of us would agree with Lindauer that we, too, learn "in safe and supportive situations."

Several titles and authors of wordless books have been mentioned here. But the number of wordless books available is surprisingly large and varied. A wonderful resource is a reference book by Richey and Puckett (1992). *Wordless/Almost Wordless Picture Books* has well over 500 subject headings for locating a wordless book to complement your topic or theme (each title has a brief description of plot and characters). Its contents should give the reader a sense of the magnitude and variety of wordless books available for use in theme units, in whole-class or small groups, or even by pairs or individuals; there are enough titles to go around! This reference book or a librarian can assist you in making informed choices about wordless book titles that might be included in your regular program.

Valuable Tools

Although the use of wordless books is not new, we must continually revisit, revive, and revise successful practices, especially those that seem to lend themselves well to current classroom situations. Wordless books can provide the stimulus for creative writing and for successful reading. Wordless books have helped struggling readers of all ages and linguistically and culturally different readers. Simply because of their visual appeal and lack of words, these little books ensure successful interaction with text—reading and writing experiences—for middle-grade students. They have been shown to be valuable for developing reading, writing, and oral language with virtually all students who have the proper guidance and encouragement. These attributes make wordless books ideal tools for literacy development in the multileveled, multicultural, multitalented middle-grade classroom.

REFERENCES

Caroff, S.F., & Moje, E.B. (1992). A conversation with David Wiesner: 1992 Caldecott Medal winner. *The Reading Teacher*, *46*, 284–289.

Ellis, D.W., & Preston, F.W. (1984). Enhancing beginning reading using wordless picture books in a cross-age tutoring program. *The Reading Teacher*, *37*, 692–698.

Flatley, J.K., & Rutland, A.D. (1986). Using wordless picture books to teach linguistically/culturally different students. *The Reading Teacher*, *40*, 276–281.

Fowler, G.L. (1982). Developing comprehension skills in primary students through the use of story frames. *The Reading Teacher*, *36*, 176–179.

Gitelman, H.F. (1990). In the classroom: Using wordless picture books with disabled readers. *The Reading Teacher*, *43*, 525.

Larrick, N. (1976). Wordless picture books and the teaching of reading. *The Reading Teacher*, *29*, 743–746.

Lindauer, S.L. (1988). Wordless books: An approach to visual literacy. *Children's Literature in Education*, *19*, 136–142.

McGee, L.M., & Tompkins, G.E. (1983). Wordless picture books are for older readers, too. *Journal of Reading*, *27*, 120–123.

Richey, V.H., & Puckett, K.E. (1992). *Wordless/almost wordless picture books: A guide*. Englewood, CO: Libraries Unlimited.

Swan, A.M. (1992). In the classroom: Wordless picture book buddies. *The Reading Teacher*, *45*, 655.

Helen L. Johnson, Susanna Pflaum, Ellen Sherman, Patricia Taylor, and Patricia Poole

Focus on Teenage Parents: Using Children's Literature to Strengthen Teenage Literacy

She waited patiently outside the room with two books she had selected. She tapped her foot, moved from side to side, cleared her throat. She was very anxious. She began practicing as she waited...nervously looking around. She wondered. Will they listen to me? Will they understand the book that I have selected to read to them? Will they bite me? Will they laugh? Will they run away? Suppose....

The time came. She entered the room and sat on the floor with her two books. A small boy immediately came over to her and stood watching. She opened the book. He stood watching. She opened up her arms and he jumped into her lap.

As she read, the little boy laughed. He pointed to the pictures and laughed some more. She read, he listened. They talked. "I'll see you next week." She beamed at the small boy. He smiled and gave her a big hug.

What a great experience!

This description is from the notes taken by a teacher in the Family Literacy Project: Focus on Teenage Parents on a student's initial experience reading in the school's childcare center. This anecdote captures the essence of what the Family Literacy Project is trying to provide for students: the experience of literacy as active and interactive and of seeing themselves as competent and successful in literacy activities.

The Family Literacy Project: Focus on Teenage Parents is a privately funded collab-

orative effort by college faculty and New York City Board of Education teachers and administrators to address the needs of student parents and their children. As evident in the previous example, the project provides opportunities for students to develop and share their literacy skills in a generative way, thereby increasing their sense of personal competence and their motivation to succeed.

The project began as a pilot program in 1989 at one high school in Queens, New York; over the past 4 years it has been implemented in New York City at two comprehensive high schools, four alternative high schools, and one community site, a residential shelter for teen parents who are studying for the General Equivalency Diploma.

The Family Literacy Project: Focus on Teenage Parents has two complementary goals: to strengthen the literacy skills of student parents, and to accomplish this through activities that also enrich their understanding of child development and parenting issues. Children's literature is uniquely suited to meeting these two goals (Doneson, 1991; Goldsmith & Handel, 1990) and plays a central role in the project.

Although many of the project students have limited literacy skills and have had unpleasant reading experiences in school, the project's collection of literature for children and young

Reprinted From the *Journal of Adolescent & Adult Literacy*, *39*(4), 290–296, December 1995/January 1996.

adults exposes them to books that address their concerns (family relations, friendship, growing up) at an accessible reading level. Reading becomes productive and rewarding, and awareness of the developing child's changing needs becomes clearer and fuller.

Many students today do not see connections between the demands of school and the issues confronting them in their personal lives (cf. the April 4, 1993 education supplement to *The New York Times*, "Kids of the 90's"). This feeling of alienation is heightened for students whose family and culture differ from those presented in mainstream educational programs (Norton, 1990; Quintero & Velarde, 1990). The Family Literacy Project: Focus on Teenage Parents engages students in serious consideration of their family histories and the links between their own childhood experiences and their behavior as parents. They examine the changing needs of growing children and explore parenting practices that respond to these needs in ways that support healthy development. Project activities, such as reading to young children and writing books for children, allow students to share their literacy skills and encourage them to view literacy as empowering (Freire, 1970).

How the Project Works

The faculty team. At each participating site, an interdisciplinary faculty team consisting of one classroom teacher (English or social studies) and one staff member from the Board of Education's Living for Young Families through Education (LYFE) program designs and implements project activities. The academic subject teacher has primary responsibility but relies on the support of the LYFE teacher, especially for coverage of child development and parenting issues. Project staff work closely with each faculty team to adapt activities to the needs and interests of the population at each site.

The book collection. An extensive collection of children's books (roughly 200 titles) has been established at each school. Multiple copies of each title are purchased for each site so that students can do joint book projects. The collection includes many classics and Newbery and Caldecott medal winners, as well as books representing the experiences of adolescents and of different ethnic groups. Lists of selections used for two of the most popular themes, "family" and "fairy and folk tales," appear in the sidebar on the following pages. Other themes that have been used include "growing up," "celebrations," and "migration experiences."

In response to requests from the project teachers, we have added more selections of poetry, folk tales, and books suitable for infants. Also, on the basis of our discussions with the faculty teams, we have begun to add nonfiction—primarily biographies and material about child development and parenting—to the collection.

Coursework. At each project site, a credit-bearing course, "Children's Literature," is offered by the faculty team. The course immerses students in children's literature and takes a holistic rather than a skills-centered approach to reading and writing (Cutting & Milligan, 1991). In addition to the children's literature class, we have developed a unit on children's language and literacy development to be incorporated into student internships or guided independent study. At several sites, we have also sponsored an after-school club that engages in project activities led by the faculty team.

Staff development. During the summer prior to implementation of the project at their school, faculty teams participate in intensive workshops on project goals and activities. The workshops cover many topics, including child development, early language and literacy, writing process activities, ways of using children's literature in the classroom, and storytelling. The workshops also provide opportunities for new teachers to talk with continuing teachers about the project, and a continuing teacher is assigned as mentor for each new faculty team. A summer workshop for continuing teachers is held to evaluate project activities and plan for the next school year.

During the school year, the staff development component continues through Saturday morning workshops where faculty teams share ideas and concerns with other project participants. Toward this same end, we have begun a project newsletter featuring brief descriptions of class activities from each school.

Recognition ceremony. To highlight the accomplishments of students in the project, an annual recognition ceremony is held at a central location. Students from all participating sites display their work and have an opportunity to view the work done at other schools. All students who participate in the ceremony receive a memento of the day.

This opportunity to receive recognition for their work from a broader community reinforces the project's identity and value for students and teachers. At the most recent recognition ceremony, James Ransome, the noted African American illustrator of children's books, gave a slide presentation about his career and students received autographed copies of one of his books.

Reading Activities

Most readings are from the project's library of children's literature. All students read a range of books, from picture books to young adult selections. Additional readings in child development are used in most cases.

Selected Readings

The family

Angelou, Maya. *I Know Why the Caged Bird Sings*. Random House, 1970.

Brown, Margaret. *The Runaway Bunny*. HarperCollins, 1942.

Christiansen, C.B. *My Mother's House, My Father's House*. Macmillan, 1989.

Cisneros, Sandra. *The House on Mango Street*. Random House, 1991.

Clifton, Lucille. *Everett Anderson's Goodbye*. Henry Holt, 1988.
Everett Anderson's Nine Month Long. Henry Holt, 1978.

DePaola, Tomie. *Nana Upstairs and Nana Downstairs*. Puffin, 1978.
Strega Nona. Simon & Schuster, 1979.

Dr. Seuss. *Horton Hatches the Egg*. Random Books for Young Readers, 1940.

Eastman, P.D. *Are You My Mother?* Random Books for Young Readers, 1986.

Freeman, Don. *Corduroy*. Viking, 1968.

Hoban, Russell. *Baby Sister for Frances*. HarperCollins, 1964.

Jenness, Aylette. *Families: A Celebration of Diversity*. Houghton Mifflin, 1993.

Johnson, Angela. *Tell Me a Story, Mama*. Orchard Books/Franklin Watts, 1989.
When I Am Old With You. Orchard Books/Franklin Watts, 1990.

Keats, Ezra. *Peter's Chair*. HarperCollins, 1967.

Kellogg, Steven. *Much Bigger Than Martin*. Dial, 1976.

Kunhardt, Dorothy. *Pat the Bunny*. Western, 1942.

MacLachlan, Patricia. *Sarah, Plain and Tall*. HarperCollins, 1985.
Through Grandpa's Eyes. HarperCollins, 1971.

Mohr, Nicholasa. *Felita*. Dial, 1979.
Going Home. Dial, 1986.

Oxenbury, Helen. *Family*. Simon & Schuster, 1981.

Simon, Norma. *All Kinds of Families*. Albert Williams, 1976.

Williams, Vera. *A Chair for My Mother*. Greenwillow, 1982.   *(continued)*

Selected Readings (continued)

Fairy and folk tales

Aardema, Verna. *Bringing the Rain to Kapiti Plain*. Pied Piper, 1981.

Princess Gorilla and a New Kind of Water. Dial, 1988.

Why Mosquitoes Buzz in People's Ears. Pied Piper, 1978.

Aesop. *The Lion and the Mouse*. Troll Associates, 1981.

Andersen, Hans. *The Emperor's New Clothes*. Houghton Mifflin, 1979.

Brown, Marcia. *Stone Soup*. Macmillan, 1979.

DePaola, Tomie. *Tomie DePaola's Favorite Nursery Tales*. Putnam, 1986.

Galdone, Paul. *Three Billy Goats Gruff*. Houghton Mifflin, 1981.

Three Little Pigs. Houghton Mifflin, 1979.

Goldberg, Whoopi. *Alice*. Bantam, 1992.

Lobel, Arnold. *Mouse Tales*. HarperCollins, 1972.

Mosel, Arlene. *Tikki Tikki Tembo*. Henry Holt, 1968.

Peet, Bill. *Ant and the Elephant*. Houghton Mifflin, 1980.

Scieszka, Jon. *The Stinky Cheese Man*. Viking, 1992.

Shute, Linda. *Momotaro the Peach Boy*. Lothrop, 1986.

Steptoe, John. *Mufaro's Beautiful Daughters*. Lothrop, 1987.

Wildsmith, Brian. *Mother Goose*. Oxford University Press, 1987.

Wolkstein, Diane. *The Banza*. Dial, 1981.

---

class. At two sites, students prepared favorite stories for presentation at a storytelling contest that the students themselves judged.

Reading to young children. An essential part of the class experience is reading to young children. Each student is required to read regularly to a young child. Those who do not have children of their own must "adopt" a child with whom to do this weekly home reading. Students keep journals about these reading experiences and class discussions cover such issues as how to choose a book for a particular child and how to sustain a young child's attention to a story.

At one of the sites, students prepared a puppet show. Students wrote their own scripts, made puppets, and performed for the children in the child care center. Students also visit the LYFE child care centers to read to the toddlers.

Reading to elementary school children. Each project site establishes a relationship with an elementary school in the neighborhood and students make regular visits to read to the children. The books that are read on these visits have been selected from the Family Literacy library, and students practice reading them before they visit the elementary school.

These visits address key elements of the project. For example, preparing to read for an older, unknown child requires that the student consider a book's possible interest, relevancy, appropriateness as to complexity, etc. Students engage in considerable critical exchange of views about the various books and their suitability. Moreover, issues of child behavior and response arise and often lead to reconsideration of the reading activities and even of parenting practices.

Both the teenagers and the young children have benefited from these shared reading experiences. Project participants are encouraged by the children's positive reactions to their reading—they experience success. This

At some sites, classes are organized around themes or units of study.

Storytelling. The project emphasizes storytelling as a way of acknowledging the rich oral traditions of many cultures. Students in some project classes have interviewed family members and then presented family stories in class. At other sites, students select favorite stories from the book collection to tell to the feedback motivates them to read more on their own and to their own children.

Writing Activities

Writing activities are a crucial component at all sites, with heavy emphasis on writing process. Project teachers are encouraged to have their students prepare preliminary drafts of their writing and to then revise them in response to teacher and peer feedback. At some sites, students use the computer lab for their writing, which facilitates their involvement in editing and revision.

The experience in the pilot project revealed the importance of clear demarcation between writing for publication (the students' books) and writing for personal reflection. Students at all sites do both kinds of writing.

Journal writing. At most sites, students engage in journal writing. They are given a notebook at the beginning of each new term and are expected to make entries regularly. In some cases, these involve reactions to the children's books they have read. In others, students reflect on their experiences reading to young children.

Topical writing. Students at some of the sites have prepared nonfiction pieces about child development issues. Sometimes, this involved reading articles on a parenting issue (e.g., schedule vs. demand feeding, toilet training, discipline) and then preparing a report that was presented to the class. In other cases, students gathered information on child safety issues and prepared manuals (e.g., how to childproof your home). Some teachers have distributed newspaper and magazine articles on child development topics (e.g., parental discipline styles) and students have written reaction pieces to them.

Children's books. Students at all sites develop a children's book, a project that requires the integration of ideas and experiences from the entire course. Students are challenged to consider issues of interest, plot, character, and language use while drawing upon their own or imagined experiences to produce a high-quality book. The books produced have covered a broad range of topics, from "The day I got lost from Mommy" to "Why Kevin is afraid" to "Kedesha's girl."

Issues of presentation lead students to consider the appropriate integration of art work with their texts. At several sites, workshops led by teachers from Doing Art Together, an outreach program in conjunction with the Metropolitan Museum of Art, are incorporated into the project class. In addition to helping students become more comfortable with art techniques and materials, these workshops encourage students to consider strategies for illustrating their stories. Students are then given class time to combine their stories with the artistic techniques they have learned. The finished books are displayed in the schools and at the annual recognition ceremony before becoming part of the libraries of the authors' families.

Notes From Project Sites

Although certain activities—reading to a young child at home, reading to elementary school children, and creating a children's book—occur at all project sites, each faculty team creates an experience that is uniquely responsive to the interests and needs of its students. (The names of the following schools have been changed to maintain confidentiality.)

Adams School. Adams School is an alternative high school in a Brooklyn neighborhood that is characterized by high levels of crime, unemployment, and illiteracy. The 550 students are predominantly African American. Students frequently transfer to Adams School after having difficulty in more traditional settings. Adams School has the largest Board of

Education-sponsored program (LYFE) for teenage parents in the city.

The project provided notebooks for student journals. With the help of the project assistant, the teacher grouped some of the books by subject so that students could compare how different authors handle topics. The students entered their critiques in their journals and later discussed them in class.

Much class time was devoted to discussion of issues raised by the students. These have included prenatal care, methods of discipline, developmentally appropriate behaviors and expectations, and what, how, and when to read to a child. Several students raised concerns about how to protect their children from abuse and violence, and this became a focus of several class activities. Reading newspaper and magazine articles on questions raised in class, students talked about the advantages and disadvantages of alternative approaches. The teacher directed the students to selections in the book collection that illustrated the situations they were discussing. In this way the reading activities were closely linked to the concerns expressed by the students.

The class explored many different types of children's literature. They discussed the origins of myths, folk tales, fairy tales, and fables, and then students created their own myths and fables. These writings were shared with the class, giving students the experience of having their creative efforts acknowledged and valued.

A storytelling contest was a highlight of each semester. For the contest, each student selected a story to tell to the class. Students had to accurately recreate the story's sequence of events but were given free rein to embellish upon the original storyline and could retell the story from any character's point of view. One student's retelling of *The Runaway Bunny* elicited cheers from her classmates.

Hancock School. Situated about two miles east of Yankee Stadium, Hancock School is an alternative high school that enrolls about 350 African American and Latino students. Every student had previously attended another high school. In addition to a social studies teacher and the LYFE social worker, the faculty team included an art teacher. The class met for a double period three times a week and twice a week for single periods. Students earned both English and art credit.

The semester started with whole-class reading and discussions of a selected novel—one semester it was If *Beale Street Could Talk* (Baldwin, 1986); another, *The Friends* (Guy, 1983). These readings raised issues of family, parenting, and friendship. The students recognized the lifestyles being presented in the readings, and connected strongly with characters, their decisions, and contexts. Class discussions made an immediate connection with the students' lives, encouraging students to become more reflective about their own upbringing so they could more clearly define themselves in their role as parents.

Literature became a tool for learning about parenting; students simultaneously developed a critical enjoyment of reading for themselves and for their children. After the novels were completed, there was greater individual selection, reading, and sharing of children's literature. By the end of the semester, when students were developing their own books, they were able to integrate their experiences reading the novels and books for children with the sense of literature gleaned from the children's books.

Students also wrote in class daily, based on structured thought questions about the literature they were reading. Most of these questions involved comparing characters in their reading to the students' own lives ("Have you ever felt the way this person did about being in school") and issues of values and morals

("Do you think this behavior was justified"). Through the art component of the course, students got the opportunity to transform their expression of what they had read, written, and discussed. The class also developed a comic book.

Several guest speakers were brought in to help explore issues in literature and child development. The speakers were obtained through the Board of Education and the Writers' Collaborative, and included noted children's author Camille Yarborough.

The Value of the Project for Nonparents

While the Family Literacy Project: Focus on Teenage Parents was designed to address the special needs and concerns of student parents, we found that limiting the class to student parents did not work well, for several reasons. On practical grounds, because the student parents are not scheduled as a block, not all of them were available to take the class at the same period. More importantly, restricting the class to student parents did a disservice to them and to other students as well. Student parents and nonparents benefit from discussing the issues together; they bring different perspectives to the discussion, and each learns from hearing the other's viewpoint.

Classes made up exclusively of student parents "ghettoize" them, heightening their isolation from normal school activities. It is important for student parents to feel connected to other students; they need to be encouraged to continue to view themselves as students as well as parents. Moreover, given the high rate of pregnancy in the schools in which the project has been implemented, every student must be considered a potential parent; and many who are not parents still carry substantial child-care responsibilities for other family members.

It is therefore important for all students to be engaged in consideration of child development and parenting issues. Indeed, several teachers have remarked on the richness of the discussions that ensue when parents and nonparents engage in dialogue around issues of child welfare and education.

The Power of Children's Literature

The Family Literacy Project: Focus on Teenage Parents began with the notion that student parents would be attracted to children's literature because it presents important issues in engaging and accessible ways, and that student parents could respond to the content of children's literature without embarrassment because they were acting on behalf of their children. All of this has proven to be true. But what we did not anticipate was the extent of this literature's power. It has been apparent in the progression of students' reading.

Initially, students reacted to the children's books as "baby books" that they considered for their infants. Later, they began to read and recommend particular books to one another. Their involvement with literature grew as they selected and prepared books to read to young children. Personal engagement with reading emerged, as evident in the comment of one student who, in requesting a young adult book, remarked, "I'd like to read some books that are for me now."

At our recent recognition ceremony, the excitement and energy of the students led our keynote speaker to comment on their positive sense of power and purpose. For student parents, as for others, literacy and empowerment are intertwined. Thus supporting literacy as an active, communicative process enhances both the positive sense of self and the capacity to nurture.

REFERENCES

Baldwin, J. (1986). *If Beale Street could talk*. New York: Dell.

Cutting, B., & Milligan, J.L. (1991). Learning to read in New Zealand. In C. Kamii, M. Manning, & G. Manning (Eds.), *Early literacy: A constructivist foundation for whole language* (pp. 83-90). Washington, DC: National Education Association.

Doneson, S.G. (1991). Reading as a second chance: Teen mothers and children's books. *Journal of Reading*, *35*, 220-223.

Freire, P. (1970). *Cultural action for freedom*. Cambridge, UK: Center for the Study of Development and Change.

Goldsmith, E., & Handel, R.D. (1990). Children's literature and adult literacy. *Interracial Books for Children Bulletin*, *19*, 3-5.

Guy, R. (1983). *The friends*. New York: Bantam.

Norton, D.E. (1990). Teaching multicultural literature in the reading curriculum. *The Reading Teacher*, *44*, 28-40.

Quintero, E., & Velarde, M.C. (1990). Intergenerational literacy: A developmental, bilingual approach. *Young Children*, *45*, 10-15.

Barbara Erickson

Read-Alouds Reluctant Readers Relish

"Miss, when are you gonna read us a whole book?" a frustrated ninth grader begged after I had read aloud the hooking chapter from yet another young adult novel. Because I was attempting to show the wide spectrum of books available in my reading-writing workshop for reluctant high school readers, I had been reading aloud enticing chapters for weeks. These chapters included several from Gary Paulsen's novels *The Monument*, *Canyons*, *Tracker*, *The Crossing*, *Hatchet*, *The River*, and *Popcorn Days and Buttermilk Nights*. Other chapters came from Robert Cormier's *We All Fall Down*, Joan Lowery Nixon's *The Other Side of Dark*, Phyllis Reynolds Naylor's *Send No Blessings*, and several from R.L. Stine's Fear Street Series books. This teen's question made me realize I was overdoing a good thing.

Beginning Read-Aloud Guidelines

Adjusting to this student's request, I began reading short stories, following the guidelines reported by John W. Conner in "Stories to Be Read Aloud" in the February 1989 issue of *English Journal*. According to Conner, stories must meet the following criteria:

- hold the interest of both teacher and students
- stimulate discussion
- require just 15–30 minutes to read
- lead to additional readings
- involve dilemmas whose solutions are open ended.

After taking risks with hundreds of selections, I have abandoned many pieces but have kept many that students enjoyed. Although every class is different, perhaps knowing my successes will help make your read-alouds more successful.

Titles That Work

The beginning short story was Todd Strasser's "On the Bridge," a story of a boy's realization that his idol, the school's toughie, is actually a coward unworthy of his respect. For the many Hispanic students in my classes, I read two stories by Gary Soto. "Mother and Daughter" describes a poor girl whose clever mother provides her daughter with a new look for an old party dress using black dye, only to have the dye weep black tears onto her legs at the dance. In the other story, "Two Dreamers," a grandfather and grandson both dream of having more wealth, but money eludes them.

Mildred Taylor, a contemporary Black author, was the next focus with *The Gold Cadillac*, a novella describing how her own

Reprinted From the *Journal of Adolescent & Adult Literacy*, *40*(3), 212–214, November 1996.

(continued)

Suggested Read-Alouds for Reluctant High School Readers

Action Magazine. Jefferson City, MO: Scholastic.

Aurandt, P. (1978). *Paul Harvey's the rest of the story*. New York: Bantam.

Avi. (1986). *Wolf rider*. New York: Bradbury.

Cormier, R. (1991). *We all fall down*. New York: Delacorte.

Cormier, R. (1992). *Tunes for bears to dance to*. New York: Delacorte.

Crutcher, C. (1989). *Goin' fishin'*. In Athletic shorts: Six short stories (pp. 81–103). New York: Greenwillow.

Dunning, S., Lueders, E., & Smith, H. (Comps.). (1967). *Reflections on a gift of watermelon pickle*. New York: Lothrop, Lee, & Shepard.

Dunning, S., Lueders, E., & Smith, H. (Comps.). (1969). *Some haystacks don't even have any needles and other complete modern poems*. New York: Lothrop, Lee & Shepard.

Fulghum, R. (1988). *It was on fire when I lay down on it*. New York: Ivy.

Gallo, D. (Ed.). (1990). *Center stage: One-act plays for teenage readers and actors*. New York: HarperCollins.

Gardiner, J.R. (1980). *Stone fox*. New York: Harper.

Garner, J.F. (1995). Twas the night before Solstice. In *Politically correct holiday stories: For an enlightened yuletide season* (pp. 1–10). Thorndike, ME: G.K. Hall.

Greene, B. (1983). *American beat*. New York: Atheneum.

Larrick, N. (Ed.). (1968). *On city streets: An anthology of poetry*. New York: M. Evans & Company.

Naylor, P.R. (1990). *Send no blessings*. New York: Puffin.

Nixon, J.L. (1986). *The other side of dark*. New York: Delacorte.

(continued)

---

family's pride in their new Cadillac turned to fear during their trip to visit relatives in the southern U.S. Another Taylor favorite was a novella entitled *The Friendship*, published in the same volume. *Mississippi Bridge* was a short tragedy about prejudice.

My students' favorite short story was Chris Crutcher's "Goin' Fishin'," a story about love-turned-to-hatred for a friend who accidentally kills the protagonist's family. When this oral reading ended, the most resistant reader leaned over, tugged at my sleeve, and said for my ears alone to hear, "Good story, Miss, a really good story." I knew this student was finally hooked.

Along with short stories, poetry was popular for quick oral readings. Gary Soto's poems were popular with my students. Dan Kirby and Tom Liner in *Inside Out* (Boynton Cook, 1988) recommended two compilations, *Some Haystacks Don't Even Have Any Needles* and *Reflections on a Gift of Watermelon Pickle* and Nancy Larrick's *On City Streets: An Anthology of Poetry*. Of course, many high school students still enjoyed old favorites from Shel Silverstein's *Where the Sidewalk Ends*, which inspired courageous students to write their own poems and share them orally. Happy poetry listeners want to read for variety and pleasure instead of for explication.

Richard Abrahamson and Betty Carter promote current nonfiction suggestions for independent reading in their book *Nonfiction for Young Adults* (Oryx Press, 1990). I also recommend nonfiction read-alouds because they appeal especially to reluctant male readers. Paul Harvey's *The Rest of the Story* includes unique but little known scenes about famous people. Bob Greene's *American Beat* shows common people performing uncommon feats, and the Readers Digest's *Great Lives, Great Deeds* includes short accounts about famous people. Robert Fulghum's *It Was on Fire When I Lay Down on It* has a humorous account of a wedding ceremony that goes amiss. Even factual newspaper articles about teenagers can capture adolescent ears. A humorous holiday favorite was "Twas the Night Before Solstice" in James Finn Garner's *Politically Correct Holiday Stories: For an Enlightened Yuletide Season*. So short stories, poetry, and nonfiction can provide successful content for oral presentation.

For variety, fluency, and oral recitation, however, students can read literature aloud for themselves and their classmates to enjoy. Every issue of *Action Magazine* (published by Scholastic) contains contemporary plays for such activities. In another successful strategy, Readers Theatre, students choose scenes from their favorite novels and after rehearsal, they read these scenes to an audience, using expression but not props. One group of dedicated juniors, however, insisted upon acting out a scene from R.L. Stine's *The Girlfriend* in which the upset boyfriend carries a comatose girl over his shoulder. Finally, published one-act plays, such as those in Donald Gallo's *Center Stage*, can be shared. Once students have selected their plays, they read, rehearse, and ultimately read them to fellow classmates and my unobtrusive tape recorder. They are pleased with their professional-sounding oral readings and the adulation of their peers.

Not only are short stories, poems, plays, and gripping chapters read out loud, but sometimes whole books are shared. In the *New Read-Aloud Handbook* (Penguin, 1989) Jim Trelease says Avi's *Wolf Rider* is an ideal whole book to share. I found that male listeners enjoyed John R. Gardiner's *Stone Fox*, and Robert Cormier's *Tunes for Bears To Dance To* was a favorite of freshmen students. In fact, when my voice faltered in the final chapter, an eager student jumped up, took the book, and continued reading to the last page.

Suggested Read-Alouds for Reluctant High School Readers *(continued)*

Paulsen, G. (1983). *Popcorn days and buttermilk nights*. New York: Puffin.

Paulsen, G. (1984). *Tracker*. New York: Puffin.

Paulsen, G. (1987). *The crossing*. New York: Dell.

Paulsen, G. (1988). *Hatchet*. New York: Puffin.

Paulsen, G. (1990). *Canyons*. New York: Delacorte.

Paulsen, G. (1991). *The monument*. New York: Delacorte.

Paulsen, G. (1991). *The river*. New York: Delacorte.

Readers Digest. (1964). *Great lives, great deeds*. Pleasantville, NY: Readers Digest Association.

Silverstein, S. (1974). *Where the sidewalk ends*. New York: Harper.

Soto, G. (1990). Mother and daughter. In *Baseball in April* (pp. 75–85). Holmes, PA: Trumpet Club.

Soto, G. (1990). Two dreamers. In *Baseball* in April (pp. 29–41). Holmes, PA: Trumpet Club.

Soto, G. (1995). *New and selected poems*. San Francisco, CA: Chronicle.

Stine, R.L. (1990). *The girlfriend*. New York: Scholastic.

Strasser, T. (1987). On the bridge. In D. Gallo (Ed.), *Visions* (pp. 122–128). New York: Dell.

Taylor, M. (1990). *The friendship* and *The gold Cadillac*. New York: Bantam.

Taylor, M. (1990). *Mississippi bridge*. New York: Bantam Skylark.

Adjusted Guidelines

After hundreds of read-alouds, I have added to Conner's guidelines. I feel that read-aloud stories must meet the following criteria:

- They should include both male and female protagonists.
- They should reflect authors from many cultures.
- They should match listeners' social and emotional stages.

To story requirements, I have added other general guidelines for the reader:

- Always practice the entire read-aloud first.
- Stop the reading if students do not enjoy it.
- Keep the reading under 15 minutes.
- Pictures and props help when used occasionally.
- Vary the reading pace.
- Allow students to doodle during the reading.
- Students must keep their heads up during reading.
- Encourage but do not insist upon discussion following reading.
- Jim Trelease says that occasionally stretching students intellectually is good.

Effects on Students

Imagination and variety are necessary in selecting successful read-alouds. Listeners become curious about contemporary literature written for and about them, so they are stimulated to finish a book on their own. In fact, they often read numerous titles from the same writer, with R.L. Stine, Gary Paulsen, and Joan Lowery Nixon the most popular among my students. After hearing myriad selections modeled by their ideal reader—their teacher—they become more fluent, expressive readers. They often discuss issues introduced in read-alouds, and perhaps even shed a tear or lengthy sigh at a powerful scene.

I believe, as was written in *Becoming a Nation of Readers* in 1985, that oral reading creates readers.

Bruce H. Eldridge

The Quick Book Share

What books are being read in the reading workshop? What do our middle school students have to say about their latest "good read"? What opportunities do we provide for them to share their passion for a book? These are key questions to be addressed if we want the reading workshop to be a place where students discover books on their own and share titles and information with one another.

For the past 3 years students in my seventh-grade reading classes have had the opportunity to talk about their books through the quick book share. Even though I am constantly exposing students to different genres and authors, they want to know what their classmates are reading and what they would recommend. The quick book share was developed to meet that need. It was not designed as a format for in-depth discussion of a book or topic.

The sharing takes place in randomly selected groups of three students. After the groups are formed and seated, one member is designated the recorder and given a simple recorder's sheet. He or she writes down each student's name and the book he/she will be recommending.

At this point I give the following instructions: "Each of you will have the opportunity to talk for 2 minutes about a book you are reading or have read during the past month.

It should be a book that has been a good read; in other words, you couldn't put it down. It is a book you want to share with two of your classmates. Share anything about the book that you want your two partners to know. At the end of the 2 minutes your two partners will have a total of 1 minute to ask questions or make comments. While you are talking they may not interrupt you. This means we want you to talk for 2 minutes straight. There will be a total of three rounds of sharing, which will allow each of you to share. The total share should take us about 10 minutes."

The first time we do the sharing I place prompts like the following on the chalkboard to assist students: What type of book is this? Describe one or two of the central characters. How do you feel toward him/her? Who was your favorite character? Describe a scene from the book which really captured your attention.

Initially, I model the roles of each of the members in the group. During my 2 minutes I share a book I enjoyed that I know few students have read. I then listen carefully while the two students talk about their books and ask questions or make comments about the books each has shared. It is at this time that I emphasize an acceptable tone of voice. There will be productive noise since there are usually seven to nine groups talking at the same time. The length of sharing and responding

Reprinted From the *Journal of Adolescent & Adult Literacy*, *41*(6), 473–474, March 1998.

for the students to talk. The use of a stopwatch makes the process more official, and most students enjoy the challenge of working within the time frame.

At the end of 9 minutes the sheets are collected from each of the groups and read to the entire class. This allows students to hear what everyone is reading. Finally, when all six sections of seventh-grade reading classes have completed the process, we develop a Top 25 list of the books that were recommended most. This list is read to the students and then posted by the library of books in the room for future reference. The Sidebar contains one of the lists from the past year.

As the year progresses, students often ask when we will have another book share, until they realize that it is an ongoing component of the reading workshop. Generally, we hold a book share every 4 to 6 weeks.

In the reading workshop we want to provide our students with a variety of experiences, including opportunities to interact with one another. The quick book share serves several purposes:

1. In a short time, everyone in the class has shared a book and been exposed to two other possible titles. The next day they are also able to view the Top 25 list of books their peers are reading.

2. Teachers can see what books their students are reading and how this might affect their teaching.

3. The time frame allows equal participation among the three students, with no single student dominating the interaction.

During the 1994–95 and 1995–96 school years our students read an average of 27 books per student. This year's students are ahead of that pace. With that much reading taking place in the course of a year, it is evident our students have a thing or two to say about the books they have been reading. Most middle school students thrive on social interactions

time could be changed to meet the needs of the students or material covered.

While the students are sharing I walk from group to group listening to their comments. I keep the process moving by announcing the start and finish of each round. I do not join the interaction, because this is solely a time and are active learners. If there is one thing that we as middle school teachers have learned it is that if we don't involve our students, we lose them. The sharing of books in small groups on a regular basis is a strategy that involves our students as active participants.

The love of reading a good book is contagious. When that passion comes through, it invites others to read. The quick book share is one small activity that allows the opportunity for that passion for books to spread from student to student.

Sharon Morley

Faculty Book Talks: Adults Sharing Books and Enthusiasm for Reading With Students

Voices soften to whispers, students hustle to their respective classroom seats, and the silence of anticipation fills the room. Students know that today is Readers' Workshop and that a faculty person will be doing a book talk. The man smiles, takes his sportcoat off, folds it neatly over a chair, and rolls up his sleeves; on the table before him lies a copy of David Maraniss's book *First in His Class*, a biography of Bill Clinton (Simon & Schuster, 1995). He thanks the class for inviting him, explains what classes he teaches and, with book in hand, begins to speak. The social studies teacher within him emerges and he fills the room for the next 40 minutes with his love of history, his attraction to politics, and his fascination with political beings.

Book talks are scheduled in my ninth-grade English classes at the beginning of Readers' Workshop sessions, which occur each Monday and Tuesday in a Readers'/Writers' Workshop schedule similar to the set-up presented in Nancie Atwell's book, *In the Middle* (Heinemann, 1987). Atwell professes that if teachers value reading, they should provide classroom time for reading on a regular basis and model their love of reading by reading with the students.

In an attempt to create a reading environment, faculty and administrators are invited to bring a favorite book to share with my English

classes during one of these reading days each week. Some presenters use 5 or 10 minutes; some use the entire period, spinning the book talk into an encompassing lesson about history, about life, or about what happens when one loves to read. A spontaneous dialogue usually emerges at the close of each book talk; students see the presenter as a fellow learner. Titles of books on related topics and vicarious as well as actual experiences are shared; books are exchanged. The boundary between teacher and student is dissolved.

Oswego High School, in rural upstate New York, USA, has an amazingly diverse faculty. When I first began faculty book talks in an effort to create a "community of readers," it seemed sensible to begin with these people: teachers and administrators who mold young people's minds in their respective disciplines and positions each day. Historically, in our traditional high school setting, students meet only the five or six teachers they have in class each year; the other 100+ people remain unknown and become generically grouped under the heading "faculty" in students' minds. Book talks by faculty expose students to a plethora of secondary staff members with varied interests and reading habits. Faculty book talks would allow students to see the humaneness of teachers and administrators in addition to the usual exposure to their professional interests.

Reprinted From the *Journal of Adolescent & Adult Literacy*, *40*(2), 130–132, October 1996.

One faculty member reads books in anticipation and preparation for upcoming vacations. The novels of Louis L'Amour and Tony Hillerman transport him to the southwestern U.S. long before he arrives in his favorite locale. His book talk expands to include reminiscences of characters he has met, side trips that turned into tall tale adventures, and descriptions of desert and canyon scenery that are emblazoned in his memory. Reading is a preparation for travel and encourages people to venture forth.

The English department chair and his wife return with their family to Cape Cod, Massachusetts, each summer and in anticipation of their travels tease themselves with the mysteries of Mary Higgins Clark. One of her recent publications, *Remember Me* (Dell, 1993), is set in Cape Cod. Restaurant and street names known to Cape dwellers punctuate the pages of her tales, providing the reader who has traveled there with a comfortable familiarity. This teacher warns the students that often his eyes scramble across the pages eager to place certain locations; sometimes as a visitor to the Cape, he even launches on personal adventures seeking out places mentioned in the novel. Reading challenges readers to create and explore.

A fellow reader who teaches health and psychology and who coaches soccer admits that part of his reading agenda includes magazines. He feels a responsibility to keep abreast of changes in medicine and current health-related research findings; magazines such as the *Harvard Review* allow him to continuously update his curriculum with current information. Textbooks alone could not provide this service. Reading keeps us current.

The principal is an avid U.S. Civil War buff. He isn't still fighting the war, but he is still reading and researching it. He admits that table talk at family gatherings back in Tennessee is still replete with war stories,

war strategies, and arguments galore. The principal's stories transport students to a different time in the southern U.S. and they are caught up in firsthand accounts of segregation and integration as their principal remembers his own high school days. He shares book titles that portray the ravages of a war-torn nation. Books such as Michael Shaara's *Killer Angels* (Ballantine, 1974) allow students to formulate a more "human hold" on their own history as well as perceive a humanistic picture of their principal. They now envision him as a man with interests apart from school and seek him out in the hall with more than common courtesy for conversation. This visit also provides me with an excellent backdrop for my introduction to Mark Twain's *The Adventures of Huckleberry Finn*. Reading reveals our past and shows us our history.

The drama teacher not only reads to the students, but uses her gift for performance to show that some books nourish the soul. She shares her love of fantasy by introducing students to J.R.R. Tolkien's *Fellowship of the Ring* (Ballantine, 1966). As she reads, the book slowly comes to rest on the table in front of her, but the narration continues uninterrupted...no need for pages; no written cues are necessary. This book has been read and reread so often that the words belong to her. She and the tale are one; her mental remote control replays the text at her command. Reading provides escape.

An anthropology teacher exits the country each summer and travels both to fulfill personal needs and to do research for his doctorate. He has read extensively about shamanic healing in remote areas of the world; such healing often involves altered states of consciousness and always involves an intense sympathetic understanding of the mind/body connection. His areas of interest also take him to the Yucatan where he volunteers on archaeological dig sites, enhancing his knowledge of ancient civilizations. Reading gives his curiosity a foundation, a place to grow from and to return to when he journeys back to the confines of upstate New York. This teacher reads for a multitude of reasons, but chooses to share Wilber Smith's *River God: A Novel of Ancient Egypt* (St. Martin's, 1993). This book talk not only weaves a brilliant tapestry of Pharaohs, the Valley of the Kings, and life in Egypt 2,000 years before Christ, but for a moment, the teacher is as inspired with the imaginings of his next trip as he would have been had he drunk the nectar of the gods. Reading provides inspiration.

Students use these classroom faculty presentations as a means of getting ideas for books to read as well as a model for how to do a book talk. Once a week, after school, two of the students in the classroom audience work in conjunction with students in a telecommunications course at the high school and tape a teamed book talk on the school television station, WBUC. Two new students from each of my five classes team each week to tape their book talk and share it with the school and the surrounding community. The book talk is aired citywide once a week as part of the morning announcements for the school. By the end of the school year, approximately two thirds of the 125 students in my classes have volunteered to do a televised book talk. The remaining students have the option to participate by signing up on a large classroom calendar and sharing a book talk with their own

English class as they have seen faculty do so often during the course of the year. These efforts all help to expand our respectable goal of creating a "community of readers."

As their regular classroom teacher, I give frequent book talks in class. I remind students that adults read according to mood; I share the fact with them that my nightstand has a variety of books and magazines waiting to match my current interest or frame of mind. Too often students think recreational and leisure reading are wrong; acceptable reading means reading a book (preferably a thick, academic one) from beginning to end. Students too often have never known the joy of not wanting to let go of characters; they have not experienced saving the last pages of a book, the hesitancy to let a story end. Reading for pleasure is validated.

Outside my classroom door on the corridor wall, students have designed a "faculty family tree" with each of the academic disciplines clearly delineated. On the "branches" are placed photocopied faculty pictures from current yearbooks reminding all of those faculty people who have shared books in our community of readers.

Adults talk books to other adults and thrive in the volley of the exchange. I've watched friends scramble for pencils and scribble titles and authors onto checkbook pages or grocery lists. They display an eagerness, an intensity to read about topics that stimulate their reading curiosity. Don't students deserve the same stimulating exchange?

SECTION 6

Connecting In-School and Out-of-School Reading

Connecting readers to the world outside of school enhances learning inside of school. This section explicitly addresses connections among in-school and out-of-school reading, and does so in a number of diverse and interesting ways.

First, the authors of these articles echo our own sentiments on the importance of involving adolescents in classroom talk about texts. If there is anything that research on middle school and high school students has taught us, it is that adolescents feel deprived of their right to express themselves orally in content area classrooms. Whether due to a lack of time, a highly constrained learning environment, or an overly burdened curriculum, classroom discussions are truly rare occurrences at the secondary level.

A second point on which we feel a professional kinship with the authors of these articles is the need to involve parents in the reading process. To paraphrase an old adage, the family that reads together stays together. And here we do not equate reading together as being limited to processing printed texts; rather, we include family sharing of texts rich in visual information, such as those found on the Internet, in videos, at art museums, and during theatrical performances.

Finally, we applaud the authors in this section who have found ways to connect adolescents with other readers their own ages or a bit younger. The motivational aspects of such "connecting" speak well for a group of literacy professionals intent on making school a place where struggling readers need not feel alienated and left to their own devices when it comes to succeeding at reading.

Ruth D. Handel

Family Reading at the Middle School

"Can a classroom be a family?" That was the first question posed by a member of the teaching staff when I introduced a proposal for Family Reading at a new middle school in Newark, New Jersey, USA. It took me a moment to understand. I had been thinking only in terms of the family-friendly way students might interact with elementary school children when serving as reading helpers and the way to bring adult family members into the process. Family Reading, a national program, had been successfully implemented for families with children Grades pre-K–3 at many sites throughout the U.S. including 34 elementary schools in Newark (see Handel, 1992, for a description). Both adults and young children had benefited from the experience. My proposal now was to adapt the program for the middle school—a particular challenge because few family-focused programs exist for the upper grades and because early adolescence is a crucial time for continued family support and for the development of higher levels of literacy and positive attitudes toward learning (Carnegie Council, 1989; "Parent and Community Involvement in the Middle Grades," 1993). The vision which I was bringing to the school was of a comprehensive program including instruction of middle school students in read-

ing strategies using interesting children's books, reading sessions with primary grade children, the participation of other family members as colearners in both school and home settings, institutionalization of Family Reading as part of the language arts curriculum, and collaborative staff development to support and refine the program. The goals were to develop higher level reading skills and enhanced self-concept of middle school students, and to foster participation of other family members in the reading process.

The middle school is located in a low-income, predominantly African-American neighborhood of Newark where decades of neglect are being countered by an infusion of new housing, a supermarket, and other community resources. The school, only 3 years old, has yet to establish itself as a center for parent involvement. Opening as a new middle school, Grades 6–8, the school also began a simultaneous collaboration with Montclair State University as a professional development site. Teachers from other schools cycle through for staff development; the resident faculty works with those teachers and also participates in staff development activities of their own. Classes average 20 students. There is a collegial atmosphere, energy, and enthusiasm for new ideas. However, teachers

Reprinted From the *Journal of Reading*, *38*(7), 528–540, April 1995.

are extremely busy and scheduling is more than usually difficult.

The complexity of my proposal together with the school context necessitated a step-by-step approach. Of major importance was the principal's wholehearted endorsement of the plan, her assignment of a staff member as coordinator, and her agreement that Family Reading should be integrated into the language arts curriculum. Staff development and workshops for seventh-grade students would be the place to start. Family Reading's focus on higher-level reading strategies accorded with the school's goals for critical thinking. Similarly, the concept of students as reading helpers of younger children was welcomed by teachers and administrators who saw the potential for increased self-esteem and maturity that fulfillment of a responsible service would bring.

As I began to know the school better, it seemed likely that for some students the classroom provided their most stable social group. Some students come from disorganized homes; others move frequently to live with a variety of relatives or in shelters for the homeless. Many students were reported to be angry and unable to manage their feelings; in my own visits to classrooms I observed several seventh graders sitting with their thumbs in their mouths. The school subscribes to the African maxim, "It takes a whole village to raise a child." Perhaps the village and family ethos would have to start with the classroom and build outward from there.

In this article, I will describe the first phase of an innovative program and present preliminary research results. I will discuss Family Reading as it exists at one middle school with particular focus on children's literature and strategy learning, on students' reflection on the Family Reading experience, and on the family component of the project.

The Middle School Adaptation

Family literacy programs aim to develop the literacies of two generations or two age cohorts. The Family Reading program began in 1986 as part of a movement in adult education that recognized the intergenerational nature of literacy learning (Handel & Goldsmith, 1988). As Family Reading moved into elementary schools the following year, it joined forces with efforts to increase home-school collaboration particularly in underserved urban neighborhoods. What was discovered during those years was the enormous appeal and value of children's literature and the power of enjoyable reading relationships among adults and between adults and children. Opportunities for book reading and sharing ideas with others led to increased engagement with literacy, the learning of higher level skills, and more positive attitudes toward literacy and the self. Family Reading built on the strengths of the family members, promoted self-efficacy of its participants, and, in integrating instruction with enjoyment, mobilized the power of affect in the service of cognition (Handel, 1992; Handel & Goldsmith, 1994). The task now was to make this work for middle school students and their families.

Adaptation of models. Family Reading in the Middle School draws on two models: the Family Reading model for families of preschoolers and elementary school children (Goldsmith & Handel, 1990; Handel, 1992; Handel & Goldsmith, 1994), and the Adolescent Helpers program of the National Center for Service Learning in Early Adolescence (n.d.; 1991).

The Family Reading model includes a series of workshops in children's literature and in reading comprehension strategies that are integrated into the literature reading. The participants learn how to read and discuss quality children's books using cognitive strategies applicable to readers of all ages.

Following their workshop, participants share books and strategies in reading sessions with children. This interactive, social model is informed by the foundational work of Vygotsky (1978) in which more expert learners (teachers, parents, or older students) mediate the learning of those less expert through careful scaffolding. All the various sites of Family Reading draw on the same basic model. The difference is that in programs for families of young children, parents or other adult caregivers attend the workshops; in the middle school adaptation, the participants are seventh-grade students who learn ways to become reading helpers to younger children and to develop their own reading competencies in the process (Heath & Mangiola, 1991; Labbo & Teale, 1990).

The work of the National Center for Service Learning in Early Adolescence was a second major influence in the middle school adaptation. The concept of service as fulfilling both emotional and academic needs of young adolescents was adopted as a guiding framework. The service concept is endorsed by many literacy researchers also. Duffy (1990) advocates socially meaningful reading tasks for middle school students and Davidson and Koppenhaver's (1988, 1993) studies of successful literacy programs for young adolescents describe linkages to developmental needs including tasks that are "intrinsically meaningful" (p. 43). Developmental needs outlined by Davidson and Koppenhaver (1993) that were influential in formulating the program are need for competence and achievement; exploration of ways to use new capacities in future adult roles; meaningful and responsible participation in school and community; and environments that allow for diversity of abilities and interests (pp. 18–19). Important contributions from the National Center for Service Learning were the "reading helper" termi-nology, student sessions anticipating the reading helper experience and reflection sessions afterward. Those elements were incorporated into the Family Reading model which is distinguished by a focus on reading strategies, a more structured workshop format, and family involvement. An ethos of collaboration and warmth characterizes both models.

The family component. The family component expresses itself through and beyond the elements described above. First, a familylike atmosphere of attentiveness and helpfulness to others would characterize student interaction during preparatory workshops and reading sessions with elementary school children. Second, transfer to the home setting would be fostered by opportunities to take the storybooks home and encouragement to read with siblings, parents, and elementary school partners who lived in the neighborhood. In particular, reading would help with the caretaker responsibilities many students had for younger brothers and sisters. A more speculative transfer might look to the students' literacy behaviors when they become parents themselves.

Participation of adult family members in program activities is a third and more problematic aspect of the family component. Parental involvement typically declines in the middle grades despite its continuing importance to student achievement (Carnegie Council, 1989; Davidson & Koppenhaver, 1988, 1993; Office of Educational Research and Improvement, 1993), and young adolescents seek independence from family ties while still needing guidance. Because of the importance of their involvement, Family Reading in the Middle School would recruit adult family members to participate as colearners in the preparatory workshops in seventh-grade classrooms and in the reading sessions with elementary school children. In addition, informational activities would familiarize adults with the program and enable them to be supportive at home.

Goals and essential program elements. Family Reading in the Middle School set goals for all participants. Goals for students included the development of positive attitudes toward reading and the learning of higher level reading comprehension strategies. That was to be accomplished through a social context that created a use for literacy, namely, the reading helper sessions, the enhanced self-efficacy that might come with the assumption of the new role, and a collaborative classroom atmosphere in which students assisted one another and exchanged ideas freely.

Staff development for teachers was an integral part of the program. Teachers would become familiar with Family Reading, participate in shaping the program, and draw connections to the language arts curriculum in their classrooms. The involvement of parents and other family members would be of personal value to participants and also foster positive home-school relations. Transfer to the home setting as well as a family atmosphere in the school were goals.

Essential elements of the project are: a family ethos; participatory, interactive learning environments; enjoyable reading relationships; critical reading, thinking and discussion strategies; quality children's books that appeal to both groups of students; reflection on the experience; and teacher expertise and commitment.

Table 1 sets out the overall structure of the project.

Program Operations

Family Reading in the Middle School was instituted as a pilot program in 1992–93, and continues to date. The first year, two seventh-grade teachers volunteered to participate in the staff development; they conducted a se-

Table 1
Program structure

1. Ongoing staff development
familiarizes teachers with Family Reading methodology

enables teachers to collaborate in shaping, refining and evaluating the program

fosters application of reading strategies in the language arts curriculum

2. Middle school students as reading helpers
preparatory Family Reading workshops conducted by classroom teachers

practice in reading and discussing children's picture books

anticipating the experience of reading to a child

experiencing reading sessions in the elementary school

reflecting and debriefing after each elementary school session

recognition of their service at a Family Reading celebration

3. Family involvement
collaboration and caring in the classroom

students sharing books at home

parent participation as colearners

ries of three preparatory workshops for their language arts students ($n = 30$), three reading sessions in the elementary school, and reflection and debriefing sessions afterward. Those activities took place during the school day, during the 2-hour block of time for language arts. In the 1993–94 school year, the principal made Family Reading a seventh-grade mandate; all four seventh-grade language arts teachers and their classes participated.

Program operations were defined and refined during staff development sessions too numerous to be detailed here. As might be expected, teachers exhibited some healthy initial skepticism and concerns as well as insightful suggestions for goal achievement. Teachers generated creative ways to integrate Family Reading strategies into their literacy curriculum to foster critical thinking and gave writing assignments on Family Reading topics and responses. When they saw how responsible and eager the students were, apprehensions about student behavior vanished after the first visit to the elementary school.

The following sections describe the classroom workshops, reading strategies, and books.

Preparatory workshops in the classroom. Preparation for reading to children, an essential part of Family Reading, takes the form of a workshop. It is an informal but focused and structured experience, offered for each book to be read to the elementary school children. The workshops are designed to generate enthusiasm for the program, help students anticipate the reading sessions with younger children, familiarize students with the books, teach reading strategies to use with the books, and provide opportunities for practice and discussion. Teachers discuss the family focus of the program, explaining the provisions for mutual help, and the concept of care for others in the classroom and in the community.

After an orientation to the program, the students participate in an activity that evokes oral and written memories of early experiences with books, reading or story telling. Student responses have varied from a brief "I do (or do not) remember someone reading to me," to details of favorite books and home reading situations. Very often the memory is of hearing an oral story told by a parent or other family member. The reading memories activity helps students get in touch with their younger selves and prepares them for reading the children's book.

Next, the children's book is presented followed by a demonstration of a reading strategy by the teacher using the children's book. In keeping with whole language tenets, reading strategies are never presented as isolated skills, but are integrated into the presentation and reading of the workshop book. Students read the book and practice the strategy together in pairs. That is a social occasion with students responding to one another, pointing out the illustrations, smiling and laughing over the book. The whole class then discusses the book and, with teacher guidance, students draw connections to their personal experience and form generalizations or conclusions about issues or important points suggested by the book. Students help one another in the workshops and share ideas. Respect for differing viewpoints is encouraged.

The next-to-last step prepares students for reading in the elementary school. Anticipations of the experience are evoked. Knowledge about young children is shared and students are encouraged to generate and express their expectations, positive or negative, about reading to them. Since many students have attended the elementary schools to be visited, they are stimulated to remember their own early school experiences and feelings.

Finally, for further practice and as a transfer to the home setting, students are encouraged to borrow the children's book to read to a younger sibling or relative at home. Despite fears of being mocked for being seen carrying a "baby" book, one half of the students have done so.

These activities are outlined in Table 2.

The reading strategies. The reading strategies are intended to foster critical thinking and exchange rather than one "right" answer. As set out in Table 3, generic reading strategies appropriate for readers of all ages are used in Family Reading workshops. They are operationalized in the form of questions or directions; their wording is varied according to the book being read and the age of the reader. The strategies derive from a constructivist approach to learning and are meant to promote active participation.

Most students report that they enjoy the strategies. Prediction-making is the one easiest to learn and most likely to be reinforced by teachers in their regular curriculum lessons. Asking for the basis for predictions may be unfamiliar, however. The second strategy, which derives from Singer's (1978) work in active comprehension, has proven difficult for students who are used to being on the receiving end of questions rather than being asked to generate questions of their own. Some adjustments in teaching this strategy were necessary. Making Predictions and Asking Our Own Questions were taught as strategies to use while reading. Relating Reading to Personal Experience and Learning New Information were incorporated into the discussion component of the workshops.

The children's books. Over the 8 years that Family Reading has been operating, adults as well as children have been delighted with the children's picture books the program has offered. The seventh-grade participants in the middle school adaptation were no exception.

In addition to providing pleasure, the simple text appeared to be an effective vehicle for learning cognitive strategies. Teachers helped seventh graders apply those strategies when reading more difficult curricular material as well. Other instructional uses of the children's literature include using the bare bones structure of a picture book to introduce story grammar and writing text for wordless picture books.

The books to be used in the project had to be appealing to both sets of students, seventh graders as well as the first graders to whom they would read. They also had to be short enough to be read and discussed in a 30–40 minute session. Beyond that, two other important criteria governed. Text and illustrations had to be of high quality, and the subject matter had to deal with or suggest important issues.

For the population in question, books with African or African American themes were considered most likely to capture the stu-

dents' immediate interest. The books selected were: *Anansi the Spider* (G. McDermott, Holt, 1972), a Caldecott winner, one of a series of folktales about the traditional African trickster figure; *Tar Beach* (F. Ringgold, Crown, 1991), written and illustrated by a prominent African American artist, a story that combines fantasy with contemporary

---

Table 2
The program for students

1. Preparatory workshops
  Introductory activities
    Orientation to Family Reading
    Reading memories
  Presentation of the children's book
  Demonstration of the reading strategy
  Practice in pairs
  Book discussion
  Anticipating reading to children
  Book borrowing for sharing and practice at home

2. Reading sessions in the elementary school

3. Debriefing and reflecting after each reading session

4. Curriculum applications

Table 3
Reading strategies used in the program

Making predictions
  1. What do you think will happen next?
  2. Why do you think so?

Asking our own questions
  1. What questions do you have about this (story, page, event)?
  2. What puzzles you? What would you like to find out?

Relating reading to personal experience
  1. Does this (story, character, event) remind you of anything in your own life?
  2. Does it remind you of anything you have heard about or learned?

Learning new information
  1. What do you already know about this topic?
  2. Let's read to learn more.
  3. What did you learn that was new?

and historical aspirations for freedom and justice; and *Amazing Grace* (M. Hoffman, Dial, 1991), a Reading Rainbow selection preferred by many students because of its realistic illustrations, a story of a little girl's perseverance. *Amazing Grace* also contains references to other children's stories, including *Anansi*. Through narratives and illustrations, all three books suggest broader themes for discussion or study.

The *Anansi* folktale raises issues of cooperation within families and the distinctive gifts each family member has, but it was felt that students' personal families would not be the most comfortable discussion base. In discussing the book in the preparatory workshops, three themes were emphasized: the classroom as family, the differing special abilities of students, and elementary school children as part of the community family. Allusions to racism in *Tar Beach* (the little heroine's father was barred from the union) and the links to old stories of flying to freedom were additional discussion topics. Each of the three books suggested developmental issues important for early adolescents: individuality and responsibility for others, aspirations and hope, and the need for perseverance and support.

In addition, two of the books contain informational text written at a higher level, thereby providing an opportunity for more challenging reading and a broadened perspective.

Anticipation, Reading, and Reflection

This section presents a descriptive analysis of anticipations of the elementary school reading sessions, the sessions themselves, and students' reflections on the experience. Observations, teacher reports, and student reports are the data sources.

Anticipating the reading session. In both project years, teachers and students expressed apprehension about reading in the elementary school. The teachers wondered whether their students would behave appropriately. Students wanted to do well and were nervous about their ability to perform. For both teachers and students, the experience turned out better than expected. Teachers reported that students who misbehaved in class or fooled around on the short walk to the elementary school became responsible, conscientious individuals upon entering the schoolhouse door. Students were pleased with the contribution they were able to make. All agreed that the process was easier the second time around.

Use of the reading strategy was identified as one source of concern. Since some students worried whether they would do it "right," we considered omitting the strategy teaching in hopes that interactive techniques would emerge spontaneously during the reading session. However, it was decided that the strategies represented both important learning for the seventh graders and support in their attempts to help the younger children interact with text. Students were reassured that enjoyable reading relationships, rather than correct procedures, were paramount, that they could use their own creativity in presenting the text, and that teachers would always be on hand to coach and help. Fine tuning of the strategies continued during staff development.

The reading sessions. Over the first 2 years of the project, six classes of seventh graders participated in five reading sessions in kindergarten or first-grade classrooms. The elementary classrooms varied in capacity to accommodate the visitors as well as in evidence of a literate environment. Upon entering, some students spotted relatives or neighbors and asked to be paired with them;

teachers paired the others. A few seventh graders were assigned to two children each. Students shared desks or sat with their partner on the reading rug in the corner. All read the same book. As in other Family Reading sites, students shared the instruction and enjoyment experienced in the preparatory workshop when they read with younger children.

Teachers helped with conversation starters and coaching as needed. Some children were shy or inattentive; a few awkward situations arose, but most pairs enjoyed sharing the book together. Teachers observed that most students used the reading strategy or engaged in discussion or elaboration of the text. Students seemed delighted when the children wanted to try reading to them or brought them a favorite book from the classroom collection. On the return trip, one boy expressed his pride of achievement by saying, "When I walked into that classroom, I felt 10 feet tall!" Any initial shyness during the first session evaporated at subsequent meetings. The reading partners quickly recognized one another and joined up eagerly.

Reflection—Year 1. Students engaged in reflection and debriefing after each of the elementary school sessions to analyze and learn from their experience, solve problems, share ideas, and give feedback to teachers. Their reflections provide a window on the affective and cognitive impact of the program.

After the first reading session in year 1, 25 students provided written descriptions of what they had learned from the experience. Eight students reported that they had learned to do something ("read to a child," "ask for predictions," "make up my own ending to the story"); 9 reported on their feelings while reading ("I read to a child and learned it was fun," "I was scared at first"); 2 commented on teaching ("It was hard," "I was proud to feel like a teacher"); 2 students had negative reactions because the child was not respon-

sive; and 4 students noted something they had learned about the child. In addition, 8 of the students supplemented their initial reflection with observations about the child. These categories would reappear in subsequent responses.

After the second session, a majority, 19 out of 29 students in the two classes, reported using the reading strategy in the elementary school reading session. One student reported explaining the theme of the story to the child, a transfer from language arts learning. Responding in writing to a general question about how the reading session and strategy use went, one of the classes (n = 14) provided such positive details as "He wants me to be his reading parent," "a great relationship," "She answered some of my questions," and the child "liked the story." Many commented with pleasure that they had gotten to know the child better. Only one student commented negatively on an experience with a difficult child. Students in the second class (n = 15), participating in an oral debriefing, also remarked on progress in their relationship with the child ("more at ease," "talked more"). Displaying empathy, one boy noted that the child had been nervous and remembered his own nervousness at that age: "Then I asked questions and he got into it," he said.

Reflection—Year 2. More systematic data collection was possible in Year 2. Students were asked to respond in writing to four open-ended, general questions designed to evoke thoughtful and descriptive responses. We hoped to learn whether the students enjoyed the experience and why; what they gained in terms of relationships; their attitudes toward reading and learning; and whether they had been able to put the reading strategies into practice. Responses ranged from a phrase to 4–5 sentences for each question, with most students falling between those extremes. Although students varied in their ability to handle the mechanics of written language, the writing of all but a few was expressive and communicative.

Question 1. How did the reading with children go? Of 61 responses to question 1, the overwhelming majority (*n* = 53) reported a positive reaction to the reading experience in the elementary school saying it was "successful," "fun," or "great." Two responses were noncommittal and six were negative. Of the latter, one student thought the experience "terrible" because of the noise in the room, two were not comfortable reading aloud, and three did not like their reading partner because the child was inattentive or disruptive.

More than half of the students who enjoyed the experience gave reasons for their positive response. The most frequent reasons related to interaction with their reading partner, namely, that the child was respectful or cooperative ("followed my directions") (*n* = 17); that the child seemed smart ("answered all my questions," "a real pro") (*n* = 12); or that the child was interested in the story or reciprocated by reading to the seventh grader (*n* = 4). One student reported learning that "a young child can be a friend." Typical positive responses were:

> It was fine because my student participated and respected me by being interested in me and the story. (Shadell 11/93)
>
> The reading with the child was great he listen he understood and payed attention to the words I was trying to teach reading with the child was a great experience. (Dashona 11/93)
>
> I learned about how we can help younger people in away of reading to them or teaching something out of a book or just from our mine. (Sharonda 11/93)

As indicated by the last two, an additional reason for liking the reading session related to the experience of teaching. Six students noted they "felt proud" or "good" to be a teacher or to "teach someone something." "If you want-

ed to be a teacher this is a great experience," one wrote. In addition, in conversation as well as the written responses, many students expressed new empathy for their instructors now that they knew what teachers "go through." Some students vowed to act better.

Ten students indicated they were happy that the reading session had gone much better than expected. Those students described their nervousness and shyness at the prospect of reading to a younger child. Three anticipated the experience as one of embarrassing self-disclosure like reading aloud in front of a class, and, in one case, fear of a negative reaction from the child. That student, whose language skills are poor, wrote:

> Befor I whent to 18th Avenue (school) I was telling my self that I was not going to go. But when all of my frenid where going I change my mine....To read infont of alot of people that's why I whent so I can get that feelling out....
>
> Whe I was reading I was very scard and I tought the little girl was going to cruse me out. But instead she listen to me and she said everything I said....
>
> I felt close to getting a A for that asingment even if didn't do so well....I had a lot of fun getting kind of close to that little girl...(James 11/93)

Another, more competent writer also progressed from being scared to having a gratifying experience. She wrote:

> Before I left, I felt a bit scared, because it was my first time reading to a first grader...I was pretty nervous....
>
> When I got there I was very nervous, now I received a little girl named Dianna who was very fidgety, and did not want to pay attention so I let her read to me. Which was a good idea because she paid attention and I listened.
>
> When I left I felt good because I had taught someone something and it actually felt good... A day later I felt like it had been a year since I had seen Dianna and wanted to see her I wondered how she was doing. I also wondered how

she did on her book report. Hope she did good. (Darnitah 11/93)

This student expressed commitment to the little girl, extending beyond the reading session to hoping she did well on a book report due the following day. Also of interest is her flexibility and inventiveness in responding to the child's restlessness, possibly because she has a younger sister the same age.

Question 2. How was the relationship with the child? Forty-six students responded to questions 2–4. The second question evoked positive responses from 44 students and negative responses from 2 who felt the child did not pay attention to them. Positive comments ranged from the approving ("nice," "good") to the warmly enthusiastic ("the child liked me," "seemed like I knew the child all my life"). Two students described the process of relationship building and their own patience ("At first I thought the child didn't really like me, but when I started to read it got better"), and 2 were relieved the relationship turned out better than expected ("I thought first graders were going to be mean").

Question 3. What were the child's reactions to the story? The third question was intended to evoke descriptions of the child rather than the relationship, but students could not keep the two entirely separate. Here, also, all but 2 of the 46 students felt that the child reacted positively to the reading. Eighteen students elaborated by reporting that their child asked for the story to be read again (n =5), asked questions, knew answers or summarized the story (n = 7), or liked particular parts of the story (n = 6). One student wrote that the child's talkativeness made him feel that the child really connected with him.

Question 4. Did you use the reading strategy and how did it work out for you? The intent of the last question was to investigate whether the classroom preparation was carried over into the reading session. We had been particularly concerned about the extent to which students had incorporated a higher level thinking strategy into their reading behavior and whether they would be able to use it amid the distractions of the elementary classroom. In two of the classes, the strategy of making predictions had been taught in the preparatory workshops. In the third, the teacher concentrated on expressive reading as a means of communication and comprehension.

Of 46 students, a total of 29 reported that they had used the strategy taught in their preparatory workshops; 18 of those students substantiated their report by describing the strategy in detail. The responses of 5 students indicated that they had not used the strategy or had not understood the question. Ten other students indicated that they had used a general questioning strategy which was not specifically taught to them for the elementary school session but which is common in many classrooms. Those questions appeared to be literal level questions related to story events or word knowledge.

In sum, a majority of students indicated that they used the technique taught in their preparatory workshops, predicting (n = 24) or expressive reading (n = 7). Those who used the prediction-making strategy were pleased when the child made correct predictions and tended to focus on correctness and feedback on the child's understanding rather than helping the child explore reasons for the predictions being made. The 10 students who adopted questioning as an alternate strategy were all from the class that focused on expressive reading in the preparatory workshops; apparently, they felt the need of an additional way to engage the children in interaction with the text. Observations also showed most pairs of students engaged in text-based discussion.

The more impressionistic results from Year 1 forecast and support the reports of Year 2. Since the use of interactive reading strategies is a goal of the project for the seventh-grade students, it is encouraging that a majority are indeed applying them when reading to children. The issue remains as to the extent to which students will integrate strategic and critical thinking into their approach to other types of text throughout their schooling.

As to the affective dimensions of the project, students were conscientious and engaged. They were interested in the child with whom they had worked. Most felt they had done a good job and expressed feelings of self-efficacy. With this taste of teaching, students enlarged their understanding of teachers and the instructional enterprise.

The Family Component

As previously stated, there are three aspects to the family component of the middle school adaptation: a familylike classroom atmosphere, transfer of Family Reading activities to the home setting, and participation of adult family members in the project. All are important, but only the first could receive full attention in the beginning years of the project.

Classroom atmosphere. A familylike atmosphere of attentiveness and helpfulness to others characterized student interaction during preparatory workshops and in reading sessions with elementary school children. Given the often disorderly lives of the middle school students, that seems important in its own right. As described, in the classroom workshops students worked together on enjoyable tasks for a common goal, watching and taking cues from one another, often smiling and encouraging others with whom they did not usually interact. Student responses to the reading helper experience—physical posture and facial expressions as well as written reflections—clearly showed intent and pleasure in establishing positive relationships with younger children.

An additional example of the seriousness with which the students approached relationship-building occurred during an early debriefing session; students generated suggestions to help them get to know the children better and expressed indignation that they had not been fully prepared in that respect by their teachers. Similarly, when a reading session had to be cancelled, students seemed genuinely disappointed. Another touching demonstration of close relationships came at end of the year when the first graders visited the middle school. Waiting in the hallway to enter the room where a Family Reading Celebration was to be held, the seventh and first graders paired up with one another spontaneously and held hands. Later, the older students proudly and protectively took their young friends on a tour of the school.

In a final piece of anecdotal evidence that points to transfer beyond the project, several seventh-grade boys were observed in the school cafeteria helping special education students with their reading. Since interaction of that type was uncommon, it is likely that the Family Reading experience had prompted the students' helpfulness.

In an interesting parallel with elementary school teachers, the students' primary focus and source of gratification was interaction with the child. Also, as many teachers know, the implications of conscientiousness and interest in the child are double-edged. While the students' attitude is gratifying, and in some cases wonderfully surprising, the stakes are high for student self-confidence and may be tied to the child's response. "The child's reaction to the story was great. I had great confidence in myself," wrote one student linking the child's response and self-efficacy in sequential sentences. However, if the child did not appear responsive, seventh graders were crestfallen:

> It took a long time for me to gain his respect or have a understanding...he didn't want to pay attention. I tried to be courteous to him but it didn't matter. I couldn't tolerate the way he ignored me. It was like every time I turned the page his attention lessened. (Anwar 11/93)

Another student was able to manage her feelings; the child eventually responded:

> Well, the child at first didn't care if Mickey Mouse was reading the story to her because she constantly was looking around the room. It got me a little annoyed but I kept myself calm. Then I started asking her alot of questions about the story and then she seemed to get into the story. (Erica 11/93)

In the main, the younger children seemed thrilled to receive attention from the seventh graders and awkward experiences were relatively few. However, such experiences underline the need for thoroughgoing preparation for the reading sessions so that students may express their hesitations, anticipate what the relationship with a younger child might be like, and, together with the teacher, offer one another suggestions for dealing with the possible scenarios. Students need to be aware that young children may vary in personality type, level of articulateness, and modes of responding and that some may initially be shy in a new situation. Students who have younger siblings may be of special help in discussions of this nature.

The reflection and debriefing sessions after the reading provided an opportunity for students to learn from one another, troubleshoot, explore alternatives, and reflect on what the experience meant to them. Students were eager to do so. Teachers had a major role in assisting with the problem-solving, prais-ing the students, and validating their contribution. Those students who worked with a difficult child needed special recognition for their efforts.

Finally, it is of great importance that many students expressed interest in the child with whom they worked. As Noddings (1991) and others have pointed out, attentiveness to another person is the basis for caring human relationships; it is also a sign of the type of maturity we hope young adolescents will begin to achieve.

Transfer to the home. Logistical factors and a decision to lodge the program in seventh-grade classrooms as soon as possible have left issues of home transfer and adult involvement still in the process of development. The fact, previously noted, that 50% of the students voluntarily brought the Family Reading book home to share with siblings, other relatives, or neighbors is a promising beginning. In the future, this activity will be strongly encouraged and the capacity of middle school students to serve as literacy resources in their home will be documented.

Participation of adult family members. Since involving parents of older students is always a challenge, it is important to recognize that adult caregivers may be involved in programs such as Family Reading in a variety of ways. Levels of involvement include awareness, monitoring, support, and participation in program activities on site and at home. Some basic awareness was assured since responsible adults had to sign permission slips for the elementary school visits. They also were sent information about the program. In addition, "good news" letters praising the students' efforts were sent home and parents were invited to learn more about the program and express support. A special Family Reading demonstration was held for interested adults, but most were parents of elementary-age children.

There was also active participation on a small scale. A mother and grandmother of one student and a father of another participated in preparatory workshops and in reading sessions in the elementary school. By entering directly into the literacy arena, these adults served students in several ways: as colearners and role models in their classroom participation; as instructors when they shared effective ways to work with children in the debriefing sessions; and as community validators of the students' efforts when they praised the seventh graders' purposefulness and behavior. The adults indicated that they, too, had learned something from the program.

Quite obviously, more active recruitment is needed to involve adults. To this end, we are joining forces with other key teachers, community workers, and project leaders in the school. Special events are planned and outreach to parents in the home setting will be increased. While adult participation in school-based activities may never be extensive, the goal is to offer a variety of ways in which adults can enter the literacy arena and enhance their own literacy development and serve as literacy resources to their families.

A Classroom Can Be a Family

This article has described Family Reading in the Middle School and some of the processes of its implementation. Preliminary results show that the seventh-grade participants developed close relationships with younger children, recognized their special role, became aware of reading strategies and demonstrated flexibility in their use. Students enjoyed the reading helper experience. The affective dimension appears to be integrally connected to cognitive learning and a powerful determinant of program success.

Teachers learned Family Reading methodology and the workshop format and began to integrate it into their language arts curriculum. Given the opportunity to view their students outside the middle school walls, they noted differences in student behavior in the new context and role.

Adult family members who participated in school-based activities served as role models, as instructors and as validators of the seventh graders' efforts. Efforts are underway to reach out to more adult family members in the future. Transfer to the home setting occurred when many students brought Family Reading books home to share with relatives. Reading relationships with younger siblings is another promising area for development.

Can a classroom be a family? Yes, if family implies an atmosphere of caring, mutual help, and shared interests. The family feeling of the project has manifested itself in the caring relationships between older and younger students, and in cooperative work in seventh-grade classrooms. Family Reading has created a social context for the use of literacy and given students a reason for reading. It has fostered the development of positive relationships with elementary school children and with younger relatives to whom students read at home. For many students, the program appeared to foster attentiveness to others and enhancement of self-efficacy. While the theoretical relationships between the latter two constructs have not been explored, it seems likely that Family Reading encourages their simultaneous development by the seventh-grade students. Data collection is continuing and analysis may yield additional insight.

Family Reading at the Middle School is a small intervention still in its early stages that is contextualized within a particular innercity school. Given life circumstances that have restricted the students' opportunities to enjoy books, gain recognition from sharing books with others, and develop critical reading skills in an enjoyable fashion, a program that offered those benefits was met with enthusiasm. Whether Family Reading would have the same impact on an economically advantaged middle school population of the same or other ethnicity is an open question.

Programs such as Family Reading in the Middle School are particularly important in view of the negative behavior of increasingly younger adolescents in high risk neighborhoods and in view of the potential for productive lives on the part of those same young adolescents.

Author Notes

Family Reading at the Middle School has been supported by Montclair State University and grants from Citicorp and Public Service Electric & Gas. My colleague, Professor Jennifer Robinson, provided helpful comments on this article and participated in every phase of the project; her expertise in working with schools was invaluable. I also thank the administrators, teachers, and students at the middle school for the pleasure of working with them.

I gratefully acknowledge the generous assistance of Joan G. Schine, director of the National Center for Service Learning in Early Adolescence, and Felicia George, clearinghouse coordinator, who shared their considerable expertise and insight at several stages of the project.

REFERENCES

Carnegie Council on Adolescent Development. (1989). *Turning points: Preparing American youth for the 21st century*. Washington, DC: Carnegie Corporation.

Davidson, J., & Koppenhaver, D. (1988, 1993). *Adolescent literacy: What works and why* (1st & 2nd eds.). New York: Garland Publishing.

Duffy, G.E. (Ed.) (1990). *Reading in the middle school* (2nd ed.). Newark, DE: International Reading Association.

Goldsmith, E., & Handel, R.D. (1990). *Family reading: An intergenerational approach to literacy*. Syracuse, NY: New Readers Press.

Handel, R.D. (1992). The partnership for family reading: Benefits for families and schools. *The Reading Teacher, 46*, 116-126.

Handel, R.D., & Goldsmith, E. (1988). Intergenerational literacy: A community college program. *Journal of Reading, 32*, 250-256.

Handel, R.D., & Goldsmith, E. (1994). Family reading: Still got it: Adults as learners, literacy resources and actors in the world. In D. Dickinson (Ed.), *Bridges for literacy* (pp. 150-174). Cambridge, UK: Basil Blackwell.

Heath, S.B., & Mangiola, L. (1991). *Children of promise: Literate activity in linguistically and culturally diverse classrooms*. Washington, DC: National Education Association.

Labbo, L.D., & Teale, W.H. (1990). Cross-age reading: A strategy for helping poor readers. *The Reading Teacher, 43*, 362-369.

National Center for Service Learning in Early Adolescence, Adolescent Helpers Program. (n.d.). *Reading, writing and reviewing*. New York: Center for Advanced Study in Education and Graduate School and University Center of the City University of New York.

National Center for Service Learning in Early Adolescence, Adolescent Helpers Program. (1991). *Reflection: The key to service learning*. New York: Center for Advanced Study in Education and Graduate School and University Center of the City University of New York.

Noddings, N. (1991). Stories in dialogue: Caring and interpersonal reasoning. In C. Witherell & N. Noddings (Eds.), *Stories lives tell: Narrative and dialogue in education* (pp. 157-170). New York: Teachers College Press.

Parent and community involvement in the middle grades. (1993). Papers and literature review commissioned by the Office of Educational Research and Improvement, U.S. Department of Education and RMC Research Corporation, Denver, CO.

Singer, H. (1978). Active comprehension. *The Reading Teacher, 31*, 901-908.

Vygotsky, L.S. (1978). *Mind in society: The development of higher psychological processes*. Cambridge, MA: Harvard University Press.

Martha D. Rekrut

Peer and Cross-Age Tutoring: The Lessons of Research

Peer and cross-age tutoring are as natural as sibling relationships and occur whenever a more accomplished student aids a lower achieving classmate, or when an older student instructs a younger one. Pupil-to-pupil teaching is probably as old as instruction.

An early institutionalization of peer and cross-age tutoring was the monitorial system developed separately in England during the first quarter of the 19th century by Joseph Lancaster, a Quaker schoolmaster, and Andrew Bell, an Anglican clergyman. Each claimed the idea originated with him, though it was Lancaster who eventually developed the more workable system of instruction.

In the monitorial system, one schoolmaster had responsibility for a large number of children, so older and abler students were trained to teach what they learned (largely the basic 3 R's) to younger children, and monitor their practice. Lancaster drew up elaborate instructions for organizing and conducting monitorial schools, such as the importance of careful planning, assigning 1 monitor for each 10 students, and concentrating work in reading, penmanship, and arithmetic. Lancaster's schools were founded on the principle that children learned most efficiently from one another (Gutek, 1972).

Recent decades have seen a return to this early version of peer and cross-age tutoring.

In the 1970s, a period of teacher scarcity in the U.S., pupil-to-pupil teaching was regarded as a way to stretch thin teacher resources. Better students could be taught concepts or strategies and in turn teach others, especially their lower achieving peers or students in lower grades. This period spurred research into various aspects of peer and cross-age tutoring—which student combinations worked best, whether students should be gender paired, what content tutors could effectively convey whether tutors should be trained, and the like.

In the 1980s, school systems feeling the effects of tight budgets explored the cost effectiveness of peer and cross-age tutoring. Indeed, a meta-analysis by Levin, Glass, and Meister (1984) found that pupil-to-pupil tutoring was more effective as an instructional method per US$100 of cost per pupil than computer-aided instruction, reducing class size, increasing instructional time, and adult tutoring. The researchers observed that a traditional labor intensive method, cross-age tutoring, yielded a cost-effectiveness ratio nearly four times that of reducing class size and increasing instructional time.

Currently, peer and cross-age tutoring are in vogue as applications of one of the central principles of collaboration: students in control of their own learning. This is an altogeth-

Reprinted From the *Journal of Reading*, *37*(5), 356–362, February 1994.

er appropriate return to Joseph Lancaster's belief that children learn most efficiently from one another.

Research Answers to Teacher Questions

The history of peer and cross-age tutoring reflects the concerns of practitioners. Lancaster and Bell sought a method for the mass education of children during the reform stages of the Industrial Revolution. Today's teachers are interested in ways to personalize instruction, enable students to reach their potential, and provide for individual differences. Researchers have responded with some answers to teacher questions about peer and cross-age tutoring.

What Subjects Are Most Amenable to Pupil-to-Pupil Instruction?

In reading per se, most studies have been done at the elementary level, although a few have dealt with secondary reading. A substantial number have focused on elementary mathematics. Other subject areas that have been explored include a wide range—principles of high school physics (Miller, 1989), writing about college psychology (Levine, 1990), secondary composition (Reigstad & McAndrew, 1984), teenage health practices (Steinhausen, 1983), computer literacy (Crist, Whitzel, Dasho, & Beckum, 1984), and second language acquisition (August, 1987).

There are a number of reasons for the preponderance of work on elementary reading: the availability of study populations, the importance of reading as the foundation of success in other subjects such as science and social studies, and the measurability of reading achievement. Within reading, a number of aspects have attracted considerable attention, most linked to strategy instruction or metacognitive awareness in one form or another: (a) sight word identification (Maher, 1984; Robertson & Sharp, 1971); (b) oral reading and comprehension (Limbrick, McNaughton, & Glynn, 1985; Trovato & Bucher, 1980); (c) use of a story grammar as a recall apparatus (Rekrut, 1992); (d) text look-backs to locate information (Garner, Wagoner, & Smith, 1983; Hahn & Smith, 1983).

What Age or Grade Students Are Best as Tutors?

Students of any age or grade level can be either tutor or tutee, but cross-age tutors examined by researchers were usually at least fifth graders, since their achievement patterns have stabilized, they have usually developed specific skills that lower achievers and younger students must attain, and they are sufficiently mature to undertake responsibility for younger children. Most often they taught third graders who needed help but who were not entirely dependent learners, and who could work with another student without active adult monitoring.

After fifth graders, the next largest group of cross-age tutors was high school students, often 9th or 10th graders, tutoring intermediate or middle school students, the age gap being at least 2 years.

Peer tutors can be any age or grade, even Grade 1, though many programs are concentrated at upper elementary levels and above. In a recent story grammar acquisition study I conducted, teenage tutors taught older students. The study found that tutoring was an effective strategy-enhancement tool, even though the 11th-grade tutors taught 12th graders (Rekrut, 1993).

Is Peer or Cross-Age Tutoring Only for High-Achieving Students?

The most common configuration in both peer and cross-age tutoring programs has been the superior student teaching his or her less-accomplished schoolmate. An example is a nationally recognized New York City program in which high-achieving high school seniors tutor younger high school students who have failed to reach specified levels in reading and mathematics (New York City Board of Education, 1990).

There are a number of other models of pupil-to-pupil partnership, however. Reciprocal reading programs (Palincsar & Brown, 1984) and the "tutor huddle" (Howard, Heron, & Cooke, 1982) are examples of classrooms in which every student is both tutor and tutee. Wasserman and Stanbrook (1981) studied what they called "inverse tutoring" in which the tutor was a low-achieving 9th grader who taught a shy 2nd grader who was having difficulty putting words together for comprehension. My own studies have been of low-achieving 9th, 10th, and 11th graders in Providence and Warwick, Rhode Island, who tutored their normally achieving peers or low-achieving 4th and 5th graders.

The preponderance of 1970s studies examined the cognitive benefits of peer and cross-age tutoring; much work has also been done that deals with affective goals—the improvement of self-esteem (Myrick & Bowman, 1983; Pino, 1990; Porter & Hamilton, 1975), reduction of truancy and tardiness (Lane, Pollack, & Sher, 1972; Lazerson, Foster, Brown, & Hummel, 1988), dropout prevention (Sosa, 1986), or the reinforcement of positive psychological factors such as altruism and empathy (Yogev & Ronen, 1982).

An excellent example of an ongoing cross-age tutoring program is one begun by Hoffman and Heath (1986) in which fifth-grade Mexican-American girls tutor first-grade boys and girls from recently migrated Hispanic families in reading, and who examine their own teaching and reading behavior by writing about it. Learning becomes a valued activity for these girls through their interactions with their young tutees.

How Should Students Be Paired?

Researchers who have examined the gender issue in establishing both peer and cross-age pairs suggest same-sex partners, primarily for comfort and modeling reasons (Berliner & Casanova, 1986). Gender pairing is regarded as especially important for girls (House, 1988; Pillen, Jason, & Olson, 1988). In a recent study at Hope High School in Providence, Rhode Island, ninth-grade female tutors indicated they were more comfortable with same-sex peer tutees (Rekrut, 1992). In cross-age tutoring done by 10th graders, the most successful pairs were of the same sex.

If it is impossible to make same-sex pairings, it is more effective to have older girls act as tutors to younger boys.

How Should Tutors Be Trained?

Most tutoring programs provide at least some initial training for tutors. Highly successful programs train tutors in three areas: (a) interpersonal skills: how to help without telling, ways to give encouragement, using positive statements about tutee work and attitudes; (b) management skills: how to sit with the tutee (usually side by side for paired reading, for example), having the proper materials for the lesson, finding a quiet place for work; and (c) content skills: preparing lesson activities in advance, prior reading of what tutor and tutee will read together, thinking up questions for parts of the story, and creating follow-up activities for the next session such as writing a prediction.

Some tutor training is quite formal. Reigstad and McAndrew (1984) described workshops during which students practiced critiquing each other's work in preparation for service as writing tutors. Hoffman and Heath (1986) trained their fifth graders by having them read with adults who modeled appropriate tutor behavior. Tutors and adults then discussed what they had done, and the tutors used the results of this analysis with their first-grade tutees.

Many tutoring programs have produced guidebooks that detail tutor training activities. Bohning (1982) provided a multistep plan for implementing a tutoring program, one step of which involves training the tutors in desired instructional behaviors. Johnson (1977) made tutorial training a central part of her *Cross-Age Tutoring Handbook*. Berliner and Casanova (1986) described a "pause, prompt, and praise" procedure that tutors practiced on each other and then used when working with remedial readers; they also suggested role playing as an ideal tutor training method.

When Is Tutoring a Useful Instructional Method?

Teachers' objectives govern their decisions to use peer or cross-age tutoring. Some forms of collaborative practice employing paired activities are essentially peer tutoring. Providing practice of a learned strategy by having one student reiterate it to another and monitor the tutee's performance and vice versa (reciprocal) is another common format.

Teachers who want to encourage self-confidence and self-esteem or other affective goals such as cooperation and sharing might organize cross-age reading with younger pupils. Students who have difficulty learning a concept may do so when they must instruct another in it, as borne out by my own study of the effectiveness of cross-age tutoring. I taught two classes of 10th graders a story structure (story grammar), but only those who later taught 4th and 5th graders internalized the strategy of using the story structure to aid story recall. During their tutoring sessions with their elementary partners, the high school students pointed out the elements of the story grammar in the trade books they were reading. Because they had to rehearse the strategy and apply it to an easily manageable text, the high school students who taught the strategy to others learned it significantly better than those who had been instructed in the strategy but hadn't taught it.

Peer tutoring may be easier to manage than its cross-age counterpart because it can be done within the teacher's classroom. Cross-age tutoring requires at least two teachers cooperating to determine objectives, create pairs, and find appropriate time during the day. However, cross-age tutoring is ideal for enrichment as advanced students gain experience in cooperation and understanding of students for whom learning is not easy. Both peer and cross-age tutoring are useful methods of providing additional practice for students needing further reinforcement of concepts, both as tutors and tutees.

Guidelines From Research

The following guidelines are based on the insights provided by researchers. These guidelines may serve as a foundation upon which teachers can build their own cross-age or peer tutoring programs.

(1) *Many elements of reading are amenable to instruction and practice* via peer and cross-age tutoring, ranging from word recognition

or identifying story structure elements, to such metacognitive skills as looking back at a text for information or using context clues to word meaning.

(2) *Any age student may be either tutor or tutee*, depending on the situation. In an elementary school where I have had my low-achieving high school students tutor fourth and fifth graders, a high-achieving second grader works comfortably with students several years older than he as they read and write together about science. Most elementary cross-age tutoring programs engage intermediate students as tutors to primary students; most secondary programs use 11th and 12th graders as tutors of 9th and 10th graders.

(3) *Peer and cross-age tutors are often high-achievers, but any level achiever may serve equally well*, especially in cross-age programs in which secondary students tutor elementary students. A more important quality than achievement in peer tutors is the ability to instruct the tutee without making value judgments.

(4) *Same-sex partners work best in both cross-age and peer tutoring.* If same-sex pairs are not possible, older girls may tutor younger boys. In peer tutoring among older students, cross-gender pairing sabotages both content and skill acquisition.

(5) *Tutors should be trained* in interpersonal, management, and content skills. This training is especially important prior to the initial tutoring session, and should be ongoing. Posttutoring debriefing through discussion is a helpful way of sharing and solving problems tutors may have.

(6) *Tutoring can be used to reach both cognitive and affective objectives.* Additional content or concept practice, skill reinforcement, strategy learning enhancement, and self-confidence and self-esteem building are all goals which can be attained with cross-age and peer tutoring.

REFERENCES

August, D.L. (1987). Effects of peer tutoring on the second language acquisition of Mexican-American children in elementary school. *TESOL Quarterly*, *21*(4), 717–736.

Berliner, D., & Casanova, U. (1986). How to make cross-age tutoring work. *Instructor*, *95*(9), 14–15.

Bohning, G. (1982). A resource guide for planning, implementing, and evaluating peer and cross-age tutoring. *Reading Improvement*, *19*(4), 74–78.

Crist-Whitzel, J., Dasho, S.J., & Beckum, L.C. (1984). *Achieving equity: Student-led computer training.* San Francisco, CA: Far West Laboratory for Educational Research and Development. (ERIC Document Reproduction Service No. 248 848)

Garner, R., Wagoner, S., & Smith, T. (1983). Externalizing question-answering strategies of good and poor comprehenders. *Reading Research Quarterly*, *18*, 439–447.

Gutek, G.L. (1972). *A history of the western educational experience.* Prospect Heights, IL: Waveland.

Hahn, A.L., & Smith, T. (1983). Students' differentiation of reader-based and text-based questions. *Journal of Educational Research*, *76*, 331–334.

Heward, W.L., Heron, T.E., & Cooke, N.L. (1982). Tutor huddle: Key element in a classwide peer tutoring system. *The Elementary School Journal*, *83*(2), 115–123.

Hoffman, D.M., & Heath, S.B. (1986). *Inside learners: Guidebook in interactive reading and writing in elementary classrooms.* Stanford, CA: Stanford University.

House, J.D. (1988, November). *An investigation of the effect of student and tutor gender on grades earned in college mathematics and science courses.* Paper presented at the annual meeting of the Illinois Association for Institutional Research, Rosemont, IL. (ERIC Document Reproduction Service No. ED 301 480)

Johnson, S. (1977). *Cross-age tutoring handbook.* Corcoran, CA: Corcoran Unified School District. (ERIC Document Reproduction Service No. ED 238 826)

Lane, P., Pollack, C., & Sher, N. (1972). Remotivation of disruptive adolescents. *Journal of Reading*, *15*, 351–354.

Lazerson, D.B., Foster, H.L., Brown, S.I., & Hummel, J. (1988). The effectiveness of cross-age tutoring with truant, junior high school students with learning disabilities. *Journal of Learning Disabilities*, *21*(4), 253-255.

Levin, H.M., Glass, G.V., & Meister, G.R. (1984). *The cost-effectiveness of four educational interventions.* Stanford, CA: Stanford University, Institute for Research on Educational Finance and Governance. (ERIC Document Reproduction Service No. ED 246 533)

Levine, J.R. (1990). Using a peer tutor to improve writing in a psychology class: One instructor's experience. *Teaching of Psychology*, *17*(1), 57-58.

Limbrick, E., McNaughton, S., & Glynn, T. (1985). Reading gains for underachieving tutors and tutees in a cross-age tutoring programme. *Journal of Child Psychology and Psychiatry and Allied Disciplines*, *26*(6), 939-953.

Maher, C.A. (1984). Handicapped adolescents as cross-age tutors: Program description and evaluation. *Exceptional Children*, *51*(1), 56-63.

Miller, K. (1989). Cross-age tutoring in science. *Paired Reading Bulletin*, *5*, 63-68

Myrick, R.D., & Bowman, R.P. (1983). Peer helpers and the learning process. *Elementary School Guidance and Counseling*, *18*(2), 111-117.

New York City Board of Education. (1990). *Chapter 1/Pupils with compensatory educational needs: 1989–1990 peer tutoring end-of-year report.* New York: Author. (ERIC Document Reproduction Service No. ED 326 599)

Palincsar, A.M., & Brown, A.L. (1984). Reciprocal teaching of comprehension-fostering and monitoring activities. *Cognition and Instruction*, *1*, 117-175.

Pillen, B.L., Jason, L.A., & Olson, T. (1988). The effects of gender on the transition of transfer students into a new school. *Psychology in the Schools*, *25*, 187-194.

Pino, C. (1990). Turned on by tutoring. *American Educator*, *14*(4), 35-36.

Porter, T.J., & Hamilton, E. (1975). *Junior-senior high tutor/aide program at Malcolm X Elementary School* (ESEA Title III Evaluation Final Report). Washington, DC: District of Columbia Public Schools, Department of Research and Evaluation. (ERIC Document Reproduction Service No. ED 120 249)

Rekrut, M.D. (1992, April). *Teaching to learn: Cross-age tutoring to enhance strategy acquisition.* Paper presented at the annual meeting of the American Educational Research Association, San Francisco, CA. (ERIC Document Reproduction Service No. 348 363)

Rekrut, M.D. (1993). *Strategy acquisition through peer tutoring.* Unpublished manuscript.

Reigstad, T.J., & McAndrew, D.A. (1984). *Training tutors for writing conferences.* Bloomington, IN: ERIC Clearinghouse on Reading and Communication Skills. (ERIC Document Reproduction Service No. ED 240 589)

Robertson, D.J., & Sharp, V.F. (1971). *The effect of fifth grade student tutors on the silent word vocabulary attainment of first graders.* (ERIC Document Reproduction Service No. ED 055 735)

Sosa, A.S. (1986, November). Valued youth partnership program: Dropout prevention through cross-age tutoring. *Newsletter*, Intercultural Development Research Association. (ERIC Document Reproduction Service Nos. ED 279 764 and ED 279 765)

Steinhausen, G.W. (1983). Peer education programs: A look nationally. *Health Education*, *14*(7), 7-8, 10.

Trovato, J., & Bucher, B. (1980). Peer tutoring with or without home-based reinforcement for reading remediation. *Journal of Applied Behavior Analysis*, *13*, 128-141 .

Wasserman, S., & Stanbrook, C.M. (1981). Inverse tutoring: An alternative strategy for remedial readers. *Phi Delta Kappan*, *62*(9), 72-73.

Yogev, A., & Ronen, R. (1982). Cross-age tutoring: Effects on tutors attributes. *Journal of Educational Research*, *75*(5), 261-268.

Sharon Benge Kletzien and Lynda Baloche

The Shifting Muffled Sound of the Pick: Facilitating Student-to-Student Discussion

The students have just read a line from Melville's *Moby Dick* "The subterranean miner that works in us all, how can one tell whither leads his shaft by the ever shifting muffled sound of the pick?"

Shelly: I think he's talking about what's inside us.

Kerry: You mean what we are thinking inside?

Shelly: No, I mean what we are really like inside, what our real self is.

Rachel: I think he means like our conscience or something.

Kerry: What we are telling ourselves we should do?

Shelly: What does that mean, "whither"?

Rachel: Maybe he spelled it wrong, maybe it's "whether."

Shelly: That doesn't make sense, "whether leads his shifting muffled sound of the pick."

Kerry: What's the "muffled sound of the pick"?

Rachel: Maybe he is talking about the direction our lives should go, like we are meant to do certain things or something. Like the path we are supposed to take. How do we know what we are supposed to do, like, how can we tell if we are really supposed to do something because it's in us or if we're just doing it because others tell us to?

Kerry: I don't think we're "supposed to" do anything; we can choose whatever we want to do with our lives. We aren't programmed like robots or something. We don't have a path we're supposed to follow.

Rachel: No, but there're things that we, that our lives should be, that we were probably meant to do. You know, like we were meant to be a certain way.

Shelly: But maybe he's meaning that we can't always tell when it is really our own...well, look, it says that the sound of the pick is muffled so it has to be muffled by something. Maybe it's muffled by what other people are telling us so we can't really tell what our true self thinks.

Defining Discussion

While most teachers agree that classroom discussion is a valuable teaching technique (Alvermann & Hayes, 1989; Alvermann, O'Brien, & Dillon, 1990), they sometimes disagree about what constitutes discussion. In many instances, "discussions" are really recitations in which teachers control the turn-taking, do most of the talking, ask low-level informational questions, and limit students to two- or three-word answers (Alvermann, Dillon, & O'Brien, 1987). In "discussions"

Reprinted From the *Journal of Reading*, *37*(7), 540–545, April 1994.

such as these, the structure of what is said is largely predetermined by the teacher, and student responses do not significantly influence outcomes (Nystrand, Gamoran, & Heck, 1993). In fact, these discussions are used to evaluate students comprehension, not to exchange ideas about text. Teachers ask questions to which they already know the answers and lead students to the "correct" response.

By comparison, a *true* discussion is an open exchange of ideas and opinions about topics that may not have easy answers. Students, not teachers, ask questions. Students respond directly to each other rather than to or through teachers. Students learn to explain their reasoning for differing interpretations and to value these differences. Teachers frequently play a minimal role, as student participants determine the direction they need or want to take to construct meaning (Cintorino, 1993).

Using Discussion to Clarify and Expand Thinking

Kerry, Shelly, and Rachel are 10th-grade students who have just completed reading *Moby Dick*. Their attempts to understand Melville's view of the meaning of life, by examining quotes and relating them to the overall theme of the novel, illustrate the kind of small-group discussion that is possible in classrooms where true student-to-student dialogue is encouraged. In these exchanges, students clarify and refine their thinking and expand their views by hearing others' interpretations.

At the conclusion of their discussions, their English teacher, Joe, asks students to explain how the quotes fit within Melville's theme. Then he asks his students to reflect on how their interpretation of the text has been influenced by discussions with peers. Discussion seems to help Kerry clarify her thinking. "I didn't really have an interpreta-

tion before I began to talk. I don't know really what I think until I try to tell somebody."

Shelly expands her initial interpretation through discussion. "I was thinking about our consciences, but then when they started talking about where our lives should go, it made me start thinking on another track. I didn't have that interpretation at first. Sometimes it helps me get out of a rut when we talk about things."

Text-based discussions often require that students return to the text to support or to clarify their interpretations. Rachel's comment supports the value of reexamination combined with discussion. "I sometimes don't read something the same way others do. I have to go back and see how they came up with what they thought. Sometimes it's because I've read it wrong, or they've read it wrong, but sometimes there really are lots of ways to understand it."

Discussions that encourage students to return to the text to justify their interpretations help students take control of their learning and become independent readers. Goodlad (1984) observed that most secondary students depend on their teachers, rather than on the text, to help them comprehend essential concepts. In fact, this dependence is so strong that in many secondary classrooms, students are able to grasp enough concepts to succeed without reading at all (Ratekin, Simpson, Alvermann, & Dishner, 1985).

Dependence on the teacher is not the norm in Joe's classroom. He has developed a classroom climate that encourages the free exchange of ideas; his students understand that they have an obligation, to their peers and themselves, to come to class prepared; and he encourages his students to develop a critical reliance on the text and on each other, not on him.

Discussions that encourage students to evaluate texts and peers' interpretations for accuracy, biases, and assumptions, help students become critical readers. In spite of the fact that critical reading is an essential characteristic of a mature reader, many secondary students are deficient in this ability (NAEP, 1984).

Joe encourages critical reading not only through discussion and reexamination of single texts, but also through assigning multiple works by the same author. Early in the year, Joe's students read Tennessee Williams' *The Glass Menagerie*. Because Joe wants his students to develop a more complete picture of the dramatist, he assigns each of his students one of five additional plays. In "jigsaw" (Aronson, 1978) groups of five, students present their new plays and then discuss similarities in plot, character, setting, and theme. Through the use of multiple texts, Joe's students are able to evaluate Williams' work, their own understanding, and their peers' reactions in a way that invites deep comparisons and meaningful evaluation.

Down the hall, in Terry's room, 11th-grade students are discussing Maya Angelou's poem for the U.S. Presidential inauguration of 1993, "A Rock, A River, A Tree." First, in groups of three, they talk about the meaning of the poem. Then the chairs in the classroom are arranged in a "fishbowl" of two circles, one inside the other. Half the class sits in the inner circle and discusses Angelou's poem while the other half sits and observes. Interpretations are offered hesitantly at first and then with increasing momentum. Students support and build on each other's comments. A common phrase is "He said...and I agree, and I also think..."

A common interpretation of the poem grows as different students add to the group's creation. New meanings develop out of the combined understandings, a typical result of good discussion (Pinnell, 1984). After about 10 minutes of discussion, Kim comments, "I'm just beginning to see this,

but I think that she is bringing together all the different parts of our country." Kim's "beginning to see" something new in the poem is a direct result of the interaction of the students' interpretations.

Using Discussion to Review Content

The discussions in Terry's and Joe's classes have been structured to help students clarify and expand their interpretations of literature. Discussion also helps improve long-term concept memory and recall (Alvermann, Dillon, & O'Brien, 1987) and can be used to help students review or master subject matter (Gall & Gall, 1976).

When we walk into Marilyn's class, we find students standing, facing each other, in two concentric circles. They are reviewing events and character development in *Huckleberry Finn*. Each student holds an index card that has been prepared for homework. First, each student in the inner circle talks to a partner in the outer circle. They use their cards to help them describe an event from the story and to help them interpret what this might indicate about the character involved. Students in the outer circle listen intently and ask clarifying questions. Next, students in the outer circle share their events and interpretations. After both sets of explanations, the students trade cards, and the students in the outer circle rotate clockwise so that each student in the class now faces a new partner. Students must now explain the event and characterization represented by the new card they hold, the card given to them by their previous partner. With little teacher intervention, the students review many of the novel's critical events and share many interpretations of the characters as they continue to move around the circle—listening, offering explanations, and trading cards.

Structuring Discussion With Cooperative Learning

Joe, Terry, and Marilyn all make frequent use of discussion in their English classrooms. Many teachers would agree that this student-directed approach results in better learning, but many teachers also find it difficult to establish classroom routines that encourage quality discussions. Problems develop that discourage teachers and students alike: two or three students dominate a conversation; discussions degenerate into emotional arguments; students just don't have anything to say.

Joe, Terry, and Marilyn all make regular use of carefully structured cooperative learning groups, based on the cooperative learning model of David and Roger Johnson, to minimize such problems and to provide students with opportunities for meaningful discussion. According to Johnson, Johnson, & Holubec (1993), five basic elements need to be included if a lesson is to be truly cooperative: positive interdependence, face-to-face interaction, individual accountability, interpersonal and small group skills, and group processing.

Positive interdependence. Positive interdependence helps create a climate in which students truly believe that they can work together to maximize learning. Joe, Terry, and Marilyn are all very careful to structure positive interdependence into their lesson designs. In all three classes, *goal* interdependence is fundamental. Students understand quite clearly that working together helps them to construct meaning. They also understand that developing meaning through discussion is up to them; they are not expected to follow their teacher's preconceived interpretation.

In Marilyn's class, students share *resources*—the notes they bring to class on index cards. In Joe's class too, students share resources. Each group of three works at a single computer terminal. Joe has prepared disks that included several quotes from *Moby Dick*, and students work together to analyze and respond. Joe assigns each member of the group a role: one student is the typist, one the synthesizer of ideas, and one the reader.

Students in Terry's class assume different roles also: While some students discuss the poem, others observe and record how the conversation progresses.

In all three classes the teachers structure the environment by assigning students to computers, by placing chairs in circles, or by clearing space so that students can stand together comfortably.

Face-to-face interaction. Teachers in all three classes make instructional decisions designed to maximize the quality of face-to-face interaction. Joe has students discuss Melville in groups of three. Marilyn utilizes a series of partner sharings to review *Huckleberry Finn*. Terry has her students first discuss Angelou's poem in groups of three before coming together in the fishbowl. All three teachers understand that by keeping their groups small, they give students more opportunity—and more responsibility—for the discussions. They also understand that heterogeneity helps insure that discussion is lively and diverse. Students in these classes don't just pick the people with whom they want to work. Joe, Terry, and Marilyn all assign students to groups, at times deliberately and at times randomly. These variable groupings insure that, over time, students have opportunities for discussion with everyone in their class.

Individual accountability. Individual accountability is a fundamental feature of successful cooperative discussion. In all three classrooms, students know that they need to come to class prepared. Marilyn heightens this sense of accountability by requiring students to bring index cards describing character involvement in an episode from the book.

At the conclusion of Joe's class, students make printouts of their group's ideas and are individually responsible for expanding on these ideas for homework. All teachers occasionally ask individual students to summarize. This too helps keep all students actively engaged.

Interpersonal skills. But every teacher knows that merely arranging the room, having students share materials, assigning individual homework, and telling them to discuss cooperatively is not enough. The interpersonal skills that are needed to work together productively don't just magically appear when they are needed. Joe, Terry, and Marilyn have all identified skills that they know their students need for productive discussion. The skill of paraphrasing, which Marilyn emphasizes when she uses the structure Inside-Outside Circle (Kagan, 1992), is but one example of an important skill for discussion.

Joe's students seem quite adept at ensuring that all members of their threesomes have opportunities to share their ideas. In the past, Joe has used the structure "Talking Chips" (Kagan, 1992) to help sensitize students to differing levels of participation. When he uses this structure, he gives each student several plastic chips and instructs them to "spend" a chip each time they talk. Students know that once their chips are gone, they must remain silent until the other members of their group have contributed their ideas and chips.

Terry uses observers when she facilitates a fishbowl discussion. Each observer is given an observation form and asked to record who contributes ideas, asks questions, jokes, summarizes, expresses support, encourages others to contribute, or gives direction to the work of the group. Over time, all her students have opportunities to observe and identify the use of their peers' positive interactional skills in discussion. Both observers and discussants benefit from this practice.

Processing. Joe, Terry, and Marilyn regularly ask students to reflect on, to process, their work together. When Terry uses the fishbowl, she initiates processing by asking the observers to report what they have seen. We know how Kerry, Shelly, and Rachel have been influenced by their groups' discussion because they have been asked to reflect and write about it. In Marilyn's class, the final 2 or 3 minutes are spent with students talking about their sharing, making general observations and comparisons, synthesizing different viewpoints, and generally just talking freely as a whole class. This processing helps students develop their ability to reflect on their own and others' thinking.

Awareness of how they have constructed meaning through both interaction with the text and with each other contributes to these students' metacognitive knowledge. This awareness enables students to generalize thinking processes so that they may be used in other related activities. The sharing of cognitive processes enables all of the students to benefit from each others' thinking and encourages them to expand their own repertoires of comprehension strategies.

Making It Work

Classroom discussions based on cooperative learning work in Joe's, Terry's, and Marilyn's classes because they work at it. They carefully plan individual lessons to ensure that students practice appropriate interpersonal skills, feel both interdependent and individually accountable, and reflect on their work. They also present their students with discussion topics, questions, and activities that encourage autonomy and in-depth discussion of texts. Their students report that they read differently when they know that they will be asked to engage in such in-depth discussion. One student commented:

"When I read for a test or something, I really try to remember all the details, but when I know we are going to have a discussion, I have to understand the major concepts in what I am reading."

Colin, a 12th grader, explained it this way: "If I am preparing for a test, I look for facts and other plot related things, but when sharing in a group, I get more ideas in my head that I can share."

Cooperative, small group discussions have the potential to provide students with "more ideas in their heads that they can share"—a worthwhile goal for any reading assignment.

The authors gratefully acknowledge Joseph Filinuk, Therese Willis, Marilyn Lee Mauger, and their students at Haddonfield High School, Haddonfield, New Jersey, USA, for openly sharing their classrooms and ideas.

REFERENCES

Alvermann, D.E., Dillon, D.R., & O'Brien, D.C. (1987). *Using discussion to promote reading comprehension*. Newark, DE: International Reading Association.

Alvermann, D.E., & Hayes, D.A. (1989). Classroom discussion of content area reading assignments: An intervention study. *Reading Research Quarterly*, *24*, 305–335.

Alvermann, D.E., O'Brien, D.G., & Dillon, D.R. (1990). What teachers do when they say they're having discussions of content area reading assignments: A qualitative analysis. *Reading Research Quarterly*, *25*, 296–322.

Aronson, E. (1978). *The jigsaw classroom*. Beverly Hills, CA: Sage.

Cintorino, M.A. (1993). Getting together, getting along, getting to the business of teaching and learning. *English Journal*, *82*, 23–32.

Gall, M.D., & Gall, J.P. (1976). The discussion method. In N.J. Gage (Ed.), *Psychology of teaching methods* (pp. 166–216). National Society for the Study of Education, Seventy-fifth Yearbook. Chicago: University of Chicago Press.

Goodlad, J.I. (1984). *A place called school*. New York: McGraw-Hill.

Johnson, D.W., Johnson, R.T., & Holubec, E.J. (1993). *Cooperation in the classroom*. Edina, MN: Interaction Books.

Kagan, S. (1992). *Cooperative learning*. Laguna Niguel, CA: Kagan Cooperative Learning.

National Assessment of Educational Progress. (1984). *The reading report card*. Princeton, NJ: Educational Testing Service. (No. 15-R-01)

Nystrand, M., Gamoran, A., & Heck, M.J. (1993). Using small groups for response to and thinking about literature. *English Journal*, *82*, 14–22.

Pinnell, G.S. (1984). Communication in small group settings. *Theory into Practice*, *23*, 246–254.

Ratekin, N., Simpson, M.L., Alvermann, D.E., & Dishner, E.K. (1985). Why content teachers resist reading instruction. *Journal of Reading*, *28*, 432–437.

Josephine Peyton Young, Samuel R. Mathews, Anne Marie Kietzmann, and Todd Westerfield

Getting Disenchanted Adolescents to Participate in School Literacy Activities: Portfolio Conferences

Interviewer: What do you think of the portfolio process?

Liz: I think it's important. Important 'cause they're about my grades.

I: Are they fair?

L: It's fair 'cause the teacher and I determine what I'm supposed to get and sometimes I'm just like, damn, I could have done better. I write down what I think I should get and she pretty much agrees with me. We agree on the grades.

I: How do you think the portfolio conferences help you?

L: By letting me know what I should work on more, and makes me and Ms. Young be more closer—like friends. Not just student and teacher.

I: Why do you think Ms. Young does the portfolio conferences?

L: I guess to help you figure out what you need to work on.

The above excerpt is from an interview conducted at the end of a school year in which Liz had participated in the portfolio process. Liz was one of the ninth-grade students enrolled in Josephine Young's reading and English class at an alternative secondary school in northwestern Florida, USA. The students in Young's class said they did not like to read and, when given the opportunity to read or write, initially chose not to do so. Most of them reported having had few positive experiences with literacy-related activities in school and spending little time, if any, reading outside of school. Because many of the students in Young's literacy classroom typically chose not to read and write, we sought to identify and develop classroom practices that would encourage them to participate in literacy activities.

The goal of this article is to describe the role the portfolio process played in Young's classroom and to report the students' reactions to their participation in this process. Reactions such as Liz's allowed us to see the utility of the portfolio process, particularly of the portfolio conferences, in classrooms where students typically resist reading and writing activities.

Portfolio Assessment

Portfolios have been defined as collections of students' work or artifacts selected by the individual students and teacher to represent the students' efforts, progress, and achievements over time (Gillespie, Ford, Gillespie, & Leavell, 1996). In addition to a collection of

302

Reprinted From the *Journal of Adolescent & Adult Literacy*, *40*(5), 348-360, February 1997.

work and artifacts, many portfolios include the students' written reflections about their criteria for selecting the artifacts and for judging merit (Northwest Evaluation Association, 1991; Rief, 1990; Tierney, Carter, & Desai, 1991; Valencia, 1990).

In a recent review of literature on literacy portfolio assessment, Gillespie et al. (1996) stated that a major advantage of portfolio assessment over traditional assessment is the active involvement of the students in their own evaluations. Other advantages included the use of portfolios as a means for students to reflect on their own development as readers and writers; to understand the relationship between reading, writing, and thinking; and to become more independent learners.

As we observed students throughout the portfolio process and listened to their comments about it, we noted similar advantages for the students in Young's class. It seemed to us that the process, especially the portfolio conferences, was important in helping disenchanted learners (often referred to as "at risk") become motivated to *engage* in school-like literacy activities and become more aware of themselves as learners. For these reasons, we valued the portfolio process as an important element in our ever-evolving classroom environment.

In an effort to understand the role the portfolio process played in Young's classroom, we conducted a content analysis of the written records and transcripts of the portfolio conferences. We hoped that, with a better understanding, we would be able to express to other teachers how the portfolio process could become not only an alternative assessment method, but also a valuable tool to encourage disenchanted learners to participate in literacy activities and assume responsibility for school literacy use and learning.

Our analysis began when Young, now a doctoral student, was a teacher at the alternative secondary school. Other members of the research team were Sam Mathews, a psychology professor, and Anne Marie Kietzmann and Todd Westerfield, who are both recent graduates of the master's degree program in the department in which Mathews teaches. We used a qualitative content analysis procedure (Guba & Lincoln, 1981) to analyze the data that had previously been collected. In this article, we will present the results of our analyses.

Disenchanted Learners, Motivation, and Goal Orientation

Many of the disenchanted adolescent students in Young's classroom exhibited behaviors associated with learned helplessness and passive failure (Johnston & Winograd, 1985). These students typically fail to monitor their performance and make accurate attributions for personal success and failure. They tend to give up easily on school-like tasks. Many do not believe that there is a connection between their actions or efforts and their performance or outcomes. These individuals do not think they have much control over their thinking, learning, or motivation. This leads to decreased interest and motivation to participate in classroom activities. They feel defeated and hopeless. Among the students in Young's classroom, many simply would not attempt tasks associated with school-related literacy. They appeared to have given up on literacy learning.

We believe that all students under the right conditions possess a natural propensity to learn, even disenchanted adolescent students. Like McCombs and Pope (1994), we view motivation "as an inherent, natural capacity and tendency within the person to learn and grow...it needs to be elicited rather than established" (p. 15). This view implies that teachers cannot instill motivation within their students. However, teachers can establish classroom environments that enhance students' natural desire to learn. In such environments, students can become aware of the control they have over their own learning, thinking, behavior, and motivation (McCombs & Pope, 1994).

Recent articles discuss the influence of learner-centered classroom environments on students' motivation to learn and the goals they adopt (Ames, 1992; Boggiano et al., 1992; McCombs & Pope, 1994; Oldfather & Dahl, 1995). Environments in which teachers relinquish some control and the learners assume more responsibility for making decisions in the classroom have been observed to increase learner motivation. Within these classroom environments, students are given choices and participate in making decisions about learning activities, strategy use, and goal setting (Ames, 1992; Boggiano et al., 1992). Evaluation also plays a key role. Ames's (1992) synthesis of research on motivation identified evaluation practices within classroom environments that affected student motivation and sustained mastery goal orientation. These practices helped students to focus on individual goals of progress and improvement rather than a final grade.

Mastery goals tend to focus more on the process of learning and students' efforts than on performance outcomes. When mastery goals are adopted students appear to spend more time on learning tasks (Butler, 1987), expend more effort to learn the materials, and adjust strategies for learning when faced with a difficult task or failure (Ames, 1992). In contrast, students who adopt performance goals are primarily interested in making a good grade and comparing their performance with peers'. The process of learning is viewed by students adopting performance goals as less important than their final grades (Hagan & Weinstein, 1995).

Portfolios have been mentioned by Blumfeld (1992) as a possible answer to sustaining mastery goal orientation in classrooms. Portfolios are designed to show a student's progress, efforts, and achievements over time, not to compare one student with another. They encourage self-evaluation of progress or attainment of one's mastery goal. This kind of self-evaluation can lead to increased student awareness of their thinking processes, strategy use and selection, and motivation (McCombs, 1986). It encourages learners to attend to the relationships between effort, the use of strategies, and performance outcomes. It can also affect the learner's self-efficacy or perception about his or her ability to perform. In turn, perceived self-efficacy affects one's attributions for success and failure, self-evaluations, goal setting, and activity choices (Ames, 1992; McCombs, 1986; Schunk, 1990).

Many of the students in Young's classroom had been referred to the alternative school because their choice in other educational settings had been to "do nothing." So the task before us was to develop classroom practices that would encourage students to choose literacy tasks over "doing nothing." The portfolio process and the culminating experience of the portfolio conference became such a practice.

The Context of the Study

The alternative school and its students. The ninth-grade reading/English classroom in which our study took place was part of an alternative high school in northwestern Florida. Students were referred to this school from other district middle and high schools because they met one or more of the district's criteria for being at risk of dropping out of school. These included retention in one or more grades, irregular school attendance, parent who dropped out of high school, pregnancy, and experiencing emotional stress or trauma. Most of the students were from the lower socioeconomic levels as evidenced by the 67% participation in the free or reduced-cost lunch program. The diverse student body was represented by 40% African American females, 11% African American males, 23% European American females, and 22% European American males. The average daily attendance was approximately 50% of the total students enrolled.

The alternative school offered a schoolwide competency-based curriculum. Students who were motivated and capable could move quickly through the self-paced curriculum. A few students finished classes as quickly as in 6 weeks. Some took 2 or more years to finish a class. Others never finished at all.

The classroom and staff. Young's classroom was akin to a school within a school. The classroom housed a Student Literacy Volunteer program (SLV), a collaborative project between the University of West Florida and the alternative school. SLV was partially funded by a U.S. Department of Education Student Literacy Corp grant. University students volunteered 6 hours a week in the classroom to work with the students individually or in groups. The volunteers and Mathews, the university-based director of SLV, became trusted mentors and tutors to the adolescent students. Mathews was present in the classroom at least 3 days a week. His role included being a participant observer, tutor for the high school students, and trainer/supervisor of the university volunteers. Young's role, in addition to being the classroom teacher, was to train and supervise the university volunteers with Mathews. Kietzmann and Westerfield were tutors in the program. Kietzmann was a volunteer in the reading/English classroom for 2 years and knew most of the students well. Westerfield volunteered 1 semester. They both were mas-

ter's students in psychology and interested in adolescent behavior and learning. The volunteers, Mathews, and Young sat at tables with the students and modeled participation in the daily literacy activities such as silent reading and journal writing.

The students in Young's classes generally scored in the lower 50th percentile (many scored at or below the 25th percentile) when given a standardized test of reading achievement. Most of the students reported on the personal preference inventory (Figure 1) administered their first day in the reading/English class that they disliked reading, never read for enjoyment, and had not read an entire book since elementary school.

Upon enrollment in the reading/English class, students were given a list of required reading and writing activities to be completed before earning credit for the class. (For an example of a management sheet see Figure 2. Students in Young's class had a reading and an English management sheet to guide them through the course.) The requirements included reading a certain number of books and writing a certain number of polished drafts. Students selected the books to read and topics to write about. In addition to completing the management sheets, they were expected to participate in the daily silent reading period and whole-class discussions or mini-lessons. During the 10- to 15-minute silent reading period, students selected materials to read from the classroom library. Materials included daily copies of the local newspaper, young adult paperbacks, adult literacy high-interest books, public health brochures, and magazines. They could also read materials from home or the school library.

Whole-class lessons and discussions focused on reading comprehension and writing strategies. Each day, time was allotted for students to work independently, with a volunteer, or with a peer on the required man-

Figure 1
Personal preference inventory

Name: _____

Name you prefer to be called: _____

1. List your favorite in each area below:
   Movie _____ Music _____
   Sport _____ Hobby _____
   Books _____ Magazines _____
   Subject in school _____

2. List three goals you have for yourself in the next 5 years: _____
   _____
   _____

3. What are your goals for this school year? _____
   _____
   _____

4. What happened to get you to this school? _____
   _____
   _____

5. How do you think this school can help you? _____
   _____
   _____

6. What must you do to attain your goals? _____
   _____
   _____

7. How do you think a reading class can help you in school and in your life? _____
   _____
   _____

8. When was the last time you read a book? _____

9. What was the title? _____

10. Why did you read it? _____
    _____

11. I read (check all that apply)
    when I have to at school _____
    for fun/pleasure at home or at school _____
    when I need information _____

Complete these sentences.

1. I think reading _____
2. I'd rather read than _____
3. When I have to write a paper _____
4. Pictures in books _____
5. When I read and come to a word I do not know I _____
   _____

Mathews, Young, & Giles (1992)

Figure 2
Reading management sheet

Student name _____ Grade _____ Birthdate _____ Enrollment date _____

Completion date _____

Newspaper unit

Activity sheet	Grade	Date
1. Who, what, where, when, why, and how	_____	_____
2. Main idea	_____	_____
3. Classified fact/opinion	_____	_____
4. Word groups	_____	_____
5. Classified search	_____	_____
6. Following directions	_____	_____
7. Other	_____	_____
Newspaper unit final grade	_____	_____

Map reading unit

Activity sheet	Grade	Date
1. Where do you live?	_____	_____
2. *Where in the World Is Carmen Sandiego?* (Solve three mysteries)	_____	_____
3. Plan a trip	_____	_____
4. Using compass directions	_____	_____
5. Compass points	_____	_____
6. Reading charts, graphs, diagrams, and schedules	_____	_____
7. Other _____	_____	_____
Map reading unit final grade	_____	_____

Reference unit

Activity sheet	Grade	Date
1. Timeline "Famous Person"	_____	_____
2. Timeline "My Life: Past, Present, and Future"	_____	_____
3. The Yellow Pages	_____	_____
4. Using the dictionary	_____	_____
5. Field trip to public library	_____	_____
6. Other _____	_____	_____
Reference unit final grade	_____	_____

Record of books read

Title	Type of book*	Date completed	Book conference/Project remarks
1.			
2.			
3.			
4.			
5.			
6.			
7.			
8.			
9.			
10.			
11.			
12.			

* Type of book: **A** type = 100 pages or less; **B** type = 100–150 pages; **C** type = over 150 pages. For one semester credit in Reading a minimum of 2 **C** type books, 3 **B** type books, or 6 **A** type books must be read and the student must demonstrate comprehension of the book in the form of a book conference with the teacher and/or a book project. For a year credit in Reading a minimum of 3 **C** type books, 5 **B** type books, and 12 **A** type books must be read and comprehension requirement met. Mathews, Young, & Giles (1992)

agement sheet activities. The order for doing the activities was up to the students. Each activity had to be deemed satisfactory by the teacher or volunteer and the student before being considered complete and having a grade recorded on the management sheet.

The portfolio process, as we defined it (Gillet & Temple, 1994; Young, Mathews, Kietzmann, & Westerfield, 1995), begins when the teacher examines the instructional environment to ensure there are opportunities for students to demonstrate their learning and to reflect on the experiences and products of their learning. In the next phase of the process students review their work and experiences, select examples for evaluations (e.g., writings, favorite books, activities), and write reflections on their criteria for selections. The conference is the pinnacle of the portfolio process. During conferences, individual students and teachers evaluate the selected works, and students describe their reflections and selection criteria. Students also discuss previous literacy goals, set new goals, and identify strategies for attaining their goals.

This phase of the portfolio process expanded the function of portfolios in Young's classroom to instructional by providing opportunities for students and Young to make explicit and public their individual criteria for determining success and failure. It also provided opportunities for students to identify and state their literacy goals and proposed strategies for achieving them.

The portfolio process became an integral part of the classroom environment. Conferences were held at Young's desk (one of the few uses found for it) and became a special time for the students. Since the students were used to working on their own, they held off individual questions for Young until she was not in conference with a student. Each 6-week period students prepared for the portfolio conferences by selecting artifacts that represented their most important or best works; they also wrote their criteria for selecting the artifacts. The selection of an artifact was guided by a question or statement posed by Young. One such guiding statement was "Select the writing you feel is most important to you. Mark it in your journal and write your reasons for selecting that writing." The students were asked to reflect about their own performance in various components of the class (see portfolio record, Figure 3). The portfolio record was used as a guide for the portfolio conferences.

Students shared with Young their written and oral reflections about their selected artifacts during their individual portfolio conferences. They also evaluated their participation in literacy activities, reflected upon their uses of literacy strategies, assessed progress toward attainment of their goals, and set new goals at this time. Each student and Young together reviewed the student's work folder and attendance records. They discussed student, teacher, and district criteria for grading and reached consensus on a grade and/or progress report in each area of focus.

Data Sources

The data for our study come from three sets of records: written records of portfolio conferences, personal preference inventories, and transcripts of interviews with students. Not considered in this analysis are the artifacts in the portfolio itself. The emphasis of this study is on what the students said during the portfolio conferences and the follow-up interviews. We distinguish records from documents in that records are derived from "official chronicles" rather than a document that arises from a motivation "to make others aware of a point of view, to persuade, to aggrandize, to explicate, or to justify" (Guba & Lincoln, 1981, p. 230). Although the records

Figure 3
Portfolio record

Student name_____ Course name _____ Grading period_____

Birthdate _____ Current grade placement_____

Below is a written record of student reactions to their work and student-teacher assessment conferences.

A. Reading response journal
1. What do you feel is important about your RRJ's?
2. Do you write in your RRJ each opportunity?
3. Do you include a summary about what you read?
4. Do you write your opinion or feelings about what you read or about why you didn't read?

Teacher comments:
Reading response journal grade

B. Writing workshop
1. Put a star on the writing that represents your most important writing and describe why you believe this.
2. Show me evidence of prewriting activities (concept map or brainstorming).
3. How do they help you write drafts?

Teacher comments:
Writing workshop grade

C. Class and group activities
1. Group projects and whole-class activities
a. Describe the activity you liked best and tell why.

Teacher comments:
Grade
2. Participation and ability to use K-W-L* and other comprehension strategies independently
a. Which strategy helped you the most and why?
b. Show me the notes from the K-W-Ls or other comprehension activities in which you have participated.

Teacher comments:
Grade
Combined class and group activities grade

D. Sustained silent reading
1. What kind of material did you like to read most and why?
2. Why do you think we read every day?
3. Do you read the entire SSR period? Why or why not?

Teacher comments:
Sustained silent reading grade

E. Have you met your goals for this 6 weeks? Why or why not?

F. Goal for next grading period
1. What do you want to accomplish in the next 6 weeks?
2. How do you plan to do this?

Teacher comments:

Teacher signature _____ Date _____

Student signature _____ Date _____

*A strategy developed by Donna Ogle; the term K-W-L derives from what I know, what I want to learn, and what I have learned.
Mathews, Young, & Giles (1992)

of the interviews and portfolio conferences were produced as an ongoing part of a classroom process rather than a systematic research effort, we viewed them as records.

The data sources collected over a school year include the following:

1. *Written records of portfolio conferences*. Records consisted of the teacher's written comments and transcripts of student comments during the portfolio conference. For the purpose of this study only the goal-setting and attainment questions on the record were analyzed. The 25 student portfolio records were chosen because these students had been enrolled and present at the third and fourth grading period portfolio conferences. Third and fourth grading periods were selected to sample because they were typically the best attended grading periods at the alternative school.

Four questions on the portfolio record had to do with goal setting, strategies for goal attainment, and reflection on actual goal attainment. The questions were added during the previous school year in an effort to help the students focus on the requirements for completing the class. We also hoped that by our asking goal-centered questions students would begin to take more responsibility for their learning. Analysis of videotaped conferences conducted the previous year showed that Young rarely commented about the "appropriateness" of the goal or evaluated the students' suggested strategies for goal attainment or reasons for not completing a goal. Instead, she acknowledged the goal by writing it down on the portfolio record and asked the student to state a plan to attain the goal.

The goal-setting part of the portfolio conference went fairly quickly. Young asked the questions and recorded students' responses on the portfolio record. She then posted the students' goals on bright paper in their work folders. In this way, the notes acted as a daily reminder of the students' stated goals.

2. *Personal preference inventories* (PPI). These were records of students' reasons for attending the alternative school, reasons for leaving their previous school(s); interests in movies, music, reading, and leisure activities, and other relevant information. They were taken on the first day of attendance in the reading/English classroom.

3. *Student interviews*. Kietzmann and Westerfield conducted interviews with a sample of the students in Young's classes. The interviews took place during the last 6 weeks of school. Students selected had participated in the portfolio process for at least two grading periods. Twelve males and 9 females were interviewed. Ethnic backgrounds of the students included European and African American.

The purpose of the interviews was to find out the students' perceptions of the portfolio process. The interview consisted of the following questions: (a) What do you think/feel about the portfolio process? (b) Is it fair? (c) How do you think the portfolio conferences helped you? (d) Why do you think Ms. Young does the portfolio conferences? The results of the interviews were transcribed for analysis.

Analysis Procedure

The unit of analysis for the coding procedure was the individual student's response. Student responses to each question that pertained to goal setting, goal attainment, and the portfolio process in the portfolio record sheets, the personal preference inventories, and the transcripts of student interviews were analyzed. Our analyses began with all of us reading and reviewing the data individually and identifying key categories of statements. Then, as Guba & Lincoln (1981) suggested, we devised a set of rules to govern the categorization of the data. We identified these rules and categories through consensus and outlined the following five classes of statements:

1. Statements of goals or desired outcomes such as completion of a task, reading a book, writing a story.

2. Statements of strategies and conditions for accomplishing a task; that is, coming to school, reading, doing drafts, using concept maps.

3. Statements of assessments and evaluations made by Young or the students.

4. Statements of evaluation criteria or justification for assessment or grade made by Young or the students.

5. Statements of affect toward the portfolio process.

These classes of statements reflect the major components of the portfolio process as we conceived it—goal setting, strategy selection, self-assessment, and reflections about the process itself.

We then individually categorized the data following the rules we devised. Once this was completed, we met as a group to share our individual understandings and to discuss what we saw as emerging themes in the data. Six months after an initial analysis, Young and Mathews reread the data separately and refined the wording of the themes.

The findings from the analysis of each data set are consistent. The themes emerging from data sets represent students who voiced an increased sense of control and responsibility over goal setting, academic evaluation, and completion of work. Although many of the students' stated goals could be classified as performance goals, we believe that the students saw the process toward goal attainment to be as important as its completion. The basis for our judgments lies in the students' expressed views of personal control over goal and strategy selection and positive affect expressed toward the process. Positive affect and perceived control within the classroom environment indicated to us that the students in Young's classes had, at the very least, be-

gun to perceive a connection between effort and outcome and to feel less hopeless in the face of school literacy activities.

We present our findings in two sections: (a) portfolio records—conversations between Young and individual students during the portfolio conferences, and (b) interview data—records of students' responses to interview questions about the portfolio process. It is our goal in the analyses that follow to provide descriptions and interpretations of the reactions of a small group of disenchanted adolescent students who participated in the portfolio process.

Portfolio Records

The goal-setting part of the portfolio record revealed two themes. Students voiced more specific goals as they participated in the portfolio process and their strategies for attainment became more detailed. Whether the change in students' goal statements was the result of a change in teacher questioning or a change in students' goal-setting skills cannot be determined from our data.

Students voiced more specific goals. Roger, a 16-year-old European American, enrolled at the alternative school because he previously dropped out of school and wanted to return. He stated he enrolled there so that he could work at his "own speed." He hoped the reading class would help him read faster and better. He stated on the PPI that his goal was "to learn" and he thought he could accomplish this "by working." His goal to learn and his strategies for attainment of that goal were abstract and lacked the specificity needed to guide his behavior.

By the third grading period a noted change had taken place. In the excerpt below, Roger explains to Young why he had not met his goals and set new goals.

Young: Have you met your goals for this 6 weeks?

Roger: No.

Y: Why?

R: I was not here.

Y: Yea, you weren't here much. What do you want to accomplish in the next 6 weeks?

R: To be here. To do some worksheets. To read more.

Y: How about reading two books?

Y: How do you plan to do this?

R: Come to school, do some worksheets, and check out a book.

[portfolio record sheet, third grading period, December 1993]

Young's comment to Roger about his absences was nonjudgmental, and she modeled a more specific goal. She suggested that he try to read two books. These goals were also not met by the fourth portfolio conference. However, during that conference, Roger stated that he had almost completed his goal of reading more, but he kept switching books, trying to find one he liked. He had not completely met his goals, but recognized that he had made some progress. His statement shows that he was becoming aware that he had control over his learning and progress in the class. Roger's new goal—to complete five activity sheets (one a week) and read one short book—was even more specific than the previous goal.

Students voiced more specific strategies for goal attainment. Lawanda was a 16-year-old African American female who enrolled in the alternative school because she was pregnant and wanted to take advantage of the prenatal educational program offered there. Her goal when she arrived was "to do my best" (PPI). She thought if she worked hard she could accomplish this goal. Lawanda's goal for the third grading period was to finish the news-

paper reading unit (see reading management sheet, Figure 2) and read two books. She didn't think she would complete her goal because she would probably transfer to the adult high school. Her prediction that she would not complete her goal was correct, but she did not transfer schools. Her baby had gotten sick, and so she had been unable to attend school. Her new goal was to read two books and do activity sheets. Her strategy for attainment was to "work when I'm here." Outside factors hindered her from obtaining literacy goals. However, she did work while at school instead of socializing, but attended school rarely. She didn't complete the reading/English class that school year.

Interestingly, Lawanda did set another goal for herself. During the portfolio conference she told Young that she didn't want any more babies. Lawanda took action to prevent any more babies by "getting a Norplant" that grading period. Although the change observed in Lawanda's conference was not a literacy goal, she did set a goal, identify a strategy, and take action to meet the goal. Working while in class and using birth control were actions focused on enhancing her progress and learning in school. Given that Lawanda's actions were focused on the opportunity to learn and not the product of learning, she reflected a mastery goal orientation.

Interview Data

Interviewer: What do you think of the portfolio process?

Bob: Makes your brain think.

Cindy: Ms. Young don't really give us bad grades, but we do it ourselves, and I think that's pretty good.

Timmy: It's okay. They're fair.

Tanika: I think it's good what she is do-
            ing—get a chance to talk to your
            teacher.

Joshua: If I get a good grade, I like
            them. If I don't, it sucks.

We found it interesting that the interview transcripts revealed that the students thought of the portfolio conferences as synonymous with the portfolio process. None of the 21 students interviewed mentioned the other phases of the process; that is, selecting artifacts or reflecting on the selection of artifacts. What they did emphasize was the content of the discussions during the portfolio conferences, not the contents of the portfolio. The salience of the conference is not surprising. It was a time when individual students commanded Young's individual attention. This was a time when students could make their case for a grade or progress report and see an immediate impact of *their* efforts on outcomes.

Analysis of these discussions led us to classify student responses about portfolio conferences into three broad themes: (a) students perceived themselves as partners in assessment, (b) students said setting their own goals was fair, and (c) students perceived the portfolio process as helpful.

Students perceived themselves as partners in assessment. In virtually all the interview responses, students reported that they considered themselves to be partners in assessment and grade assignment. As one student said, "Ms. Young don't really give us bad grades, but we do it ourselves…if you get a bad grade, you give yourself a bad grade for a reason." Another student, Christopher, also considered the grading process collaborative as the following statement suggests: "I like the way she graded it 'cause she didn't put the grade on it herself. We went over it, and after we get finished, she asks 'what do you think you deserve?'"

During the portfolio conferences the student and Young negotiated the grades. The negotiation process began when the student stated his or her proposed grade and the rationale for that grade assignment. Young then commented on the student's proposed grade and rationale. Her comments took into account district standards and individual student progress and achievement. The student was then invited to continue the negotiation until both Young and the student were satisfied that the grade reflected the student's progress, efforts, and achievements.

As the students analyzed and evaluated their own performance, they evidenced the antithesis of learned helplessness. They weighed their performance against their goals, identified what remained to be done to meet their goals, and finally integrated information about their performance to assign a grade. The self-evaluation within the portfolio process helped the students attend to the relationship between effort and outcome. Given that the students were legitimate partners in the assignment of grades and that they selected the artifacts to be graded, the focus of grades changed from a performance evaluation to an evaluation that reflected process, effort, and achievement.

Students said setting their own goals was fair. They expressed a sense of fairness in being active participants in the process of goal setting and assessment. For instance, Jim, a European American 15-year-old, came to the alternative school because he said he was "having trouble with the people" at his high school. He told us that setting your own goals was fair.

I guess…well, yea [they are fair] 'cause… you can't say they [the teachers] are putting too much pressure on you 'cause you're setting goals for yourself of what you need to be doing. You're telling her [Young] what you think you can handle. You're doing what you said you could handle...helps you set responsibility for yourself—learning responsibility at the same time. Doing these goals 'cause you told her you would do them, and I guess that's your responsibility.

Like Jim, many of the students interviewed spoke about their responsibilities for setting goals and noticed a difference between what they experienced in other schools and the reading/English classroom. In answering the interview question about the fairness of the portfolio process, one student replied, "I reckon so. 'Cause in the regular school they just give you anything...we get to pick our goals." Another, reflecting on Young's assistance in goal setting, said, "she helps them [the students] set goals, tell you what you're missing....She explains more to you."

As these comments suggest, the students expressed the belief that setting their own goals was fair and acknowledged that Young assisted them in setting goals. Young pointed out course work already completed and additional work required to complete the course. This, they thought, helped them to set more attainable goals and complete the required course work. The students' remarks supported what researchers have written about the relationship between students' being involved in decision making in the classroom and motivation (Ames, 1992). When students set their own goals and expend effort accordingly, they evidence a sense of personal control over learning and acting.

Students perceived portfolio process as helpful. Students found the portfolio process helpful and perceived it positively. They reported that the portfolio conference helped them to determine what they needed to do during the coming grading period. This is especially important in a competency-based curriculum in which the students govern their own progress. For most of the students, choosing which activity to do in class on a given day was a new experience. The goal-setting part of the conference helped them to focus on course requirements. Students told us that the conferences helped because, "We get to pick our own goals.... Help you to know...what you need to do" and "'cause it sets your sights on what you need to finish."

In addition to helping students focus on necessary activities, goal-setting was also seen as helpful in obtaining good grades. Tonya, a European American 16-year-old, saw a connection between goal setting and making good grades,

> Well, I think they [portfolio conferences] help you because like when you get the goals you know what you need to do to get a good grade for the next 6 weeks. If you do your goals you get a pretty good grade and you get your work done. If you don't, you don't get punished or nothing, but you're hurting yourself by not getting your goals.

Some students, however, did not think that goal-setting helped them to complete their work. As one student so aptly stated after being asked if the conference helped him to finish his goals, "No, you ain't gonna do it, you ain't gonna do it." But for others, like Artie who would rather use his time to read fantasy and science fiction than to write or complete a reading activity sheet, goal-setting served as a much needed guide. Each 6 weeks, he set the goal of completing the reading activity sheets and failed to attain it. Finally, during the fourth portfolio conference Artie stated he thought that he was reading too much and would try to read only during the silent reading time. Young had waited patiently for him to realize that in order to complete the class, he had to do something other than read books. Once he realized this on his own, Artie completed the activity sheets and other course requirements.

Most of the students interviewed perceived the portfolio process positively. At first, however, students thought it was "weird" but eventually liked it "'cause you can grade yourself." Others worried that they would "grade themselves too easy." As they grew accustomed to the process they expressed fondness and respect for the process. Jim's thoughtful response to the interview question about why Young does the portfolio process sums up this respect.

> I guess so you can discuss what you've done and what you need to do…so if you're doing bad, she [Young] can talk to you about it and see if there is anything she can do to help you get a better grade. Other schools give you a grade, can't improve it. Make an F, get an F…I mean if you make an F, they should at least discuss it with you…I think it's good because you discuss what you've done…and give yourself a grade.

Young made the course requirements explicit to the students. During the portfolio process students were asked to select particular types of work representative of their mastery of those requirements and to reflect on their criteria for selections. Students verbally justified their criteria to the teacher and assessed their works in conference with Young. In return, Young expressed her agreement or disagreement with the students' judgements. If a discrepancy occurred, the final assessment was typically found in a consensus agreement between the teacher and student. This process provided a bridge between the mastery orientation associated with positive outcomes in classroom environments and the inevitable demand for performance data (e.g., grades) to meet the need for administrative accountability.

Opportunities for students to set academic and personal goals emerged as a potent element of the portfolio process. During the conferences, the students reflected on their goals and the degree to which they attained them in a given reporting period. Students' academic goals typically began as a general statement about finishing the course or finishing school and moved toward more specific goals such as reading one book. The interview data and transcriptions of portfolio conferences revealed a transition from general goals to more discrete goals, including specific tasks to be completed.

The students in Young's classroom reported a sense of responsibility and efficacy in selecting and attaining their own academic and personal goals and in evaluating their own work. Responsibility and efficacy in academic pursuits are not characteristic of students who are classified "at risk," and so this finding is exceptionally important. While it is unclear that the responses were totally dependent upon the portfolio process as we implemented it, the structure of the portfolio conferences guided students' self-monitoring and self-assessment.

According to our observations, a contribution to students' responsibility and motivation to set goals and complete work came in the evolving relationship between Young and the students. The students expressed positive affect toward the conference phase of the portfolio process. They often included comments about Young's willingness to listen, reach consensus, provide useful feedback, and respond respectfully and honestly to their concerns.

The portfolio process provided opportunities for students to self-monitor and self-assess, to set and attain goals, and to develop a personal relationship with the teacher. More importantly, it became a classroom practice that encouraged this group of adolescent students to make the choice of participating in school-related literacy activities a viable one.

REFERENCES

Ames, C. (1992). Classrooms: Goals, structures, and student motivation. *Journal of Educational Psychology, 84*, 261-271.

Blumfeld, P.C. (1992). Classroom learning and motivation: Clarifying and expanding goal theory. *Journal of Educational Psychology*, *84*, 272–281.

Boggiano, A., Shields, A., Barrett, M., Kellam,T., Thompson, E., Simons, J., & Katz, P. (1992). Helplessness deficits in students: The role of motivational orientation. *Motivation and Emotion*, *16*, 271–296.

Butler, R. (1987). Task-involving and ego-involving properties of evaluation: Effects of different feedback conditions on motivational perceptions, interest, and performance. *Journal of Educational Psychology*, *79*, 474–482.

Gillespie, C.S., Ford, K.L., Gillespie, R.D., & Leavell, A.G. (1996). Portfolio assessment: Some questions, some answers, some recommendations. *Journal of Adolescent & Adult Literacy*, *39*, 480–491.

Gillet, J.W., & Temple, C. (1994). *Understanding reading problems: Assessment and instruction* (4th ed.). New York: HarperCollins.

Guba, E.G. & Lincoln, Y.S. (1981). *Effective evaluation: Improving the usefulness of evaluation results through naturalistic approaches*. San Francisco: Jossey-Bass.

Hagen, A.S., & Weinstein, C.E. (1995). Achievement goals, self-regulated learning, and the role of classroom context. In P.R. Pintrich (Ed.), *Understanding self-regulated learning* (pp. 43–55). San Francisco: Jossey-Bass.

Johnston, P.H., & Winograd, P.N. (1985). Passive failure in reading. *Journal of Reading Behavior*, *16*(4), 279–297.

Mathews, S.M., Young, J.P., & Giles, N. (1992). *Student literacy volunteers: Providing 'tools' for brighter futures*. Unpublished training manual, University of West Florida, Pensacola.

McCombs, B.L. (1986). The role of the self system in self-regulated learning. *Contemporary Psychology*, *11*, 314–332.

McCombs, B.L., & Pope, J.E. (1994). *Motivating hard to read students*. Washington, DC: American Psychological Association.

Northwest Evaluation Association. (1991). *Proceedings of the Fourth Annual October Institute: Alternative assessment*. Lake Oswego, OR: Author.

Oldfather, P., & Dahl, K. (1995). *Toward a social constructivist reconceptualization of intrinsic motivation for literacy learning* (Perspective in Reading Research No. 6). Athens, GA: National Reading Research Center.

Rief, L. (1990). Finding the value in evaluation: Self-assessment in a middle school classroom. *Educational Leadership*, *46*(6), 24–29.

Schunk, D.H. (1990). Goal setting and self-efficacy during self-regulated learning. *Educational Pyschologist*, *25*(1), 71–86.

Tierney, R.J., Carter, M.A., & Desai, L.E. (1991). *Portfolio assessment in the reading-writing classroom*. Norwood, MA: Christopher-Gordon.

Valencia, S. (1990). A portfolio approach to classroom assessment: The whys, whats, and hows. *The Reading Teacher*, *43*, 338–340.

Young, J.P., Mathews, S.R., Kietzmann, A.M., & Westerfield, T. (1995, April). *Alternative purposes for the portfolio process: Beyond assessment for high risk adolescents*. Roundtable presentation at the annual meeting of the American Educational Research Association, San Francisco, CA.

Arlene L. Barry

High School Reading Programs Revisited

During the spring of 1940 Glenn Myers Blair, a professor at the University of Illinois, posed the following question to 1,090 U.S. high school principals: "What do you do with pupils in your high school who are unusually poor in reading ability?" He received responses from 379 schools in 38 states and the District of Columbia (Blair, 1941). While more recent studies have focused on exemplary reading programs (i.e., American Institutes for Research in the Behavioral Sciences, 1975; Lang, 1995; Office of Educational Research and Improvement, 1991) none have provided an update of common practice across the United States as Blair did. It is important to provide such an analysis for many reasons, one of them being that we, as educators, cannot make decisions about what we need to change if we do not step back and examine what we do.

Also, as I work with teachers in the field, I find that they simply want to know about the daily practices of other educators. They ask such questions as "What books are your students reading?" "How long are your class periods?" "Do you team teach?" Unfortunately, teachers don't always have time to talk with one another. Perhaps the information presented here can allow reading teachers to vicariously touch base with others who teach similar populations.

The purpose of this article, then, is two-fold: (a) to report on a nationwide U.S. survey in which I asked principals to identify programs and practices in place for high school students who have difficulty reading (i.e., those who are two or more grade levels below their peers in reading achievement) and (b) to present comparisons between current practices and past ones. It is this second factor that I have personally found most encouraging—the changes in practice from past to present. While they are not overwhelming in scope, I find the changes significant.

In earlier decades, for example, there was often little respect for either the student or the abilities of the teacher in the remedial reading program. As one curriculum director who oversaw secondary reading programs during the 1940s told me,

> In those days it was not really respectable [to teach remedial reading] and so the teacher really took an awful lot of gaff from her colleagues. They thought she was just capable of teaching people who were mentally deficient.... Her colleagues sort of put the onus on her that she wasn't capable of teaching bright students. (A. Morann, personal communication, June 1988)

Certainly, reading specialists/teachers today are considered knowledgeable, respected pro-

Reprinted From the *Journal of Adolescent & Adult Literacy*, *40*(7), 524–531, April 1997.

fessionals. Credentialing and widespread education about reading processes and problems have undoubtedly done much to dispel misconceptions such as the one Morann related.

Finally, I believe this survey highlights the concerns of secondary reading teachers across the United States for increased support (monetary and administrative) and the need to advocate for content reading programs.

Particular survey questions used here were developed by reviewing surveys like Blair's (1941, full text, 1946), and ones carried out by the National Education Association (1942) and the North Central Association (1946). Items from these older surveys were chosen so that results could be compared and the differences between early reading programs (1920–1950) and present ones discussed. It is, of course, important to reflect on the progress (or lack thereof) we have made. Questions used in this survey were altered to eliminate unacceptable (e.g., use of the term "retarded reader") and vague language. Eight questions (multiple choice and open ended) that focused on regular education programs were constructed and piloted. Adjustments were made to the survey based on feedback from the pilot, and the final questionnaires were distributed to a random sampling of 2,287 principals across the United States. The results of this mass mailing were responses from 737 principals, reading specialists, teachers, and curriculum directors in 48 states and the District of Columbia.

What follows, then, is summary information of survey questions, combined with conclusions based on changes over time and trends that have emerged. The questions asked focus on structure (i.e., Is a program in place? What is it called? What grade levels are served? How are students placed in programs?); evaluation (often reported by respondents in terms of student progress); organization and staffing (i.e., Which teach-

ers in which departments are responsible for programs and what credentials do they hold?); and instruction (reported largely in terms of materials used). This discussion is organized by categories of responses to those survey questions. Implications for literacy educators are explored.

Structure

First, 67% of the 737 respondents said that they maintain a program, as part of their regular education department, for secondary students who have difficulty learning to read. Seventeen percent said that such reading assistance programs existed only as part of the special education department and 11% said their high schools had no programs to assist adolescents who struggled with reading. Nine percent (of the 11%) reported that while they had no particular reading assistance program, classroom teachers made efforts to somehow accommodate students who struggled. Some of the accommodations noted were creative lesson planning, hands-on experiences, individualized instruction, alternative means of assessment, team teaching, reading to students before and after school, tape-recording for students, use of guided questioning, smaller classes, peer tutors, after-school tutoring, cooperative learning, extra study time, Reader's Workshop, and extensive staff development to help teachers teach reading in the content area. In a similar vein, while Blair reported that 20% of the 1940s respondents had no formal program, plans were "under consideration for caring for this problem in the near future" (p. 33).

Some schools also provided several different types of reading programs within their regular education departments. For example, one Virginia school proudly noted, "We have a great program to reach all levels of reading ability: (a) Applied Reading and Learning

Strategies (At risk students); (b) Study Skills (Average readers); (c) College Reading and Study Skills (College bound)."

Program titles. Current programs are given many different names, 143 in all, from the "X Program" to the "Tiger Club." Numerous respondents used "reading" in their program titles (28%), with such labels as "Reading Improvement" (17%) or "Developmental Reading" (11%) appearing nationwide. Several schools noted that programs formerly called "remedial" were now being called "developmental." The opinion among many districts was similar to that of the Missouri educator who said, "No 'remedial' or special classes are held anymore—they were not effective." While the concept of the pull-out remedial class appears to be losing favor, 4% of respondents did still specifically designate their program as remedial (e.g, "Reading Remediation," "Remedial English," "Remedial Reading"). This movement away from the remedial class appears to be in line with what has been occurring throughout the U.S. over the past several years.

Grade levels served. When reading assistance programs are available in a district, they tend to be available across multiple grade levels. In other words, while the greatest number of programs (64%) serve adolescents in 10th grade, similar numbers are served at 9th (62%), 11th (58%), and 12th (54%) grades. This is a change from practices in pre-1950s high schools when the remedial reading class temporarily served students in Grade 9 and then the frustrated reader often dropped out (Barry, 1992). Increases in high school graduation rates over the decades (National Center for Education Statistics, 1994), society's demand for a high school diploma, and the ever-increasing reading demands of the workplace have undoubtedly increased the range of reading assistance programs to cover Grades 9 through 12.

Student placement. In terms of placing students into programs, a determination of a high school student's eligibility to participate in a special reading program was made primarily on the basis of standardized test scores (61%) and teacher recommendation (58%). Other criteria (38%) such as grades in content courses, cumulative grade point average, prior enrollment in Chapter 1, and parent or student request for assistance were considered to a lesser degree. The tests used for placement decisions were extremely varied (70 different tests reportedly were used by respondents). However, tests most frequently cited to determine program placement included specific state exams (19%, e.g., New York City Regents Competency Test, Virginia Literacy Test, Maryland Reading Test); Comprehensive Test of Basic Skills (12%); Iowa Test of Basic Skills (10%); California Achievement Test (9%); Gates-MacGinitie Reading Test (9%); Degrees of Reading Power (7%); Stanford Achievement Test (6%); Stanford Diagnostic Reading Test (5%); Nelson-Denny Reading Test (4%); Test of Academic Proficiency (4%); and the Woodcock-Johnson (4%).

One difference noted between use of tests in current reading programs and programs in earlier decades is that teachers in pre-1950s programs regularly said that they used intelligence tests in combination with reading tests to identify adolescents for reading assistance programs (Barry, 1992). Whether or not IQ data were actually taken into consideration for current programs, neither intelligence tests nor their scores were mentioned in connection with current program placement. Fortunately, we now know that students may be poor readers but possess normal intelligence. Frequently, this was not the case with programs of earlier decades.

Evaluation

Generally, the same criteria used to place students in reading programs (i.e., test scores, teacher feedback) were used to evaluate their progress. Fifty-eight percent checked test scores and 63% teacher feedback as being used to determine student progress in reading programs. The particular standardized test used to determine program eligibility tended to serve as a posttest. Overall use of standardized reading tests was widespread and, as one respondent put it, "we use any standardized test." Only 4% of survey participants said they used no test data for either placement or evaluation. A very small percentage of respondents reported that they used teacher-made tests (2%) or Informal Reading Inventories (<1%) for placement and/or evaluation.

This widespread use of objective tests appears to be in line with the findings of Barton and Coley (1994), who recently examined assessment practices in U.S. schools. "Seventy percent of tests given in statewide systems are multiple-choice" (Barton & Coley, 1994, p. 6). Twenty percent of those who said they used data other than test scores or teacher/ student feedback to evaluate progress cited use of such performance-based measures as portfolios, writing samples, and student journals for evaluation purposes. Parental feedback was another source of information noted for evaluating student progress within programs (16%). One difference between placement and evaluation criteria was the significant amount of student feedback (37%) reportedly taken into consideration in order to determine program success.

Organization and Staffing

Most programs for students with reading difficulties are, and historically have been, organized as part of the school day (64%), as opposed to before (4%) or after (6%) school. Depending on the number of class periods a school had (respondents noted between 4 and 17 periods), particular programs were mentioned as being available during one specific period during the day (i.e., lunch period, study hall, English period, 25%); available during several class periods (32%); or available during all periods of the school day (19%). Programs were available to students anywhere between 1 and 5 days each week, with time frames varying from 10 minutes to 120 minutes. Other specifics ranged also; students in some programs received course credit and others received none; some courses were mandatory and others elective; and yet other programs were optional; for example, a "peer tutor contacts [the] student and they make their own arrangements."

In regard to amount of time allocated for programs, a trend was noticed when respondents' additional remarks were analyzed. When the responses of those who offered positive comments about their programs (18% of the 50 who included additional remarks) were compared to those who made negative comments about their programs (48%), a difference was noted in the amount of time allocated for reading assistance. It was not a surprise to find that respondents in districts with more time allocated for student reading needs tended to make positive comments about their programs and those with little time to meet adolescent reading needs were frustrated. For example, a midwestern respondent, who said "Our school used to have a 'strong' remedial and enrichment program in reading but when 'funds' became tight our staffing changed," described a program that was "catch as catch can." By way of contrast, a Virginia respondent, who said "We have a great program to reach all levels of reading ability," described a program with "1 or 2 classes offered, determined by need...classes [that] can be taken for 4 years...teacher available to help after school in study hall or one-on-one" and a reading specialist available to model strategies in content classrooms.

Collaboration. While describing their program's organization, 22 respondents offered additional comments stating that they team taught with a content teacher (usually English, but social studies, science, math, and geography were mentioned also). This movement by a reading specialist to collaborate with content teachers is a change from the isolationist practices in earlier decades. The current move toward collaboration appears to bring with it greater satisfaction, as evidenced, once again, by comparing survey responses of those who indicated program satisfaction and those who indicated dissatisfaction. Educators who indicated a high level of satisfaction with their program also reported that their districts used collaboration or "interdisciplinary teams." Here is an example from Illinois: "Our PACE program involves all classes save [physical education]... each class is taught in tandem by the Regular classroom teacher and a Special teacher... we are rather proud of it."

Teacher expertise. Also contrary to former practices in high schools where the new, inexperienced English teacher was the one who staffed the special reading program, respondents in this survey report a different trend. For example, reading teachers and specialists (39%) and those who have additional reading endorsements (27%) currently staff special high school reading programs. Blair (1941), on the other hand, found that "the brunt of the teaching of remedial reading falls to the teachers of English [61%]" (p. 32). This staffing arrangement was a particular problem because, as one 1940s English teacher explained, "A high-school classroom teacher with a prescribed course of study to cover does not have time to develop elementary skills in reading or to do remedial reading" (Tabackman, 1948, p. 521). Presently, only 13% of program respondents report that their programs are staffed by regular education teachers with 0 to 5 years' teaching experience. While this is an improvement over past practices, perhaps 13% is still too large a number considering the needs of the population with which these novice teachers are working.

Instruction

Approximately half of respondents provided written information about the specific materials they used in their programs. (Educators were asked to check whether they used commercially produced or teacher-made materials and then to describe them.) Some talked about using "bottom-up" materials like *Hooked on Phonics*, worksheets on word attack, flashcards, workbooks, Dolch sight lists, skill builders, spelling lists, grammar, basal readers, controlled readers, Barnell Loft Specific Skill Series, and McCall Crabbs Readers. (The McCall Crabbs readers were found to be the most frequently used texts in pre-1950s secondary reading programs [Barry, 1992] with the first set of readers published in 1925.) Computer use appeared frequent (27%) and, based on the specific software mentioned (i.e., *Word Attack III*, *Skills Bank II*, *Increasing Your Vocabulary*, *Learning to Spell*), computers seem to have been used often as a vehicle for skill and drill.

Contrary to practices described by the previous group, other respondents made a point to say, "I use no workbooks or programmed materials," "nothing is taught in isolation," "not kill and drill," or "we have found that a whole language reading/writing-in-the-content-area approach is the best." Reading materials such as books (25%, including high-low books, trade books, adapted classics, and novels), newspapers (26%), and magazines (13%, especially *Read* and *Scholastic Scope*) were noted. Two especially popular authors were S.E. Hinton and, as one educator put it, "anything by Gary Paulsen."

Based on yet other comments made by respondents with regard to materials chosen, a third philosophy appeared to emerge—one that might be referred to as an "interactive" reading framework. This framework is probably best exemplified by a midwestern high school teacher who said, " some [students] work on skills and drills, all work on vocabulary, and all must do free reading."

Many types of commercially produced materials were listed, especially materials by Jamestown, (this publisher was clearly the favorite, as it was specifically named by 12% of respondents who cited the materials they used), Scholastic (10%), SRA (9%), Reader's Digest (4%), EDL (4%), and Globe (4%). Other materials whose names came up repeatedly were Barnell Loft Specific Skill Series (7%) and *Be a Better Reader* (4%). Dozens of other publishers, kits, and materials were noted less frequently.

Just as with reading, different philosophies about writing were evident. For example, in describing his writing assignments, one educator noted, "This is real, purposeful writing that students take pride in—unlike when they're given those bogus 5-paragraph essay tasks!" On the other hand, though, some teachers did specifically mention assigning "writing exercises," "grammar exercises," and "5-paragraph essays." The number of respondents who noted engaging their students in writing was 11%. One cannot help but wonder if there is any connection between this 11% and the fact that 12% of tests given in statewide systems are writing samples (Barton & Coley, 1994). Noting the historically small amount of writing (Applebee,

1981) in which high school students have been engaged, perhaps classroom writing practice is more closely tied to assessment than to what is known about the connections between reading and writing (Atwell, 1987).

While teachers in the 1940s remedial reading programs and those in present ones used a wide variety of materials to help their adolescent charges, subtle differences appear in the ways these materials were used. Based on teachers' descriptions of what they did in their classrooms in pre-1950s programs, it appears that most students did not spend time reading whole pieces of literature, talking about books, writing in connection with reading, or using text to learn to comprehend. In general, it seems that little connection was made for students between what they did in reading class and what they did in other content classes. As Scarlet (1939) said, all students seemed to be doing was "measuring rates and answering 10 questions" (p. 11). Due to the range in behaviors and learning problems, and lack of teacher training in early programs, teachers did the best they could by keeping students busy with lots of skill and drill work—management supplanted instruction (Barry, 1992). In current programs, with a trend toward integration of content areas, collaboration, writing across the curriculum, and implementation of whole language philosophies, I am hopeful that more disabled readers are seeing reading as a meaning-getting process. Qualitative studies are needed to more carefully examine what teachers really do on a day-to-day basis in today's special reading classrooms.

Trends

While, indeed, "there is no such thing as a typical remediation program" (Johnston & Allington, p. 988), particular trends in program components may be gleaned from this analysis.

Structure. Despite the fact that a majority of respondents said they maintained a program for students who struggled with reading, educators across the country expressed concern about the reduction in secondary reading services. An educator from the northeast, for example, reported, "We used to have an excellent program, with a reading teacher in every school. However, we went to site-based management and reading teachers were included as part of staff allotment. As a result, as budgets were cut, reading teacher positions were given up." A midwestern teacher said, "We used to have a reading lab where kids could sign up for a semester and work on improving reading skills. This was an elective class, open to anyone. An individual program was written for each student. Our central administrators decided that it was no longer fashionable to do this, and they closed the lab." "Even in Alaska," a respondent noted, "program was very strong in 70s and 80s. Has been drastically reduced to one section of remedial reading."

Perhaps allocations for secondary reading programs need to be rethought in light of recent findings from the National Assessment of Educational Progress (NAEP). NAEP researchers concluded, "The most striking finding from the 1994 assessment is that the average reading proficiency of twelfth-grade students declined significantly from 1992 to 1994. This decline was observed across a broad range of subgroups" (Williams, Reese, Campbell, Mazzeo, & Phillips, 1995, p. 6).

Evaluation. The significant role of standardized tests in both program placement and evaluation has remained constant across decades. However, there appears to be a growing awareness of and use of other viable tools in the decision-making process (e.g., teacher, student, and parent feedback; portfolios; writing samples; journals; teacher-made tests). Also, reliance on standardized test scores alone for placement decisions appears to be decreasing. For example, while 61% of respondents in this survey said that test scores were used to place students in reading programs, 90% of programs analyzed prior to 1950 used reading tests and one fifth used three or more reading tests in placement decisions. In addition, the majority of respondents presently making placement decisions report that they use both quantitative (e.g., standardized tests) and qualitative (e.g., teacher feedback) data to make those decisions. Once again, this was not the case with pre-1950s programs where the majority of placement decisions were reportedly made on the basis of test data.

Organization and staffing. There appears to be a movement away from the homogeneous pull-out program previously thought to be an effective organizational structure (e.g., Billett, 1932; Goodrich, 1931) to a more collaborative and consultative model. Undoubtedly, teachers and researchers alike have been concluding that the pull-out is largely ineffective (e.g., Magner, 1991; Singer, Balow, & Ferrett, 1988). Perhaps the fostering of teacher collegiality that had been a focal point of previous reform efforts (e.g., Smith & Scott, 1989) has begun to take hold. These efforts are exemplified nicely in the comments of one Philadelphia educator: "I am working my way to dissolving isolated classes of reading and including myself in classes where the students and staff need my help with modifying curriculum...I co-teach 10th and 11th grade general Science and co-teach 9th grade English." While considered a valuable instructional approach by some, however, simply recommending that teachers team is not, as this southwestern teacher points out, going to ensure that high school teachers will do so:

This school opted to drop remedial reading from its curriculum 3 years ago, in the hopes of emphasizing a strong content area reading program, with the support of the reading specialist and other reading staff. The content area teachers refused to cooperate and the program was dropped.

While there may be many reasons for content teachers to refuse to cooperate, perhaps one barrier to change is similar to one noted in secondary content reading programs back in the 1930s and 1940s. This problem has been more recently researched by Duffy and Anderson (1984) and Vacca (1983), who explain that teachers' instructional decisions are influenced more by the pressures they encounter in the work setting than by their beliefs about reading and classroom instruction. In other words, with early content reading, while every teacher was encouraged to be a teacher of reading, educators resisted this notion because they did not have the additional time, money, training, or support to do so. The same kind of situation with the same resistance may be occurring again.

Along with the time and support to incorporate reading into the content area, teachers must also be provided with the knowledge to do so. "By 1996," one upper midwestern teacher complained, "all classroom teachers will be expected to teach and assess student reading abilities. However, little preparation or inservice has been offered so far. Students will have to pass a reading proficiency test before graduation; however, reading classes are being phased out." On a more positive note, current personnel changes that help students have to do with the level of specialization of those who staff secondary reading programs. In contrast to present staffing practices, the high school remedial reading teacher of the pre-1950s had primarily been a novice English teacher who did not want the job (Barry, 1992). Perhaps the current employment of specialized personnel reflects a general change in attitude about a child who

struggles with reading. Fortunately, information about reading processes and those who have difficulty reading has been more thoroughly disseminated via content reading courses due to requirements for those who seek secondary certification (Mastain, 1988).

Instruction. Unfortunately, in early and even in more recent programs, "Remediation has come to mean primarily skills-based teaching" and often a "reduction in the quantity of reading instruction" (Johnston & Allington, 1991, pp. 994 & 992). However, a number of respondents in this survey claim to have moved away from solitary skill instruction (e.g., "nothing is taught in isolation," "all must do free reading," "not kill and drill"). Of course, it is only through direct observation that I will know if words and practice are in sync.

Future Work

The next step, then, is to accept invitations extended and determine exactly why some are able to report that "We've had spectacular success." Also, results need to be sent to respondents who specifically requested them, so that those like the New Yorker who said, "I am interested in hearing that the situation is not so desperate elsewhere" can know what others are doing. Through an analysis of past practices and present ones, I can also tell the respondent from New York that I believe we have made gains over the years in understanding and instructing adolescents who struggle with reading. However, we certainly need to keep moving forward. We have a long way to go.

REFERENCES

American Institutes for Research in the Behavioral Sciences. (1975). *Effective reading programs: Summaries of 222 selected programs*. Urbana, IL: ERIC Clearinghouse on Reading and

Communication Skills. (ERIC Document Reproduction Service No. ED 112 346)

Applebee, A.N. (1981). *Writing in the secondary school: English and the content areas*. Urbana, IL: National Council of Teachers of English.

Atwell, N. (1987). *In the middle*. Writing, reading and learning with adolescents. Portsmouth, NH: Heinemann.

Barry, A.L. (1992). *The evolution of high school remedial reading programs in the United States*. Unpublished doctoral dissertation, University of Wisconsin, Madison.

Barton, P.E., & Coley, R.J. (1994). *Testing in America's schools* (Policy information report). Princeton, NJ: Educational Testing Service, Policy Information Center. (ERIC Document Reproduction Service No. ED 366 616)

Billett, R.O. (1932). *Provisions for individual differences in marking and promotion* (Bulletin #17, National Survey of Secondary Education). Washington, DC: U.S. Government Printing Office.

Blair, G.M. (1941). Remedial-reading programs in senior high schools. *The School Review*, *49*, 32-41.

Blair, G.M. (1946). *Diagnostic and remedial teaching in secondary schools*. New York: Macmillan.

Duffy, G.G., & Anderson, L. (1984). Editorial comment: Guest commentary: Teachers' theoretical orientations and the real classroom. *Reading Psychology*, *5*(1-2), 97-104.

Goodrich, T.V. (1931). Influence of homogeneous grouping on pupil personality. *School Executives Magazine*, *50*, 259-263.

Johnston, P., & Allington, R. (1991). Remediation. In R. Barr, M.L. Kamil, P. Mosenthal, & P.D. Pearson (Eds.), *Handbook of reading research* (pp. 984-1012). White Plains, NY: Longman.

Lang, G. (Ed.). (1995). *Educational programs that work. The catalogue of the National Diffusion Network* (21st ed.). Tucson, AZ: National Dissemination Association. (ERIC Document Reproduction Service No. ED 381 535)

Magner, M.M. (1991). *Academic progress of selected middle school students after release from remedial reading programs*. Unpublished doctoral dissertation, Fordham University, New York.

Mastain, R.K. (Ed.). (1988). *The NASDTEC manual: Manual on certification and preparation of educational personnel in the United States*. Sacramento, CA: National Association of State Directors of Teacher Education and Certification.

National Center for Education Statistics. (1994). *Digest of education statistics*. Washington, DC: Office of Educational Research and Information.

National Education Association, Research Division. (1942). Reading instruction in secondary schools. *Research Bulletin of the National Education Association*, *20*.

North Central Association, Subcommittee on Reading. (1946). A second attack on reading problems in secondary schools. *The North Central Association Quarterly*, *21*(1).

Office of Educational Research and Improvement. (1991). *Educational programs that work. A collection of proven exemplary educational programs and practices* (17th ed.). Washington, DC: National Diffusion Network. (ERIC Document Reproduction Service No. ED 338 618)

Scarlet, W. (1939). Tendencies and practices in the teaching of reading in the high schools. *High Points*, *New York City*, *21*(5), 6-11.

Singer, H., Balow, I.H., & Ferrett, R.T. (1988). English classes as preparation for minimal competency tests in reading. *Journal of Reading*, *31*, 512-519.

Smith, S.C., & Scott, J.J. (1989). *Encouraging school staff to collaborate for instructional effectiveness*. Eugene, OR: Oregon School Study Council.

Tabackman, S.P. (1948). Can we make nonreaders like to read? *English Journal*, *37*, 517-524.

Vacca, J.L. (1983). How to be an effective staff developer for content teachers. *Journal of Reading*, *26*, 293-296.

Williams, P.L., Reese, C.M., Campbell, J.R., Mazzeo, J., & Phillips, G.W. (1995). *1994 NAEP reading: A first look-findings from the National Assessment of Educational Progress*. Princeton, NJ: Educational Testing Service. (ERIC Document Reproduction Service No. ED 381 749)

SUBJECT INDEX

A

ABSENTEEISM, 113

ACADEMIC ACHIEVEMENT: absenteeism and, 113; attitudes toward reading and, 34, 111; classroom behaviors and, 41–42, 48; and cultural diversity, 58; Family Literacy Project and, 259; parent involvement and, 58; and risk levels, 128. *See also specific area*

ACADEMIC CONFIDENCE: and authentic instruction, 213–214; and building literacy, 39–50, 51–52; and ownership in learning, 215

ACADEMIC ENGAGEMENT: attitudes toward reading and, 34, 111; and coping strategies of poor readers, 51–56; and K-W-L strategies, 222; and literature-based vocabulary development, 180–182, 186–187; and mock participation, 52; and social context of school, 41; with verbal-visual word association strategy, 111, 114

ACHIEVEMENT, in school. *See* academic achievement

ADULT READING SHARED WITH STUDENTS, 272–274

ANTHOLOGIES, and student learning, 215–216

ASSESSMENTS: Comprehensive Test of Basic Skills (1989), 110–111; diagnostic spelling inventory, 13; informal reading inventory (IRI), 9, 10*t*, 19–20; letter identification task, 19–20; literacy portfolio assessment, 302–303; Literature Project Evaluation Form (LPEF), 130–133; Metacomprehension Strategy Index (MSI), 20, 23–24; The Piers-Harris Children's Self-Concept Scale: The Way I Feel About Myself, 130, 133; posttesting, 14, 23–24; reading interest inventory, 129; spelling inventory, 34; of students' own work, 48; teacher-constructed dictation task, 19–20; of Teaching for Understanding (TfU) model, 158; "thick" description of observed behaviors, 52. *See also* standardized tests; *specific name*

"ASSISTED LEARNING," 16

AT-RISK STUDENTS, 17; motivation for reading of, 128–135; teaching reading comprehension to, 138–147. *See also* high school remedial reading programs and practices surveyed; learning disabilities and difficulties; reading disabilities and difficulties

B

BANDURA, A. *See* self-efficacy theory

BILINGUAL EDUCATION. *See* cultural and linguistic diversity; English as a second language (ESL); English language learners (ELL)

BOOK DISCUSSION GROUPS, 182–185

BRAINSTORMING, 88–89, 91, 120

C

CAI, M., AND LITERATURE CATEGORIES, 97–98

CASE STUDY: of intervention for student "at promise," 19–26; of middle school reading disability, 8–18

CHEYENNE WAY, verbal-visual word association strategy and, 107–115

CLASSROOM BEHAVIORS, and academic success, 41–42, 48

CLASSROOM DISCUSSION: book discussion groups, 182–185; peer-led, 70; student-to-student, 296–301; whole-class questions for, 69. *See also* student-to-student discussion

CLASSROOM ENVIRONMENTS, and student motivation to learn, 304

COGNITIVE STRATEGIES, 74–82

COLLABORATIVE CONVERSATION, 113–114

COMMISSION ON ADOLESCENT LITERACY (IRA), 2–3

COMPREHENSION STRATEGIES, 16; for at-risk students, 138–147; for cultural diversity, 74–82, 84, 92; and Metacomprehension Strategy Index, 20, 23–24; Rapid Retrieval of Information (RRI) technique, 171–173; story frame, 223–224; student-developed questions for group discourse, 168–170; for students with learning difficulties, 148–156; in subject-specific study, 137–196; "think aloud," 20. *See also* K-W-L; metacognitive strategies; reading comprehension instruction, in subject-specific study

COMPUTERS: and benefits for reading intervention, 22–23; and TTALL Program, 61

CONCENTRATION, timed trials and, 13

CONFIDENCE, ACADEMIC. *See* academic confidence

CONTENT AREA INSTRUCTION, 107–115, 238–243; and peer and cross-age tutoring, 291; and textbooks for ESL classrooms, 92; using wordless books, 254–255

COOPERATIVE LEARNING APPROACH, 70, 85, 116

COPING STRATEGIES, of unsuccessful readers, 51–56

CREATIVE WRITING, 89–90, 247

CRITICAL THINKING AND PROBLEM SOLVING SKILLS, 112–114, 177, 198–199, 204

CROSS-AGE TUTORING: peer and, 290–295; using wordless books, 254

CULTURAL AND LINGUISTIC DIVERSITY, 39, 57–135; and cognitive strategy instruction, 74–82; and ESL classrooms, 74–82, 83–95; and ethnic-specific literature, 96–106; and holistic instruction for LEP students, 116–121; and home-school partnerships, 58–65; influences on self-efficacy of, 48, 49; literacy plans for, 68; and mainstream curriculum, 111; in a Mexican American school, 66–73; and popular culture, 122–127; and self-concept of at-risk females, 128–135; and strategies for ESL classrooms, 83–95; and strategies for Latina/o students, 74–82; and strategies for Native American communities, 107–115; and verbal-visual word association strategy, 107–115; wordless books and, 253–254, 256. *See also* The Literature Project

D

DECODING SKILLS, 189–196

DIRECT INSTRUCTION, and vocabulary development, 178–182

DIRECTED-READING-THINKING ACTIVITIES, 33–34

DISADVANTAGED SCHOOLS, state funded programs for, 60–61

DIVERSITY. *See* cultural and linguistic diversity

DYSLEXIA, reading disabilities and, 8–9

E

EDUCATORS. *See* teachers

EFFECTIVE PARTNERS IN SECONDARY LITERACY LEARNING (EPISLL), 60–61, 62–63

EMBEDDED QUESTIONS, metacognitive strategies using, 157–167

EMPOWERMENT: and classroom cultural symbols and materials, 124–125; and classroom literacy practices, 63–64; and cultural diversity, 59; and stress reduction, 20

ENGAGEMENT, ACADEMIC. *See* academic engagement

ENGLISH AS A SECOND LANGUAGE (ESL): among Latina/o students, 74; classes for, 74; effects on self-efficacy of, 39, 48, 49; and figurative language, 88–89; holistic instruction for, 116–121; informational picture books and, 83–95; in Mexican American community, 67

ENGLISH LANGUAGE LEARNERS (ELL), instructional strategies for, 83–95

ENGLISH ORTHOGRAPHIC SYSTEM, 15–16

ENVIRONMENTS: atypical home, 85; classrooms and motivation to learn, 304; for learning, 41; for reading disabilities and difficulties, 30–31. *See also* cultural and linguistic diversity

ETHNIC DIVERSITY. *See* cultural and linguistic diversity

ETHNOGRAPHIES, SCHOOL, 52

EXPLICIT INSTRUCTION, MODEL OF, 149

F

FACULTY BOOK TALKS WITH STUDENTS, 272–274

FAILURE, breaking cycles of, 3–4

FAMILY LITERACY PROJECT: FOCUS ON TEENAGE PARENTS, 257–264; and academic recognition, 259; and effects of children's literature on parents, 263–264; goals of, 257–258; how it works, 258–259; at particular project sites, 261–263; reading activities of, 259–261; selected readings for, 259*t*–260*t;* and value for nonparents, 263; writing activities of, 261

FAMILY LITERACY TRAINING. *See* home-school partnerships; parent and family literacy programs

FAMILY READING (NATIONAL PROGRAM), 276–289; adaption to middle school of, 277–279, 286–288; classroom as a family in, 288–289; family component in, 286–288; program anticipation, reading and reflections, 282–286; program operations, 279–282; school background, 276–277

FEEDBACK, ON PERFORMANCE: and graphing of results, 13; from learning logs, 217; self-efficacy and, 46; and self-monitoring, 55

FIGURATIVE LANGUAGE, and ESL students, 88–89

FLUENCY. *See* reading fluency

"FREE CHOICE" READING, 124–126

FRUSTRATION LEVELS, 15

FUNDING PROGRAMS, Disadvantaged Schools Program, 60–61

G

GRAPHIC ORGANIZER TECHNIQUE, 86, 87, 88

GROUP JIGSAW METHOD, 91, 93

H

HARVARD UNIVERSITY'S PROJECT ZERO, 157–158

HIGH SCHOOL REMEDIAL READING PROGRAMS AND PRACTICES SURVEYED, 317–325; evaluation of students in, 320, 323; instruction in, 321–322; organization and staffing of, 320–321,

323-324; purpose of survey, 317-318; standardized tests used in, 319; structure of, 318-319, 323; trends in, 322-324

HISPANIC STUDENTS: cross-cultural literacy plans for, 68. *See also* cultural and linguistic diversity

HOME-SCHOOL PARTNERSHIPS, 58-65; developing programs for, 59-60; ethnic-specific literature and, 102-104; in Mexican American community, 68-69

HOW-TO BOOK PROJECTS, 206-214; definition and rationale for, 206-207; process of, 207-210; reflections and evaluations of, 210-214

I

INCLUSION MODELS, AND ALTERNATIVES TO, 17

INFORMAL READING INVENTORY (IRI), 9, 10*t*

INQUIRY CHART (I-CHART), FOR STUDENT RESEARCH, 198-205

INQUIRY METHODS, FOR STUDENT RESEARCH, 198-205, 206-214, 220

INSTRUCTIONAL MATERIALS: content textbooks for ESL classrooms, 92; for literature-based programs, 175; for motivating lifetime reading habits, 238-243; picture books for ESL classrooms, 83-95; picture books for middle-level classrooms, 244-250; popular culture and, 124-125; for Recycled Words strategy, 120-121. *See also* reading materials; resources

INSTRUCTIONAL METHODS AND STRATEGIES: alternatives to total inclusion models, 17; and appropriate instruction, 15-16; book discussion groups, 182-185; brainstorming, 88-89, 91, 120; cognitive and metacognitive strategies, 74-82, 157-167, 204, 220; collaborative conversation, 113-114; for content areas, 107-115, 238-243, 254-255; and cooperative learning approach, 70, 85, 116; creative writing, 89-90, 247; critical thinking and problem solving skills, 112-114, 177, 198-199, 204; decoding skills, 189-196; Directed-Reading-Thinking Activities, 33-34; easy reading, 11-12; for ESL students, 83-95; and experience *vs.* ability, 30; and frustration levels, 15; group jigsaw method, 91, 93; guided practice, 112-114; guided reading, 10-11, 14, 17; holistic, recycled words strategy, 116-121; how-to book writing, 206-214; inclusion models, 17; independent problem solving, 112-114; inquiry chart (I-chart) method, 198-205; inquiry methods for student research, 198-205, 206-214, 220; and instructional levels, 14-15, 16-17; journal writing, 68, 99-100; K-W-L/K-W-L-S, 198, 204, 217, 219, 220-222; literature circles, 99-100, 102-103; literature-based activities and strategies, 74-82, 83-95; model of explicit instruction, 149; one-on-one intervention (Clay), 20-23; oral reading activities, 33, 69, 75-76, 116-117; partner or paired reading, 14, 70; peer editing strategies, 119-120; peer-led discussion, 70; picture books, 83-95, 244-250; poor reader coping strategies, 51-56; portfolio process, 302-316; and "pull-out" programs, 17; pupil-to-pupil teaching, 254, 290-295; and purpose, 32; quick book share, 269-271; Rapid Retrieval of Information (RRI) technique, 171-173; read-alouds, 25, 30-32, 87-88, 103-104, 133, 171-173, 265-268; Reading Rescue, 19-26; recycled words strategy, 116-121; repeated readings, 12-13, 14, 25; and responses to individual adolescent identities, 7-56; round-robin reading, 32-33; sample lesson plans, 11*f*; Scaffolded Reading Experience model, 148-156; self-selected reading materials, 2, 33-34, 226-237; sharing reading experiences, 30, 269-274; skill-and-drill approach, 32; small-group instruction, 16-17, 51-52; student centered reading, 124-126; student-to-student discussion, 296-301; Sustained Silent Reading (SSR), 29, 177-178; taped reading, 14, 17; teacher-student interactions and, 51, 52, 54-55; and teaching effectiveness prescriptions, 51–52; Teaching for Understanding (TfU) model, 158–167; think-aloud procedure, 75–82, 112–114; timed trials, 13; tutoring programs, 14–15, 16–17, 19–26, 116, 254, 290–295; verbal-visual word association strategy, 107–115; visual-verbal technique, 86; vocabulary development programs, 107–115, 116–121, 174–188, 246–247; and whole-class discussion questions, 69; word attack skills, 189–196; word recognition, 16, 75–76, 79; word study, 11, 17; writing strategies, 11, 17, 71, 217–219; written conversations between participants, 99–100; zone of proximal development, 47, 149. *See also* assessments; comprehension strategies; reading fluency; standardized tests; *specific method*

INSTRUCTIONAL RESOURCES. *See* resources

INTEGRATED PARENT INVOLVEMENT PACKETS (IPIPs), 69

INTERGENERATIONAL LITERACY DIFFICULTIES, 59. *See also* parent and family literacy programs

INTERNATIONAL READING ASSOCIATION (IRA), and adolescent literacy, 2–3

INTERPRETING CONFLICTING INFORMATION, IN STUDENT RESEARCH, 198

INTERSUBJECTIVITY, 59

INTERVENTION, for literacy improvement, 19–26, 128–129. *See also* Reading Rescue

J

JOURNAL WRITING, 68, 99–100

K

K-W-L/K-W-L-S, 198, 204, 217, 219, 220–222

L

LANGUAGE EXPERIENCE APPROACH, 76–82

LATINA/O STUDENTS, literacy instruction for, 74–82

LEARNER-CENTERED CLASSROOM ENVIRONMENTS, 304

LEARNING DISABILITIES AND DIFFICULTIES: Scaffolded Reading Experience and, 148–156. *See also* reading disabilities and difficulties

LEARNING DISABILITIES TEACHERS: problems of, 17. *See also* Title I teachers

LIMITED ENGLISH PROFICIENCY (LEP) STUDENTS. *See* English as a second language (ESL); English language learners (ELL)

LITERACY FOR TEENAGE PARENTS. *See* Family Literacy Project: Focus on Teenage Parents

LITERACY PORTFOLIO PROCESS, 302–316; analysis procedure for, 310–311; context of the study, 304–308; data analysis and evaluation, 311–312; data sources for study of, 308–310; interview data and results of, 312–315; portfolio assessment, 302–303; students, motivation and goals of, 303–304

LITERACY VOLUNTEERS OF AMERICA, 3

LITERATURE: Cai's categories of, 97–98; as a psychoeducational intervention tool, 128–129

LITERATURE CIRCLES, 99–100, 102–103

THE LITERATURE PROJECT, 128–135; activities used in, 133*t;* assessment tools of, 130–133; goals of, 128–129; instruction of, 129–132; motivation of subjects, 128, 132–134; participants and curriculum development of, 129; recommendations for future implementations of, 134; results of, 132–134

LITERATURE-BASED COGNITIVE STRATEGY INSTRUCTION, 74–82

P

PARENT AND FAMILY LITERACY PROGRAMS: Effective Partners in Secondary Literacy Learning (EPISLL), 60–61, 62–63; ethnic-specific literature and, 104; Family Reading (national program), 276–289; goals of, 277; and posture of reciprocity, 63–64; Talk To A Literacy Learner (TTALL), 60–61. *See also* home-school partnerships

PARENT INVOLVEMENT. *See* home-school partnerships

PARTNER OR PAIRED READING, 14, 70

PEER AND CROSS-AGE TUTORING, 290–295; content areas amenable to, 291; cost-effectiveness of, 290; guidelines for using, 293–294; pairing of students for, 292; situations of usefulness of, 293; students as tutors, 291–293

PEER EDITING STRATEGIES, 119–120

PEER-LED DISCUSSION, 70

PERFORMANCE FEEDBACK. *See* feedback, on performance

PHONICS, Reading Rescue and, 24

PICTURE BOOKS IN MIDDLE-LEVEL CLASSROOMS, 244–250; for creative writing, 247; purposes of using, 244–245; universal appeal of, 250; using in all subject areas, 245–250; for vocabulary development, 246–247. *See also* wordless books in middle-level classrooms

POPULAR CULTURE, 122–127; and questions of textual ideology, 126–127; social and political uses of, 124–127; strategies for responding to, 122–124

PORTFOLIO PROCESS. *See* literacy portfolio process

POSTURE OF RECIPROCITY, 63–64

PROBLEM SOLVING SKILLS, 112–114

PROXIMAL DEVELOPMENT, ZONE OF, 47, 149

"PULL-OUT" PROGRAMS, 17

PUPIL-TO-PUPIL TEACHING. *See* cross-age tutoring, using wordless books; peer and cross-age tutoring

Q

QUICK BOOK SHARE, 269–271

R

RAPID RETRIEVAL OF INFORMATION (RRI) TECHNIQUE, 171–173

READ-ALOUDS, 25, 30–32, 87–88, 103–104, 133, 171–173, 265–268

READING COMPREHENSION INSTRUCTION, IN SUBJECT-SPECIFIC STUDY: for at-risk students, 138–147; for students with learning difficulties, 148–156

READING DISABILITIES AND DIFFICULTIES: case study of, 8–18; characteristics of those with, 40; and coping strategies, 51–56; and dyslexia, 8–9; environments for, 30–31; and ESL, 74–82; generalizations about, 28–36; metacognitive strategies for, 157–167; wordless books for, 251–253, 256. *See also* high school remedial reading programs and practices surveyed; learning disabilities and difficulties

READING EXPERIENCE, *vs.* reading ability, 30

READING FLUENCY: and culturally relevant text, 74; and repeated readings, 12–13

READING INTERVENTION PROGRAMS, 19–26, 128–129

READING MATERIALS: acceptability of, 29; access to, 29; and culturally relevant text, 74–82; self-selection by students of, 226–237. *See also* instructional materials; resources

READING RECOVERY, 16

READING REQUIREMENTS, of states, 2

READING RESCUE, 19–26; computer benefits for, 22–23; implementation guidelines for, 24–25; instructional model for, 20–23; language experience approach (LEA) of, 22–23; preliminary literacy assessment of, 19–20; reading aloud to student in, 22; reading familiar material in, 21–22; reading new material in, 23; running record in, 22; study results of, 23–24; words and letters in, 22; writing in, 22–23. *See also* Metacomprehension Strategy Index

READING/WRITING CONNECTION, reinforcing, 25

RECYCLED WORDS STRATEGY, 116–121; advantages and disadvantages of, 121; evaluating word knowledge, 119; focused word study, 119; free writing, 118–119; Invisible List activity, 117; jump-in reading, 117–119; Literary Response Journals, 118–119; oral reading and responses, 117–119; prereading activities, 117; writing workshop, 119–121

"REFLECTIVE PRACTITIONER," 16

REMEDIAL READING PROGRAMS AND PRACTICES, survey of high school. *See* high school remedial reading programs and practices surveyed

REPEATED READINGS, 12–13, 14, 25

REPORTS. *See* organization skills for student research

RESEARCH PROJECTS, STRATEGIES FOR. *See* how-to book projects; organization skills for student research; "skinny books" for student learning

RESOURCES: children's books, 35t–36t; criteria for selecting ethnic-specific books, 100–102; ethnic-specific literature and writers, 96–97, 100t–101t; literature about women/girls, 130t; picture books, 246t–249t; read-alouds for reluctant high school readers, 266t–267t; wordless books, 252t

RISK LEVELS, ACADEMIC, 128. *See also* The Literature Project

ROUND-ROBIN READING, 32–33

S

SCAFFOLDED READING EXPERIENCE (SRE), 148–156; activities of, 150t, 151t, 152–155; model for, 149–150; planning and implementation of, 150–151

SCHOOLS, U.S. PUBLIC: ethnic-specific literature in, 96; success of remediation systems in, 17–18

SELF-CONCEPT/-ESTEEM: breaking cycles of low, 3–4; cross-age tutoring and, 293; enhancing, 3–4, 71; Family Reading (national program) and, 276; and Literature Project Evaluation Form (LPEF), 130–133; and The Piers-Harris Children's Self-Concept Scale: The Way I Feel About Myself, 130–133; as a reader, 11; uses of literature to improve, 128. *See also* academic confidence

SELF-EFFICACY THEORY: and approaches to reading and writing, 42; and building literacy, 40–41; and characteristics of learners, 43–46; cultural and language influences on, 48; teachers' influences on, 41–42, 46–48, 49. *See also* academic confidence

SELF-SELECTED READING, 2, 33–34, 226–237

SHARING READING EXPERIENCES, 30; of faculty with students, 272–274

SHORT TERM SURVIVAL, as a coping strategies of unsuccessful readers, 52–53

SKILL-AND-DRILL APPROACH, 32

"SKINNY BOOKS" FOR STUDENT LEARNING, 215–216

SMALL-GROUP INSTRUCTION, 16–17, 51–52

SOCIAL STUDIES, AND LIFETIME READING HABITS, 238–243

SPECIAL EDUCATION. *See* learning disabilities teachers

SPECIAL EDUCATION ASSISTANCE PROGRAMS, 8–9

SPELLING, and diagnostic spelling inventory, 13

STANDARDIZED TESTS: explaining scores on, 3; 1998 NAEP Reading Report Card, 1–2; scores on state-mandated, 67. *See also* assessments

STATE GOVERNMENT FUNDING PROGRAMS, Disadvantaged Schools Program, 60–61

STATES, reading requirements of, 2

STATISTICS, on adolescent reading, 1–2. *See also* standardized tests

STORY FRAME COMPREHENSION STRATEGIES, 223–224

STRESS, reading and, 20

STRUGGLING READERS. *See* reading disabilities and difficulties

STUDENT CENTERED READING, 124–126

STUDENT PARENTS, and motivation for learning, 257–258

STUDENT PARENTS' LITERACY. *See* Family Literacy Project: Focus on Teenage Parents

STUDENT RESEARCH. *See* how-to book projects; organization skills for student research; "skinny books" for student learning

STUDENT-PREFERRED READING MATERIALS, 226–237

STUDENTS: adult reading shared with, 272–274; and attitudes toward/feelings about reading, 1–5, 20, 34, 111, 226–233; and beliefs about themselves, 42–45; and contextualized observations, 52; effects of read-alouds on, 268; and evaluation of their own work, 48; and focus of social context of school, 41; and peer and cross-age tutoring, 291–293; sharing reading experiences among, 269–271. *See also* academic confidence; motivation for learning; motivation for reading; motivation for research and writing; self-concept/-esteem; self-efficacy theory; *specific type*

STUDENTS WITH LEARNING/READING DISABILITIES AND DIFFICULTIES. *See* at-risk students; high school remedial reading programs and practices surveyed; learning disabilities and difficulties; reading disabilities and difficulties

STUDENT-TO-STUDENT DISCUSSION, 296–301; to clarify and expand thinking, 297–298; discussion defined, 296–297; problems that hinder, 299; purposes of, 297–298; to review content, 298; skills students need for, 299–300; structuring for cooperative learning, 299–300

SURVEY OF HIGH SCHOOL READING PROGRAMS AND PRACTICES. *See* high school remedial reading programs and practices surveyed

SUSTAINED SILENT READING (SSR), 29, 177–178

T

TALK TO A LITERACY LEARNER (TTALL), 60–61

TAPED READING, 14, 17

TEACHERS: characteristics of, 58; and contextualized observations, 52; education and training of, 16, 17, 36–37; and ethnic-specific literature, 96–97; quality of, 16–17; of renegade readers, 233–235; roles in academic confidence, 39–50, 51–52; roles in creating lifetime readers, 242; roles in introducing wordless books, 255–256; Title I, 16, 17, 27–37; and use of informational picture books, 92–93, 94. *See also* home-school partnerships

TEACHING FOR UNDERSTANDING (TfU) MODEL, 158–167

TEACHING METHODS AND STRATEGIES. *See* instructional methods and strategies

TEENAGE PARENTS' LITERACY. *See* Family Literacy Project: Focus on Teenage Parents

TESTS. *See* assessments; standardized tests

THINK-ALOUD PROCEDURE, 75–82, 112–114

TIMED TRIALS, 13

TITLE I TEACHERS, 16, 17, 27–37

TUTORING PROGRAMS, 14–15, 16–17, 19–26, 116, 254, 290–295

V

VERBAL-VISUAL WORD ASSOCIATION STRATEGY, 107–115

VISUAL-VERBAL TECHNIQUE, 86

VOCABULARY LEARNING/DEVELOPMENT: in a literature-based classroom, 174–188; picture books for, 246–247; recycled words for, 116–121; with verbal-visual word association strategy, 107–115; and vocabulary square, 112–114. *See also* literature-based vocabulary development programs

VOCABULARY SQUARE, 112–114. *See also* verbal-visual word association strategy

W

WHAT I KNOW/WHAT I WANT TO KNOW/WHAT I LEARNED (K-W-L). *See* K-W-L

WHOLE-CLASS DISCUSSION QUESTIONS, 69

WINNER (WAYS OF INTEGRATING THE NEW TO THE KNOWN BY EVOKING REFLECTION), writing strategy, 71

WORD ATTACK SKILLS, 189–196

WORD PATTERNS, study of, 14

WORD RECOGNITION, 16, 75–76, 79

WORD STUDY, 11, 17

WORDLESS BOOKS IN MIDDLE-LEVEL CLASSROOMS, 251–256; content area instruction and, 254–255; cultural and linguistic diversity and, 253–254, 256; reading disabilities and difficulties and, 251–253, 256; teachers' roles in introducing, 255–256; tutoring programs using, 254

WRITING STRATEGIES, 11, 17, 71, 99–100

WRITING STRATEGY, WINNER, 71

WRITING-TO-LEARN STRATEGIES, 217–219; admit/exit slips, 217–218; cinquains/progressive cinquains, 218–219; K-W-L, 219; looping, 218

Z

ZONE OF PROXIMAL DEVELOPMENT, 47, 149